THE FINAL CHOICE

And so, Glaucon, the tale was saved,
and did not perish; and if we trust the tale,
it will save us.

PLATO,
The Republic

THE FINAL CHOICE

PLAYING THE SURVIVAL GAME

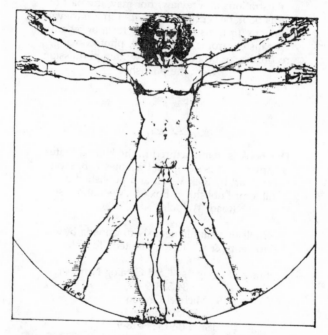

MICHAEL GROSSO

STILLPOINT PUBLISHING
WALPOLE, NEW HAMPSHIRE

This book is manufactured in the United States
of America. It is designed by James F. Brisson,
cover art by Rick Veitch and published by
Stillpoint Publishing, Box 640,Meetinghouse
Road, Walpole, NH 03608.

Published simultaneously in Canada by
Fitzhenry & Whiteside Limited, Toronto.

Library of Congress Card Catalog Number:
84-52879
Michael Grosso
Final Choice
ISBN 0-913299-18-9

0 9 8 7 6 5 4 3 2 1

ACKNOWLEDGMENTS

Some, though not all, of my debts are acknowledged in the
list of references—meant, by the way, to be suggestive, not
exhaustive. In particular, I want to pay special thanks to
these pioneer researchers: William Roll, Kenneth Ring,
Karlis Osis, Rhea White, Ian Stevenson, and the late Laura
Dale.

To my father, Carmine Grosso

NOTE TO THE READER

This book is for people who like to dream. And for people who believe in the truth of dreams. In it I try to dream about life and death in a new way. Why bother? First, the love of truth. Certain facts don't square with the orthodox dream picture. There's also the love of life. The orthodox picture puts a cramp on the spirit.

About method, my rule is to be bound by none. First principle: allegiance to no school of philosophy, no religious or political sect. My non-method has its uses. It enables me to draw on the whole, the healing well of truth. In this venture, it meant helping myself to the riches of opposing but reputable disciplines, religious and scientific; and to disreputable but daring disciplines like parapsychology. In the book are tales of Mind at Large. You could call it a kind of conceptual artwork—a sketch of a New Age Metaphysics of Death and Enlightenment.

Michael Grosso—1985

CONTENTS

THE FINAL CHOICE

INTRODUCTION

Death In Search Of A Myth

Beneath the ceaseless changes of history, death remains a changeless fact of life. The fact of death is constant; the meanings change from culture to culture and from age to age. Whether seen as life's black hole or the gateway to unknown paradise, we live our death in the meaning we give it.

Death is a border concept, pointing to the other side, the unseen, the unknown. We observe the obvious; but there remains a gap, a dark hinterland of the unobserved, or of the less readily observed. Imagination, unafraid to leap into the unknown, may help us find the full meaning of death.

We pause before the cave of death, anxious to peer into its shadows. We'd like to turn away but are drawn back, knowing it's our fate, sooner or later, to go inside. We stand at the entrance with lanterns of science and reason, but we cannot see very far. Sometimes we peer inside with the light of our mythical imagination.

Myths are the maps we make to guide our gropings in a world riddled with uncertainties. We are feeble creatures—mere reeds as Pascal said, but thinking reeds. Because we think, we reach beyond ourselves, disturb ourselves with questions of our origins, our desti-

1

nies. We are restless weeds with longings to travel, to uproot ourselves and wander into the openness of space. We like to abide comfortably in our terrestrial roots; but we have inklings of cutting loose
and are full of lofty yearnings.

The medieval philosophers understood the thirst to know and
love the Transcendent. All desires—even the shady and disreputable
ones—they claimed, gravitate toward a Source of Ultimate Satisfaction. We may pause in the evening at an inn; but in the morning,
after sleep and restless dreams, we set out again, unaccountably
driven toward a new horizon. Wisdom, they said, was to aim for this
Ultimate Satisfaction, to set out on this Road toward Ultimate Well-
Being.

The further we wander, the more we are driven to speculate on
what lies beyond. Indeed, we build machines, launch ourselves into
outer space, probe the planets and beyond as a way of exploring
what we are, what we can reach. Still, there's the question of what
lies beyond physical space itself, and so we send imagination probes
into the outer spaces of the spirit, the possible worlds of afterdeath.
Born space travelers, our myths are the starcrafts we use to explore
the edge of reality.

Why We Need a New Myth of Death

The old myths of death have been dying since the rise of modern
science. Science has detailed maps of the atom, the human body, the
earth, the forms of life, the stars and so forth; but it lacks even a
rough map of the thing we call death.

Yet this isn't quite accurate. We have been given a map, a pointer
to what lies beyond. On the question of the final frontier, the bulk of
scientific workers agree in giving us a "myth" of nihilism—an image
of nothingness at the heart of our future.

The steps by which we inherit all this are familiar. It is said, for
instance, that Copernicus shattered our man-centered vanity by
proving a sun-centered cosmology. The old Western myth of death,
in Dante's Divine Comedy, had earth as the center of the universe.
Our myths of the afterlife were tied to this outlook. In this picture,
the damned were dispatched to the bowels of the earth, while the
blessed were assigned happier stations in heaven. Of course, it is
hard to take this medieval story seriously today. After Copernicus,
the wicked of the world may roam free from disquieting thoughts of
hellfire. One can now pursue the survival game unruffled by

thoughts of posthumous justice. One could, depending on one's point of view, hail the passing of the old hells as progress. One could also fear that to lift too many clamps from our dark side is to court hell on earth.

As the new science won the day, the old myths of the beyond faded. Final causes dropped, the world became a clockwork mechanism. In Dante's universe, the motive force behind all things was divine eros; the end of the human adventure was the consummation of love. The wizards of the Renaissance hexed the old vision. Love was degraded to a secondary quality, a mere ripple in the meandering streams of human subjectivity.

Modern behaviorism carries on the reduction: banishing human consciousness, along with soul, mind and spirit to the limbo of superstition. The old belief that human consciousness survived bodily death is, practically speaking, near death. Worse, belief in the reality of mind itself is threatened with the same fate. Modern science may have opened vistas of outer space; but it also shrank the worlds of inner space.

Despite the dogmas of the official world view, we still entertain questions unanswered, or unanswerable, by current science. Copernicus, Galileo, Darwin, Freud, Watson and other masters notwithstanding, we still feel perplexed before the mystery of death and need a more complete picture of reality. The average understanding of the world, based on orthodox science, fails to touch, even in outline, the needs of our whole selves.

For this we have to turn to the depth psychologists and the parapsychologists. Carl G. Jung, the great explorer of inner space, found, below the Freudian personal unconscious, evidence of transcendent instincts of Mind. Frustration of that instinct—the damming up of the spirit—could make us sick, Jung believed, as surely as the damming up of any vital impulse.

Hemispheric brain research also shows the need for image-thinking, for holistic ways of living our meanings. The tendency to reach past the known toward the unknown, past the fragmented picture toward wholeness, is built into the brain itself.

Further, there are *collective* risks in living with the wrong outlook on the life-and-death connection. Death demythologized enlarges the potential for violence. Death robbed of significance cheapens life. A human being, according to the old view, is an embodied spirit, a center of inviolate value, made to evolve beyond the grave. From this comes the imperative to respect the life of each human being. Deny our sacred status, and the temptation to regard people as mere things grows considerably.

Our myths need to be judged as part of the struggle for survival; in this book we look at things in the light of evolution. The world is changing faster than ever before. We need general ideas that help us to adapt to the changing world.

On balance, we find our world degraded, drained, impoverished by war and massive preparations for war. Acts of destruction become a source of self-affirmation. Sucked down into the whirlpool of non-being, we strike wildly for proofs that we are. Our nihilism is a revolt against the murder of hope and has its own appealing dynamics.

Two things might dull this grotesque attraction. One is the fear of losing our souls. But in an age that denies the soul, this restraint lacks force. The second is the fear of losing material advantage. For the many who are poor, this also has little force. The double loss, inner and outer, leaves us exposed. Nihilism is tempting under these circumstances.

The ruling world view is materialism, but the means to enjoy the fruits of materialism are waning. Materialism becomes an empty creed in a double sense. It empties people of hope in a spiritual reality; but it is also empty of real—*material*—promise. Materialism is a creed especially suitable for those who can afford to reap its this-worldly benefits. One can tolerate the idea of death without redemption if one has, in the meantime, the material means to enjoy life.

This theft of spirit and matter is unique. First, the poverty, thanks to science, of the way we think and feel about reality: the mechanization of life, the assault on quality; the degradation of feeling, intuition, subjectivity. Surrounded by dead symbols, broken connections, the ancient highways of the spirit are roadblocked; stranded at the crossroads of history, the human soul looks a bit ragged and forlorn. The inner landscape is bleak but no bleaker than the average external scene: a world of diminishing resources. Natural science, enemy of the supernatural, is a poor friend to nature. Natural science denatures nature. It's one thing to talk of the survival of human personality; the survival of nature itself is also at risk. Survival "beyond" is derided; survival here and now is also menaced.

To "survive," to "live beyond," is not just to conserve our own personal being; it means reaching out beyond our personal boundaries. We survive backwards as well as forwards, inwards as well as outwards. As living beings it is our right to play the game to the hilt; our deepest aspirations are grounded in living bodies, traced in the DNA code, in the "mechanisms" that propel us to duplicate, to multiply. We're primed to adapt, to learn, to expand our being. The search for new environments, other worlds, higher dimensions, all, I believe, spring from the demands of living process. Life itself has a stake in honing our myths of death and rebirth.

In these circumstances, a new myth of life-in-death could prove useful. The survival game is total; it encompasses both our inner and outer lives; it cares about the here and the hereafter.

In this book I try to describe a certain formal dynamic of the collective mind, an archetype of inner transformation: an item of possible use in a world struggling to be reborn. There are signs everywhere of impulses toward being "born again." The belief that we are on the threshold of a New Age is alive and flourishing.

In the New Age our prophets and dreamers describe, there is talk of a universal consciousness—what I call, following Aldous Huxley and a tradition among parapsychologists, Mind at Large. As we shall see, there are signs of a Helping Intelligence, a kind of agency of Mind at Large; it is acting upon us and seems to be part of a system superior to our normal human functioning.

We could use this help, this wisdom of a higher mind, for the wisdom of the present age is based on a precarious Balance of Terror—the wisdom of Mutual Assured Destruction. This established metaphysics of survival is summed up under the acronym: MAD!

According to the Russian sociologist, Pitirim Sorokin [1], ours is a disintegrating sensate culture on the threshold of becoming a new ideational culture, a culture of higher consciousness. We are, we could say, in the midst of the near-death experience of our sensate civilization. Is the Bomb the trump card in a master plan to raise us to a new consciousness? If so, we need to expand our image of the possible and to open ourselves to the process of collective rebirth.

To survive the nuclear age, we may have to choose to enlist the aid of a new spirit. But this means we must stop clinging to half-ideas and learn to handle opposites: science and religion, art and technology, reason and intuition, personal and collective, masculine and feminine.

Certain things complicate the survival game. Not only are societies everywhere changing so rapidly, humans reproducing to an alarming degree, but an incredibly destructive technology is growing day by day. The great powers are massing for what can only be the *last war*. A new age metaphysics of life and death should face this prospect: the final move in playing the survival game.

Why "game"? Play is basic to all living substance. Play is useful in learning to inhabit new environments. Oddly, those who struggle too hard to save their lives often put themselves at increased risk. The struggle to preserve the security of the world powers is a case in point. Effort to achieve greater security seems only to increase our peril.

The hands of the Doomsday Clock move inexorably toward midnight. And yet the human psyche was never less prepared for death. Two historical moments are converging: first, we find ourselves at an all-time low of inner resources for coping with death, orthodox science having rejected the classic redemptive myths. At the same time, scientific ingenuity places before us the specter of global death.

This book is a study of our inner "arms" race: it looks at some neglected resources for coping with this uncanny situation.

Summary and Plan of the Book

The book is divided into six parts. The one purpose: to draw a picture of Mind at Large and to show how that concept may relate to our survival, both here and hereafter.

First, let me say what I do *not* do. I don't review in detail evidence for life after death; I don't discuss the mind-body problem; and I don't try to make a case for parapsychology in general.

What I do attempt is to use psi and related data to sketch the large picture. I stress the synoptic, not the analytic, side of philosophy: the need to see things whole, in a way, to create a "myth," a whole, a healing picture.

The book is an exercise in the healing imagination. However, it is based on matters of fact. In particular, I focus on out-of-body and near-death experiences, on certain types of apparition, on what depth psychology calls archetypes, and on "miraculous" phenomena of Christian saints and mystics. I also try to keep within focus the biological framework, the evolutionary drama in which human life finds itself playing a leading role.

In Part One, I outline the idea of a modern deathcraft: the art of dying and the survival game. In the first chapter, I track some hints from old deathcrafts, such as Plato's and the Tibetan *Bardo Thodol*. We look for ways of coping with death, new perspectives, psychic "technologies"—what's usable in everyday life. Chapter Two looks at the Resurrection as a model for deathcraft. We end this first part by talking about why a modern "art of dying" would be useful in the nuclear age.

A modern art of dying would, in my view, have to take in the findings of psychical research. Part Two of the book deals with research on postmortem survival. Disregarded by orthodox science, it offers material for enlarging the science of life. Chapter Three looks at the parapsychology of transcendence. No attempt is made to argue the case for ESP and psychokinesis. This is done adequately elsewhere; the reader may turn to the many proceedings and journals of the English and American Societies for Psychical Research. There are good anthologies: Wolman's *Handbook of Parapsychology* [2], *Advances in Parapsychological Research* [3] and the *Philosophical Dimensions of Parapsychology*, edited by James Wheately and Hoyt Edge. [4] For a careful analysis of psi concepts and data, the reader may use Stephen Braude's *ESP and Psychokinesis*. [5]

After discussing in Part Two the importance of a *synoptic* view of psi, survival research, altered states of consciousness and biological theory, we turn in Parts Three and Four to two sets of connected data: the out-of-body experience (OBE) and the near-death experience (NDE).

In Part Three I attempt to show that the out-of-body process permeates the higher games of the "spirit"—art, philosophy and mysticism. The OBE is a way we explore the fringes of Mind at Large.

Part Four tackles near-death phenomena. Next we come to the core idea of an archetype of death and enlightenment. The NDE leads us, via phenomenology, to the hypothesis of a collective psychism: to mystical experience, classic mystery rituals, visionary and high dream life and so on. Near-death turns out to be an important inlet to Mind at Large. In this chapter we make two important moves. First, we show there is a general mechanism, triggered by near-death, which may work during any crisis of transformation. The second move is to push the talk into the arena of *collective* psychology.

So far we find a network of increasingly inclusive phenomena. Psi itself is the first sign of our potential for going beyond the limits of space, time and matter. Psi appears again in the context of the OBE, which, as we shall see, is goal-directed. The OBE reappears in the near-death process, which awakens the archetypes of the deep unconscious. The near-death psychisms, the most inclusive so far, are powerfully transformative; they help adapt us to the future, a sign, we shall argue, of their evolutionary significance.

In Part Five we mount the spiral of our theoretical scheme; NDEs are part of a larger class of apparitional phenomena whose function is to assist, reassure, encourage, guide and direct individuals, or groups of individuals, in times of crisis. These we call Messengers from Mind at Large. This chapter, needless to say, is a thumbnail sketch. Helping apparitions occur in the lives and fortunes of peoples and individuals. If we see these goal-directed epiphanies as showings of Mind at Large—of the collective will of the human species—we may infer a benevolent trait in the evolutionary intelligence. We do not, however, see any signs of omnipotence in the operations of Mind at Large.

After sketching a typology of helping apparitions, the focus in the next chapter is on a uniquely paranormal apparition—namely, what seems like a kind of photograph of the man known to history as Jesus. We may think of the Shroud of Turin as a psychokinetic effect associated with an unusual death. The Shroud is therefore grist for near-death research. It is also of interest to students of archetypes, helping apparitions and the idea of Mind at Large.

Now, with evidence before us of a Helping Intelligence, we turn in the last part of the book to the question of *global near-death*. This is a hard topic, although it is on the minds of many today. To begin with, some near-death experiencers are having visions of global catastrophe. More to the point, global near-death is believed by many, experts and non-experts, to be increasingly probable in the form of nuclear war.

Chapter 13 looks at the threat of nuclear war as a psychospiritual problem. Not to see it in this light may well be fatal. Ordinary reason, morality and "realistic" political thinking seem helpless before an impersonal, collective march toward military showdown. This chapter stresses the "demonic" side of the global death dance—and the need for a higher, a "divine" perspective, to deal with it.

Chapter 14 develops insights of E. P. Thompson, Robert Lifton and Richard Falk on the *totality* of the battle against the threat of nuclear war: the fact that weapons are symptoms of a way of life, a general way of thinking and feeling, of organizing reality itself. The "Bomb," in short, is the symptom of a metaphysical disease, and as such cries out for metaphysical healing. This pattern of destructiveness is dubbed the *thanatos* conspiracy. In this chapter we also use the analogy of near-death to imagine forms of awakening the collective higher self.

In Chapter 15, *A Morphology of the Apocaplypse,* we compare near-death, UFO and Marian visions. Something appears to be mobilizing the Higher Collective Mind *before* catastrophe. The increasing risk of global near-death is, I believe, awakening our evolutionary potential. This chapter, in fact, resumes the typology of helping apparitions. It extends the idea of a higher adaptive mechanism in dying from the individual to the group. The final question is whether this mechanism might work for the largest unit of mental life, the species mind.

The last chapter outlines a theory of healing truth: the "poetics" of conscious evolution.

PART ONE

THE MIRROR OF TRANSFORMATION

1
Notes on the Art of Dying

She knew how to live rarely well,
and she desired to know how to die;
and God taught her by an experiment.

—Jeremy Taylor

The Muse of Death

Seeking inspiration from the muse of death is an old habit of reflective people: whether to discover the goad to authenticity, the grace for stoic resignation or the passion to pursue the divine. It is a habit that goes back to Gilgamesh, the ancient Babylonian king, who went on a long journey in quest of the flower of immortality.

But what of us moderns in the scientific age? After all, aren't we on the verge of colonizing space? Of escaping the womb of earth at last? Of gliding out beyond the tether of gravity and sailing among the stars?

"Wonders are there many but none more wonderful than man," cries the chorus in Sophocles' play *Antigone*. Man is *deinoteron*—"the more wonderful," as it is usually translated; but the word really means "ingenious, clever." The chorus sings of everything clever that man can do—farm the land, trap wild beasts, sail the high seas and battle the elements. But the one thing on which all this cleverness founders is death. Death, after all, is cleverer, if you like, more wonderful than man. In spite of modern technology, nothing has changed since the days of Sophocles. Like Nachiketa in the *Katha Upanishad*, we can still dialogue with Yama, Lord of Death, and learn something of use.

True to the spirit of the age, even science—on a small scale to be sure—has begun to throw out a few stammering queries to Lord Yama. Research on death and dying raises basic questions about life and what it means to be a human being. True, the amount of research is miniscule compared with the mammoth outlays for the physical sciences, for industry and for the arts of war. Men have been busy exploring the frontiers of physical space but neglectful of the equally challenging frontiers of inner space. Knowledge expands, though great mysteries remain—above all, the mysteries of the knower. Biology probes the *origin* of life. But what of the *end* of life? A true science of the human must also probe *that*.

Unfortunately, the fundamentalists of modern science see no mystery here at all; death is the end of life, they assert with curious confidence. But the word "end" is ambiguous. The "end of life" is a phrase that conceals an enigma.

The new research on death and dying, I believe, is reaching out toward the goal and meaning of life—the "end" in its positive sense. The quest for the "end" of life is what guides the new breed of poet-scientists, explorers of an exotic republic of the improbable: near-death experiences, deathbed visions, reincarnation memories; ecstatic, mystical, out-of-body states; supernormal powers of the human mind. Others look to the "end" in different ways: by laying bare the denial of death in an age of science; by exposing the dangerous effects of a twisted will to immortality; by exploring the dialectic of love and the death-instinct.

All these words, books, studies of death—what do they forebode? Are they perhaps premonitory of the end of humanity as we know it? Are they foreshadowings cast up from the collective unconscious—harbingers of a convulsion, a catastrophe of the biosphere? What sort of animal is man anyway? A dead-end on the tree of evolution or a bridge between human and parahuman?

An Experimental Link Between Life and Death

Death, it would seem, is the opposite of life. For this reason, the inner side of death would have to elude our grasp. It would appear to lie on the other side, an impassible frontier. Yet there may be a method of exploring the fringes of this frontier. It is to treat the elusive "something" we call death as if it were a peculiar state of consciousness—a suggestion which at first glance may seem far-fetched.

What sense can we make of it? One way is as follows: just as biologists study the border between living and nonliving—for instance, viruses—in hope of divining the secrets of the origin of life, so do near-death researchers study the border between living and being dead in hope of divining the secrets of the end of life.

The border condition, dying or near-death, as research shows, is associated with a unique pattern of experience. This pattern may be an important clue, a kind of foothold to what lies beyond, a way of bringing the mystery of death into clearer focus for study.

Regardless of the final outcome of this research, the border condition allows us to drive an experimental wedge into a place normally thought of as unknowable. By means of this method, we may learn to detect signals from the undiscovered country from which no traveler returns.

Once we forge this experimental link between death and consciousness, new possibilities of exploration arise. As we shall see, features of near-death experience may be observed in many unusual states of consciousness. In short, the hypothesis underlying this method is that the inner side of death is, under special conditions, open to human experience before bodily death. There are ways of being in the world that may form an inner bridge between life and death, enabling us to explore the "undiscovered country."

A Craft of Dying

Once we grant a connection between dying and altered states of consciousness, the idea of exploring, preparing for death, acquires a new dimension of meaning. It would even make sense, in the light of this, to speak of gaining skill, a kind of knowledge in the art of dying. Perhaps the new research on death and dying could be of service here. Even if it is unlikely that science can provide exact knowledge of death, it may be able to provide some insight and guiding principles based on probabilities.

It would be pretentious to speak of science here, where science means anything like exact knowledge. But perhaps we could speak of a *craft* of dying. Such a craft might supplement what it can glean from science with the wisdom of the great spiritual traditions.

A modern craft of dying, like the ancient Platonic one, would revolve around strategies for altering the quality of our consciousness. Dying—and possibly death itself—may be thought of as a change of consciousness. In one sense, of course, the materialist won't dispute our claim. Death is a change in consciousness, all right; it's the end of it! Our craft entertains a more hopeful view, however. While we admit that our ordinary personal consciousness must change drastically at death, afterdeath may yet reveal a new, and possibly higher, form of consciousness.

One could, of course, see almost the whole of religion and much of philosophy as expressing the struggle to cope with human mortality. All we hope to do here, however, is to note a few specific illustrations of early deathcrafts.

Philosophy as Deathcraft

The classic pagan craft of dying is seen in Plato's *Phaedo*, which tells the story of the death of Socrates and gives a model for heroic, philosophical death. Other philosophers went to death for the sake of their ideas. Bruno died a martyr to the new Renaissance cosmology. When the Inquisition burnt Vanini at the stake for his heresies, he is said to have boldly exclaimed: "Let us die happily for philosophy." But in the case of Socrates, the relation between death and philosophy was deeper than Vanini's accidental heroics. Philosophy itself is defined as the practice of death—the highest wisdom being achieved through death.

At first this may seem morbidly fanciful. How does one go about practicing death, and to what end? Everything hinges on the definition of death as the separation of the soul from the body. We can practice death by learning how to separate ourselves from our bodies. Such a program sounds suspiciously schizoid to modern ears, but when we look closely at Plato's language, his meaning becomes clearer. *Chorismos* is his word for separation, but he also uses *lysis*, loosing or freeing, and *appallage*, which means departure. The freedom of the soul depends on readiness for departure, on looseness, flexibility, ease of movement. The essence of the soul, of life as the Greek philosophers understood it, was self-movement, autonomy of personal energy. The highest life—the life that is godlike—as taught in Aristotle's *Nichomachean Ethics*, is marked by *autarkia*, autonomy, essentially, freedom from servitude to the body.

Normally, however, we live deeply enmeshed, identified with the anxieties and demands of our bodies. We not only have bodily experiences, we attach exclusive importance to them. We become imprisoned by our body-egos, engrossed by our needs for comfort, security and pleasure.

Plato says we can break the bonds of this hypnotic state and so, in a way, learn to anticipate that great "departure" defined as death. This "loosening" of the soul requires a special way of life, a spiritual discipline. Freedom from mindless immersion in bodily existence is the way to freedom from the fear of death, the secret to a radical courage based on wisdom and self-knowledge. (Socrates rejects courage not based on philosophic insight.) A soul consciously detached from the body, Plato tells us in the *Phaedo*, "is not likely to feel that it will be torn asunder at its departure from the body and will vanish into nothingness, blown apart by the winds, and be no longer anywhere."

The Platonic craft helps us to anticipate the divorce of our self from the body in different ways. For instance, pain and pleasure are said to "nail" the soul to the body. Violent emotions increase our bondage, habituate us to a delusive concept of reality. "The evil is that the soul of every man, when it is greatly pleased or pained by anything, is compelled to believe that the object which caused the emotions is very distinct and very true; but it is not. These objects are mostly the visible ones . . ." [6] Plato makes the interesting observation here that world views, or metaphysical biases, are state-bound. If we identify ourselves exclusively with everyday sensory modes of being, we automatically tend to think of them as the only reality—i.e., as "very distinct and very true."

Materialism would thus tend to be the by-product of a materialist *habit* of consciousness. A person who broke that habit, who experienced states going beyond the ordinary sensory mode, would feel less bound to hold a materialist world view. He might be tempted by an alternate view of reality even if it clashed with the prevailing view. If Plato is right, the battle between world views is a battle between different kinds of experiences that people have, and that they think are real, true and clear. If materialism prevails today, it may be less a sign of its truth than of the limitations in the sorts of experiences people are having.

In line with this "state-specific" epistemology, Plato recommends abstention from unnecessary indulgence in bodily pleasure. Unfortunately, the rhetoric sometimes seems to encourage unwholesome repression of the natural instincts.

A modern craft of dying should remain true to the needs of the body without succumbing to the delusions of state-bound materialism. An ignorant and sometimes malicious neglect of the body is a fault of the earlier deathcrafts. By condemning the body as an inferior vehicle, we expose ourselves to the oppressive forces of history. Anything that validates the repression of the body also serves to validate the general repression of life. Plato seemed to underestimate the wisdom of the body.

Yet in defense of Plato we might point out that the leading idea of Platonic metaphysics is harmony, not power. This is the main teaching of the *Republic*. The climax of the quest for truth is an intuition, a direct awareness of "justice," the pattern of the harmony of being and the template of human "happiness." When the soul divides itself from the body in the practice of death, it does so for the sake of its own integrity. The integrated soul orders itself in tune with the *kosmos*: the "ornament" or pattern of the universe. In the cosmology of Plato's *Timaeos*, the universe itself is said to be a "single animal comprehending in itself all other animals, mortal and immortal."

Science, according to Plato, is supposed to teach us to imitate, not dominate, the cosmic pattern. The goal lies in "learning the harmonies and revolutions of the universe." Intellect, our divine part in kinship with the Creator, strives to "assimilate" these harmonies which afford the model for "the best life which the gods have set before mankind." To the extent that one succeeds in this assimilation, one already shares in the realm of the "deathless." The whole enterprise of science is given to harmonizing individual life with cosmic life. This contrasts starkly with the paradigm of modern science. Modern scientific materialism, though it claims identity of mind and body, is committed to the Baconian ideal of lordship over bodily nature. The Platonic deathcraft, based on the separation of soul from body, is yet guided by the ideal of harmony with the "divine animal" of nature as a whole. The practice of death is a prelude to living in harmony with the universe.

The Medieval *Ars Moriendi*

The late Middle Ages of Western Christendom created a different kind of craft of dying, based on the liturgical office *De Visitate Infirmorum*. The generic title *Ars Moriendi* (art of dying) refers to two basic texts. One is a block book version consisting of eleven woodcuts depicting the deathbed drama of *Moriens* (the dying person). The other, a longer version, had an English exemplar commonly referred to as the *Crafte of Dyinge*. Both versions were extraordinarily popular. The artistic climax of the tradition was Jeremy Taylor's *The Rule and Exercises of Holy Dying* of 1651. [7]

Historical factors paved the way for the *Ars Moriendi*. The fourteenth century, in particular, witnessed a rise of virtual necromania. The obsession with death and transience was due in part to the ravages of the bubonic plague in Europe, to war, political upheaval and widespread apocalyptic expectations. Preaching styles, especially in late-medieval England, savagely stressed the perils of hell and purgatory. The earlier, more primitive, *Crafte* made ample use of such tactics to subjugate the wayward conscience of the populace. Churchmen of the day exploited the gruesome side of death to combat the new wave of secularism. As one scholar wrote:

> Hence the Last Things easily became emotional bludgeons with which to combat ignorance, individualism, immorality. Closing ranks against these common foes, all the religious orders found that skulls, worms, fire, and brimstone were, in one way or another, singularly useful weapons in the battle for God and the Church. [8]

In the wake of the Middle Ages, it is hardly surprising that we moderns are so eager to bury the idea of death in the dustbin of the unconscious. A modern craft of dying, while refusing to coddle the impulse toward denial, would wish to avoid the macabre obsessiveness of the medieval *Ars Moriendi*.

Jeremy Taylor's devotional masterpiece on holy dying gets past the shortcomings of the earlier tractates. Taylor would have us meditate calmly on the universal doom of death and cultivate a pious detachment from the world. Taylor iterates the common (admittedly dismal) wisdom of the ages: "As our life is very short, so it is very miserable, and therefore it is well it is short." His tone is somber, not fanatical.

The omnipresence of death is a favorite theme in Taylor's craft. Death penetrates to the core of life. Here we find no amiable talk of the "joy of living." Taylor would set us straight with the grim rhythms of his prose:

> Death meets us everywhere, and is procured by every instrument, and in all chances, and enters in at many doors; by violence and secret influence, by the aspect of a star and the stink of a mist, by the emissions of a cloud and the meeting of a vapor, by the fall of a chariot and the stumbling at a stone, by a full meal or an empty stomach, by watching at the wine, or by watching at prayers, by the sun or the moon, by a heat or a cold, by water frozen into the hard-

ness and sharpness of a dagger, or water thawed into the floods of a
river, by a hair or a raisin, by violent motion or sitting . . .

Language is almost magical in Taylor's *Ars Moriendi*. The point of
this "word magic" was not to eject the idea of death from awareness
but to focus on it. The modern rational mind, stripped of metaphor
and sounding power, finds it hard to contemplate death. Taylor's
relentless realism sharply differs from modern evasiveness.

Although Taylor's deathcraft is otherworldly in intent, it offers
"hints" on the art of living. For example, he alludes to a technique of
recollection that dates back to the ancient Pythagorean brotherhood.
"He that will die well and happily," we read, "must dress his soul by
a diligent and frequent scrutiny; he must perfectly understand and
watch the state of his soul; he must set his house in order before he
be fit to die." The daily practice of self-observation prevents one from
falling into the habit of sin. Recollection is a form of behavior modification. According to Taylor, anyone who dies in good conscience—
properly self-recollected—dies well.

In some ways, daily recollection anticipates the hour of death. It
is now known, for instance, that persons near death often report having a kind of panoramic memory of their lives. The practice of daily
recollection, urged by Taylor, would be a rehearsal of near-death recollection. The near-death experiencer gets a new lease on life as a
result of the play-back experience, a chance to "set his house in order." Taylor and the Pythagoreans of old make self-recollection piecemeal, a gradual, daily process.

The lesson of Taylor's deathcraft for us comes to this: if we hope
to make dying a more conscious process, we shall have to begin by
making living more conscious. Daily self-recollection is a simple exercise to that end.

Or consider the following. "He that would die well and happily
must exercise charity during the whole of his life." This at first seems
like a step beyond the Platonic deathcraft. Plato knows the yoga of
eros—as in the *Phaedrus* and the *Symposium*—but falls short of the
mysteries of Christian charity. Unfortunately, as Taylor describes it,
charity seems mostly a negative exercise; it doesn't express an altogether disinterested outlook. *Charity* here is motivated by the wish to
be forgiven our own sins. "For we receive absolution of our sins in
proportion to our forgiving our brother." It is a way of guaranteeing
the mercy of God on our "day of dissolution."

The general drift of Taylor's holy dying is to devalue worldly existence. "Since we stay not here, being people of a day's abode, and our age is like that of a fly, and contemporary with a gourd, we must look somewhere else for an abiding city, a place in another country." It would seem that "holy," as used by the great Anglican preacher, is less than "holistic" in the modern sense. It is a one-sided "holiness" that celebrates the hereafter at the expense of the here and now. This form of one-sidedness is the counterpart to our modern secular fixation on present-centeredness. Neither satisfies the needs of a holistic metaphysics of death.

A Tibetan Manual for Dying

The *Bardo Thodol* [9], recited by Tibetan lamas over a dying or dead man, is both map and guidebook for the intermediate stage between death and rebirth. The word *bardo* means gap, place of transition, literally "the lake between two islands." Unlike Dante's *Divine Comedy*, also a cartography of the postmortem journey, the *Bardo Thodol* is an open-ended manual. The Tibetan picture is more fluid than Dante's, where our afterlife adventures are fixed by the deeds we perform in this life. Here is a definite eschatological divide: the East is in no hurry and allows many lives to learn the lessons of enlightenment. The West would have us go promptly to doom or paradise; once the die is cast, it is cast, and our fates are sealed.

Church doctrine has not been uniform in its opinions on this. For instance, the early Church father Origen held that all souls, even the Devil himself, would be reconciled in the end to the Divine Source. The official Church doctrine came out against this optimistic heresy. An even more ferocious simplification is evident in the Fundamentalist who wants to get rid of the Catholic purgatory. The Oriental view is plainly the most encouraging. Nobody need fret over the risk of eternal damnation; even the most hopeless cases may derive some consolation from this.

The *Bardo Thodol* describes three stages, gaps or bardos in the postmortem state: *Chikhai, Chonyid* and *Sidpa Bardos*. The three stages progress from the high point of the first moment of death downward through increasingly terrible experiences which end in reincarnation. The Eastern idea of death, we should recall, differs from ours in at least one striking way. The fear of birth—we are led to believe— outweighs the fear of death. Our entry into the world is seen as a greater calamity than our exit. Thus everything in the teachings of the

Bardo Thodol is directed toward avoiding the disaster of rebirth. Embodied existence is itself hell. This twist, curious for most Westerners, may be seen as expressing either the bleakest pessimism about human life or the greatest confidence in the reality and superiority of the next life.

According to the *Tibetan Book of the Dead*, the best chance of enlightenment comes during the *Chikhai Bardo* which occurs at the moment of death. The moment of death is our best chance for permanent escape from rebirth. At that moment, one is said to behold the Reality of the Fundamental Clear Light "wherein all things are like the void and cloudless sky, and the naked spotless intellect is like a transparent vacuum without circumference or center." We are instructed to abide in the consciousness of the Clear Light, to merge with and know it to be our true nature.

But this is not easy. It implies maximum consciousness of the dying process itself. The difficulty here is obvious, given our tendency to deny death, to associate it with the loss of consciousness. The Tibetan craft requires the dying person to remain conscious, and even describes physiological techniques for staying alert. Anything detracting from that alertness might interfere with the experience of the Fundamental Clear Light. This claim about the need for alertness is confirmed by modern findings; for instance, K. Osis and E. Haraldsson [10] and B. Greyson [11] found that narcotics or organic brain dysfunction decreased the incidence of deathbed and near-death visions. The less impaired our consciousness is, emotionally or physiologically, the greater the probability of enlightenment experiences at the hour of death.

In Plato's view, the problem of death is a problem of false identification. We falsely identify with our bodies, which restricts our potential range of consciousness. In the *Bardo Thodol*, we also falsely identify, but with our psychic projections. The difficult thing is becoming clear about our projections. The Tibetan craft maps the obstacles we are said to meet in the postmortem state. After the tremendous initial encounter with the Light arises the *Chonyid Bardo*, the stage of the dawning of peaceful and frightening apparitions.

At first the deceased is not aware that he is deceased (an idea confirmed by spiritualist teachings); he hovers in an astral or dream body in the neighborhood of his corpse, confused, vaguely aware of the presence of mourning relatives and religious functionaries. If, after the first glorious encounter with the Clear Light, we fail to recognize we are one with that Light, the text recommends that we meditate on our guru or tutelary deity with intense fondness and humble trust.

The Tibetan system is flexible. Characteristic of Buddhism, it first advocates the path of self-reliance: know that the source and ground, the supreme consciousness, is within. But if for want of training or insight we fail in the saving quality of awareness, then it's alright to fall back on devotional practices, trusting in external support.

The sequence of events in the intermediate state is: first, we encounter the Clear Light; second, the peaceful apparitions appear; third, the wrathful appear. The apparitional stage is called the *Chonyid Bardo*. The last, *Sidpa Bardo*, is the most unpleasant, the onset of rebirth. Let us again note a parallel with empirical findings. The Tibetan Clear Light is a good match for the Being of Light of near-death research. Given the proper cultural variations, the peaceful apparitions of the *Bardo Thodol* compare well with friendly take-away messengers, Christlike visions and transcendental landscapes. A few empirical reports also indicate signs of the third stage of wrathful apparitions.

The empirical data doesn't take us much further than the threshold of death; and what we observe is rather pleasant, so much so that critics complain that the research romanticizes death. In fact, nothing in the work of serious investigators justifies this censure. In any case, if anyone extracts sanguine fantasies from near-death research, I recommend reading the *Bardo Thodol* as a corrective. For if the parallel between the Tibetan and the modern empirical maps holds all the way, then the romantic fantasy is a spin-off from incomplete data. What may await the unwary, unprepared soul is a psychic battle with "flame-enhaloed, wrathful, blood-drinking deities," none of which sounds like much fun.

The *Bardo Thodol* justifies no self-deceptions concerning death. The Tibetan teaching, however encouraging in tone, offers no easy path to enlightenment. The message, in fact, seems to be that the great majority of us are unprepared for death and the sudden change of consciousness it will bring. The cost of enlightenment is a lifetime of cultivated self-awareness, and in this respect scarcely differs from Plato or Jeremy Taylor. How we experience the afterlife state depends on whatever psychological insight we manage to bring with us.

In the afterdeath bardos we become our own worlds, as liberated as we are liberated or as hell-bound as we are hell-bound. The paranoid-compulsive mind intent on sharply-focused distinctions (me versus the other, for instance) would founder horribly, for in the *Chonyid Bardo* the other *is* me; I create-project my enemy. The more unyielding, mistrustful and hostile I become toward my phantom foes, the more relentlessly they would assail me. The skill I need here is not divisive, separative, but dialectical and unitive. My job is to learn that the wrathful and peaceful apparitions are two sides of the same coin and that both reflect my own unconscious self.

Skills for overpowering and manipulating others would be a hindrance in the possible world of the *Chonyid Bardo*. Surviving the "ambushes" in the bardo realms calls for a skill with oneself, especially with the self normally concealed beneath our everyday persona. Violence is a self-destroying program in the *Chonyid Bardo*. "Through the power of anger," the text says, "you will beget fear and be startled at the dazzling white light and will wish to flee from it; you will beget a feeling of fondness for the dull smoke-colored light from Hell." In ordinary life, anger and violence may be profitably exploited; here, in the presence of the "dazzling white light," they are self-defeating.

The old, routine strategies for coping with hazard and crisis won't work in the afterlife. We'll have to adapt to a different set of rules, use different mental "skills." It's not unreasonable to suppose that if we enter a spiritual universe after death, quite different principles and laws will operate there. They are most likely to be mind-dependent. Dreams, art and mythology give good models for imagining a postmortem spiritual universe.

Traditional wisdom urges renunciation of the worldly mind, becoming like a child. The wisdom of this world would indeed be foolishness when it came to obstacles in the spiritual world. What happens when we meet the monsters of the deep? Is there a secret principle for handling our adversaries—the inner demons, the outer enemies? The *Bardo Thodol* advises: "Be not attracted to them; be not terrified; but abide in the mood of non-thought formation."

This is strange advice. Do nothing, think nothing. In fact, a tradition of creative nonaction is widespread. The modern Mexican shaman, Don Juan, speaks of nondoing, of "stopping the world." Turn the other cheek, declares the shaman of Nazareth. Among the Chinese sages, the principle of *wu wei* or nonaction is also held in high esteem.

This ancient wisdom appears even in the popular consciousness, for instance, in the Hollywood spectacular *Star Wars* of 1977. The young hero, Luke Skywalker, faces the challenge of his life; he has to fly his space vehicle in a pinpoint attack on the evil forces of Darth Vader, a wrathful divinity of the *Chonyid Bardo*. About to zero in on the target, Luke's disembodied spiritual mentor commands him to let go of the controls, to trust his feelings and the Force.

This scene inspired contempt in Ben Bova, a science fiction writer who disliked the movie. One reason was the "philosophical" point *Star Wars* made. " 'Trust the Force' is the philosophy of the slave," Bova proudly proclaims. "Here is a movie produced with the latest and best technology that you can buy and the punch line is that when you're in a crisis, switch off the computer and wait for Alec Guiness to whisper in your ear." Bova would have us trust the computer when we're in a crisis but certainly not the "Force" (a thinly disguised expression for Lord or Spiritual Power). Unfortunately, there is little evidence that trust in technology, even the "latest and best . . . you can buy," has helped to resolve the perennial crises that beset us. In any case, the *Star Wars* fantasy looks more like an episode in the *Chonyid Bardo*. Seen in that light, Luke Skywalker was right to hearken to the "whisper" of the Force.

In the *Sidpa Bardo*, or last stage before reincarnation, the soul wanders helplessly, blown about by the "karmic winds." The intellect, having no object to rest upon, "like a feather tossed about by the wind," is driven toward re-embodiment, seeking to lose or entrap itself in a new body. In this way we get caught up in a new cycle of suffering. The job of enlightenment is to shatter the bonds of this cosmic repetition compulsion.

An important theme of the Tibetan deathcraft is paralleled in Plato's Allegory of the Cave. Humankind cannot bear too much consciousness. The reincarnated body and Plato's cave are symbols of retreat from the Clear Light. But according to both Greek and Tibetan traditions, death is a road to the Clear Light. Death is the necessary, though not the sufficient, condition for being in the Greater Consciousness. Yet we flee from the Greater Consciousness, as Plato's Allegory shows. The cave-dwellers are prepared to kill any would-be liberator, so disinclined are they to be led out into the Light of the True Sun. If Plato and the *Bardo Thodol* are right, then what we really fear in death is not extinction but *too much consciousness*.

The *Bardo Thodol* is not just a guidebook for a possible afterworld journey. Human relations, personal and political, are prone to the same projections, the same ignorance, aggression, desire, fear of life

and death, and flight from autonomy. The Tibetan deathcraft applies
to the art of living. Existence is inescapably transitional, *bardo*-like.
Making our way through the "gaps," across the "lake between the
islands," is our common lot, both here and hereafter.

2
The Resurrection Model

The hint half-guessed, the gift half-understood, is Incarnation.

—*T. S. Eliot,* The Four Quartets

We have looked at several models of deathcrafts. All seem to share a deep mistrust of life lived in bondage to abstractions and projections. The tradition of the great death revisers is based on the belief in a new reality principle. Deathcraft at bottom is lifecraft. Perhaps the most important idea linking earlier and modern crafts of dying is the search for a new form of consciousness. The Greek and Tibetan tradition called for *transcendence* of the body. The Christian called for a *transformation* of the body. Whether these represent real opposition is unlikely. It makes more sense to view them as aspects of the same tendency to revolt against the limits of bodily existence, against death itself.

Platonic, Christian and Tibetan deathcrafts are all, in different ways, preparations, rehearsals for death. In all death is a goal that promises a chance for enlightenment, for enlargement of self. In all we find the assumption that there is something beyond death. We need not assume that this implies a degradation of this life, as writers like Feuerbach automatically do. It would be more accurate to say that the transcendent focus of classic deathcrafts serves as an ordering device for this life.

Although a good deathcraft must, at least in principle, carry over into the art and craft of living, the Christian way, based on the resurrection model, has the strongest implications for the transformation of this life. Christian doctrine values the psychophysical unity of the person. Moreover, the "resurrection," the incarnation of the higher spirit, is supposed to take place here and now. Theoretically, therefore, the Christian deathcraft is the most "this-worldly" of the death-preparing disciplines. History itself becomes the field for practicing the art of dying, the art of bringing the creative spirit into the world process. Christian deathcrafts thus introduce a fresh dynamic to the existential venture.

Earth in Transformation

A glance at some historical examples of deathcrafts shows one thing clearly: any attempt to make sense of the idea of practicing death leads to the question of how to live. Merely preparing for death does not satisfy the needs of the spirit. Spirit is more ambitious. There's a need to be active before death, to learn to see ourselves as more than helpless victims of a dark implacable power. In the Christian belief in the Resurrection we observe the impulse to assume this active stance. If the Platonic strategy was to master the body of death by deserting it, by identifying the whole of one's being with the realm of Mind and Idea, the Christian strategy is to transform the body itself, to eliminate the sinful cause of its fall into mortality. *The Christian solution is to materialize a new spiritual body on earth.*

The Christian way of life, thus understood, is the practice of freeing nature from the "wages of sin"—from death itself. Christian belief sees in death something neither self-evident nor necessary.

Greek and Oriental metaphysics never challenge the dominion of natural death. The human body remains subject to death; only the *soul* is immortal. The Christian idea radically breaks with this view. If we accept the gift of the New Spirit, we may ourselves begin to reap the first fruits of the Resurrection. In Romans, Paul says: ". . . as Christ was raised from the dead by the Father's glory, we too might live a new life. If in union with Christ we have imitated his death, we shall also imitate him in his resurrection. We must realize that our former selves have been crucified with him to destroy this sinful body and to free us from the slavery of sin" (Rom. 6:5).

This may mean that we begin to imitate the Resurrection at the end-time of history when the Kingdom of God is established on earth. But there is another interpretation that stresses the immediate presence of the Kingdom, beginning perhaps with the first pouring out of the Holy Spirit on the Apostles during the Feast of the Pentecost. On this view, the *anastasis* or resurrection of nature, which overcomes the power of death, has already begun with the gifts of the Holy Spirit.

In the Gospels this transfiguration of death-and-matter is highlighted in the deeds of Jesus. Thus the first miracle at the feast of Cana is a sign of this new power at work: the transmutation of water into wine. Healings and raising the dead are more dramatic signs of the coming resurrection of nature. This new power is not restricted to the agency of Jesus; thus, at the prompting of Jesus, Peter walks on water. The power is awakened in Peter himself—although in a faltering way, due to hesitancy and lack of trust.

In the Acts of the Apostles, we see the beginnings of the New Spiritual Principle unfolding itself. Reports abound of miraculous healings and escapes, of prophecy, telepathy and other prodigies. Peter himself is now said to have raised the woman Tabitha from the dead (Acts 9:36-38.) Primitive Christianity claims the revelation of a New Spirit. The new spiritual dynamism transcends matter, time and space. Thus, during the first outpouring at Pentecost, the "men living in Jerusalem from every nation under heaven" were amazed and confounded when the Apostles spoke of the "marvels of God" *in their own languages:* Parthians, Phrygians, Elamites, Cretans, Arabs, Pamphylians, Cappadocians, Egyptians, and even Romans. Skeptics laughed. "They have been drinking too much new wine," they said (Acts I:1-13.) Others were possessed by the New Spirit. Thus the primitive community grew on the wings of a miraculous new power, a new kind of intoxication. The Kingdom of God is within you, Jesus said. It has already begun. A newness of being, a Holy or Healing Spirit: this is the theme of Acts. The world psychokinetically transformed by love is becoming "Love's Body," in N. O. Brown's phrase. In the chapter entitled "Resurrection" [12], Brown writes:

> To rise from history to mystery is to experience the resurrection of the body here now, as an eternal reality; to experience the *parousia*, the presence in the present, which is the spirit; to experience the recincarnation of the incarnation, the second coming; which is his coming in us.

THE FINAL CHOICE

These words sum up the forgotten Christian craft of dying. For Brown, True Christianity means the death of a fundamentalist adherence to the letter and the rebirth of the polysemous spirit, Spirit incarnate, spirit alive in a loving body.

The Christian deathcraft is the practice of being radically alive in a loving body. The ultimate goal is to spiritualize the body, to create what Paul called the *soma pneumatikon*.

Modern liberal Christianity is embarrassed by miracles; it shies away from signs and wonders. But to the primitive Christian, the sensible sign was essential. It was the experimental "proof" of the reality of the New and Holy Spirit. The early Christians were radical empiricists. They needed concrete evidence of the Higher Power they worshipped and trusted. Lofty ethical ideals and philosophical reasons were by-products of an encounter with a living Force, experiences that "sounded like powerful wind from heaven," noises that "filled the entire house," the appearance of "tongues of fire" (Acts 2:1-4.) The roots of the Christian deathcraft were powerful transformative events.

The need for concrete evidence of the supernatural continued throughout the Middle Ages and is part of the Roman Church to this day. Criteria for sainthood include such evidence. Miraculous power is surely not the whole story of heroic sanctity, but, consistent with Christian belief in the Resurrection, i.e., in the power of a new and transcendent force in nature, extraordinary disciples of the Christian way are expected to demonstrate the reality of this New Spirit. And indeed the rules of canonization call for evidence of miraculous power in all candidates for sainthood, evidence, let us say, that the *anastasis* of nature is already in process. Sainthood is the acme of the Christian deathcraft.

Levitations, bilocations, stigmata, healings, discernment of spirits, prophecy, bodily incorruption and other saintly phenomena may be taken as powerful signs of the Christian *ars moriendi*. Perhaps one of the most powerful signs of Resurrection at work in nature is the phenomenon of bodily incorruption. It is a matter of ascertainable fact that many Catholic saints have either escaped or delayed the natural course of bodily corruption. Some cases have been meticulously attested by medical reports and eye-witnesses. Normal accounting for these preservations is often difficult to provide.

The incorruptibles—they are a distinguished company including Theresa of Avila, John of the Cross, Francis Xavier—are dramatic expressions of the peculiarly Christian idea of the spiritual potential of the body. It is as though the incorrupt bodies of the saints are a sensible foretaste of the Resurrection, signs that a unique power has incarnated itself in nature, undermining the dominion of death. Let me offer one (among many possible) examples: St. Andrew of Bobola. The description is from Joan Carroll Cruz's [13] study:

> Prior to his martydom he [St. Andrew] was partially flayed alive, his hands were hacked off and his tongue was torn from his head. Splinters of wood were driven under his fingernails, and his face sustained such mutilations that he was scarcely recognizable. After hours of further tortures and mutilations, he was dispatched by a sword's blow at the neck. His body was hastily buried by Catholics in a vault beneath the Jesuit church at Pinsk, where it was found forty years later perfectly preserved, in spite of the open wounds, which would normally foster corruption. Although his grave had been damp, causing his vestments to rot, and in spite of the proximity of decaying corpses, his body was perfectly flexible, his flesh and muscles soft to the touch, and the blood which covered the numerous wounds was found to be like that which is freshly congealed. The preservation was officially recognized by the Congregation of Rites in 1845. Even though the relic was roughly handled during its numerous translations, the body remains after more than three hundred years in a marvelous state of preservation.

The rebellion against death and fallen nature, against the tyranny of the "corrupt" body, continues to manifest in a wide assortment of "miracles." [14] Evidence of a Higher Power periodically erupts into our world: the levitations of Theresa of Avila or Joseph of Copertino; the stigmata, healings and bilocations of Padre Pio; the dried blood relics of Januarius that periodically, inexplicably, liquefy in the Naples Cathedral. [15] Dramatic phenomena are claimed by modern charismatics. Examples are plentiful for those willing to investigate the facts. The original Easter message, the original vision and transforming power, is the source of a continuous process of renewal and transformation. The evolution of Western civilization remains under the spell of this powerful spiritual impetus.

These extraordinary phenomena are the *by-products* of the Christian way of life. The Cross is the symbol of the way, the symbol of love that triumphs over death. The Christian idea of resurrection, understood as the founding of a new order of psychophysical reality, goes beyond Platonic and Eastern conceptions of immortality. The Christian Good News invites us to partake in the ultimate experiment: to live in such a way that we gradually incarnate the divine on earth.

This primordial Christian vision, in contrast to the narrower medieval and eighteenth century model of *ars moriendi*, is especially relevant to a modern craft of dying. First, the accent is on existential transformation, the most dramatic symbol of which is the Resurrection. Second, in line with the scientifically minded, New Age spirit, the Christian transformation deals in observable, psychophysical effects. The Holy Spirit—the psychokinetic agency of concrete transformation—actively produces empirical phenomena which, however exceptional, are subject to impartial verification.

It should be noted, however, that liberal Christianity has so far shown little interest in using psychical research in its effort to reconcile ancient faith with modern rationality. The liberal theologians have demythologized Christianity. Yet it was the belief in the supernatural, the living mythology of the resurrection, and the reality of the miraculous, that inspired the primitive Christian communities. Psychical research offers the key to remythologizing Christianity and a way to enrich a new Christian deathcraft.

The Future and the New Age

The idea of a New Age, a powerful force in the modern consciousness movement, can be traced back to the New Testament. The fact that our calendar dates from the birth of Christ testifies to this debt. The idea of a new mind—of *metanoia* or psychic transformation—is rooted in the Christian tradition. The vision of a New Age, once born in Western consciousness, has haunted men and women of all periods in our history. The bulk of human cultures have usually placed the Time of Best Things, the Golden Age, back in the days of old, the days of auroral beginnings. The Western tradition is driven by goal-oriented energies. Like the proverbial phoenix, the magical bird of the Christoform spirit is continually reborn. The lure of the future draws the West eternally on.

The goal-oriented spirit is at work in the apocalyptic tradition. "And I saw a new heaven and a new earth; for the first heaven and the first earth were passed away," writes John of Patmos, and further, "Behold, I make all things new," (Rev. :21). Out of this evolved the idea that the world would witness a final conflict between the forces of Christ and Antichrist, that a warrior Christ with miraculous powers would triumph over the wicked and that the elect of God would be saved. A new life of peace and justice was envisaged, a life in which nature would be pacified, spiritualized. "And God shall wipe away all tears from their eyes; and there shall be no more death." (Rev. 21:4) This is the most radical promise of the Christian New Age Vision.

Throughout centuries of the Christian era, the New Spirit has inspired diverse historical movements animated by the belief that a new world was coming. The writings of the eleventh century Calabrian prophet, Joachim of Fiore [16], became a model for apocalyptic spirituality. According to Joachim, there are three stages of history, each stage under the dispensation of one of the three persons in the Holy Trinity: the Father, the Son and the Holy Spirit. The Father signifies the reign of law and servitude; the Son presides over the age of faith and filial concern; under the aegis of the Holy Spirit the last age of history would commence and be marked by freedom, love and contemplative joy. The implications of this view of history are radical; the reign of the Holy Spirit is the reign of freedom from the letter of the law.

Joachim was a loyal son of the Church, but the Joachite philosophy of history appeared in secular theories of social evolution, especially among the nineteenth century German idealist philosophers. Thinkers like Lessing, Schelling, Fichte, Hegel, Comte and Marx were influenced by the Joachite view of the three ages of history. Some scholars even trace the spirit of National Socialism to the trinitarian archetype. Thus, according to Norman Cohn [17], the idea of the Third Reich, "adopted as a name for that 'new order' which was supposed to last a thousand years, would have had but little emotional significance if the phantasy of a third and most glorious dispensation had not, over the centuries, entered into the common stock of European social mythology."

The fact is that Joachim's thought—quite apart from the author's intentions—lent itself to anti-ecclesiastical and anti-establishment sentiment. The Church was identified with the fearful and submissive stage of history. The vision of spiritual apocalypse spawned millenarian cults, mystical anarchists and eschatological revolutionaries: movements like the Flagellants, the Franciscan Spirituals, the Brethren of Free Spirits, the Amaurians and many others. What these movements had in common was a belief in the power of a New Spirit to renovate human life and society.

In one pattern, the belief in a new spiritual body took the form of release from conventional sexual restraints. The quest to abolish bodily death became a search for the erotic innocence of Adam and Eve before the fall. If the overcoming of death were not immediately feasible, one could at least struggle to release the paradisical potential of the human body. In fact, this theme of New Age erotics recurs in modern social theories in Herbert Marcuse's *Eros and Civilization* [18] and in the works of Norman O. Brown. The problem of transcending death becomes the problem of the resurrection: the full recovery of the erotic body, the body freed from repression and death-anxiety. The new dispensation, the new heaven, was envisaged as a liberated sensuous existence on earth.

Feuerbach, Death and the New Age

We can see this translation into temporality in the New Age speculations of the nineteenth century German philosopher, Ludwig Feuerbach. Feuerbach's conception of the birth of the New Age was closely tied to his philosophy of death. In 1830 he published a book called *Thoughts on Death and Immortality* [19], an energetic mixture of brilliant insight and acerbic rhetoric.

Feuerbach, along with Stirner, Marx, Kierkegaard, Bakunin and others took upon themselves the task of destroying the edifice of Hegelian philosophy. The philosophy of Hegel represents a grand effort at synthesis of many opposing strands of European thought, a struggle to generate new life out of the fractured consciousness of the post-scientific world. Hegel strove mightily to reconcile history with God, the organic Greek conception of the city-state with the apocalyptic spirit of Christianity, the discords of time and becoming with the harmonies of eternity. A critic of romantic individualism, he nevertheless affirmed the value of the human subject. For Hegel, the essence of philosophical dialectic was to break down the one-sidedness of thought. Truth, he said, was the Whole. Hegel was a prophet of modern holism.

The thinkers that followed Hegel were uncongenial to the ideals of synthesis and holism. Feuerbach, like other young Hegelians, spun his philosophy out of a few pieces of the whole Hegelian fabric. In his *Thoughts on Death and Immortality*, the chief problem is the divided consciousness. (Marx would speak, especially in the early philosophical writings of 1844, of *alienation*.) The Christianity of false pietism causes us to project our spiritual energies into a vague future state; sentimental fantasies of an afterlife drain life from our present, sensuous existence. We become alienated from our true powers, enthralled by the abstractions we forge. The most damaging abstraction is the selfish ego, which hinders us from full participation in communal life.

For Feuerbach, the concrete human community is the locus of love and liberty. The abstraction of God must also be overcome. God is the projection of the highest powers of humanity: the supreme symbol of the divided consciousness. The radical challenge is to recapture the displaced energies of our consciousness. Like the *Bardo Thodol*, Feuerbach urges us to become aware that we ourselves are the Fundamental Clear Light and, to recognize our projections, self-veilings and self-imprisonings.

The *Bardo Thodol*, however, like Hegel, doesn't predicate the concepts of either/or but in terms of both/and. The Divine is not *only* a projection of the psyche; it also has a life of its own in a world beyond time and space. Jung notes how hard this idea is for the Western mind: "But though the European can easily explain away these deities as projections, he would be quite incapable of positing them as real." [20] Feuerbach—and later Freud—certainly hit upon important psychic mechanisms of religious life. But it remains for Jungian thought and parapsychology to show that the psychic realm stretches deeper and wider than physicalism and personalism allow.

Feuerbach was no doubt justified in railing against the false piety of his day. Here is one of his epigrams: "For these gentlemen, religion is a life-insurance company. Even sacrifice relates only to one's good; and God for them is the grease on the squeaky wagon of life that makes the wheels turn more easily." Religious ideas can be exploited for selfish reasons. Nietzsche and Freud made similar points: religion sometimes becomes an instrument for both disguising, and inflicting, one's neurosis on the world. Fear, even hatred of life, may conceal itself behind religious behavior; human energies are vainly spent on the abstractions and projections of religious experience.

According to the left-wing Hegelians, the poison seeps into all aspects of life. The whole of organized society falls prey to self-alienating abstractions and projections. For the philosophical anarchist, government itself was such a mental artifact. A product of *nomos* (to use the ancient Sophist word), of mere convention, government is the creation of the human mind. It does not derive its sanction from *nature* but from essentially arbitrary human fiats. It may serve us to be reminded of the conventional and mind-dependent status of these constructs. Governments are also projections in the *Chonyid Bardo* of political life, and we can free ourselves from their enchantment. Since we made them, we can also unmake them. Ultimately, the authority of government is not rationally justifiable, the anarchist argues. [21] The first step is to recognize the Clear Light of this fundamental anarchist truth: governments are human constructs, legal fictions, dreams of authority. When they become nightmares, we are entitled to "wake up" from them.

We who watch the planet around us changing into a nuclear battlefield might learn something from these rebels against Hegel. For in current times the human race, as never before, is hostage to the governments of the world. Worse, it is as though the human race is hostage to a world-government—but not to one bound by universal reason or international law.

And yet, the young Hegelians remind us, we have made the monster with our own hands: labor, taxes and votes. We sink into the lower bardo of global politics, confused and terrified by our own awesome fictions: the Wrathful Atomic Divinities. Through our own labor, as Marx said, we create the world that oppresses us. The hope expressed in these philosophies of freedom was that we can uncreate the nightmare we dream into existence, the nightmare we incarnate through our daily deeds.

Unfortunately, Feuerbach got snared in one of his own projections, namely, "religion"—that vast catchword which hides so many worlds of human experience. Feuerbach displays a fundamentalist cast of mind when he states, "As they posit a future life, they negate the actual life." But *must* it be either/or? "For if there is life after death," he goes on, "there cannot be life before death; one excludes the other; the present life cancels the future life, the future life cancels the present life."

But there is no incompatibility between being present-centered and engaging in a life of dialogue with the Transcendent. (Some might say that the two need each other.) As a matter of fact, Feuerbach did distinguish between a certain species of false piety, between purveyors of the divided consciousness and a more authentic, visionary strain of religious consciousness he associated with primitive Catholicism. He once remarked that a "senseless visionary" is more equipped to understand the Bible than a scholarly theologian. The idea, I take it, is that one must be in the right state of mind to fully appreciate writings that were, at least in part, the product of people in extraordinary states of mind. Genuine Christian ethics is an ethics of inspiration. Those who merely fake it become candidates for the psychoanalytical couch.

Feuerbach's revulsion against false piety resulted in a disabled openness to the Transcendent. Nevertheless, Feuerbach, like Nietzsche and all great rebels against traditional religion, is still brimful of immortal longings. He still craves to behold the "heroic shapes of reality." His writings quiver with talk of infinity, immortality and universality. The difference is that he struggles to squeeze all the old categories of transcendence into the shrunken frame of sensuous, time-bound existence.

Sometimes Feuerbach falls back upon the old romantic conceit that in death we might experience the triumph of love. In self-transcending, self-giving love we acquire a kind of immortality. This is why the idea of community was crucial to Feuerbach. The collective structures of society become a vehicle for a rather elusive form of temporal immortality. But for me, Feuerbach's temporal immortality is as "insubstantial" a shadow as ever drained the vital spirits of the false pietist.

Still, a modern craft of dying has much to learn from Feuerbach. We do need today, as always, to address the ills of the divided consciousness. The Craft we envision must, as Neitzsche and Feuerbach would have it, be faithful to human life on earth, to its needs and meta-needs. But there is nothing in this fidelity to the quality of earthly existence that need close us to the possible beckonings of the Transcendent. The attempt to extract immortality from history makes impossible demands on history and at the same time perverts the idea of immortality.

Deathcraft in the Nuclear Age

According to Elizabeth Kübler-Ross [22], friend and healer of the dying, the stage of dying is also a stage of intense growth. The terminal situation is a challenge to growth; dying shakes up the basic structure of personality, throws open the door to new possibilities of perception and relationship. Now if indeed we are a terminal civilization, then we may be (collectively) caught up in a forced challenge to personal growth. By terminal civilization, I mean—as we shall see in Part Six—a civilization threatened by extinction through nuclear war.

The nuclear age, which in one sense threatens to be terminal, in another sense promises to be seminal, primal; a "new" age. The nuclear age, by threatening us with collective catastrophe, is also forcing us to face the radical necessity of inner change.

There is a growing, global movement inspired by this awareness. It flows from different sources and goes under different names: secular and religious peace movements, the scientific search for a new paradigm, the consciousness revolution. Under the banner of a new age outlook, these currents are converging as a collective response to the dangers of the nuclear age. The idea of a new deathcraft is particularly relevant to a civilization in the throes of nuclear terminalism, and there are several reasons for this.

It is generally acknowledged that our secular culture is beset by the denial of death. [23] Now, the inability to face personal death is likely to make it all the more difficult to face the idea of planetary death. The pervasive denial of death makes it hard to face the prospects of nuclear war. But, if we cannot psychologically deal with these large-scale threats to life, we are apt to remain passive before them. A new outlook on death might help us to overcome nuclear paralysis of the will. It might help us to take a more active stand against the forces that threaten life itself.

Cultivating a personal deathcraft implies taking responsibility for our deaths. That would be a way of taking responsibility for our lives. We especially need to do this at present, as we increasingly give up responsibility for our lives to the military and political establishments. Security is supposed to lie in trusting the experts, yet the actions of a handful of men could wipe us all out. We need to reappropriate responsibility for our own lives and deaths.

As we shall see later, a new conception of death played a creative role in founding the new Christian civilization in the ancient world. I believe that founding a new civilization today also calls for a new conception of death. The roots of the nuclear disorder are spiritual; a new vision of life and death is needed to help us get to the bottom of the nuclear dilemma.

In the past few years, the medical profession has joined the worldwide anti-nuclear movement. Thousands of physicians have organized in an effort to educate the public on the medically catastrophic implications of nuclear war. The anti-nuclear physicians have concluded that the only cure for nuclear war is prevention.

The prevention of nuclear war is the greatest challenge to the healing and helping professions. Prevention, however, requires the right diagnosis of the disease. The disease, as I attempt to show in Chapters 13 and 14, pervades the whole of our modern culture; the epidemic of arms is a symptom of a systemic dis-ease of spirit. It is part of a syndrome I label "the thanatos conspiracy." It is my hope that the anti-nuclear physicians movement will follow through with a diagnosis of our culture's nuclear pathology, recognizing in it the need for a total interdisciplinary healing project. Part of this total project, I think, must be a critique, a revision of the prevailing nihilistic metaphysics of death.

The importance of a new deathcraft in the nuclear age may also be seen in this way. Science and the arms race are intimately allied. Science has made itself part of a deadly conspiracy against life. Science therefore needs to recover its "con-science." "Con-science"—to know *with:* to be con-scious of community. A glance at the interplay and etymology of these words is illuminating: science, conscience, consciousness. All three stem from a common matrix. To be "whole" they need each other. "Science" is a fragment of "conscience" and "consciousness." Science has lost its conscience. The millions who devote themselves to the science of murder and threatening murder are proof of this claim.

A metaphysics of death in the nuclear age must address this perilous splitting apart of science, conscience and consciousness. A modern deathcraft would base itself on research into those states of consciousness conducive to a transcendent outlook, conducive to a new kind of courage, a new respect for life. It would try to mobilize the inner forces we need to survive the crisis of the present age and to assist in the birthing of a New Age. It would explore the forms of consciousness that point the way back toward recovering the lost conscience of science.

A Healing Parable of Death

Let us imagine that life is a road whose end is obscure and whose direction is changing, shadowy and full of unpredictable twists and turns. And let us imagine that at the end of the road—what we call death—there waits an unknown monster. Imagine the most hideous of possible fates—conjure the Lord of Doom in whatever form you like. Or make your monster formless, a chilling presence. But know that this Lord of Doom whom you shall meet threatens to spring without warning on you, the wayfarer on the road of life. And the threat is constant: the risk of being attacked by the monster of death.

Such an unpleasant fantasy would seep into your bones; it would hinder you as you strode, or let us say skulked, with misgivings, on the road of life. With such a picture—mulled on or beaten to the back of the mind—you might hesitate to venture on the way. Under the burden of this dark anticipation, the timid soul (that we all sometimes are) could not, with Walt Whitman, say: "Afoot and light-hearted, I take to the open road!" No, far from it. You might be reluctant to step out at all. You might just dig a hole in the ground or bury yourself in a tree trunk. You might even use your own body to armor yourself against the weathers of the open road, against all possible adventures, any one of which might bring you face to face with Death, Monster of the Road, Lord of Doom.

Let us call this the Old Myth of Death. The Old Myth has modern secular and old religious versions. The common part is death viewed as negation, extinction, risk of damnation. The Old Myth—as strong today as ever—constricts our mode of being in the world. It cramps the swiftest runner and chills the warmest tropical spas. The image of the end of the road casts a shadow on every step of the journey. No matter where we happen to be standing—far away under open sky and dazzling sun—death still casts a long shadow, an ever-lengthening shadow.

The myth of death we cherish deeply colors the whole fabric of our life, and there are many ways we could shade in our sketch of wayfarers of the road. Some we might portray as studiously cultivating their shelter, until they were barely visible and hardly emerged to meet the world around them. Then there might be those who set out to trick fate by trying to inch their way backwards in a kind of inconspicuous terror, impeding their own progress and that of others. Still others in sudden bursts of bravado might charge forward, daring the Monster, so to speak, and trampling in heroic desperation on other wayfarers. It is easy to imagine these or other possibilities.

So let us now place a different picture before the wayfarer flung without choice on the road of life. Now suppose the traveler believes that instead of a Monster, a beautiful and mysterious Lover lies in wait at the road's end. Say that this Lover holds the key to the gates of paradise. Remember now that you can meet this keeper of the key, but not without first passing over the Bridge of Death. Indeed, there is a way to this mysterious beauty, a way that opens the heart of this enigmatic personage, Friend of all pilgrims of the universe. The way lies close at hand, no further than the span of a breath, but invisible and beyond the reach of human hands.

Now we can advise travelers to say farewell, to go forward and not to fear what lies ahead. Let us choose for the moment to trace such an image of Unknown Splendor, of Sublime Attractive Force.

Suppose now this image or myth of death pulsed in the blood of the wayfarer: instead of the old tightness, there would be a new looseness in the traveler's limbs. Perhaps now the wayfarer is ready to climb out of his hole, to leave behind the musty little burrow of your world and to head out on the road of life. The road, far less menacing now, beckons the traveler. At every turn, the signs say: Advance! The road of life now welcomes exploration. However obscure and unpredictable its winding detours and overpasses, the traveler will be drawn on by longing for the mysterious Lover. Trusting that a great Friend is waiting at the end of the road, it will be hard to discourage him from taking the risks of the way. No obstacle will be too great, no fear too strong and no sadness too deep to stop him from a brave and bold journey. He will feed on the spring of hope and grow stronger with the passage of time.

PART TWO

SURVIVAL: GOING ALL THE WAY

3

Sketch of a Science of
Transcendence

It is true that advance is partly the gathering of details into assigned patterns. This is the safe advance of dogmatic spirits, fearful of folly. But history discloses another type of progress, namely the introduction of novelty of pattern into conceptual experience. There is a new vision of the great Beyond.

—*Alfred North Whitehead*

The Riddle of the Sphinx

This curious center of experiences I call myself—will it cease and come to nothing with the death of my body? Or will it flicker on somewhere and somehow after death? Does our center of awareness persist, contract, or widen perhaps (as Plato, Butler and Bergson held), grow more dull or more brilliant, divide by fission into a plurality or fuse in new ways with other centers of consciousness? The survival problem raises the riddle of the Sphinx, the riddle of what it is to be a person, what is nowadays dryly treated by analytic philosophers as puzzles about personal identity, and what the rishis of the Hindu *Upanishads* treated as a psychological experiment of saving importance.

The orthodox scientific answer to the riddle of the Sphinx is well known. A human being is a physical object, unique in many remarkable ways, but essentially a complex machine. Nor can we say that a human being has or is a mind, soul or spirit; moreover, it is absurd, or at best immensely improbable, to say that human consciousness survives bodily death.

The evidence of psychical research—especially the more challenging survival data—clashes with this orthodox answer to the riddle. If indeed there were strong evidence of the persistence of consciousness after death, it would be hard to maintain the current scientific dogma that I as a person can no more be separated from my body than roundness can be separated from the penny in my pocket. Admittedly, the results of survival research are not conclusive. There may be special difficulties in this kind of research, but they need not be insurmountable.

The Hidden Face of Death

Owing to advances in medical technology, it is becoming increasingly difficult to agree on the definition of death. There are bewildering reports of people being resuscitated after lapses of time believed medically impossible. Life-sustaining techniques used with comatose patients create further difficulties. Nevertheless, medical definitions of death typically use behavioristic criteria such as flat EEG, absence of vital signs and so forth; they rely exclusively on what is publicly observable.

This is natural from the pragmatic standpoint. But unless philosophical behaviorism is true, there is an inner side to the human organism. An adequate definition of death ought to take into account the essentially *occult* side of the person. Flat EEG, expiration and other publicly observable signs of death don't of themselves imply that the curtain goes down on the hidden side of the person.

Whether or not the inner person continues to function after behavioral death is a question that psi science could help decide. If the weight of evidence inclined toward the survival hypothesis, then a redefinition of death would be in order. A redefinition of death would call for a new terminology. Along with a new vision, a new language of death is at stake. Survival research challenges us to rethink and rename the concept of death; it forces us to attempt to sketch the hidden face of death and to acknowledge the hidden meanings in our public language.

Death in modern society, like much of life, is one-dimensional. Survival research challenges our one-dimensional view of death. As such it also challenges our one-dimensional view of Self.

The Origins of Psi Science

The origins of psychical research were linked to a quest for the multi-dimensional Self. Frederic Myers, for instance, wrote in his great work, *Human Personality and Its Survival of Bodily Death:*

> The 'conscious Self' of each of us, as we call it,—the empirical, the supraliminal Self, as I should prefer to say—does not comprise the whole of the consciousness or of the faculty within us. There exists a more comprehensive consciousness, a profounder faculty, which for the most part remains potential only so far as regards the life on earth, but from which the consciousness and faculty of earth-life are mere selections, and which reasserts itself in its plenitude after the liberating change of death. [24]

Myers called this "more comprehensive consciousness" the *subliminal Self*—an idea close to that of Jung's *objective psyche* or *Self*. These terms are reincarnations of the older, religiously derived, *soul*, a word rejected by scientific orthodoxy. The work of Myers and the early psychical researchers, and the more recent work of Jung and, his associates, have helped to verify empirically the reality of the world-old notion of the human soul. The overarching concern of the early psi scientists was, in effect, to found a new science of the spirit. As Myers wrote on the first page of his *magnum opus*, the method of science "has never yet been applied to the all-important problem of the existence, the powers, the destiny of the human soul."

But when science interrogates nature, unexpected answers are often given, answers that lead toward new directions of enquiry. Indeed, modern parapsychology has wandered from the original goal of the first psi researchers and is pursuing new questions in new ways. The shift in focus took place by 1934 with the publication of J. B. Rhine's *Extra-Sensory Perception*. [25] Although the original impetus behind Rhine's work, like that of the British founding fathers, was to validate religious belief through empirical science, the focus shifted to experimental parapsychology. The card-guessing paradigm with its stress on statistical evaluation of controlled experimental results displaced the big but intractable concerns of Myers, the Sidgwicks, William Barrett, Oliver Lodge and the rest of the soul-seeking pioneers. The problem became the experimental validation of psi and the conditions under which it could be observed and possibly controlled. Do moods, states of consciousness, personality traits, physical barriers and so forth influence the way psi manifests in nature? Increasingly, modern technology and methodologies were used for detecting and, hopefully, controlling psi occurrences. Slow but steady progress is visible here.

The comprehensive vision of the early researchers, however, is no longer an explicit part of recent work in this field. In particular, the concern for the "destiny" of the soul that Myers spoke of is the concern of few contemporary researchers. Survival research is no longer at the center of psi science, no longer the informing spirit of research. Virtually none of the (apparently provocative) near-death research is being done by parapsychologists; among some of the people in the near-death field there even seems to be an anti-parapsychological bias. Among those who show a pronounced interest in the spiritual implications of psi research—and there are growing signs of this interest—the experimental concerns tend to be unduly neglected. In short, the current scene shows a fragmentation of interests with tension, sometimes amounting to antipathy, between "pure" science and "pure" spirit.

In spite of much bold theorizing by rigorous experimentalists today, none of the new models or theories is directly concerned with survival; with few exceptions most researchers prefer to shelve the problem. The argument usually voiced is that we cannot probe the question of a possible otherworldly psi until we know more about this-worldly psi. Nevertheless, if there *is* an "otherworldly" dimension to psi, it may well be crucial to our understanding of this-worldly psi. Survival research may occupy a strategic position for understanding psi and its place in nature. On the chance that this is so, psi research in general should bear in mind its possible connections with the survival hypothesis. Psi data may make more sense if looked at in relation to survival data; an approach that unifies this-worldly and "transcendent" psi may prove to be more fruitful than the present fragmented approach. Let us consider why this may be so.

Psi and Transcendence: A Unified Framework

Suppose, for instance, that the primary function of psi in nature is to mediate an order of being distinct from and higher than that of our embodied existence. But before we try to develop this idea, we might ask why anyone, given the present climate of thought, would be tempted to entertain such a view?

At least two reasons suggest themselves. First, psi itself stubbornly resists physical explanation. Parapsychologists have long noted certain facts that militate against a physical explanation of psi. Further, there is a growing body of argument that points to logical difficulties in any physical explanation of psi. [26, 5] The combination of logical and empirical objections to a physical explanation of psi have thus led to recent attempts toward new types of models and theories of psi functioning based on nonmechanist notions such as correspondence, conformance behavior, synchronicity and the like. [27] Despite much disagreement among writers over details, there is a broad consensus pointing toward dissatisfaction with conventional mechanist-materialist models of psi functioning.

The second, more positive, reason that favors entertaining such a hypothesis is that a massive testimony of human experience speaks of a nonphysical or supernatural order of reality. Whatever may be the ultimate interpretation of this testimony, there is a primordial tradition of human response to the Transcendent. Mystic, seer, saint, poet, prophet and shaman converge in descriptions of their encounters with a transcendent spiritual reality. The nonphysicality of psi is consonant with this universe of over-belief. Psychic and spiritual experience both refer beyond the known landmarks of physical reality. Each in their own way is testimony to the reality of transcendence.

Let us then assume that the function of psi is ultimately to serve a higher order of spiritual reality. Let us further assume that the spiritual order, although it intersects with the physical order, comprehends it the way that perhaps the Jungian Self comprehends the ego or Myers' Subliminal Self comprehends the supraliminal self. There are different ways of trying to conceptualize this "higher" order of spiritual reality. One typical ploy is to talk of a higher "dimension" extending beyond the three-dimensional world of sensory experience which would account for the properties of "extended" human potentialities. For the moment, however, we need not attempt to clarify in detail the concept of a higher spiritual order. Our aim here is just to think of psi as an expression of that order.

Once we assume that the main function of psi lies in a transcendent spiritual world, the consistent elusiveness of psi effects begin to make more sense. If the function of psi is essentially otherworldly, then we need not be surprised how transient and marginal an effect we find it to be in *this* world. In this world, we normally rely upon the sensory-motor system for engaging the environment. Despite some evidence that occasionally psi serves the needs of the organism—sometimes without conscious awareness—its *day-to-day* survival value in the terrestrial struggle for existence seems to be slight by comparison with our bodily senses. Clairvoyance, for instance, could never compete with the eye of an organism; not, at least, if reliability is any index of survival value.

One way we can look at the present hypothesis is by talking of the goal-oriented nature of psi. Helmut Schmidt, the physicist-parapsychologist, has defined psychokinesis as "a goal-oriented principle, one that aims successfully at a final event, no matter how intricate the intermediate steps." [28] Subjects in Schmidt's experiments influenced the outputs of complex machines based on electronic and radioactive emissive behavior just by concentrating on the final outcome. Success was independent of task complexity; results were achieved merely by mentally picturing the goal, not by calculating steps for arriving at the goal. In a typical experiment, a subject directs attention at a circular panel of nine lights, consciously willing that the lights move in a clockwise or counter-clockwise direction. To succeed, the subject has to modify random radioactive behavior of a random event generator, a machine of which he may not have the slightest understanding. Schmidt produced successful experiments with immense odds against the chance hypothesis. In these experiments, thought has modified physical reality *directly*. In a sense, this is "magic," a demonstration of the primitive belief in the "omnipotence of thought." All the subject does is goal-direct consciousness, and somehow the goal is expressed in a physical state of affairs.

Psi, let us then assume, is a goal-oriented process of living substance. We may now ask if life as a whole is goal-oriented. One answer to this question is that the goal of life essentially is *more life*. The life process consists of the reproduction, expansion and increasing complication of itself. For example, the tendency among mammals, and man in particular, is toward greater mobility and greater detachment from the environment. Human life is especially mobile and already has begun to move beyond the planetary habitat to explore new habitats in outer space.

But must we suppose that the goal-oriented process of life halts at the limits of the physical world? If the goal of life is more life—in a word, survival—and if psi serves the needs of life's goals, then psi may be an instrument for mediating survival of bodily death itself. The spiritual order we hypothesize would name the stage at which the evolution of life transcends the earthly environment. Once we are willing to entertain this logical extension of the goal-oriented nature of life and psi, and postulate a transcendent evolutionary tendency, we may look at several kinds of phenomena in a fresh and unified light. Artworks that exemplify autonomy of form, utopian spiritual communities, plans for space colonization, psi and survival data, may all be seen as expressing the same push toward transcendence.

All modes of creative activity would, by our hypothesis, be animated by a single goal: the creation of a transcendent environment, an environment in tune with the aims of infinite life. Parapsychology cuts across and, in a sense, underlies our creative life by demonstrating that mind can, in effective ways, function independently of the normal constraints of physics and chemistry.

If the goal of life is more life, higher, freer and more complex forms of life, then psi may represent the next medium of self-transcending life. Psi, thus understood as a transcendent function, is the wedge of life driving through the most fundamental obstacles to the evolutionary process: the inertness and resistance of mechanical reality, the boundaries of time and space. Psi, the transcendent function of mind, may also be viewed as the medium in which new forms of life are carrying us beyond the restrictive boundaries of the earthly environment.

Human existence is amphibian. As bodies we must adapt to the earthly environment; but as psi-mediated minds or spirits we may be evolving toward a transcendent environment, a world freed from the physical limitations of time and space. The non-physicality of psi and the experience of the Transcendent, taken together, invite us to consider psi as a transcendent function. The plausibility of this hypothesis in increased when we consider the biologically puzzling side of psi.

Gardner Murphy, the great American psychologist, wondered why, on Darwinian principles, living organisms do not develop increasing psi ability, which would obviously be of great survival value. For instance, an animal could escape a predator. If psi ability were genetically coded, moreover, we would expect natural selection to work toward a growing incidence of psi function, at least among some favored species. But there is no evidence of psi becoming a *biologically stronger* function; further, the consensus among parapsychologists is that psi, unlike most normal psychological abilities, is unlearnable. In fact, almost all the empirical evidence indicates that psi abilities decline with use; one of the most reliable bits of knowledge about psi functioning is enshrined in the expression, "decline effect." Psi functions in a way that seems to be almost inversely proportional to normal biological functioning. Murphy is right, then, in speaking of psi ability as a "profound biological enigma." [29]

Driven by the paradox of the sheer existence of this biologically quirkish psi function, Murphy goes on to speculate that "behind these apparently capricious expressions of a power beyond the ordinary, there is good reason to believe that there exists a *deeper level of function*, a level at which, perhaps, the paranormal is the normal." Murphy suggests that there are two modes in which an organism is capable of functioning: one, the sensory mode, in space and time; another, the psi mode, independently of space and time. In the deeper psi mode, the paranormal is the normal, but this could only be a mode in which the sensory mode were suspended or, as in death, superseded. The psi that appears fitfully and elusively in the terrestrial environment would be the essential mediator of the transcendent environment.

More recently, the English philosopher and psychologist, John Beloff, has again called attention to the biological enigma of psi. "There is an evolutionary niche to correspond with almost every conceivable mode of life on Earth and yet, so far as we know, there is no species which depends critically on using extrasensory perception. One is entitled to ask why, if psi is a reality, it has not been exploited in the struggle for existence." [30] Like Murphy, Beloff is puzzled by the biological enigma of psi. How indeed does psi stand with respect to the phenomenon of life? If we could get clearer on this question, we might begin to understand psi with respect to the phenomenon of death.

Unfortunately, few biologists show much interest in the problem of psi; yet the challenge is as great as any in modern times. Men like Freud, Einstein and Darwin have forced us to refashion our thinking on aspects of the familiar worlds of time and space. Psi science, in an even more radical vein, may force us to face the possibility of unfamiliar worlds in some sense beyond ordinary time and space.

The Theory of Natural Selection

Nevertheless, some biologists and biology-minded people have begun to think about the implications of psi for the science of life. There are puzzles about the end of life, survival-related phenomena, that just don't jibe with the mechanist view of things, and there are puzzles about the origin and development of life. My object is simply to juxtapose these puzzles and to attempt, as seems natural, to look at them as if they were related, as pieces belonging to a larger puzzle. What follows is not a comprehensive review of what has been said on this subject; my more limited aim is to mark that thought is on the move here and that our basic understanding of life and death remains an open question.

In fact, the attempt to connect psi with the science of life came at the very beginning of modern evolutionary theory. Alfred Russel Wallace, one of the co-founders of the modern theory of evolution, was an early researcher into spiritistic phenomena, even before the founding of the English Society for Psychical Research. In 1874 Wallace said that natural selection "is not the all-powerful, all-sufficient, and only cause of the development of organic forms." [31] In the Tenth Chapter of his *Contributions to the Theory of Natural Selection*, he cites certain residual phenomena which he thought might be accounted for by a psi factor or by the operation of "preternatural intelligences." Wallace describes how by education and temperament, he was exposed to the most hard-boiled materialism but that acquaintance with certain facts "beat" him. Some of the facts concern the physical mediumship of Mrs. Guppy, a lady whose psi feats gave pause even to the redoubtable sceptic, Frank Podmore. Thus, psi and biological theory were linked up from the very start, as may also be seen from the Baron Carl du Prel, the early investigator who coined the word "parapsychology." He believed that the next step of human evolution lies in the sphere of psychic development.

The English biologist, John Randall, has made several bold and comprehensive hypotheses concerning the parapsychology of life. [32] Randall's overall strategy is as follows: first, he reviews problems in biological theory which Darwinian orthodoxy cannot handle. Second, experimental evidence is cited for the influence of psi on living systems. Third, a transcendent psi factor—Randall calls it Mind at Large—is advanced as a hypothesis to account for aspects of life neglected by the orthodox view.

Among the chinks in the mechanist armor that critics like Randall focus upon, three in particular stand out: the problems of the origin, the development and the forms of life. To begin with, there is the problem of the origin of life. The orthodox view is that living matter arose by chance from a combination of inanimate molecules. But if the origin of life was a random event, it must have also been, as Sir Frederick Gowland Hopkins, the discoverer of vitamins, once said, "the most improbable and the most significant event in the history of the universe." One of the founders of population genetics, Sir Ronald Fisher, once remarked that evolution was a device for generating improbability.

The truth is that extraordinary improbability argues against the chance hypothesis; and the orthodox view is that life is a product of chance. A number of writers, using different approaches, have tried

to specify in exact mathematical terms the improbability of life originating by chance. For what it is worth, we might mention some of
these numbers. For instance, H. Quastler, [33] a prominent biochem-
ist, came up with 10-301 as the odds against a chance derivation of
life.

The Cambridge zoologist W. H. Thorpe was willing to grant the
assumption that an aqueous solution of amino acids was formed under primordial terrestrial conditions. Others have shown by experiment how this *might* have been possible. But the real problem is how
the amino acids were built up into complex proteins and enzymes.
According to Thorpe, the improbability of the formation of any enzyme by chance is fantastically high. [34] The claim is that in the
combinations of molecules essential to enzyme production, each separate molecule would have had to have occupied a volume of 10/50
times the volume of the earth. Based on such calculations, Thorpe
virtually ruled out the chance hypothesis of life's origin.

Such arguments need to be viewed with caution, since they cannot help being based on questionable assumptions; but they should
at least give pause to those who think the mere immensity of the
earth's age renders the chance hypothesis automatically plausible.
Many mathematicians do not think so. That same specious plausibility receives a further blow from the following: recent fossil findings
are pushing back the time when there is evidence for life on earth,
back possibly even to 3.2 or 3.8 billion years ago. Given the need for
the earth to cool to reasonable temperatures, say 4.2 billion years ago,
this seems not to give much time for the improbable chain of events
necessary for the formation of life to have occurred—less than half a
billion years. The improbability is increased by evidence indicating
that it took *three billion* years for nucleated protista to evolve from the
prokaryotes. Why did this particular step in evolution take so long
and the leap from inanimate to animate being take such a relatively
short time? Something, as G. R. Taylor [33] says, is missing in the
story. In any case, the truth is that nobody really *knows* how life began. The mechanist faith in the play of random forces is no more
justified than the theist faith in design.

Entropy and Information Theory

There are other, more general ways to argue against the chance
hypothesis of the origin of life: for instance, by using the Second Law
of Thermodynamics, according to which all physical systems tend

toward a state of maximum entropy or disorder. The physical universe as a whole appears like a vast death-bound process. Scientists have argued for the inevitability of the "thermal death" of the universe, a time when the candle of creation would be forever extinguished.

Yet despite this chilly drift toward extinction, there are exceptions to the apparent cosmic trend, small pockets of improbability where life and anti-entropy are thriving. Living things seem to be swimming upstream in the entropic current; moreover, the tendency of evolution is toward *decreasing* entropy, greater order and complexity. Life, in short, is anti-entropic, as Julian Huxley asserts in his Introduction to Teilhard de Chardin's *Phenomenon of Man*. [35] Those who dislike discontinuity are bound to recoil at this. The picture is brazenly dualistic, suggesting that reality is in conflict with itself, or at any rate that there are two opposing principles or tendencies at work in the universe.

Efforts have been made to avoid the argument around entropy. The physicist E. Schroedinger [36] said that living organisms feed on "negative entropy," in other words, that they extract order from the environment. But this would seem to beg the question concerning the origin of life. What we need to know is how the environment produced the anti-entropic systems in the first place.

Or else it is said that the Second Law of Thermodynamics only applies to closed systems; but since living systems are open, exchanging matter and energy with other systems, increases in entropy may be avoided through metabolism; even *decreases* of entropy become feasible in open systems. But this also seems to beg the question of *how* open, that is, living, systems arose in the first place. In any case, it is clear that if a system is open, it cannot become *more* orderly than it already is unless it derives the increase of order from a system outside itself.

Assuming then that the order or information essential to produce life did not derive from the nonliving physical universe, then we need to hypothesize a nonphysical ordering principle to account for the origin of life. This line is somewhat analogous to Aristotle's argument for the existence of an Unmoved Mover. For Aristotle, movement or change in the Universe is unintelligible unless we postulate a First Cause of movement; without such a First Cause, the whole chain of movements would be unintelligible.

In a similar vein, we are saying that the great mechanist chain of living being is unintelligible unless we postulate a First Cause of Life logically independent of the mechanist chain. Nothing, by the way, is gained by saying with astronomer Fred Hoyle that life arrived on floating spores from outer space; this only postpones dealing with the difficulty of trying to reduce order to disorder or of trying to extract life out of death.

The modern concept of entropy is also used quantitatively in Information Theory. Thus, a living being may be thought of as expressing a system of information; a decrease of its entropy would then constitute an increase of information. Thorpe estimates the information of a bacterial cell to be of the order of 10/12 bits and finds it hard to believe that the living world, packed with such huge orders of information, arose accidentally from a primordial gas, the most random type of physical system in nature, that is, the type with the least amount of information.

The problem of accounting for the origin of life on the basis of chance shades into the problem of the development of life. Once again we have to account for the sudden increases of information or order; the directedness, creativeness and increasing complexity of life. According to the orthodox conception, all these properties can be explained by natural selection.

Darwinism and the Development of Life

Characteristics are selected which render the organism more fit to adapt to the environment. But what does "fit" mean here? Apparently, the "fitter" organism is the one that leaves more offspring, thus insuring the replication of its genes. If it has any "goal," the goal of natural selection as the mechanism of evolution is to further the survival of the fittest organisms, the ones that successfully reproduce themselves. But if this is the ruling tendency of the evolutionary process, why should any but the simplest organisms have appeared on the scene? Bacteria, algae, perhaps the protista are obviously as "fit," if not "fitter" than the more complex metazoa; that is, they are as good at reproducing themselves as reptiles, say, or mammals. What advantage—given this concept of fitness—lay in the evolution of higher forms of life? Natural selection, the survival of the fittest, are purely quantitative concepts and fail to account for the *qualitative* evolution of life.

Gradualism, the idea that evolution takes place through a gradual accumulation of accidental variations that have adaptive value, is a cardinal principle of orthodox Darwinism. Nevertheless, biologists are amazed by the sudden leaps to new levels of adaptation. The longer the leap, the greater the number of adaptive variations and the greater the need for them to be synchronized and coordinated. The longer the "leap," the less it looks like a *gradual* accumulation of favorable variations because *one* new adaptation that doesn't afford any advantage will, on the mechanist theory, automatically select out. Mechanism relies on smooth transitions, yet even G. G. Simpson, who is an orthodox Darwinian, asserts that "the absence of transitional forms is an almost universal phenomenon," and adds that "the line making connection with common ancestry is not known even in one instance." [37] A more recent critique of gradualism comes from the work of two Americans, Stephen Gould and Niles Elredge, who see the evolutionary process as punctuated by the sudden appearance of fully evolved forms. [38]

Nothing seems to dismay believers in the omnipotence of mechanist science more than discontinuities in nature. Yet discontinuity is everywhere to be found and at the most critical junctures: for instance, at the juncture between nonliving and living processes. As the fossil records indicate, there are discontinuities at all levels of the evolutionary process. For instance, they exist between the procaryotes and the eucaryotes, between the protista and the metazoa, between life-forms of the sea and life-forms of the land.

One must, in fact, look at the details—which is beyond the scope of this book—to appreciate the problem of these biological discontinuities. Consider, to take one example, the saltation from reptiles to birds. Some of the changes required for flight include the development of feathers, a modified brain (a larger cerebellum for balance), a larger visual cortex, reduction of weight, the body condensed into a compact shape, legs and feet reduced to a minimum, the pelvis strengthened to absorb the shock of landing, a crop for reserving fuel, new air sacs and a system of thermal regulation for coping with high altitudes. All these new developments, we are supposed to believe, resulted from essentially haphazard variations, each individual variation synchronized with all the rest. The greatest difficulty is in seeing the synchronized effect of all these variations without which none of them individually would have gotten off the ground, so to speak.

For a bracing review of the specifics of saltations—such as the appearance of bone, the trilobite eye (or compound eyes in general), the amniote egg, flowering plants and so forth, the reader should turn to G. R. Taylor's *The Great Evolution Mystery*. Let us note here in passing that if Darwinian gradualism breaks down, Randall's hypothesis of a Transcendent Source of Information or Order intervening in the course of evolution acquires a greater degree of plausibility.

The Ultimate Discontinuity

But before we drop the issue of discontinuity and the hypothesis of transcendence, we should at least call attention to other, even more fundamental discontinuities noted in philosophic speculation. Pride of place belongs to the discontinuity between nonbeing and being itself. The question that many philosophers have asked is why there should be anything at all rather than nothing. The usual reply is that it makes no sense to ask such a question about the existence of the universe as a whole.

So, it is proper to ask for an explanation of a species of plant or animal, of the human brain, of the earth, of the solar system, of certain galaxies but not to ask about the existence of the universe as a totality. For my part, it seems arbitrary, though intellectually convenient, to pronounce against the right to ask the ultimate question about Being itself. When we do so, we find ourselves face to face with the Ultimate Discontinuity. The traditional way of handling this discontinuity is to invoke a Transcendent Principle; the modern scientific response is to call the question of being itself a pseudo-question, to repress the fundamental mystery of being.

In addition to the discontinuities of being erupting from nonbeing, of life and its complications from nonlife, we finally observe the discontinuity of consciousness erupting from living nervous systems. Once again, modern materialism struggles valiantly to deny, evade, repress and discredit the mystery of consciousness and its complications. This, of course, is one of the oldest problems of philosophy; and we are not going to tackle the mind-body problem here. Suffice it to say that one of the boldest solutions to this engima is comtemporary *identity theory* which attempts in one way or another to dispose of consciousness by identifying it with brain states. But philosophers find difficulties here. For instance, if consciousness is characterized by *intentionality* (as the phenomenologists say), then it cannot be identified with any brain state, since no brain state could be characterized by intentionality. Or using Leibnitz's Principle of the Non-Identity of Discernibles (things with discernible differences cannot be identical), the identity hypothesis founders, since there are things which we can assert of consciousness that we cannot assert of brain states. For instance, as already noted, intentionality is a property of consciousness that we cannot ascribe to brain states.

Biologic Utility and Consciousness

By far, the most decisive blow to a physicalistic elimination of consciousness is the existence of psi. Consciousness is a nasty stumbling block to mechanistic monism. As with psi, one wonders about the biological utility of consciousness, especially if one says with biologist John Maynard Smith that "The individual is simply a device constructed by the genes to ensure the production of more genes like themselves." [39] One wonders about the higher states of consciousness. Man, for instance, is a being of divided consciousness, capable of awareness of duty that often clashes with natural inclination. The heroic self-denial and self-transcendence of the saints, yogis and bodhisattvas is hard to see as *biologically* adaptive. Yoga, as Mircea Eliade [40] has shown, is the willed suspension of all vital functions: thought, breath and sexual impulse. Indeed, the ethics of the spiritual masters is *trans*biological, oriented to "overcoming" the world, radically rearranging and virtually subverting the natural order. All this is hard to understand as the product of a genetic device "constructed" for the sake of replicating itself. It is hard to see such spiritual behavior as adaptive to biological existence in any merely natural sense.

Life is not a conservative principle. Rather, it looks as if some creative principle were using the forms of life not merely to maintain the status quo but for the sake of evolving into more extended environments. Von Bertalanffy says that the Darwinian concept of fitness "is the projection of the sociological situation of the nineteenth and early twentieth centurys into two billion years of the earth's history" and adds that "evolution appears to be more than the mere product of chance governed by profit. It seems a cornucopia of *evolution creatrice*, a drama full of suspense, of dynamics and tragic complications." [41]

There can be no doubt that natural selection plays *some* part in the evolution of life, but it fails to account for the upward direction of life. Says Randall: "Whereas Darwinian selection will account for many of the differences between varieties of the same species (microevolution), it is difficult to see how it can account for the emergence of entirely new species." Orthodox Darwinians explain new species as the result of one species splitting up geographically. The divided populations of the original species adapt to their new environments, and two distinct species are thought to evolve. But there is a problem here: geographic splitting of a species may explain how one species becomes two but not how one becomes more highly organized than its predecessor.

Circular Reasoning

Moreover, there are more general objections to the concept of natural selection; it has, in fact, a universal applicability that is suspiciously unfalsifiable and is thus, as Karl Popper has said, not even a scientific hypothesis. How, for instance, could it be denied that any change in biological process was naturally selected? If we observe a biological change as adaptive in any conceivable way in the struggle for existence, it can always be said to be naturally selected. Natural selection is like other concepts we meet with a comparable degree of magical unassailability: for instance, psychological defense mechanisms that Freudians love to brandish. It is hard to think of any human behavior that might not be said to be defensive. Suppose a man believes in God—that will be his defense against reality. Suppose he doesn't—that will be his defense against religion. If he happens to be indifferent to the whole business, that will be his defense against the painful riddles of life and death. Natural selection is a concept that lends itself to similar abuses, a concept that is infinitely plastic and infinitely adaptable to all circumstance of fact.

Morphogenesis

The problem of the origin and development of life is related to problems of morphogenesis, that is, to new forms of life. Some of the difficulties here revolve around (1) epigenesis, the fact that the fertilized egg unfolds into an organism with a definite form; (2) regulation, the fact that the form is maintained in spite of lacerations to the embryo (Hans Driesch's maimed sea-urchin embryos being the classic experimental examples); (3) regeneration, the fact that damaged structures are restored (flat worms divided into parts which develop into new flat worms). Even more problematic, though highly controversial, would be instances of paranormal regeneration of living organs. Some well-documented instances of this phenomenon have been recorded at Lourdes and in connection with Padre Pio, the stigmatist of San Giovanni Rotonda. [42, 15]

Bergson wrote in 1907 that mechanism would be hard to accept if "it could be proved that life may manufacture the same apparatus, by unlike means, on divergent lines of evolution." [43] Yet in *On Growth and Form*, published in 1917, D'Arcy Thompson describes how shapes of animals in the same zoological group express variations of a constant, mathematically defined form. The changes in form here seem due less to pressures from the external environment but more to an unfolding of an "internal" plan or archetype.

More recently, the biologist Sir Alister Hardy confirmed Bergson's philosophic intuition when he said that the "concept of homology in terms of similar genes handed on from a common ancestor has broken down." [44] Thus, the pentadactyl limb pattern is found in the arm of a man, a bat's wing and a whale's flipper. On mechanist principles, such homologous structures must derive from the same gene-complex, but Morgan's experiments with the fruit fly *Drosophila* demonstrate that homologous organs can be produced from different gene-complexes or different species. In these remarkable experiments, pure eyeless alleles of the fly are inbred; nevertheless, perfect eyes are formed after a short while, available genes recombining to 'deputize' for the missing gene. Randall, Koestler [45] and others take this to imply the existence of an overall plan acting upon the "eyeless" genetic materials.

In 1981 Rupert Sheldrake published *A New Science of Life*, [46] which calls attention to the shortcomings of the mechanist account of morphogenesis. According to mechanists, developing systems are explained by *genetic programmes*, but Sheldrake argues that the notion of genetic programmes contains assumptions at variance with mechanistic principles. Genetic programmes imply goal-directedness, teleological causation. In the words of Sheldrake:

> The concept of genetic programmes is based upon an analogy with the programmes that direct the activities of computers. It implies that the fertilized egg contains a pre-formed programme which somehow specifies the organism's morphogenetic goals and coordinates and controls its development towards them. But the genetic programme must involve something more than the chemical structures of DNA, because identical copies of DNA are passed on to all cells; if all cells were programmed identically, they could not develop differently.

Sheldrake goes on to postulate falsifiable nonmechanist hypothe-

ses concerning the nature of life, calls attention to the challenge of psi
and reckons (like Randall) on the hypothesis of a transcendent causal
factor as one way of making sense of the phenomenon of life.

Psi in Evolution

Needless to say, we have barely scratched the surface of the critique of mechanist biology. Yet if we hope to succeed in revising our
understanding of death, some effort toward a critique of the mechanist theory of life is needed. Following Randall in outline, the next
step is to consider evidence that psi agencies may influence biological
systems. Randall [30] and the American parapsychologist, Robert
Morris, [47] provide reviews of the literature, experimental and anecdotal. For our present purpose, we note with Randall that evidence
suggests a psychic "force" capable of influencing cell division and
enzymatic activity, both of which bear on fundamental biological process. Of special interest here are Sister Justa Smith's experiments
with a healer who accelerated activity in the enzyme trypsin and
Bernard Grad's well-known experiments in which a healer accelerated the healing rate of wounded mice tissue or the growth rate of
barley seeds. Grad views his experimental results as confirming
Wilhelm Reich's and Henri Bergson's speculations on the existence of
a life force called "orgone energy" or "elan vital," respectively.

Sheldrake and Randall insist on the need for experimental confirmation of their theories. Sheldrake has specified experimental hypotheses which, if confirmed, could at least be construed as showing
the role of psi in the evolution of life. Randall has also suggested
research hypotheses with the fruit fly *Drosophila*.

The possible role of psi in evolution is indicated when we consider that mutations may arise from single microphysical events. In
the words of von Bertalanffy: "As can be shown by mathematical
analysis of the experiments, one single hit into the sensitive zone of a
gene suffices to cause a mutation. Therefore, the induction of mutations is subject to the statistical law of microphysics." This increases
the theoretical plausibility of psi-induced mutations; psi might act on
the "sensitive zones" in a gene. The plausibility is further increased
by recent discoveries in genetics.

In the late 1970's, Pierre Chambon of the Louis Pasteur University in Strasbourg discovered that genes may be split into sections of
"nonsense DNA" called "introns." What the purpose of these introns is, and how they are spliced out by RNA, is not yet known;

though some geneticists were quick to see that the "nonsense" or indeterminate genetic structures might offer opportunities for rearrangement in the evolutionary process. Once again, it is known that psychokinesis works best on indeterminate systems, i.e., on dice in motion rather than on dice sitting in a stable position. Introns are the indeterminate material of the genetic structure and thus make more suitable targets for psychokinetic action. Introns, the random sequences in genetic materials, may be the target sites of microphysical psi-induced mutations.

But now the great question is what the source of these possible psi-induced mutations may be. This brings us to Randall's third step and boldest speculative move. Given the gaps in mechanist biology and the experimental evidence that psi influences living systems, Randall states: "There is at least a possibility that parapsychology has discovered the missing factor needed to construct a general theory of life." Randall outlines several postulates for a general theory of life. The most fundamental and radical is that of a psi-factor he calls Mind at Large. Mind at Large is the transpersonal aspect of mind; it is distinct from but able to interact with matter. Although our individual minds are constantly interacting with our own bodies, Mind at Large does not normally interact with matter. Normally, matter behaves in accord with the Second Law of Thermodynamics. Though living organisms are self-regulating on a routine basis, Mind at Large intervenes at critical junctures: for instance, the origin of life, the development of new and higher species, instances of "paranormal" healing and in other circumstances where we observe psi at work. For Randall, this hypothesis is a kind of neo-vitalism empirically backed by the data of parapsychology. And indeed the case for a new and experimental vitalism—using the term broadly to contrast with mechanism—is far stronger today in the light of what is known about psi.

The concept of Mind at Large needs to be greatly clarified—for example, in regard to its relationship with individual minds. Randall at least makes it clear that Mind at Large is not identical with the traditional Western idea of God, which implies perfection. Randall's transcendent mind is more like an experimental artist-God who makes mistakes and scratches them out, discovering what it creates as it goes along. At least we can say that Mind at Large is *mind*; and minds are the kinds of process said to be *conscious* and to have *purpose* and *intelligence*. While it would no doubt be a mistake to anthropo-

morphize this Mind Factor and suppose that its mode of consciousness, purpose and intelligence were merely an enlarged replica of our
own, we may take some comfort in the thought that being *mental*, it
may be possible to engage Mind at Large in some type of meaningful
dialogue.

Psi and the Survival Problem

But let us return to our point of departure. We are now in a better
position to attempt an answer to John Beloff's question: if psi is a
reality, why is it not exploited in the struggle for existence? If Randall
is right, the answer is that organisms, though originally expressive of
psi-mediated information, normally work like self-regulating machines. Psi may indeed come into play in the struggle for existence
under special circumstances. But its overall function, if I understand
Randall, is to direct and oversee the upward thrust of the evolutionary process and to maintain the total balance and ecology of life. Robert Morris [48, 47] suggests a number of ways this might happen, as a
"homeostatic regulatory device" among populations, for instance;
Morris is also led to consider the possibility of a "supra-intelligent
regulatory aspect in psi functioning . . ."

The function of psi may be to mediate the origin, evolution and
regulation of life, though the sheer maintenance of life, the conservative mechanisms, would be governed by the laws of chemistry and
physics. Since the mass of observable life processes is conservative,
mechanists can suppose they hold the key to all of life, as long as they
ignore the discontinuities, the puzzles of creativity and the paranormal.

Now, how does all this relate to our question of the relationship
between psi in general and the survival problem? We also began, let
us recall, with a general hypothesis. Let us assume, we said, that
there is survival of bodily death and that there is a psi-mediated order
of spiritual reality. Whereas Randall leads us "outside" matter toward the origin of life, the present hypothesis leads us "outside"
matter toward the end of life. Puzzling survival data complement
puzzling data about the origin and evolution of life. Mechanism fails
to account for certain features of the terminal phase of biological existence, just as it fails to account for certain features of the originating
phases of biological existence. Psi-oriented theories of life concur in
referring to an overall plan, template, original impetus and directedness of life. The survival hypothesis calls attention to the farthermost

reach of that overall plan and directedness: the struggle of life to become radically independent of the physical environment *as such.*

Everything about the most organized and complex of creatures, man, already points in this direction: man, the master of all lifeforms, habitats, earth itself and beyond. Technology is the most obvious expression of the will to dominate matter, to make matter plastic, malleable and transparent to the aims of consciousness. Space travel, genetic engineering, satellite television, the giant computers, the great microscopes and telescopes, every technical instrument, every machine furthers the psychosocial evolution of the body and provides a way of *escaping* the mechanistic limitations of the body. In this sense, technology is the material analogue of spiritual transcendence, an expression of the Incarnation, of the quest for freedom from death and finitude. Why should this evolutionary thrust toward unlimited life stop short of the death of the body?

If indeed there is biological and parapsychological evidence pointing toward an originating entity distinct from, but interactive with, living matter, then the same entity might escape the death of living matter. In short, if we hypothesize a prebiological psi factor, it is a correlative step to hypothesize a postbiological psi factor; and indeed, they would be one and the same. One thing seems clear. If there is a prebiological psi factor such as Randall suggests, the plausibility of postbiological survival increases considerably, since whatever bears the life-originating information might well survive the life-bearing vehicle. Conversely, the stronger the evidence for postbiological survival, the greater the plausibility of a psi factor or Mind at Large behind the origin development of life.

Bergson did not shrink from seeing and stating the connection between the *original impetus* and upward evolutionary thrust of life and the possibility of life persisting after the death of the bodily organism. Thus, he wrote in *Creative Evolution:* "... behind each of us is an overwhelming charge able to bear down every resistance and clear the most formidable obstacles, perhaps even death."

Pre-adaptation

Finally, there is one further problem for the mechanist theory of evolution which relates to Bergson's remark about the life-force seeking to transcend death: pre-adaptation, the emergence of structures before they are used. Pre-adaptation, says G. R. Taylor, "completely explodes the theory of natural selection." Consider, for instance, the mesosaurs which apparently never left the water, showing that the development of the amniote egg was not an adaptation for living on land but emerged before there was any need for it. The same holds for the feathers of the archaeopteryx or the change in fins of fishes from a form based on rays to a system of bones resembling the limbs of land animals. Also, a tree-climbing apparatus developed in frogs before they began to climb trees. Indeed, as one of the great experts on the biology of amphibians, G. Kingsley Noble, says: "A detailed analysis of the many 'marvelous adaptations' in the Amphibia will reveal . . . that in most cases the modification arose before the function."

If such pre-adaptations are genuine, we could hardly account for them by natural selection. They look rather like expressions of a plan, as if they were produced for the sake of future use. Now our problem has been to account for psi ability in terms of evolution. What I wish to propose is that we think of psi ability as a pre-adaptive "structure" or "organ." Of course, these latter terms cannot be taken literally, since there is no evidence that psi functioning is anatomically based; thus only by analogy may we speak of psychic structures or organs. Perhaps then we might simply say that psychic *functioning* is pre-adaptive, leaving the question of organic structure open.

Now the idea that psychic ability may be oriented toward the future of evolution has already been suggested by Robert Morris who speculates that "psi may facilitate temporary expansion into new ecological environments, until the organism or its species develops completely effective adaptive mechanisms." The question then is what new ecological environments might psi be pre-adaptive for?

The first thing to note is how difficult it must be to guess this in advance, especially when we consider advances in earlier stages of evolution. Could the reptiles have foretold that one day they might fly? Could the fishes of the sea have divined that one day they would give rise to creatures that wandered freely on the surface of the earth? Or what hints could blind matter have had that it would one time *see* the light of the sun? It would seem that lower forms could never have cognized their own higher developments or been able to predict them in terms of the "logic" and "paradigms" of their existing worlds. It would have required a genius-seer of a reptile to know that the soarings of seagulls and the flights of eagles were in the offing. Had any one of them—perhaps some inspired archaeopteryx sensing the power of its mysterious feathers—announced a vision of flight, no doubt the most rational of his fellow reptiles would have jibed at him. With us things are different. Given the superior powers of reason and analogical thinking we possess, it may be easier to see correctly the shape of things to come.

The Noosphere

My guess is that psi ability is oriented toward adaptation of a new ecological environment, an environment that Teilhard de Chardin christened the Noosphere. There are two aspects of the Noosphere that we can logically distinguish: the premortem and the postmortem. The premortem Noosphere includes the collective life of all forms of consciousness; systems of belief, knowledge, art; movements and traditions of the spirit. Of this we have ample evidence in the cultural and transpersonal dimensions of human experience, many forms being adaptive to survival, others maladaptive and harmful to the vital interests of the biosphere.

We participate in this "layer" of the Noosphere by means of the higher powers of mind: reason, intuition and imagination, and thus we are using psi *implicitly*. We also participate less obviously and more fleetingly by using psi *explicitly*, by means of ecstasy and inspiration that shade off into telepathy, clairvoyance, precognition and psychokinesis. At this "lower level" of the Noosphere, we are still talking about embodied organisms but organisms gradually, sporadically, breaking past the barriers of time, space and matter and expanding into a new spiritual environment. Man, thus seen as astraddle the biosphere and the Noosphere, is the ultimate amphibian: a being struggling at the dividing line of two environments and two ecologies, a being barely awake to its potential, transitional and exposed to unprecedented danger.

At the next, the postmortem layer of the Noosphere, the purely noogenetic component of organisms, now extricated from the machinery of the physical body, would rely wholly on psi, the pre-adaptive "organ" or function now essential for a new mind-dependent ecology. This particular view of the role of psi in nature is compatible with the pre-adaptive nature of psi in our ordinary terrestrial existence, the fact that we don't need it to survive as biological organisms. It would also account for survival data now understood as reflecting interactions with the postmortem "layer" of the Noosphere. The present hypothesis might also explain why certain types of behavior are psi-conducive, that is, the inverse of behaviors oriented toward survival in the biosphere. Pre-adaptive psi ability would become adaptive in the transition from the biosphere to the Noosphere. As Bergson argued, access to the Great Memory or Mind at Large would increase as attention was deflected from the *physical plane of life*. [49]

We are trying to view the picture of psi relative to survival, the hypothesis being that the deep and essential function of psi, in addition to its possible roles in terrestrial life, lies in the postmortem Noosphere, the postbiological stage of evolution. Certain features of the empirical data now seem to make more sense. We already mentioned the elusive, marginal nature of most psi effects and how psi does not follow a normal learning model. Everything happens as if practice would render the more dramatic psi capacities extinct.

Living organisms are normally self-regulating and have efficient sensory-motor equipment for coping with the terrestrial environment. An unusual increase of psi capacity would disrupt routine performance. It is easy to imagine how a sudden influx of psi would disorient an organism. Too much information can be as confusing as too little.

The confusion would extend further than the individual. If there is a master plan or cosmic intelligence acting upon the biosphere, it probably wouldn't permit the untrammeled use of psi among living organisms. Untrammeled psi would wreak havoc on the ecological system. For instance, if large numbers of animals could use psi to escape their predators, the great food chain of natural being would be broken.

Far worse is conceivable with man. Untrammeled psi power in man the slave of Realpolitik, man the oppressor and aggressor, is a distressing thought. We have only to reflect on what we have already done with our great power over matter: i.e., created the nuclear arms race. If there is a master plan or cosmic intelligence—unless it is positively malefic or positively stupid—it must be averse to the human tribe acquiring extensive psi power. For what would we do, given our present state of moral development, with abnormally increased psi powers? One shudders at the prospect.

Death as Psi Liberator

The suggestion, then, is that restraints upon psi ability are built into the ecological system, which explains the elusive, marginal, unharnessable and doggedly unlearnable character of psi. Yet psi does erupt into terrestrial experience. But under what conditions? If there is anything to our hypothesis, those conditions are apt to be *trans-biological*. Conditions disruptive of normal biological functioning that reduced *attention to life* might tend to release restraints on psi ability. The most dramatic instance of this discerption from biological functioning is being near death. Here we may think of the near-death situation in a broad sense.

In fact, a variety of death-related circumstances appear to generate paranormal phenomena. The early British Census of Hallucinations [50] showed that people often have veridical hallucinations of individuals in life-threatening circumstances. It is as if dying releases a psi factor, enabling a person to communicate independently of time and space. There is an element of irony here, for it appears as if the transpersonal is released when personal unity is shattered. Normal psychophysical unity seems to hold the paranormal in check.

Precognitive dreams tend to be targeted on accidents or sudden death. Again, it's as if the restraints on psi are lifted just when the practical advantage is reduced to a minimum. There are rare exceptions to this, but my firm impression is that in the majority of cases, authentic precognition of death and disaster is practically useless. Ian Stevenson [51] reports that reincarnation memories often are associated with violent death. However we interpret these cases, it is the disruptive transition and discerption from life that seem to heighten the psi capacity. Much the same can be said for apparitions, hauntings and mediumistic phenomena; regardless of the ultimate interpretation, the circumstance of death seems to set the psi free. Ernesto Bozzano [52] collected cases in which psychokinetic events (clocks stopping, bells sounding, paintings falling) were coincident with the moment of death. The deathbed visions and near-death experiences currently under scrutiny fall into the same pattern. The onset of death liberates the subject from the customary restraints of ordinary consciousness. Not only are evidential out-of-body experiences and other psi effects reported but generally expanded spiritual states are also reported.

One effect of NDEs is particularly interesting in the light of our hypothesis of a transcendent psi factor, which we said is bipolar, stretching back to the origin of life and forward to the goal that is death. Normal consciousness, fixated upon the plane of life, is usually locked into a narrow band of the present. In the near-death experience, that fixation is broken, and consciousness dilates over the whole field of memory, just as Bergson predicted it would. It dilates beyond the present, overflowing toward the future, embracing the collective life-plan, surging beyond itself and escaping the constraints of brain-filtered consciousness.

Near-death in the Midst of Life

There is another type of transbiological experience that squares with the present hypothesis. Sometimes individuals come close to death, not through illness or accident, but through willed discipline. Here we note God's athletes, long-distance runners of the Absolute: men and women who seek, often with fanatical intensity, to annihilate their merely personal and vital stake in being in order to throw themselves at the mercy of the Transcendent.

From the viewpoint of everyday life, the behavior of such seekers of the Absolute seems strange indeed. One gets the impression of deep mistrust and hostility toward life. The saint, the yogi, the shaman—all are marked by an exaggerated development of the ascetic impulse. The body, its appetites and modes of perception, becomes the target of studied indifference or fierce abuse. The style may vary. It may be quasi-scientific or moralistic, but the goal is the same: control of biological forces.

The quest for mastery of the body takes place at all levels. The cognitive issue of the body—what we can garner of the world through our senses—is said to be defective, misleading and enslaving. Platonism and neo-Platonism, *Vedanta,* Buddhism and so forth all assail the dangers and shortcomings of bodily sense perception. Mastery is exercised through the will by direct inhibition of normal bodily impulses. Fasting may take extreme forms such as prolonged inedia. With St. Joseph of Copertino or St. Francis of Assisi, specially concocted, foul-tasting powders were placed on whatever was grudgingly ingested. Herbert Thurston [14], in his study of the physical phenomena of mysticism, describes how many Christian saints became so averse to normal eating that the mere smell of food would create sickness and convulsions. Or again, like Jean Marie, the famous French Convulsionnaire, our seeker may indulge in coprophilia.

What is behind this seemingly monstrous self-laceration? Is this war waged against the body mainly pathological? The modern, life-affirming humanist or religious liberal is likely to see nothing but extravagant perversity and morbid self-abuse here. What is the enlightened person of the space age to think of men and women who make a fetish of physical suffering, who behave like some exotic species of sado-masochists? The athletes of the absolute often glorify pain and suffering, not just with words but by wearing hairshirts, flagellating their bodies and submitting placidly to the abuse of superiors.

Nietzsche was certainly on the right track when he said that the ascetic impulse expressed an aspect of the *will to power*. The target of this exercise of power is nothing less than the most basic instincts of life itself: the deepest compulsion of life to replicate itself. But Nietzsche was inclined to see in this war of life against itself a thirst for vengeance, something primarily *negative*. Yet the power the ascetic seeks may be something positive in its own right—the power of the spirit, the power of escaping the constraints of space, time and matter.

Athletes of the absolute struggle to master two things—air and sex—and in mastering them come closest to mastering life. Yoga is known for its practice of *pranayama*. *Yama* means restraint; the yogi is an adept at restraining the breath of life. Documented cases attest to yogis who survive for days in airless, underground pits or who, under medically controlled conditions, can stop their hearts at will. [53]

Spiritual mountain climbers struggle hardest with the insuperable crags of sex. The war on sex is the most unabashedly frontal attack on life. Widespread success in this strange sphere of pursuit would lead to a speedy disappearance of the species. The ascetic impulse, carried to its logical conclusion, would lead to our biological extinction. As such, the ascetic impulse is hard to reconcile with a mechanist theory of life. The forms of life, according to Darwinian principles, have evolved with one ruthless, impersonal effect: toward survival of the species. But instead we find a will to death nurtured in the deep soul of the most complex form of life, a negation of the most basic feature of living substance: the inviolate law of physical reproduction. If we follow the great ascetics and renounce our sexual inclincations, we shall vanish from the earth, and as the Taoist sages advise, we shall indeed leave no trace of ourselves.

Needless to say, this is not a practical cause for concern. But the ascetic impulse, however rare and haltingly evolved, is nonetheless problematic for a theory of life, especially since it is often the most evolved spiritual beings that counsel indifference, even antagonism, toward bodily life. Moreover, such programs of positive negation of the body are a universal phenomenon not confined to a few eccentric desert saints like Simeon Stylites, who spent much of his life perched on top of a sixty foot pillar.

The link between the suppression of sexual vitality and the transcendence of death may also been seen in the *Tantric* ritual of *maithuna*. The object of this exercise is to engage in sexual congress while stopping short of seminal emissions; here, the vital force is not simply suppressed but deliberately aroused, played with and used. One of the effects of this curious erotico-spiritual experiment is to experience the mystic light. As Mircea Eliade notes [54], a similar mystic light is said to be encountered at the moment of death, according to Indo-Tibetan traditions. It is also known from modern near-death research that erotic, mystical lights are sometimes experienced at the moment of death. Ascetic practices that reverse the current of the vital impulse may have as their goal the experience of a type of higher spiritual energy.

Psi and the Spiritual Master

In some instances, extreme ascetic behavior may amount to little more than exalted psychosis or, if Nietzsche was right, to a subtle form of the will to power. But perhaps a deeper explanation lies in the hypothesis of a psi-mediated transcendent world. Our ascetics and body deniers may indeed be struggling to achieve a new and higher type of power. The lure of the ascetic impulse promises entry into a world of spiritual power. If normal biological functioning constrains access to Mind at Large, then the goal may be a kind of experimental death in which the constraints are temporarily lifted and the floodgates of the spirit opened. We may see in ascetic behaviors a breakthrough—sometimes with grotesque flourishes, to be sure—toward forms of life less restricted by time and space. In the *Katha Upanishad* we read, "Though sitting still, it (the Self or *Atman*) travels very far; though lying down, it goes everywhere." This is a metaphorical way of talking about the space-transcending property of psi. And we can be sure that it is a metaphor based on experience. To have this experience, the bonds between body and spirit would have to be weakened. What the near-death experiencer stumbles upon spontaneously, the ascetic and mystic pursue gradually, deliberately.

The transcendent hypothesis is strengthened by the evidence for psi occurring in a religious setting. If the spiritual master is struggling to free Mind at Large from its customary constraints, we should expect to observe unusual showings of psi ability. I think it can be shown that much of the most impressive psi phenomena have a tendency to cluster around great saints, yogis and shamans. Fully a quarter of Patanjali's *Yoga Sutras* consists of recipes for obtaining *siddhis* or paranormal powers. The ancient Hindu tradition connects psi power with spiritual development. Contemporary researchers like Osis and Haraldsson give eyewitness accounts of Sai Baba's ability to materialize objects. Biofeedback researcher Elmer Green observed Swami Rama perform feats of extraordinary bodily control and episodes of psychokinetic influence on a magnetometer. In 1977, the anthropologist David Barker gave an eyewitness account of a Tibetan shaman who stopped at will a rain storm in an area where a ritual was taking place.

Some of the most startling evidence for spiritual psi derives from the saints of the Catholic Church. The legalistic tradition of the Church inspired the creation of methods for deposing and sifting evidence. St. Joseph of Copertino, whom we mentioned earlier in regard to ascetic practices, demonstrated remarkable levitation powers for many years and in the presence of numerous credible witnesses. The modern case of Padre Pio, the stigmatized priest of San Giovanni Rotondo, abounds with reports, numerously attested, of various psi wonders: bilocation, telepathy, healings, precognition, the odor of sanctity, the power to vanish and so on. Healings at spiritual shrines like Lourdes are sometimes extremely dramatic, such as the materialization of bone tissue and the restoration of sight. Marian apparitions, like those witnessed by thousands at Fatima and Zeitoun, make another striking chapter in the story of religious psi.

In sum, extraordinary psychic ability seems to be tied to spiritual struggle. This, by the way, is not to say that all psi effects have great, or for that matter, *any* direct spiritual significance. The point is that the magnitude of psi effects in a religious setting seems to result from the odd relation to biological instinct. Those disciplined to the demands of the Transcendent produce the most dramatic and concrete signs of real transcendence. It is as if the dramatic effects are allowed to be displayed only as hints toward the ultimate function of psi; short of that larger and ultimate function, they sink back to marginal levels of significance.

Empirical Research in Psi

We can approach the transcendent function of psi from another angle, that of empirical research itself. We already noted Gardner

Murphy's suggestion that psi shows the presence of an alternate, deeper level of psychic functioning, although Murphy stops short of identifying that function with the spiritual order of being. Arthur Koestler comes close to the present view when he states that "ESP would then appear as the highest manifestation of the integrative potential of living matter—which, on the human level, is typically accompanied by a self-transcending type of emotion." Philosopher and psi researcher Ramakrishna Rao [55] concludes that the evidence for psi implies a latent omniscience in every human being.

Using a different approach, Charles Honorton [56] construes evidence for psi as evidence for Mind at Large. Mind at Large, he suggests, may be thought of as unrestricted psi potential, a potential never fully realized in any finite being, no doubt. Honorton doesn't go quite as far as Randall does in suggesting that this larger psychic entity or process has a purpose of its own, or, as I would like to suggest, that *if* it is conscious, intelligent and purposive, then it *may* speak to us as persons. The idea seems natural enough; for if minds "speak" and communicate with one another, then why not minds with Mind at Large—perhaps the most interesting of possible dialogues!

Honorton recalls a fundamental distinction, made by the Cambridge philosopher C. D. Broad, between psi *interactions* and psi *experiences*. The former is clearly the wider of the two categories. Broad suggested that we may be continuously interacting through psi at a deeper level of functioning but that only under certain special conditions are we able to detect such interactions. According to Honorton and William Braud [57], internal attention states are optimal for detecting the psi "signal." (This latter word is used metaphorically, as Braud acknowledges.) Normally, psi signals are masked by "noise" of non-psi interfering signals. The sources of this masking "noise" are the sources of mechanist life: cognitive, emotional, somatic, egoic—the "static" an organism makes when in high gear struggling for existence.

Methods for reducing bio-mechanical noise consist of controlling the various organic systems of a subject: nervous, muscular, respiratory, cardiovascular, etc. Braud gives a lucid account of the kinds of noise and ways to measure and reduce their masking effect. The aim is to reduce the "engine" to an "idle." Braud speaks of the *psiconducive syndrome*, Honorton speaks of *psi-optimizing procedures*. Specific experimental studies of the psi-conducive effects of relaxation, meditation, ganzfeld or perceptual isolation, dreaming and hypnosis are cited.

Honorton reviews over eighty experimental studies with significant results. According to Honorton, evidence that reduced sensory input enhances the ability to detect psi is "the beginning of an empirical basis of support for the filter theory of Henri Bergson." [56] According to this theory, the brain, normally a "filter" of Mind at Large, an instrument for adapting to the plane of life, sometimes relaxes its reducing function and thus permits a greater influx of consciousness from Mind at Large. Bergson speculates that death of the brain may involve the final breakdown of the "filter" that would open us to a radically expanded mental space. On this view, life after death would represent a stage in the evolution of psi.

The mystics, yogis and shamans who practice death—often in nearly literal ways by suppressing the vital functions—offer another type of evidence for the filter model. Both sensory reduction and sensory overload disrupt the filtering mechanism of the brain, thereby increasing chances of experiencing the contents of Mind at Large. This type of evidence is too extensive to discuss here. It will be enough to say that if we consider the hypothesis of postmortem consciousness along with the filter model, then we can see how the evidence for psi-conducive internal states fits well with, even supports, the notion of survival of bodily death. When consciousness disengages from the biomechanism, it leaps into a new orbit of functioning, free from the constraints of space and time. But something like this would be expected if one did survive bodily death. Near-death conditions, conditions tending toward the final breakdown of the filter, would enhance the probability of detecting "signals" from a transcendent world.

Let us consider for a moment Charles Tart's model of psi and altered states. Psi information is said to flow into awareness by several routes: directly, when the information breaks *im*mediately into the subject's awareness, or mediately, when it is routed through memory traces, somatic signaling or the subconscious mind. According to Tart, ordinary, biologically bound, consensual consciousness automatically tends to block these psi routes to awareness. Normal behavior is geared toward adapting to the physical environment. "Switching gears," however, into a different mode of psychological functioning might help the psi "signal" to break into awareness.

Altered state functioning, in effect, bypasses the biological restraints on psi functioning. One radical way of describing this—radical for the prevailing consensus—is to say with Tart that "awareness could literally be less controlled by or imprisoned with the brain." [58] Altered states are psi-conducive because they enable awareness to be less imprisoned by the body, which is another way of talking about what may conceivably happen at death. Osis and Haraldsson spoke in a similar vein when they tried to explain some of the odd effects associated with deathbed visions; consciousness, they said, may be gradually disengaging itself from the organism. The psi function would automatically take over as one approaches the post-mortem state. The upper limit of altered state functioning would be complete elimination of control and imprisonment by the brain; death, as Plato taught in the *Phaedo*, would indeed be the *lysis* or freeing of the soul from the body.

Another important model of how psi works is that of Rex Stanford's [59] Psi-Mediated Instrumental Response (PMIR). Constraints—rigid and stereotyped behavior—get in the way of using psi to our advantage. Now in a massive review of the experimental literature on extrasensory perception, John Palmer [60] found that *spontaneity* is perhaps the most useful predictor of human psi ability. Some evidence indicates this may even extend to nonhuman, animal psi. Stanford's stress on the psi-inhibitory role of constraint tallies with Palmer's conclusion: spontaneity is the antithesis of constraint. The link with Bergson is again notable, since constraints may be thought of as working through the filtering functions of the brain, and they probably permeate the ecosystem, programmed perhaps by Mind at Large. Stanford's work on constraint also tallies with Tart's on the structuring role of consensual validation. All in all, things seem arranged to make it difficult to escape the limitations of our ordinary consciousness.

Ironically, the compulsion to survive as a bodily organism apparently blocks our inlets to transcendent psi. Most researchers agree that excessive striving and egocentric effort tighten the filter and squeeze off access to our psi-potential. We have heard similar things from spiritual teachers: he who struggles to save his life will lose it; he who is willing to give it up for the sake of God or the Higher Cause may save it. Stanford has described the internal strategies which tend to reduce the constraints on psi functioning. Like the internal attention strategies, they converge on the theme of switching into an alternate mode of mental functioning, one that is relatively free from egocentric striving and allows itself to be directed by a higher, external agency. We learn of the release-of-effort-syndrome. The attitude of trusting a transcendent agency facilitates spontaneity, which in turn allows the deeper psi function to act more freely. This is confirmed by evidence that those most disciplined toward release from egocentric striving—the spiritual acrobats of the race—often display the wildest and most startling profusion of paranormal effects.

Conclusion

We are attempting to see the connections between four types of data that naturally fall together but which researchers have so far tended to view in isolation. The four types are: (1) survival data; (2) spontaneous and experimental psi data; (3) spiritual experience or the data of transpersonal psychology; and (4) biological data compatible with nonmechanistic theories of life.

First, as regards (1), mainstream parapsychologists have (for apparently sound reasons) shelved the survival problem. That is, they do not conduct their research with explicit concern as to how their findings may relate to an ultimate, survival-related function of psi. This, I am suggesting, may be a mistake. Modern cartographers of inner space, who focus on (3), are open to the reality of (1) and (2) but do not recognize their strategic importance. The tendency of these researchers is to rely on ideas from modern physics such as quantum mechanics and holography for grounding the reality-status of their claims about the spectrum of consciousness. Psi researchers, with some exceptions, have kept a respectable distance from transpersonal data. They neglect psi in a transpersonal or religious setting. Also, there have been few signs of interest in the link between biology, psi and transpersonal data. Again, there are notable exceptions that go back to Bergson and Driesch.

The biological factor, despite this neglect, merits a key role in the quest for a "new paradigm." If human beings are capable of transcending time and space, either through mystical or psi experience, then it is highly unlikely that their biological nature can be wholly explained by a mechanist theory of life. Some new, perhaps radically overarching principle, is called for. If the psi-mediated spiritual side of human organisms is not illusory, then we should be tempted to *predict* that there are grave flaws in mechanist biology. Further, if human consciousness really survives bodily death, we should again be tempted to predict that the same survival-related psi factor plays a role in the origin and development of life. We should, at least, be on the alert to look for their possible connections.

A healing vision of the human being needs to take a synoptic look at these four sets of data. At the moment I am stressing the strategic importance of survival research in this revisionary exercise. The stronger the evidence we obtain for survival, the greater our reason to doubt the adequacy of the mechanist theory of life. Psi would appear far less the biological fluke it presently appears to be; its main function we would now take to lie in pre- and post-biological spheres. The spiritual, or person-making, process would not be confined to a single biological life span.

The creative psi factor, Mind at Large, the transcendent field we postulate would (1) account for the origin and evolution of life and (2) explain, in a peculiar sense, the data of spiritual experiences. That is, in such experiences human beings interact in dramatic ways with the transcendent field. The goal of such interactions, judging from the available data, may be called *enlightenment*, a state of deep and lasting release from the tyranny of psychic entropy.

Mystics, visionaries, artists, etc. might be said to "participate" (the term is Platonic) in the transcendent field, exploring and mingling with its inhabitants out of time and space. The hypothesis of transcendence also would (3) cover data, indicative of postmortem survival. We would now assume that *some* survival data—hauntings and apparitions, mediumistic phenomena, reincarnation memories—express genuine interactions with inhabitants of Mind at Large. Finally, psi would (4) make sense as a pre-adaptive function destined to unfold fully in the postmortem Noosphere.

There can be no single argument or crucial experiment to decide if this synoptic view is correct. I recommend it as a way of looking at several sets of problematic phenomena and as an incentive to further survival research. Contrary to the dogmas of the day, we are still free to forge a vision that dares to say "yes" to the transcendent potential of life.

4

Repression of the Immortality Instinct

*I know you want to keep on living. You do not
want to die. And you want to pass from this life
into another in such a way that you will not rise
again as a dead man, but fully alive and
transformed. This is what you desire. This is the
deepest human feeling; mysteriously, the soul itself
wishes and instinctively desires it.*

—Augustine:
Sermon 344.4

Je me revolte contre la mort.

—Rimbaud

The ancient myths of transcendence, which sheltered us from
disquieting thoughts of our mortality, are crumbling away. And as
they crumble, the consequences for human life become more apparent. The old myths helped us to manage the raw *angst* of just being,
of just being conscious; they were aids to live life with the terror of
death at bay. But now these shelters of the psyche lie in ruins from
the storm-blast of the scientific revolution.

Mythic humanity, who lived in harmony with the collective wisdom of life, was as vulnerable to the pain of death as we are in the
space age. But the sharp awareness of individual existence, the sense
of being rent from the rhythmic flow of cosmic life, was not nearly as
acute. In a way, the great mythologies of the beyond were reflections,

on the psychic plane, of the deathless continuity of living substance.

Far from being neurotic and escapist, the belief in life after death is a reflex of life itself. The myths portray death as rebirth, return, reincarnation, as development on higher planes of being. They voice the fate of living substance: the self-replication of DNA, the branching out and evolution of living forms. In a prepersonal way, the idea of immortal soul merely echos the fact of immortal DNA. Indeed, there is an uncontroversial sense in which Man as Species *is* "immortal." Something of this ambiguity is caught in Plato's arguments for immortality in the *Phaedo;* the individual soul is said to participate in the Form of Life, a thing timeless, spaceless and intangible, and so immortal. Even philosophers like Aristotle and Spinoza, inclined toward rejecting *personal* survival, were willing to admit that some impersonal aspect of the human mind escaped the ravages of the grave.

Nevertheless, the individual gets lost in the shuffle of these grandiose patterns. Few spirits are quickened by the philosophers' promise of abstract immortality. Some perhaps naively think that the Law of the Conservation of Matter and Energy will preserve them from extinction. The truth is that modern science has wrecked the shelter, the buffer against feeling helpless before the winds of death.

Discord is the name of the human game. Organically, we are citizens of the physical universe; but psychically, we are strangers, thrown without apparent purpose into the world, as the existentialists liked to say. Yet one of the most striking oddities of the human animal is how demanding it is, full of insatiable ambition, a rebel against death, the feeble offspring of random gases who yet nurses the project to be God. What discord and what effrontery!

Hunger for Immortality

If a pebble on the beach became conscious of itself, would it resist the prospect of being eroded by the waves? The pebble might very well cry out in anguish against wind, wave and sky. Like any conscious being it would seek to preserve itself. Is there something about consciousness *per se* that is antagonistic to finitude? It certainly seems that way with people, the most conscious of beings we can observe, who are the least content with being finite creatures. We *do* send up our cries of anguish and rebellion against the universe. We may not advertise our discontent, and we may even affect indifference to our condition, pretend we are quite reconciled to mortality. Nevertheless, we are haunted, driven—and the worst when it is unconscious—by what the Spanish philosopher Unamuno called the "hunger for immortality." [61]

Any attempt to search out the riddle of human behavior—especially in these times of apocalyptic potential—needs to face the problem of this hunger or risk being dangerously superficial. In a pregnant phrase, Unamuno speaks of the "immortal origin of this yearning for immortality." A yearning so powerful and pervasive becomes even more problematic against the background of declining myths of immortality. What are we to make of this strange hunger for deathlessness? Is the main cause the fear of death? Or is the fear of death the effect, the by-product of something positive in its own right? Perhaps the origin of this immortal yearning Unamuno speaks of is, as suggested above, the biological mechanism of self-replication translating itself into human consciousness. Or perhaps in some sense, Mind at Large may be the "immortal origin" of the urge to immortality. Whatever we may think of its origin, it is a psychological force that must be reckoned with.

Freud focused on the evil consequences of repressing sexuality: the business of *species* immortality. But following Unamuno's suggestion, we may also need to focus on the consequences of repressing the instinct for *individual* immortality. Unamuno wrote in 1921 of the "tremendous struggle to singularize ourselves, to survive in some way in the memory of others . . ." The urge to be singular, to stand out, to be noticed at all costs, becomes, after the decline of medieval faith in immortality, a struggle that is "a thousand times *more terrible than the struggle for life.*"

Hegel probably had this in mind when he said that consciousness craves recognition more than it craves love. Recognition makes me "real" and gives me a kind of life through others, a hope of survival in the Great Memory Pool of Human Experience. If I want to survive, I must make myself noticed, known, seen; I must stand out, be outstanding. The will to power is nurtured in this psychological matrix, the force that siezes and directs the heroes, the world-shaping figures who make history, which is the memory of the race. But this is also the force that leaves the slaughter-bench of history strewn with victims.

Resistance to Surrender

Modern Western man sees himself as on his own, refusing to stoop and beseech strange and obscure agencies of the unseen world.

He holds to his own shrewd perception of the world, strives to master himself and trusts only in his own skills and possessions. He wants no part of the old "comforting traditions." At its best, we find here a certain grand stoic detachment; but at its worst, the driven man in quest of earthly power imposes his will on the world, indifferent to the hopes and comforts of *others*.

There are many forms to this conflict where the soul yearns to surrender to immortal longings, but the intellect is a beehive of disclaimers. Scientific rationalism intimidates the deepest instincts of the spirit. The appetite for transcendence lost its traditional sanctions and was forced to retreat to a kind of spiritual underground. One "underground" solution to the outlawed transcendent instinct was to create a new category of higher "illusions": constructs justified by their therapeutic and pragmatic value. One would have to learn to live *as if* there were a God, an afterlife and so forth. Such a metaphysics of glorified pretense rested on shaky foundations.

Nietzsche, who understood the need for healing illusions, believed the "illusion" of Christianity was unwholesome, a corroder of human potential, and strove to conjure new healing illusions such as Superman and Eternal Recurrence, revenants of the old God and Immortality. Freud, who knew his Nietzsche, was no less tough-minded, and treated the gods of his forefathers as symptoms of collective neurosis, as signs of the sickness of the human condition, the inability to adjust to the demands of reality. The world is not a nursery, Freud said, and humanity must outgrow its need for gods and fairy tales.

But there was another side to Freud: his fascination with the uncanny, the telepathic and the so-called "oceanic" states of consciousness. Had he pressed forward here, picking up with Myers and James, his thinking would have gone beyond the framework of mechanistic biology. But it remained for Jung to unfold the repressed side of Freud; Jung brings us closer to understanding these life-sustaining "illusions" of human culture. We shall exmaine an important class of life-enhancing "illusions" associated with death and dying, in the light of Jung's work, further on in these pages.

Narcissism and Denial

The most penetrating psychological thinkers are tied to the metaphysics of mechanistic biology. For instance, in a fascinating study, Otto Rank [62] marshalls examples from film, literature and anthropology, illustrating the phenomenon of the human double. Rank explains the primitive idea of the "soul" by the same mechanism responsible for producing the psychic double. The issue is narcissism, a pathological fixation of libido on the self. A severe threat to the self causes us to create an alternate or shadow self. Death is the most catastrophic threat to the self. "The idea of death, therefore, is denied by a duplication of the self incorporated in the shadow or in the reflected image." The belief in immortality is a reflex of the denial of death. Religion, superstition, modern cults (including spiritualism) are all creatures born of "the increasing reality-experience of man, who does not want to admit that death is everlasting annihilation." Rank comments on the narcissistic pathology of writers like Wilde, Maupassant, Hoffman, Musset, Dostoyevsky and others, to explain their preoccupation with doubles.

None of the parapsychologically relevant studies are cited. Moreover, if we follow the implications of Rank's thesis, the greatest believers in the immortality of the soul, which includes many spiritual heroes of human culture, must also be the greatest narcissists. This would include great saints and yogis, even though becoming saints and yogis at least appears to call for getting past the narcissistic ego. It's hard to think of St. Teresa of Avila or Padre Pio as narcissists; the lives of the great saints and yogis show heroic efforts to abolish the smallest traits of self-indulgence and narcissism.

The denial of death remains a problem for the theory of culture. The argument, developed by Freud, Rank and others like N. O. Brown, Alan Harrington, Herbert Marcuse and Ernest Becker, is that the entire dynamism of human culture, works of art, religion, philosophy, politics and so on, represents a gigantic revolt against death, a disguised quest for immortality. The great acheivements of civilization are said to express our wish for a godlike standoff from the clutches of the void.

Eros and Life

The body we refuse—because it reminds us of our mortality—is also the source of our erotic sense, our sense of free and expansive openness to the world around us. One would like to forget that the body is associated with excretions, with decay and death; so the flight from death ends in compulsive anality, a morbid preoccupation with cleanliness. A world without excrement would become a symbol of being death-free, untainted by the smell of corruption.

Somehow all this translates into the habit of hoarding, a sublimation of the refusal to defecate, *to spend one's vital being*. Out of this,
according to the psychoanalytic tale, evolves a certain obsessive economic energy, the capitalist spirit: the instinct to hoarde and multiply
gold. The entire historical process is demonically driven, according to
Brown's scholarly and penetrating analysis, by the inability (due to
death-anxiety) to live out the erotic and thus the satisfying and peace-
endowing potential of the body. The restless, aggressive energies of
the historical animal, man, creature of self-repression, are driving the
world toward a self-destruction. Self-destruction follows from being
at war with our own vital impulse, at war with life itself, because life
is dialectically wed to death. We cannot have the one without the
other.

There is a way to prevent the dark outcome of this demonic dialectic. There is a way to halt the compulsion to horde, to shore up
power against the anarchy of life and death. There is a way to disarm
those who would *fight to the death* for all they have hoarded. The way
is to unrepress the erotic potential of the body. The erotic potential of
the body, as Brown sees it, includes far more than genital satisfaction.
Eros embraces a whole way of being in the world—a way of wholeness, a healing way. The highest fruit of Eros, as Plato and the Christian mystics teach, is a mystical love affair with the whole world.

The fulfillment of Freudian erotics ends for Brown, not in the
narcissism of a pseudo sexual-revolution, but in a form of Christian
body mysticism. The struggle to reunite death with life is the struggle
to reunite the body with the spirit. Brown, who began with a psychoanalysis of history, is carried beyond the framework of the Freudian
reality-principle toward a new poetics of body *and* spirit. The new
poetics is anti-Cartesian. Spirit reclaims body. Rising above the fear of
death, spirit reinstalls itself in the paradise of Eden, rediscovers
friendship with the serpent. But if spirit takes matter back into itself,
matter is raised to a new grade of significance by spirit. Matter ceases
to be Cartesian, inert and mechanical; it acquires new properties, sacred and mystical. The body is resurrected. The word or *logos* becomes flesh. But how are we to take this?

What in truth do the symbols of the Christian mystical tradition
point to? *Unless we see these symbols as referring to some effective, supernormal and transcendent power, they will continue to fade in significance for
modern man*. Short of grounding such symbols in some concrete do-
main of fact, they will become beacons of empty hope—critics will

scoff at them—they will be thought of as mere fantasies of wish-fulfillment, as regression to magical modes of thought. If so, Brown's struggle to overcome the maladies of our death-denying culture ends in failure.

The Problem of Annihilation

One of the most brilliant studies of this problem is Alan Harrington's *The Immortalist*. [63] The emotional honesty of this book is remarkable. Harrington, echoing Unamuno, exposes the bad faith in repressing our hunger for immortality. Harrington takes the new consciousness of death very seriously and writes of the "problem of meaningless annihilation having become so urgent in our time, threatening world-wide violence and madness . . . All around us we have the spectacle of overflowing millions no longer praying but grasping for salvation, behind all faces of sophistication and tough-ness, each in his own style, every man for himself . . . an imperious demand to be rescued from nothingness."

There have always been people bothered by the latent absurdity of the human condition. Skepticism, atheism, nihilism have in the past been badges of a few iconoclasts. What makes it a matter of evolutionary significance today, however, is that the spector of annihilation has pierced to the "general consciousness." Harrington traces every upheaval, every menace to this growing sense of nihilism: the obsession with achievement, being on "top," gratuitous violence, paranoia on the rampage, sensuality disturbed, art and philosophy finished, etc. "An unfortunate awareness has overtaken our species: masses of men and women everywhere no longer believe that they have even the slightest chance of living beyond the grave." Harrington adds, "The species must solve the problem of death very soon, blow itself up, or blow its mind."

Harrington is quite penetrating, neither denying the immortalist project nor the consequences of its frustration, until he proposes his solution. Well, given that death is causing such a problem, let us just abolish it! After all, science has unlimited potential—why not summon the gods of medical technology, unite ourselves in a great war on death?

This is not the place to examine this proposal. It is enough to say that even if we succeeded in prolonging life far beyond its present span, death by accident or murder would remain a possibility; hence, the fundamental anxiety would remain. Neither would merely pro-

longing life solve the peculiar modern problem of the *meaning* of life. I
say nothing at all of the ethical niceties of who would enjoy the benefits of "immortalist" medical technology.

Harrington doesn't consider the possibility that parapsychology
might help to "solve the problem of death." There is a mass of challenging material available for study, and many distinguished writers
have engaged in the survival dialogue. Anyone interested in the
problem of death could begin by tackling Myers, Bergson, James,
Ducasse, Price, Hart, Sidgwick, Broad, Bozzano, Murphy, etc. Such a
keen diagnosis is provided of the sickness: why ignore potentially
good medicine? Assuming the magnitude of the problem—its tremendous implications for the future of humankind—why do Harrington (and others) ignore one hundred years of research on mind,
body and death? Is the dogma of physicalism so powerful? Is there a
secret fear that we do survive bodily death? And if so, why?

Yielding and Defenselessness

The same question could be put to Ernest Becker, another theore-
tician of death. Becker's *Denial of Death* [23] is a landmark study of the
psychological problems of modern man. His treatment of the problem of Freud's character illustrates his argument. According to Becker, Freud toyed with the idea of submission to higher powers. His
character, however, stood in the way of the act of surrender. His basic
stance toward reality, like that of many men, was antagonistic to the
idea of yielding. But "Freud not only played with yielding but actually longed to be able to shift his center elsewhere." Becker quotes a
conversation between Ernest Jones and Freud on psychic phenomena
in which Jones said: "If one could believe in mental processes floating in the air, one could go on to a belief in angels." Freud then said,
"Quite so, even *der liebe Gott*."

According to Becker, Jones was disturbed by the quizzical, almost
receptive tone of Freud's remark. But Freud remained ambivalent toward the supernatural, that is, toward his capacity for yielding. The
root of this ambivalence with Freud, as with many of us, is this: "To
yield is to disperse one's shored-up center, let down one's guard,
one's character armor, admit one's lack of self-sufficiency." To yield is
to risk losing one's defenses against anxiety. It is easy to see, in this
light, why so many educated people (and not only educated) ignore
or resist the evidence of psi. If such things are afloat "in the air," it
opens the door to angels, God and all manner of transcendent pow-

ers. Such powers threaten the self-sufficiency of one's character, one's carefully wrought system of defenses. They also bring the challenge of new, perhaps unwelcome responsibilities. The powers invite us to yield, to let go of the hold, however precarious, that we have won over ourselves.

An illustration of this is novelist Graham Greene's encounter with Padre Pio. Greene was deeply impressed by Padro Pio's mass, by his stigmata and by a "small miracle" he experienced with the priest-mystic. The novelist had prayed to the Padre for a distressing personal relationship to clear up and he obtained seemingly miraculous results. Greene had the chance to meet with Padre Pio but backed down. His reasons throw light on the question of resistance to psi and transcendent power in general: "I was so convinced of his powers of goodness that I refused to approach him and speak with him. I explained to the friends who had brought me along that I was too afraid that it might upset my entire life." Upsetting one's "entire life" is equivalent to dispersing one's character armor, one's fundamental style of coping with existence.

Superficially, we might think of this resistance as born of pride; but beneath this apparent pride is the fear of losing a *known* advantage. Ironically, the fear of death is precisely what keeps us in the bind that prevents us from transcending the fear of death. The bind lies in the tremendous difficulty man has in admitting the "hopeless lack of genuine centering on his own energies to assure the victory of his life." [23] Death renders such a victory impossible. Admission of this impossibility becomes more difficult for modern people, as may be seen in Harrington's desperate biomedical immortality project, an expression of the hope that victory after all is possible by our own energies.

The one thing we cannot, we *dare* not, do is confess that "there is no strength within oneself" to bear the overwhelming fact of life and death. The Transcendent may invite us, may perhaps throw out beckoning hints in the form of psi. But to yield to that invitation is a more threatening enterprise. "To yield is to admit that support has to come from outside oneself and that justification for one's life has to come *totally* from some self-transcending web in which one consents to be suspended . . ."

The plea for the recognition of the limits of human nature ends with a plea for a *fusion of science and religion*. Again, as with Harrington, Brown, Marcuse and others, there is no reference to the possible role of parapsychology in bringing about the fusion. Nevertheless, parapsychology is the most obvious candidate for laying the foundations of a *science* of the Transcendent.

The fear is that if we renounce the armor, the illusion of scientific omnipotence, we will end up cheated, deceived, without *any* armor or protection against death-anxiety. To renouce the armor of physicalist science for the sake of transcendent psi beckonings would be psychologically risky. After all, psi (evidence of the breach in being) is the subject of an elusive science. We need to stabilize anxiety, rid ourselves of the panicky sense of being mere creatures. We need something powerful, unequivocal, repeatable on demand. But a repeatable experiment is just what parapsychology cannot come up with. Psi is like a flirtation with the transcendent. Most grown men—grown into the radical insecurity of existence—crave a more secure marriage relationship. Like Lysius, in Plato's *Phaedrus,* modern rationalists prefer manageable and profitable relations with their loves to those riskier love-affairs with Transcendent Beauty.

If Becker and Brown are right, psychoanalysis has shown the failure of the *causa-sui* project: the humanist hope of achieving total independence from transcendent powers. Scientific technology has tried to substitute itself for the old myth of divine omnipotence. Yet neither peace nor fullness of life have come from this Promethean effort. The violence of the human spirit is flourishing; in addition, science has produced the machinery for the suicide of the human species. The paradox is striking: the amount of money available for research on life after death is practically nil; contrast this with the multibillion dollar budgets, the rush to research, develop and build weapons of mass murder.

If science is modern man's armor against the fear of death, the machinery used to repress the idea of human helplessness, then psi and survival research, which expose the limits of established science, threaten to shatter the machinery of repression and to increase the fear of death.

The Dead-end of Thanatology

Thanatology has made death an academically respectable subject. The trouble is that talking about the sociology of the funeral, the psychology of mourning, the ethico-legal status of the death certificate, skirts around the edge of the *basic question of what death itself is.* Volume after volume is produced by the academicians of death. Mountains of data are being amassed, and one wonders to what end.

In a recent example from the academy of death, the authors lavish attention on the details of the burial process. We are provided with the following fascinating observations which are typical of this volume:

> Most persons choose earth burial, where the body is placed in a casket and buried beneath the ground; a stone monument or marker is customarily placed above the grave to mark its location . . . [64]

The writers continue to discuss the materials used in the construction of coffins, the options for design, etc. It seems a good way to deaden the consciousness of death. In the middle of the book we find a *one page section* dealing with the question—*Life After Death*. A mere page is devoted to the ultimate question!

Thanatology, supposedly the new science of death, is a stillborn discipline. The professors of thanatology mostly work within a framework which assumes, without hesitation, that death is annihilation of consciousness; but surely a science of death should be open to *all* the data, including the relevant transpersonal and paranormal data. Unfortunately, most of the new wave of death experts show little acquaintance with this broader material.

One recent study examines the relationship between death and the creative life. [65] The author, Dr. Lisl Goodman, a psychotherapist, ran interviews with highly self-actualized people, famous and successful artists or scientists, as well as with numbers of "failures," people who are "drop-outs" or who lead "aimless lives." Are the successful, the self-actualized, those who fulfill their potentialities, better able to deal with death?

The writer concludes from her interviews that it *is* possible to win the race with death by achieving a kind of "immortality" through "self-fulfillment." This is an important idea, though everything depends on what is meant by self-fulfillment. Goodman's model is, in a curious way, Hegelian insofar as is relies on the notion of *recognition*. All her self-actualizers are public, *productive* personages. Those who perform, achieve, excel according to established standards are rewarded with the badge of self-actualization: their photographs appear in popular magazines, they have their epiphanies on network talk shows, they live comfortably, perhaps even opulently by world standards. We know all the telltale signs of the great self-actualizers.

But there is no room for the "drop-outs," the unfortunate mass of botched and bungled humanity, in Dr. Goodman's death-transcending society of self-actualizers. Since money is a handy tool for self-actualization, the rich seem to stand a better chance of grappling with the nuisance of mortality.

I will not press the implications of this. One might, however, think of self-fulfillment otherwise, say, in terms of self-*transcendence*. Now the central focus of the person shifts *beyond* the ordinary self. The goal of fulfillment moves from affirmation of the personal I to affirmation of a higher Will, a higher Intelligence. Call it the transpersonal will, the goal-system of Mind at Large, the long-range goal of life in evolution. Becker spoke of surrender to transcendent power, release to a superordinate intelligence.

Unfortunately, Dr. Goodman has a vague, worshipful attitude toward human potential. Says she, ". . . to one who has succeeded in reaching self-fulfillment by giving form to all the latent possibilities within, death no longer presents a threat: one has won the race with death." But this is dangerously fuzzy-minded, for "*all*" the latent possibilities within includes much that is wicked and unpleasant.

Would Goodman have us believe that Hitler and Stalin won the race with death? Nothing in the ideal of self-actualization, a possible solution to the problem of death, guards against the perils of selfism. One thinks of the ancient Greek self-actualizer, Herostratus, who put the torch to the temple of Artemis in hopes of immortalizing his name. Such a reckless solution to life's anxiety is consistent with reducing immortality to self-actualization.

But there are other difficulties with this approach. For instance, does one *ever* give form to *all* one's potentialities? If not, the whole conception falls to pieces, and one never wins the race with death. The greater the awakening of self-actualizing potential, the greater the smarting at restraints. Was Leonardo da Vinci a self-actualized man? Perhaps in the eyes of those who worship the aura of fame and "immortality," the bemusing *halo* of a Great Man. But not in the eyes of *Leonardo*, apparently! Thus, at the end of his life, he reproached himself bitterly and said, "I have wasted my days."

And what of Goethe, another giant self-actualizer? Goodman herself reminds us of Goethe's obsession with death, how he refused to see his wife on her deathbed or go to her funeral. And this was after living with her for three decades. This hardly seems like a man who has won the race with death. It seems more like denial, shabby defensiveness, behavior we might expect from neurotic failures, shirkers and drop-outs. The truth is that we can neither assign any limits to human potentiality nor can we say that any amount of self-actualizing enables us to win the race with death. Human beings are self-transcenders, not merely self-actualizers. Neither the dream of indefinite life-extension nor the secular ideal of self-actualization are bread to satisfy the human hunger for immortality.

There are other problems with self-actualization as the key to *winning the race with death*. The metaphor gives itself away. A life that is lived as a race with death must be an uneasy life, driven, full of anxiety. The best are cut off without warning. And even the swiftest long-distance runner is, in the end, overtaken. Moreover, anxiety is magnified by other runners. My self-actualizing potential, in a competing world, often depends on de-actualizing my neighbor's potential. In a race, not everyone can win. In fact, almost everybody loses. Everybody, of course, loses in the race with death. Yet we can pretend we have won the race, one seems to be suggesting, if we are number one at least with respect to our sister and fellow runners. That is, if we run faster, longer, better. But the race with death, given this view, must always be a race *away from* death, not a race *toward* a natural goal, a natural fulfillment.

In his *Search For Meaning*, Victor Frankl says that self-actualization as a model for happiness and fulfillment is self-defeating. "Self-actualization is not a possible aim at all, for the simple reason that the more a man would strive for it, the more he would miss it." This relates to Frankl's clinically derived concept of *hyperintention*. The hyperintense person is morbidly focused upon himself. This kind of *wrong* effort is self-defeating, a hothouse of anticipatory anxiety. The solution is to focus beyond the egocentric self; self-actualization and happiness come as a by-product of self-transcendence. A mundane example: a carpenter is good because he focuses on making a good *table*—he transcends himself *in making the table* and as a *result* wins a reputation for being a good carpenter. If he begins with the accent on his reputation, the table will suffer the consequences.

A Note on the Unfulfilled

Our aforementioned author, who deifies self-actualization, shows little sympathy for those she lumps together under the rubric of *the unfulfilled*. Here, of course, we encounter quite a large assortment of types. In view of the specialized criteria of fulfillment (success, productiveness, recognition, etc.), it excludes the overwhelming mass of humanity.

Professor Goodman is very strict about whom she allows to count as fulfilled. For instance, one of her unfulfilled cases, described as one of "three aimless lives," lost a leg in an automobile race and was an ardent theosophist. This man's "future orientation, so rarely encountered in any but creative people turns out, on closer examination, to be other-worldly, serving as an escape from the reality of the present." Goodman clearly does not approve of theosophy; those who do must be leading *aimless lives*. The otherworldly concern is *automatically* classified as an escape from the reality of the present. You must actualize your potentials according to Professor Goodman's conception of reality; if you do not, your life consists of aimless escapism.

This particular solution of secular selfism to the death-question speaks, at best (if at all), to a small class of privileged persons; it is silent—if not contemptuous—about humanity as a whole. There is nothing here for the one-legged victims of "aimless" life: the maimed, the hindered, the poor, those who for whatever reason are held back from developing, from evolving their personalities.

For a subtle and profound discussion of humanism and death, the reader may turn to John Hick's *Death and Eternal Life*. [66] He writes that "any morally acceptable justification of the sufferings of humanity is bound to postulate a life after death. Attempted justifications which refuse to take this step fail under the criterion of universal love." In other words, a universal humanism, not one that defines non-self-actualizers as subhuman, *cares* about the problem of evil and the sufferings of humanity at large. The narrower humanism of the privileged and successful is prepared to accept an "immensity of unredeemed and unredeemable suffering and of unfulfilled and unfulfillable potentiality." [67] This indifference is not at all surprising since, as La Rochefoucault said, we can always summon up the fortitude to bear the sufferings of others.

Western theology tries to justify belief in a benevolent God in the face of unmerited suffering. Secular humanism despairs of God because of this apparent contradiction. But when it comes to the humanist metaphysics of death, we never hear about the old problem of unmerited suffering. Apparently, there is no need to wonder about the tremendous fact of unmerited suffering anymore. The hell, the extinction of the *unfulfilled* (secular counterpart of the damned), does not rattle the conscience of the professors of thanatology.

A Stimulus to Self-perfection

The humanist metaphysics of death founders on the rock of its firmest belief: the belief in human potential. For the belief in survival is more consistent with the idea of human potential than is the belief in annihilation. Western philosophers, long before modern humanists, were passionate about human perfectibility. But the older masters of the tradition of human potential saw the connection between the ideal of human perfectibility and life after death.

In the old tradition, death was seen as a radical step in the evolution, not the extinction, of human potential. The belief in annihilation may be a stimulus to self-gratification, the belief in a life after death a spur to self-perfection.

In a passage from the *Phaedo*, Socrates makes this point and, incidentally, puts his finger on a good *motive for disbelieving* in life after death. Socrates, about to drink the fatal hemlock, says:

> We ought to bear in mind that, if the soul is immortal, we must care for it, not only in respect to this time, which we call life, but in respect to all time; and if we neglect it, the danger now appears to be terrible. For if death were an escape from everything, it would be a boon to the wicked, for when they died they would be free from the body and from their wickedness with their souls. But now, since the soul is seen to be immortal, it cannot escape from evil or be saved in any other way than by becoming as good and wise as possible.

Now the warning of Socrates reappears in a garbled form among the adversaries of the secular humanists: today's fundamentalist preachers who exploit the fear of hell to terrify millions of people into repentence and god-fearing submissiveness. The fundamentalist fear of hell is psychically equivalent to the humanist fear of nothingness—both contract us in the presence of life. The one is obsessed with sin, the other with failure.

The idea of a judgment of the dead, of postmortem rewards and punishments, especially of hell, repulses the modern mind. Especially distasteful is the commercial exploitation of the fear of hell so popular today among American electronic preachers. Some fundamentalists even object to current near-death research because it fosters the picture that death is judgment-*free*, that it is an altogether *too pleasant* affair.

In spite of all this, the notion of postmortem judgment may have an important positive content. First, it can be viewed as an expression of the deep human need for justice. Second, the punitive effect of the image of hell may help to restrain the evil leanings of some human beings.

It is a question for sociologists to decide how much the belief in a postmortem existence has conditioned the moral outlook and behavior of human societies. Many of us would be tempted to put little stock in the value of coercive morality. And it is no doubt true that philosophers can construct good moral theories without relying on the idea of postmortem judgment. But the affairs of men and women are not, for better or for worse, conducted in accord with the dictates of a philosophic slide rule.

Modern secular morality has freed itself from the threats and sanctions of a future life. Is this a boon or does it open the door to nihilism? The verdict among many is clear enough: it is a boon. An obstacle to political progress has been removed, some say. Marxism broke with French and American revolutionary traditions and proclaimed that religion was the opiate of the people. But the fear of hell, the acute sense of personal responsibility and the will to spiritual perfection hardly seem like opiates. As Hanna Arendt shrewdly remarks:

> Modern ideologies, whether political or psychological or social, are far better fitted to immunize man's soul against the shocking impact of reality than any traditional religion we know. Compared with the various superstitions of the twentieth century, the pious resignation to God's will seems like a child's pocketknife in competition with atomic weapons. [67]

In the past, mythologies of a future state were persuasive guides for a populace impervious to reason or spiritual insight. Such mythologies are out of fashion today. But none of the secular mythologies deal with the new order of criminality that Arendt speaks of. Beneath the veneer of advanced scientific civilization remains the primal condition of war of all on all, the universal will to power and the attendant systematic mutual mistrust. Nothing has changed in the deep psychic structure; only certain internal restraints are blown away.

Loss of belief in a future state has a double effect. First, it has intensi-fied the demonic drivenness, the need to singularize ourselves, to make ourselves count before the void claims us. It has also abolished the restraints on the individual conscience in the pursuit of degraded forms of immortality.

The return to fundamentalism is no answer to this problem. Still, the nihilism of orthodox scientism is apt to strengthen the appeal of such simplistic formulas. Science itself must lend a hand in rebuild-ing a universal philosophy of transcendence.

Death and a Lonely Child

I wish to end this chapter with a concrete illustration of how psi science could be useful in forming a new myth of death. The follow-ing was written by a thirty-year-old student after completing a course of mine which touched on the theme of life after death.

> The greatest problem that death presents, in my opinion, is its final-ity. When I began this course I had feelings of anger, desperation, fear and confusion. My daughter, age six, is dying of leukemia. Her fears were hard enough to deal with, but compounded by my own fears, the task was next to impossible.

> The night we discussed children's reincarnation memories was the turning point for me. *I began to see there were many possibilities I had never considered before.*

> People must examine their innermost thoughts and feelings to come to terms with death. Now I feel that when the end comes, I will still feel pain but I also feel that my child may go on to another dimen-sion. She will not be alone; there will be others to watch over and guide her to the next life.

> I have been successful in conveying some of these more positive feelings to my daughter. Now she also seems more relaxed and the anxiety she had is greatly diminished.

> Without this course I'm sure the end would have been much, much different when it comes.

> 　　　　　　　　　My thanks,
> 　　　　　　　　　Rhoda X

This calls for several comments. First, I had no idea, until the end of the semester, that Rhoda's child was dying. I had presented some data in support of the survival hypothesis. My conclusions were tentative, even skeptical, though I stressed that there *were* grounds for believing in survival, even though a complete proof was unavailable and probably always would be. Rhoda told me of her child's terror of going away, of dying in loneliness.

Rhoda's world view gave no help in coping with her child's dread of death. I had pointed out that some evidence suggests that if death is a transition to another world, then personal, benevolent guides may be part of the story. I said that these were possibilities but that they got their sanction not from traditional religious belief (which apparently was not a live option for Rhoda) but from facts impartially gathered by means of modern science.

Certain empirical findings became threadwork in the tapestry of a myth of death for Rhoda and her child, allowing them to hope, to be less overwhelmed by anxiety and to trust that in the end all would be well.

PART THREE

THE OUT-OF-BODY
CONNECTION

In the job of revising our mythology of death, the out-of-body experience (OBE) promises to be useful. We shall therefore examine the concept of the out-of-body experience, consider its utility for reinterpreting ancient and traditional thought and call attention to its spiritual and therapeutic significance. An adequate theory of evolution, and of man itself, should take into account the OBE phenomenon. In the following discussion, I try therefore to stress the evolutionary import of the OBE. I attempt to raise this question, fully aware of how odd it may seem to orthodox biologists; nevertheless, extraordinary behaviors of human beings are among the facts that a complete theory of life must account for. The philosophical anthropologist cannot help but wonder at this will to transcend, to escape the body.

5

On Going In and
Out of the Body

*Our religions make promises to be fulfilled beyond
the grave because they have no knowledge now to
be put to the test, but the ancients spake of a
divine vision to be attained while we are yet in the
body.*

—AE

A Curious Night Visit From a Lady

In 1976 I made the acquaintance of a student of anthropology,
Mrs. Elizabeth Sebben of Belleville, N. J. She often experienced the
sensation of being localized out of the body, for instance, during her
second childbirth. Mrs. Sebben didn't claim much control in starting
her out-of-body flights, but once they had begun, she felt some control over where she went. I therefore casually suggested that she try
"visiting" me in her out-of-body state. Nothing more was said of the
matter.

Within a few weeks, the following occurred. But first let me explain that at that time I had begun playing the flute; in the morning I
normally practiced for about an hour. A music stand stood by a large
bookcase in my living room. I kept the stand in the same spot, so I
was puzzled one morning when I awoke, went for my flute but
found the stand in the middle of the living room. I had no idea how it
got there; no one else was in the house nor had I received any visitors
the night before. I was puzzled for a moment but assumed I unconsciously moved the stand myself.

Within an hour, I received a telephone call from Mrs. Sebben. Without my mentioning the music stand, she recounted the following. The night before—it was well past midnight—she found herself in the out-of-body state and thought of "visiting" me. She did this merely by concentrating on me; suddenly she found herself observing me reading in the kitchen. (I was, in fact, reading in the kitchen at that time.) My out-of-body guest hovered nearby but was unable to make any impression on me. She then wondered how she could leave her mark; after straying through the house, she came upon the music stand and took hold of it in her OBE "hands," appearing to herself to succeed in moving it to the center of the living room. She then "returned" to her normal bodily self in Belleville.

Here we have at least a remarkable coincidence. On that morning or previous day, I unwittingly moved my music stand. Mrs. Sebben hallucinated paying me a visit, coincidentally noting just what I was doing at the time, and coincidentally imagining she moved the music stand I unwittingly moved. I repeat an essential point. I hadn't mentioned anything about the stand to Mrs. Sebben or anyone else. A very odd coincidence! The alternative is to say that somehow she actually did "leave" her body and was able to displace a physical object in my room. The story is one of many I have collected of OB-like incidents; I cite it because (a) I was an eyewitness and (b) the occurrence apparently involved the displacement of a physical object weighing (with music sheets) over two pounds. What are we to make of all this? Did Mrs. Sebben—and can people in general—really "leave" the body?

The Importance of Being Out-Of-The-Body

In a global cross-cultural survey, Dean Shiels [68] found that ninety-five percent of the world's cultures believe in OBEs. According to Shiels, the belief in OBEs is strikingly uniform; it appears to be a basic phenomenon of human experience. Other surveys vary, but it is clear that large numbers of people, millions perhaps, are having out-of-body experiences. For over ten years, I've been asking students of various ages and ethnic backgrounds if they ever experienced themselves located outside their bodies. About ten percent say they have. OBEs have seeped into popular consciousness through another avenue: as a component of the near-death phenomenon. Further inroads into the popular mind come through hit science-fiction fantasies like Star Wars and Return of the Jedi, which feature OBEs and other paranormal marvels. The idea of a human somehow being able to split up, form a double of itself, and then roam about freely in time and space, appeals to our longing for a magical universe. It appeals to the escape-artist in us, the spiritual Houdini that yearns for immortality.

The Mind-body Problem

As a rule, philosophers concentrate on the most trivial, and least conceptually disturbing, aspects of mind. Itches, pains and after-images are the favorite examples used to illustrate a metaphysics of mind. These are examples of mental happenings that are very close to bodily happenings. Itches and pains, for instance, are readily localized. It is just under the left shoulder blade that I want so badly to scratch. The throbbing ache in my tooth is right here and now in my mouth and not afloat in the heaven of Platonic Ideas. The truth is that even these near-body mental events are not easily digested by materialism. For instance, even our most localized sensations depend on attention. If we worry, dwell on and anxiously await pain, pain increases; a good hypnotist may decrease our experience of pain by manipulating attention.

Problems increase for materialism when we turn to the higher activites of mind, such as reasoning and imagining. Difficulties multiply when we look at paranormal and transpersonal mental happenings.

Consider especially the paranormal OBE. Suppose a person whose body is located at X in space has a veridical episode of being conscious at location Y. This would be hard to reconcile with the assumption that the person being conscious at location X is identical with the body at location Y. The verifiable OBE, in a dramatic way, seems to show that conscious process may occur as spatially distinct from brain process. There is no denying that there are knots to untie here, but if such things happen, they challenge our understanding of mind. Philosophers might profit if they brought themselves temporarily to drop their "itches" and "toothaches" and instead zeroed in on OBEs, telepathic hallucinations, mystical transports, shamanic ecstasies and the like. An adequate theory of mind must embrace the whole spectrum of human capabilities.

OBEs and Shamanism

The OBE is important because it sheds light on the shamanic roots of religion. Shamanism is the archaic response to the Transcendent. Mircea Eliade describes this as the quest for ecstasy. The sha-

man, using different techniques, is the master of out-of-body journeys. He explores the nether and the higher worlds, rescues lost or
sick souls and curries favor with gods, angels and other emissaries
from the Beyond. He guides and instructs the tribe in matters calling
for firsthand spiritual experience. The shaman is the primitive transcendent experimentalist and also the primitive poet of the Transcendent, namer of gods and demons, mapper of supernatural geogra-
phies.

Evolution?

The OBE seems a logical extension of the evolutionary ascent of
life. The records show a progressive expansion of life forms, the gradual mastery of environments: sea, land, air. Human mastery extends
to the psychosocial and extrasensory environments. The OBE is a
mutant foray into a new environment.

The present stage of evolution of life on earth indicates a mandate
for a new environment, a new space or at least, a new attitude toward
the old environment and the old space. Overpopulation, a deteriorat-
ing environment and the growing menace of nuclear war have inspired science visionaries like Carl Sagan and Isaac Asimov to speculate on interplanetary colonization and dialogue with
extra-terrestrials. There is a growing sense that maybe we are on the
threshold of carrying life to a new environment, perhaps to new
planets. But OBE and survival research also point toward the potential of new environments into which the organic capacity for living
experience may be extending itself. There are no a priori limits we can
place upon future directions in the evolution of life.

Need we feel embarrassed by such a seemingly wild hypothesis?
I think not. Sagan's and Asimov's data base is virtually nonexistent
by comparison with ours. There is virtually no evidence whatsoever
for the existence of extra-terrestrial civilizations—especially since
these authors reject the evidence for UFOs! By contrast, our more
radical "extra-terrestrial" hypothesis is based on survival, OBE and
psi data; it is evidence controversial and full of difficulties, to be sure,
but *evidence* nevertheless.

OBE research, we said, may offer insight into the shamanic origins of religion. We are also trying to look at religion, from an evolutionary perspective, as a peculiar form of behavior significant for the
life of humankind, for the future of life itself. OBEs may represent the
matrix for the *next environment* in the psychosocial evolution of man.

Even the most conservative biologists admit that the physical evolution of man has ceased; what remains, they usually agree, is the evolution of psyche and society. The idea of the psychosocial evolution of man is not an idle speculative possibility but may, in fact, be essential to the survival of life on Earth.

Survival

The experience of being localized out of the body suggests to many the possibility of surviving bodily death. The idea is that if a person can be conscious out of the body while living, the condition may persist after bodily death. This conviction is especially strengthened when a person has a close brush with death in a car accident, say, and observes his body pronounced dead by a bystander yet continues to feel alive and conscious.

In cases like this, people claim to *know* there is a life after death. They make extraordinary claims on the basis of such near-death OBEs. Things, of course, look different from the outsider's viewpoint; one could then say that the claimant was not really dead, that the experience was just an interesting hallucination, possibly mixed with psi. The position of the experiencer in a way is unassailable, however. Unless you were in my state of consciousness, he might say, it would be impossible to see as I did. It is as though you are a citizen in a country of the blind, he might add; if a few people suddenly acquired vision and claimed to see the sun, it would only be natural for the blind consensus to be skeptical of the claims of the few who could see.

The "outsider" here is not compelled to accept the claims of people who have these unusual experiences. On the other hand, it would be unwise to dismiss them out of hand. One might accept these bold claims as invitations to experiment. We could do this in a scientific setting, or we could do it in a personal way.

As a child, I used to travel "out of my body" into worlds of the imagination. Many of my childhood memories are of "airborne" places. I spent much of my school days "out of my body," dreaming of summer pennants blowing under faraway suns, staring into the foliage of trees and blank stretches of distant sky. During cold winter nights, I loved to sit with my nose pressed to the window (at prayer, you might say), lost in thought of what lay out there among the stars. There were times when I forgot myself, drifted into a strange tranquility, sailed above the rooftop of the house I lived in. I've always tried to keep in touch with the memory of my boyhood soul-travels.

One summer, not too long ago, I was vacationing on the small Greek island of Aegina. My plan was to "astral project" by loosening my imagination and learning to linger on the border between waking and dreaming. I would lay in bed half-dreaming, marveling in my mind's eye at the crystal turquoise wave of the Aegean Sea. Here was the sea that Homer sang of, and I recalled the sea-rhythms of the *Iliad's* dactylic hexameters, *menin aeda thea . . .* As I incanted to myself certain rhythms from the ancient Greek epics, I visualized the pagan gods soaring among the peaks of Olympus, gliding over emerald waters. I imagined myself flying in the company of Hermes, across the Milky Way, down among the islands of Lesbos, Patmos and Ogygia. I glided among the zephers in quest of the old red-haired king, Menelaos.

I practiced with these images of flying, humming and chanting in dactylic hexameter. I pictured myself flying above my house, floating over the outdoor cafes and I traced, as from above, the crooked moonlit streets leading to the shore's edge.

I was, in short, busy modifying my body image, exercising my cognitive map of the Island of Aegina. I increased this internal work just before going to sleep. Twice I succeeded in producing startling effects. Both experiences were pretty much the same, so I will describe the first and most vivid. The projection was brief. One morning I was half-dreaming, sensing vaguely the presences, faces and voices of the preceding day; suddenly, I seemed to shoot out the top of my head straight up through the roof into the sky. I looked around as I whirled through space; down below was the sea and the streets of the town. I noticed a man talking to a young woman. The man resembled the poet, Gregory Corso, who happened to be lecturing on the island that summer. In a flash I was back in my body, awake. Was it a dream? An illusion? Or a short leap of the spirit out of the prison of my body?

The Concept of the Out-of-body Experience

The concept of the out-of-body experience is in disarray. Current researchers are working with two apparently conflicting views of the phenomenon. *Psychological* theories hold that the OBE is like a dream, a memory or episode of the imagination. Most parapsychologists who follow this line admit that some OBEs involve a paranormal factor; but, it is insisted, the experience itself of being out of the body is just a psychological experience and must be distinguished from the psi factor that may accompany it. At most it is admitted that the feeling of being out of the body may help to liberate a person's psi potential. So the OBE is reduced to a psychological experience, occasionally accompanied by a bit of psi.

According to the rival *separation* theory, a conscious entity physically separates from the body, moves around in space, relocates itself and observes events from a particular perspective. This is hard to imagine, but perhaps remembering Cary Grant's double cavorting about in the movie *Topper* will help. The more scholarly might recall the astral, spiritual and radiant bodies of the Platonic and New Testament traditions or the fluidic bodies fancied by the mesmerists of the nineteenth century. G. S. Mead [69] has outlined a history of the doctrine of the subtle body. According to the separation theory, the subtle body is sometimes detectable and has localized perception.

Both schools of thought cite evidence in support of their views: surveys of OBE reports, phenomenological studies, experiments with gifted subjects like Ingo Swann, Alex Tanous and Keith Harary, as well as anthropological and a few psychophysiological studies. The gist of the arguments used to support the psychological theory is as follows: OBEs often occur in conjunction with sleep and dreams; OBEs may therefore be a special type of dream. It is well known, moreover, that dreams are psi-conducive, which explains why some OBEs have psi components. OBEs show perceptual mistakes, as do memories; hence OBEs are a type of memory, a construction of the imagination based on memory.

There are other, psychoanalytic approaches: people are afraid of death; hence they create a double of themselves in fantasy, narcissistically endowing this duplicate self with immortality. Still others say that when we lose the sense of our body-image, as in those twilights of waking life called hypnogogic reveries, we recreate our body-image, through memory and imagination, to sustain the continuity of our sense of self.

Whatever one may say about these theories, they make the point that we have a strong *conatus*—to use Spinoza's word—a force to preserve our being, our sense of unified self. When our normal bodily mechanisms fail to sustain the central core of this identity, as from the threat of death, imagination and memory are mobilized, and a new ego and a new world are reconstituted. This creative function of the self, this refusal to disintegrate, is itself a phenomenon worthy of study.

The separation theorists also recognize this transcendent conatus. But they hold that the OBE not only registers a psychological tendency; it actualizes one. The OBE is a projection of a separate psychic entity. To show that OBEs are real, they stress the psi components: unlike mere dreams and imagination, true OBEs interact with objective space.

Since psychological theorists agree that some OBEs may have psi components, separation theorists look for evidence that OBE vision is localized. They want to show that the OB subject is *somewhere*. Localized OB perception would differ from ESP. To test this, Karlis Osis, of the American Society for Psychical Research, used a special optical device by which subjects may correctly identify targets, but only from a position within a few feet.

The evidence accrued from these ingenious tests is neither strong nor consistent; but there are some indications supporting the hypothesis of localized OB perception. K. Osis and Donna McCormick [70] introduced another advance in methodology through a device designed to test localized physical effect from the out-of-body projector. Again, there are tantalizing hints of localized OB excursions. We will comment further on this work shortly, but let's briefly note some further studies designed to test OBE theories.

Harvey Irwin [71], an Australian researcher, has tested versions of the psychological theory. For instance, Irwin found nothing to show that fear of death correlates with having OBEs. One might quarrel with certain assumptions he works with; for instance, he assumes that verbal reports on attitudes toward death can be taken at face value. Irwin has also produced evidence at odds with Susan Blackmore's [72] psychological theory; he found that OBErs are not better at imaging tasks than non-OBErs, which they should be, if OBEs are productions of the imagination, as Blackmore believes. But D. Scott Rogo has suggested that the basic ability to form a mental image—the ability to dream, he might have said—is a sufficient condition for having an OBE. Blackmore has come up with evidence that confirms her hypothesis. One wonders if the self-confirming experimenter effect is at work here.

What does it mean to be out of the body? My view is based on two assumptions. The first is that psi occurs. The second is dualistic interactionism, according to which mind and matter are different kinds of "thing" or process. The two kinds of being interact, as when I blush from embarrassment (mind-to-body) or smart from a blow (body-to-mind). In this view, mental events do not occur in physical space, though some mental events occur in their own mental space. For instance, in a dream X is standing to the left of Y; "to the left of" is a spatial relation. Dreams occur in dream space, a space whose "geometry" awaits some Euclid to discover.

All experience is mental. No mental events occur in physical space. Hence, no experiences occur in physical space—that is, *all* experiences are out-of-the-body. It's impossible not to have an out-of-body experience because having an experience implies being out of the body. What is called the "discrete" or "classic" OBE is a special category of the general, ongoing human OBE. (We shall come back to the classic OBEs, those big whopping psychic adventures, in a moment.)

From this perspective, psychological theories of the OBE *are* separation theories. Any theory assuming the autonomy of mind is a separation theory. For such a theory, all mental events are *separate;* that is, they do not occur in the space occupied by the body.

Of course, the theory so far does not seem to account for certain features of OBEs such as the unique experience of being localized outside the body. There is a problem, but the way to solve it, I think, is to turn the question upside down and ask for an account of why we experience ourselves as in the body at all. If all experience is essentially "out" of the body, occuring in its own mental spaces, why then do we normally feel located "in" our bodies in the first place?

First, we feel we are "in" the body because most of our normal waking life is spent in sustaining, protecting and using our bodies. As I switch lanes driving, survival depends on attending to the immediate sensory environment. While I play tennis, eat lunch, saw wood—in short, use my body—I am compelled to attend to and identify with it, enjoy its triumphs and suffer its defeats. As Plato said in the *Phaedo*, it is this normal use of the body that causes us to identify with it and further, to think it most "real." Charles Tart and Harvey Irwin have raised questions about what it means to be "in" the body in the first place; Irwin has suggested that the OBE may be seen as an *attentional* phenomenon. In short, when we attend to normal bodily functioning, to what Bergson called the plane of life, we experience ourselves as "in," as integrated with, the body.

However, the sense of bodily solidarity with the plane of life is fragile. Things can disrupt the normal flow of sensory input and motor output: deep relaxation, dreaming, extreme stress and indeed, a variety of conditions. Such states drive us inward; we identify less with our bodies and our attention is directed "out-of-the-body." Going out of the body is just "going" more deeply into the mind—you return from the sensory-motor circuit, from biological immediacy. Our mental life, in fact, shows continuous shiftings of focus from "in" to "out" of the body; indeed, the out-of-body process is normal, as may be seen in the cycle of waking and dreaming. In addition to the normal cycle of the in-and-out-of-the-body process, there are abnormal and paranormal fluctuations, more precipitous tangents from the plane of ordinary life. Certain kinds of pathological hallucination would qualify as abnormal fluctuations in the OBE process. Even more radical would be the fluctuations we designate as paranormal.

One may grant that all experience is, in the sense we have specified, out-of-body; but there is a unique kind of out-of-body experience—the kind Tanous, Muldoon, Fox, Whiteman, Monroe and numerous one-time experiencers report. This type of OBE may have a psi component. What are we to make of it?

To begin with, the idea that there is a discrete, unique, classic OBE is, in my view, a myth. There are many kinds of "classic" OBE: those with silver cords and those which describe no such thing. Some OBErs report experiencing themselves in duplicate bodies, some in cloudy diaphanous envelopes, still others as balls or points of light. Yet others lay claim to a pure bodiless state. Some report the sensation of moving from X to Y; others say passage is instantaneous. Some claim they can "see" their bodies; others don't. With some, getting in and out of the body is attended by sensations of electrical-like vibrations; yet for others, transition is smooth, unconscious. Some OBErs claim to have been in parallel or higher worlds, or in fantasy worlds, or in the space nearby their physical bodies or even in outer space, as Swann and Yram and Jung said. Finally, some OB sojourners tell of environments that are peculiar mixtures of the normal, the fantastic and the transcendent worlds. Some OBEs are said to be voluntarily induced; others happen involuntarily. Some are seemingly quite subjective; others look veridical. This is quite a mix; it is not a simple, clear-cut phenomenon.

Well, obviously there *must* be something unique about the prototypical OBE; otherwise, why all the fuss? Let us then look at some of its possible distinguishing characteristics. Many experiencers insist on ascribing a sense of *reality* to their OBE. Unfortunately, it is not clear in what sense the experience is supposed to be real. One sense may be vividness—brilliance, intensity in one of the sensory modes, usually visual. But such intensity is common in psychedelic intoxication; in fact, many descriptions of OBEs sound like the psychedelic experience. In particular, both speak of sensory enhancement and of a curious noetic sense, a sense linked with mystical states.

"Real" could mean emotionally real, charged with significance. But so are some dreams and visions real in this sense, and they are able to produce striking aftereffects. Perhaps "real" means indistinguishable from physical reality; again, some dreams and hallucinations are real in this sense. Nightmares would not be so frightening if we did not take them to be real. Still, merely to say that OBEs are like dreams is not to say a great deal.

The truth is that we don't know a great deal about what dreams are; there is no scientific consensus on the nature and function of dreams. Theories run the gamut from Freudian to Jungian; some recent theories view dreams as neurological noise-cleansing mechanisms. A recent version, advanced by Francis Crick and Graeme Mitchison, implies that we should forget our dreams; but had Descartes, Kekule, Poincare and many others done so, science would be the poorer today, as these men obtained critical scientific insights in dreams.

Neuro-mechanist theories of the dream don't cover the relevant phenomena. No theory of dreams that fails to deal with dream-mediated psi phenomena, as demonstrated by Stanley Krippner and Montague Ullman [73] at the Maimonides Dream Laboratory in the 1960's, can hope to be adequate. The fact is, there are different kinds of dreams, dreams of varying degrees of vividness, coherence and meaningfulness. There are lucid dreams, high dreams, archetypal dreams, group dreams, telepathic, precognitive and near-death dreams. There are dreams that seem to be springboards for full-fledged out-of-body experiences.

It is sometimes said that during the OBE, one often "sees" one's body apart. In fact, it is a fairly common experience of mine during dreaming to sense my body beside me as a presence and sometimes to see an image of my body. I am pretty sure this experience is not peculiar to me, having made informal surveys of the matter with students. Some writers say the (very sparse) psychophysiological data concerning OBEs doesn't support the view that OBEs are dreams. For instance, characteristic REM sleep brain waves are absent. But this doesn't prove that OBEs are not a type of dreaming. The relationship between a certain type of brain wave and dreaming is contingent; other patterns might be associated with dream states or with certain peculiar types of dreaming, perhaps OBEs. If a person reported having a dream but didn't show the usual brain wave pattern, could we conclude he was not dreaming or not having a "real" dream? I think not. We would just have to adjust our idea of what brain wave patterns accompany REM sleep. For the same reason, we cannot conclude that the OBEr is not having a mental experience like dreaming if the usual brain wave doesn't turn up.

The point is not that OBEs are just dreams but that nothing about their phenomenology or physiology distinguishes them essentially from being a certain type of internal attention state. They are one of many kinds of experience that results when attention is not fixated on using the body in the everyday waking environment.

Separation theorists, however, will still object that we haven't done justice to the psi components of OBEs. But if one accepts psi, one already has a theory of mind "separation." We have seen in what sense simply having an experience implies being out-of-the-body. Psi is "projecting" out of the body in another sense. Suppose a subject scores above chance in a general ESP test. The subject has interacted with a target "out-of" or beyond the sensory reach of his body. Ditto for psychokinesis. Now he may or may not have a particular experience associated with this interaction. Suppose he doesn't; then we may distinguish between having an out-of-body *experience* and having an out-of-body *interaction*. At the very least, psi entails having an out-of-body interaction. Psi functions in a logically "separate"—i.e., independent—way; it supports the hypothesis that aspects of mind can "separate" from the body.

But we have yet to address another problem. As Robert Morris says, the separation theory is seeking "possible evidence of the capacity of some tangible aspect of the self to expand beyond the physiological body," and that there is a "demonstrably real departure of something that can be shown to be somewhere." [74] The researchers at the Psychical Research Foundation at Durham, North Carolina, used a variety of human, animal and physical detectors of a possible "tangible aspect" of the out-of-body traveler. So far, the most suggestive results have come from Keith Harary, whose OB self may have been detected by his pet kitten. The experiment produced statistically significant results; moreover, the cat did not respond when Harary only imagined himself projecting to the kitten.

As far as I can see, the separation theorist doesn't need the concept of a physically *localized* something that "departs" and moves through space in order to back the idea of genuine separation. Psi, by itself, accounts for experimental results supporting the detection hypothesis. Why not suppose, for instance, that Harary projected a quasi-material, invisible "duplicate," a three-dimensional image of himself, strictly by means of psychokinesis? We need not multiply entities beyond necessity by assuming that some mysterious and subtle double of the self exists. In a study of the psychology of psychokinesis, remarks of Colin Brookes-Smith are worth quoting in the present context. He writes,

> The reality and nature of mind may always remain an unresolved enigma, but the fact of its psychical ability to organize chemical atoms into temporary amorphous or structured forms to perform particular tasks or even to replicate by ideoplastic materialization human faces and clothed bodies as in apparitions will no longer be doubted . . . The evidence suggests that if a volitional impulse demands action or seeks information beyond the range of limbs or senses, then an appropriate tenuous-matter structure is temporarily exteriorized which not only performs mechanical tasks but also acts as a sensory organ. [75]

While this may imply a questionable model of how psi works in general, it does seem to describe in a plausible (and economical) way how psi may account for paranormal OB effects. Yet it is easy to see the appeal of the idea of a double, of a fixed entity or "tangible something." Persons, it might be thought, need some sort of double as a vehicle for inhabiting the postmortem world. Without that self-identifying vehicle, persons would evaporate into nonentity. We need to think of ourselves in solid terms. We gravitate toward the thinglike, toward substance and mechanism. The same propensity does us in in the Tibetan *bardos;* blown on the winds of freedom, we fly into the arms of lovers in the throes of passion and are born again among the stars of time and space. An afterlife of unbounded freedom is daunting. Let us have something to grab on to—*somebody!* The double is a necessary support for "fleshing out," so to speak, the survival hypothesis.

But psi is all we need to account for tangible signs that a person has "projected" out of the body. In one study, Karlis Osis and Donna

McMormick found that when star OB projector Dr. Alex Tanous exteriorized himself to a specific location, sensitive strain gauges nearby registered an unknown physical force. Tanous was not informed of the presence of the strain gauges; this suggests that the effects he produced were not the result of deliberate psychokinesis but that something of Tanous was localized at the target site, something tangible, energetic. But again, we can accept the psychokinetic effect on the strain gauge without assuming, as Osis and McMormick seem to do, that a second Alex Tanous has departed out of the first Alex Tanous.

It is more economical (at the very least) to say that Tanous used his psychokinesis to produce a transient, quasi-physical extension of himself that influenced the strain gauge. This is no less plausible because it was done unconsciously; psi mostly occurs without the exertions of conscious will. Indeed, such exertions block successful psi performance. Far from a Second Alex Tanous emerging in the Osis-McMormick experiment, there never really was a First Alex Tanous; that is, there is no thinglike, closed-system, no well-rounded essence or entity called Alex Tanous, mind or body; there is only a process, a web of interactions that, as Whitehead said, reverberates throughout the whole of reality.

The present account handles detection effects more readily than do the psychological theories; but the idea of a special OB entity may be dropped. We have tried less to explain than to describe OBEs more clearly. The idea of psychokinesis duplicating a transient "double" or symbol of the body fits a psi-modified theory of life. OBEs are a type of morphogenesis, an expression of the creative elan of Mind at Large.

6

The Flight of the Spirit

Consume my heart away; sick with desire
And fastened to a dying animal
It knows not what it is; and gather me
Into the artifice of eternity.

—*Yeats*

The last chapter argued that the out-of-body experience covers a variety of states of consciousness, some normal (like dreaming) and others paranormal (like the OBE). The OB dislocation of mind from the plane of life can be deepened through voluntary exercise—for example, in meditation. Insofar as the will refines upon a natural process, we may speak of the spiritual dimension of the OBE. In this chapter we focus on the voluntary aspect of the OB process, on its spiritual significance.

The OB process is at work in art, philosophy and mysticism. As expressions of Mind at Large, they seek to transcend the constraints of embodied life. They reveal the immortality instinct and belong in an outline of a New Age metaphysics of death. Indeed, much of our higher life is an attempt to escape time and death. The psi-OBE element puts this project into a new perspective, endowing the wings of the spirit with new strength. Spirit is the Mind at Large working on the natural body. We seek to transcend the body for the sake of a higher body. The play of evolution is toward a higher, freer, more complex body.

In art, philosophy and mysticism we struggle to detach ourselves from the natural body. The goal is always the same: to build a divine body, to transfigure the molecules of worms into the flesh of gods.

The Pathos of Distance

At first glance, it may seem odd to couple art and out-of-body experience. As Yeats said, "Art bids us touch and taste and hear and see the world, and shrinks from what Blake calls mathematic form, from every abstract thing, from all that is of the brain only . . ." [2] But experience is mediated by attention. Suppose I find myself in the midst of some portion of natural beauty; if I am depressed, obsessed by inner phantoms, the glories of the senses will be as nothing to me. Or take the opposite case where there is no sensory input at all, and still we "see" as if in the brightness of a summer afternoon, as in certain dreams, in near-death or other visionary experiences. Attention is the key.

"Where most men see the sun rise," said William Blake, "I see the sons of God shouting with joy." The most ordinary physical object—Aldous Huxley's plaid sleeve—may glow like a patch from the Garden of Eden with some assistance from mescaline. The quality of the sensuous appearance of the world depends on inner conditions. Sensory enhancement is commonly reported in OBEs. According to a study of T. X. Barber [76], the fantasy-prone personality (highly hypnotizable people with a rich inner life and psychic ability) is also marked by a rich sensuous life. Artistic and psychic ability, as is clear from such cases as Yeats and Blake, often go together. The visionary mind illuminates the world of sense as well as the worlds beyond sense.

Distance is part of the esthetic attitude. The British psychologist, Edward Bullough, wrote the classic paper, *Psychical Distance*. [77] According to Bullough, the esthetic attitude consists of maintaining the right degree of psychical distance from the object we contemplate. Psychical distance makes the object a subject for esthetic enjoyment. "Distance," Bullough writes, "is obtained by separating the object and its appeal from one's own self, by putting it out of gear with practical needs and ends." As with the OBE, one deflects attention from the plane of life.

The two dangers to the esthetic attitude are under- and over-distancing. Suppose I am watching a play; the villain reminds me of someone I know and dislike; I overreact and cuss under my breath. I under-distance, and the esthetic attitude is ruined. Under-distancing is marked by excessive involvement: envying or adoring the heroine, viscerally loathing the villain. Psychical distance favors wider sympathies, a detached, all-inclusive perspective. Art, when it is great, lifts us above the abstractions of good and evil. We end by neither hating the villain nor adoring the hero but by seeing each more fully in perspective. On the other hand, over-distancing, carried to extremes, leads to inner deadness, schizoid indifference, even catatonic stupor.

The philosopher Immanuel Kant developed a philosophy of art, which placed esthetic contemplation among the higher disciplines of the spirit. As with the English psychologist, Bullough, Kant saw in the esthetic experience a suspension of the category of existence. The first "moment" in the analysis of beauty is disinterestedness. "The beautiful is that which pleases in disinterested contemplation. Disinterestedness is pure contemplation independent of concern for the real existence of the object." [78] Interest is based on desire, which fuels our passion for pleasure and good. In disinterested contemplation of the beautiful and the sublime, we learn to rise above the opposites of pain and pleasure, evil and good.

Deflecting attention from the plane of life is an element of all great philosophies of the spirit—the New Testament word about gaining the world and losing one's soul, for instance. Kant, a Christian philosopher, yet like the Buddha, roots human bondage in desire: desire affirms the existence and non-existence of things, things tangled in time and space. One way to break the spell of ordinary life is through the counter-spell of beauty, the magic of form tracing itself in the language of the senses. Through art we detach ourselves from existence through the power of the beautiful.

Disinterestedness in the existence of the object is not just an act of negation. It releases power. The esthetic process sets our minds free. Whereas in normal life, our energies are consumed in the struggle for existence, in art they are given over to play. Passion, instinct, desire, sensation, intelligence—the esthetic process allows them to work together unhindered by divisive interests. There is a coming together of oneself, a gathering of one's internal forces in active, free play. Activity is for the sake of the powers themselves, for self-enjoyment of vital energies.

The World of Esthetic Creation

The following remarks of Kant (from the *Critique of Judgment*) bear out H. H. Price's [79] statement that often the great philosophers

were unconsciously doing theoretical parapsychology. The free play
of our psychic powers, autonomous and distinct from theoretical and
practical interest—this is the esthetic function of the spirit. Esthetic
activity is said by Kant to be purposive without purpose, not re-
strained by rules. "The cognitive powers are here in free play, because no definite concept limits them to a definite rule of cognition."
Kant's description of esthetic activity anticipates research findings on
what is psi-optimizing. Arousal without cognitive and emotional restraints, lack of ego-involvement, spontaneity and playfulness, all
promote success in psi tasks. Indeed, many talented psychics are
gifted artists.

The creative imagination, according to Kant, consists of the
power to negate nature, the given reality, and to create another in its
place. From the material supplied by nature, genius creates something that surpasses and transcends nature. Genius is the power of
"freedom from the law of association." What "surpasses nature" is
"supernatural." Art is a vehicle of the immortality instinct. In art, as
Yeats wrote, we seek to be gathered into the "artifice of eternity."

Translating into a popular Eastern metaphor, artistic genius is
akin to breaking the bonds of *karma*. Schopenhauer, influenced by
Kant and Eastern thought, saw in art the same exalted moral function: the power to stop the blind will to existence, to quiet the irrational cravings of an animal caught in the treadmill of the survival game.

For Kant and Schopenhauer, the esthetic imagination presses beyond the limits of ordinary existence. For Kant, God, immortality and
freedom are only speculative ideas of pure reason; our ordinary rational and moral faculties gives us no experience of the supersensible.
It is only in the free play of esthetic ideas that we enjoy a kind of
symbolic foretaste of the freedom of supersensible existence. The
world of art, like the world of the paranormal, foreshadows a greater
transcendence.

Art is thus a way of disengaging from the constraints of everyday
life, of beginning to create, concretely and symbolically, another nature, a transcendent environment. A work of art is a sensuous em-
bodiment of an autonomous, integrated world, constructed in accord
with the "rules" of the spirit. A landscape of Poussin or a stilllife of
Morandi are both symbols and specific sensuous embodiments of a
higher order, a more perfect world in which form, line, color and
psychic energy fit into a harmonious whole. As Oscar Wilde said,
nature imitates art. Art is the discipline we impose on nature, a foretaste of the *super*natural.

Art and Wholeness

Kant's philosophy of art took off in another direction with Friederich Schiller's *The Esthetic Education of Man* [80] and, more recently, with the radical psychoanalytic theories of Herbert Marcuse. [81] According to Schiller, art is essential to educate the whole person. Without the sense of beauty, the rational and moral dimension of human nature develops out of proportion to the whole person. Beauty humanizes reason and morality. Reason without beauty becomes mechanical; morality without beauty becomes heartless.

This theme was taken up by Marcuse, who stressed the erotic side of the beautiful. The esthetic sensibility foreshadows a new type of humanity, a new reality-principle based on the spirit of song and play instead of on aggressive competition.

With Marcuse the negative function of art is uppermost. Art creates images of a possible world, images that indict and negate established social realities. Art is the free spirit of the imagination reconnoitering the realm of the possible. It points to us and says with critical passion: this is what life could be like! Why not make life like a Mozart clarinet concerto or a painted garden of Matisse? A world subdued by orphic form; the energies of aggression subdued in the design of a self-contained artwork.

Negation under the banner of art proceeds by different routes. Each authentic artwork is an outcry of the imprisoned spirit, a quest for wholeness. The more completely the artwork expresses internal coherence, the more it will remind us of the fragmented and sordid quality of daily life. Like the duplicate body of the OB traveler, light, luminous and rejuvenated, the artwork expresses a duplicate world, transformed, enlightened by the harmonious free play of the spirit.

Marcuse ends by criticizing Kant's view of art as disinterested. He objects to art as merely contemplative. Since Marcuse, unlike Kant, rejects the supersensible, the esthetic dimension cannot be seen as foreshadowing a transcendent environment. Yet Marcuse was unable to accept a world deformed by injustice; and the visionary world of art is valued as foreknowledge of a new society on earth, of a new reality fulfilling the potential of Western humanity.

The Body Transformed

Despite Marcuse's secular framework, on two points he reveals unconscious allegiance to Christian eschatology. The first is his rejection of the established world (he calls it "reality-principle") and his vision of transcendence as a new body. He does not speak in ancient metaphors of the spiritual body but draws on psychoanalysis to construct a metaphysics of the new body. The new body is based on new social relations—on freedom from repression, aggression and exploitation. The new body is defined by its erotic, not its instrumental, potential. A similar argument appears in N. O. Brown's intellectual love feast, *Love's Body*. [12] It is a short step to the Resurrection from here; a new body transformed by divine love.

The second Christian theme is the rejection of pseudo-progress and false optimism. Optimism is intolerable as long as the bulk of humanity is oppressed. Optimism is the opiate of the middle class. Art itself becomes an opiate in a society drugged by affluence; esthetics becomes anaesthetics. In a remarkable essay, *Art as a Form of Reality*, Marcuse denounces the anaesthetizing misuse of the esthetic experience: "It seems that the esthetic sublimation is approaching its historical limits, that the commitment of Art to the ideal, to the beautiful and the sublime, and to the 'holiday' function of art, now offends the human condition." [81] Art should not sublimate but transform existence. And the way to transform existence is to liberate a new sensibility: to transform the body, to make it a vehicle of love, not a tool of dehumanizing labor.

We are opening the concept of out-of-body experience. Now we are looking at out-of-body experience as the longing for a new body. The body of routine existence is a body as tool, a body whose erotic, expressive and communicative potential is worn down, desensitized by monotonous, degrading and meaningless labor or idleness. Occult and esoteric traditions, along with both classical and radical theories of art, converge on this vision of a new incarnation, a transmutation of earthly existence.

The Metaphysics of Modern Art

Concern for an "out-of-nature" body is not always explicit with artists and poets. Still, it is not hard to detect. In general, modern art, freed from mimetic goals, is metaphysics in action.

Ad Reinhardt, for instance, a master of minimal art, was steeped in Zen thought. His final, "black" paintings, where the visible hovers on the threshold of the invisible, were evocations of the dark night of the soul, meditations on the tunnel that leads to the Being of Light. Reinhard's art was to minimize the visible content of the visible; his curious task was to make an image of no image. It was an art dedicated to the transcendence of art. Few artists were less willing to give concessions to the sensory world than Ad Reinhardt, painter of the mystical *via negativa*.

Metaphysical aims in modern art are evident in all the major movements: cubism, in its quest for the geometry of the fourth dimension; expressionism, in its revolt against reliance upon external reality; dada, in its assult on conventional logic; surrealism, in its desire to incarnate dream life; conceptual and environmental art, breaking all boundaries, bringing art into the foreground of life itself.

Georgio de Chirico, a founder of surrealism, nursed his art on the thought of Nietzsche and Schopenhauer. He was consciously devoted to cultivating the pathos of distance. In his 1912 *Meditations of a Painter*, Chirico quotes the following from Schopenhauer: "To have original, extraordinary, and perhaps even immortal ideas, one has but to isolate oneself from the world for a few moments so completely that the most commonplace happenings appear to be new and unfamiliar, and in this way reveal their true essence." [82] We are back to the Bergsonian principle of deflecting attention from the plane of life, defixating attention from the struggle for survival.

Modernist art revolts against ordinary perception, against ordinary reality. In painting, this became a revolt against the very physicality of painting. The modernist painters saw art as a transcendent act, a raid on the fourth dimension, a destruction of solidity and the familiar, a rending of the fabric of regular human associations. In a famous letter, the poet Rimbaud described his method for becoming a clairvoyant, a seer. "Je est un autre," he wrote: "I is another." Rimbaud's method was to subject his senses to a *dereglement*, literally, a *deruling*. His method was diametrically opposed to Descartes', which was to filter our perception of reality through a small, incorrigible set of rules.

Marcel Duchamp epitomizes the revolt against the rule-bound mind. Duchamp's gesture was, first, to refuse to repeat himself, a way of purging the habitual and the mechanical from his art. The final gesture was to renounce painting itself. Duchamp chose to do nothing, to act only from a motive of "amusement." Art became a playing with the will, a game of chess, a diverting manipulation of the tokens of reality. One of his "artworks" consists of a photograph of himself playing chess with a naked woman—an archetypal portrait of the artist practicing psychical distance.

Duchamp cultivated a form of painting he said was in the "service of the mind." Dada, he wrote, was "an extreme protest against the physical side of painting. It was a metaphysical attitude. It was a sort of nihilism to which I am still very sympathetic. It was a way to get out of a state of mind—to avoid being influenced by one's immediate environment, or by the past: to get away from cliches—to get free." [82]

Cultivating the esthetic attitude can be seen as a discipline for dislocating consciousness from the body. The aim varies in focus: to create psychical distance, to disengage the sense of compulsive practicality, to learn to see things in their isolated thinghood, to destabilize the rules of ordinary perception, to suspend the mechanical and merely sensual response to the world and so on. All these phrasings point to the same task. In Dante's word, *trashumanar:* to transcend humanity; to become a spectator, as it were.

The Spectator of All Time and Existence

Plato once said that in philosophy we aim to become spectators of all time and existence—what an exalted view of philosophy! And how different it is from today where philosophy labors at correcting the misuses of ordinary language. Are Plato's words the hyperbole of a proud aristocrat? Do they betray a man who took slavery, and the means to a livelihood, for granted? One might think so, on grounds that only someone who never had to work for a living could be so condescending toward all time and existence. However, there's more to it than dislike of work. The ancients placed a higher value on the life of contemplation than on the life of action.

Modern life, by contrast, is devoted to the ideal of action; we are what we achieve and what we produce. The active life is linked to world views that reject transcendence; the highest goals are placed within the framework of history. Traditional humanity, preferring the contemplative life, looked beyond history. Is there a pattern here? In fact, the process does seem to be circular: contemplative practices increase the probability of transcendent experience, while a life embroiled in action lessens such a probability. Given that modern life isn't very contemplative, it's no wonder that claims of transcendent experience are suspect. Nor is it any wonder that the extraordinary language of traditional societies should sound so strange to us down-to-earth moderns.

Talk of the philosopher as a spectator of all time and existence is a good example of extraordinary language. However, if a person even for a moment experienced an extended, psi-mediated awareness of reality, the phrase "spectator of all time and existence" would no longer seem quite so nonsensical.

The philosopher-parapsychologist, Ramakrishna Rao (the successor of J. B. Rhine at the Foundation For Research On Man), concludes an extensive review of the theories of psi with the following remarkable statement:

> Every subject is a microcosm, potentially capable of reflecting the whole cosmos. This potential is not realized because we are habitually and constitutionally given to respond to and interact with our environment rather than to probe within to discover hidden knowledge. Psi events do seem to indicate, however, that this is not an irreversible process and that on occasion knowledge can be had by tapping our inner resources. Thus we are led to postulate an omniscience inherent in our very being. [55]

The language of unlimited capacities, and perhaps the language of divine powers, may be projections of our unlimited psi potential. They point perhaps to the future of human evolution.

The metaphor of the *spectator* is common. There is an aspect of us that is *outside* the theatre of existence. We might speak of a fundamental out-of-world experience, referring to the uppermost limit on the OB continuum. Local OBEs would thus only afford a tiny glimpse of the profound out-of-world experience, the transcendent OBE reported by mystics and neglected by parapsychologists.

It is known that the *Phaedo*, which contains Plato's philosophy of death, was influenced by the school of Pythagoras. Of particular interest is the Pythagorean idea of the fusion of science and religion, especially the idea of using mathematics as an esthetic discipline for purifying the soul and contemplating the cosmos. The mystical society of the Pythagoreans was based on a lifestyle that stressed the kinship of all life-forms. Science and art, mathematics and music, as used in ancient Crotona by Pythagoreans under vow of silence, were means to the contemplative life. Pythagoreans were among the first to teach the doctrine of immortality and reincarnation.

The contemplative life and the living belief in survival go hand in hand. By contrast, the psychological difficulty in accepting the reality of survival is probably the result of seeing action, productivity and achievement as the aim of life.

Primal Greek Shamanism

The image of the spectator is primordial. We have touched on some of its early expressions: Plato and Pythagoras. We could push our inquiry further back, to the early shamanic wise men of Greece. Shrouded in obscurity and older than Thales or Heraclitus are the figures of Abaris of Hyperborea, Aristeas of Prokonnesos, Hermotimos of Klazomenai and the Cretan Epimenides, ecstatic seers and cathartic priests, said to be great fasters capable of prolonged out-of-body journeys.

Aristeas, for instance, was a man of high rank in his native city. According to Suidas, "whenever he wanted, his soul left his body and returned again." Or from Maximum of Tyre we hear that while his body lay as if dead, his "soul going out of the body sailed into the aither." In this state he was "seized by Phoibos" and given mantic knowledge of past and future.

The case of Hermotimos is intriguing. It was said that he could go out of his body for years and that he returned with much mantic lore, especially of the future. According to Pliny and Plutarch, the enemies of Hermotimos, enlisting the help of his wife, set fire to the seer's deserted body, thus making it impossible for his soul to return from its voyages.

Hermotimos, however, also figures in the history of philosophy of mind; for according to Aristotle in the *Metaphysics* (l., 3,948b), Hermotimos was among the first to clearly distinguish between pure Mind and matter. From the town of Klazomenai came another philosopher-shaman, Anaxagoras, condemned to death because he theorized that the sun was a red-hot metal; but also, like his townsman, he was a first seer into the fundamental nature of Mind. Thus, in the twelfth fragment of Simplicius: "All other things have a portion of everything, but Mind is infinite and self-ruled, and is mixed with nothing and is all alone by itself." We may thus claim Anaxagoras as one of the earliest forerunners of the notion of Mind at Large.

But what was the source of these ancient insights into the infinite and autonomous power of Mind? The words of Irwin Rhode, the great classical scholar and schoolmate of Nietzsche, might shed some light:

. . . when it is related of Hermotimos that he, like his countryman Anaxagoras, attempted a distinction between pure Mind and matter, we can see very clearly how this theory might arise out of his special "experiences." The ecstasies of the soul of which Hermotimos and this whole generation had such ample experience seemed to point to the separability of the soul from the body—and indeed to the superiority of the soul's essence in its separate state over that of the body. [83]

Behind the Platonic concept of *theoria*, the condition of being a spectator of all time and being, lies this tradition of primal Greek shamanism: special "experiences" of ecstatic flight beyond the body. Of course, the philosophy of Plato went far beyond its shamanic experiential roots; out of this matrix sprang new questions of logic, epistemology, ethics, esthetics and political theory. Nevertheless, the idea that permeates Platonic thought is the ultimate power of Mind at Large. Philosophy as a contemplative immersion in Mind at Large was behind the tranquil and totally unmodern Platonic attitude toward death.

Husserl, Jung and Reduction

The image of the spectator reappears in the phenomenology of Edmund Husserl. [84] The basic technique of phenomenology is called the reduction. A kind of meditation, it requires practice. In a way, it resembles Plato's practice of death, a "drilling" that suspends what Husserl calls the "natural standpoint."

Phenomenology is a descriptive art-science, a discipline whose goal, according to Husserl, is to "go back" to the transcendental field of pure consciousness. In the reduction, we turn to ourselves as pure subject and make an effort to detach ourselves from all assumptions of what is real, true, objective, natural. "Go within," said St. Augustine, "the truth lies there,"—words quoted by Husserl in the *Cartesian Meditations*. Phenomenology is a method of exploring the ground of consciousness, the source of our freedom. Like Plato and Duchamp, Husserl struggled to transcend the category of existence, an impediment to the freedom of consciousness.

The goal of the phenomenological reduction, as Husserl wrote in *Ideas*, is "the winning of a new region of being." Husserl, like Descartes in the seventeenth century, sought to discover a fresh point of departure for grappling with the problems of philosophy. Like Descartes, he began with the attempt to doubt everything. To doubt everything is to express of "our perfect freedom."

Husserl borrowed a word from the ancient Greek skeptics—

epoche, which means *abstention*. The aim of this abstention from beliefs, opinions and claims of knowledge is largely therapeutic. It offers a special tranquility. The Zen masters say much the same thing:
only cease cherishing opinions, and truth will illuminate your mind.
The Buddhist philosopher Nagarjaruna [85] had a similar goal: to exhaust the mind by systematically confronting all its contradictions.
The same could be said for those mind-exhausting meditative devices
called koans. Let me add to the list the study of psi, as baffling to the
ordinary mind as any skeptical argument, dialectical caper, japa or
koan. To meditate on psi is to throw a pall of skepticism on our most
cherished beliefs about the natural world.

The reduction is a type of meditation. Let us rehearse this inner
work, this silent, self-searching activity: disconnecting, dropping the
idea of the world's existence; all assumptions, habits of cognition,
passion and affection; the categories and familiar concepts of natural
science; the moral and political convictions that regularly heat and
disturb our brains; memories of past injuries, history itself; all future
forebodings, hopes, anxieties; our own inner sense, the contracted,
the inflated ego. Let us for a moment lay aside all aspects of mind
conditioned, the accidents of fate and fortune: that we are poor or
wealthy, admired as wise or mocked as foolish, powerful or the victims of power. Let us put aside all conditions that bind our consciousness, the entire standpoint of the natural world. Let us place them in
parentheses and demonstrate our perfect freedom, our ability to "go
back" to the roots of our greater self. In the words of Husserl:

> Consciousness *in itself* has a being of its own which in its absolute
> uniqueness of nature remains unaffected by the phenomeological
> disconnexion. It therefore remains over as a "phenomenological re-
> siduum," as a region of being which is in principle unique, and can
> become in fact the field of a new science—the science of Phenome-
> nology.

The field of this science is absolute consciousness, what remains after
the world is disconnected, parenthesized. The task Husserl set for
himself was to purify the foundations of knowledge, to create a new
science of the spirit. The reduction is the first step. It brackets the
natural standpoint, even the natural attitude toward our body. The
reduction is a technique for dislocating consciousness from our everyday relationship to the body.

It asserts the freedom of spirit over the claims of the natural world; it attempts to restore epistemological innocence. It is a way, paradoxically, of nullifying the traditions of spiritual life in order to rediscover them anew. The tradition has always to be rediscovered. Every Native American Indian must go on his own vision quest. Every Western philosopher starts the search for wisdom from scratch. Every Christian rediscovers the meaning of the cross. What is unique in modern times, however, is the magnitude of our oblivion to traditional meanings. There is a collective loss of capacity to read the basic scripts of the World Memory and World Traditions.

The task of rediscovering these basic scripts was central to the Jungian reduction. With regard to his own native tradition, Jung wrote:

> Not only do I leave the door open for the Christian message, but I consider it of central importance for Western man. It needs, however, to be seen in a new light, in accordance with the changes wrought by the contemporary spirit. Otherwise it stands apart from the times, and has no effect on man's wholeness. [86]

Husserl and Jung, each in their own way, spent their lives trying to stand outside the "body" of tradition. We may now speak of an "out-of-tradition" experience. Just as we normally identify with our bodies, we normally identify with our traditions; that is, we have routine relationships or attitudes toward our bodies as we do toward our traditions. We inhabit the body of Christian tradition. Jung sought to step outside that body in order to see it more clearly. Like Husserl, he had to deal with the ponderous category of existence. Does God really exist? Do angels and demons, heaven and hell, really exist? Since they do not exist the way atoms and genes do, and since they cannot be measured, there is doubt about their place in the scheme of things.

Husserl and Jung tried to renew our sense of reality by suspending our naive acceptance of existence. Husserl used logic to discredit the primacy of material existence—a construct riddled with presuppositions. The only radical certainty, the true *arche* and principle of all philosophy, is transcendental subjectivity, the most logically primitive form of "existence."

Jung took a therapeutic tack; what is real, effective and fateful is the psyche. We are immersed in a sea of psychisms, deep collective images, linked somehow to vital and cosmic forces. These exist as the living forms of internal existence; what is more, as Jung believed,

they are both "subjective" and "objective." Jung affirms a conjunctive logic of both/and over a disjunctive logic of either/or. Transcendental subjectivity is transcendent objectivity. What is deeply within
leads to what is deeply without.

Let us end this section with an example of how a conjunctive
logic of existence helps us to retrieve meaning. Suppose a man says
he "saw" an apparition of some mysterious form. If we assume that
such things "don't exist," we automatically destroy our relationship
to the phenomenon in question. We invalidate it before it even begins
to speak to us. The reduction allows the phenomenon *as* a phenomenon to reveal itself. It is a discipline in listening. It helps us cultivate
the art of understanding that comes before the science of explaining.
What did seeing the apparition mean to Jones as it appeared to *him*?
What was its appearance? How did Jones experience it? The immediate impact on the subject surely *exists*.

Jones' apparition, however elusive, lives! Let us adopt a nonviolent attitude toward it; nonviolence begins with our metaphysics. Let
us cultivate a metaphysics that begins in the nonviolence of understanding.

Our traditions have been subjected to the subtle violence of scientific explanation. Old worlds of meaning are lost to us. Yet we may
learn to listen, to understand first, to place ourselves in the presence
of our neighbor. The abstention from reality claims stretches to human relations. It offers a way to enhance dialogue, the understanding
that comes before analysis. To feel the compulsion to explain is already a sign that community is broken. At this moment in the survival game, we need to recover the peaceful art of understanding, the
listening that comes before the explaining. This, I believe, is a part of
philosophy, the love of wisdom, that we need to recover.

The Mystic as Artist

Dislocating consciousness from its ordinary relation to the body
figures in art and philosophy; it is also part of the mystic quest. The
mystical life assumes a special attitude toward the body, a progressive detachment from the plane of life where bodily survival is a con-
suming priority.

A. R. Orage [87] speculated on the idea of the "superman"—the
mystic as artist whose artwork is himself. According to his scheme,
the difference between human and animal consciousness is a difference in degree of inner detachment. Lower forms of life identify completely with the external environment; we humans, by contrast, ex-

perience ourselves as distinct, disidentified. We experience ourselves as *out of the body of the world*.

Ordinary man, although normally disidentified from the body of the external world, identifies with (a) his own body, which is part of the external world, and (b) with his own internal world, itself a subtle version of the material world. It remains for us to learn to disidentify from our bodies and from our internal worlds. The evolutionary challenge, if Orage is right, lies in learning to disengage from our interior environments as we, at earlier stages of evolution, learned to disengage from the external environment. The "superman," according to Orage, is one who stands outside his own mental life the way an ordinary man stands outside the world of external objects. The superman looks on his inner realities—passions, ideas, memories—in as detached a manner as a painter might look on the colors of his palette. He uses them to build an artwork, his higher self. Each of us is an artist, an unconscious, if not a conscious, fabricator of worlds; our life is an artwork, seen perhaps for the first time in proper perspective in the galleries of the next world.

Once we posit the evolutionary function of the imaginative life, the arts become spiritual disciplines, sensuous rehearsals for spiritual adventures in possible worlds, here or hereafter. Biologists like Sir Alister Hardy, Ludwig Bertanaffly and John Randall have likened the "intelligence" behind the evolutionary process to that of an artist's. Speaking of the mechanisms behind the transformations of life, Hardy, for instance, wrote: "It seems to me that they have all the appearance of a definite mental conception like that of an artist or designer—a pattern outside the physical world which in some way has served as a templet or gauge for selective action." [44]

If Mind at Large is an artist, and the forms of life are works of art, and if we are the clearest reflection of the work of Mind at Large, then the artist in us would reflect most clearly the meaning of life. The artist works on the raw materials of himself; the outcome is matter transformed by spirit. The mystic goes a step further, renouncing the project of producing an external artwork, and struggles to make himself a living icon of eternity. The mystic seeks to embody, to bear witness to, the designs of Mind at Large.

The Mystic as Witness

The idea of the mystic as witness appears in the writings of Vedanta. Our basic perception of the world is riddled with illusion, according to *Vedanta*; if we could rid ourselves of the illusion, upon

which normal life is based, we would experience ourselves as one
with Brahman, the source of true being. Shankara likens this awakening from the illusion of the normal mind to the sudden realization
that a frightening snake was really a harmless piece of rope. Our
deepest fears spring from a profound, persistent cognitive error.

Let me quote the extraordinary language of Shankara from
Swami Prabhavananda's and Christopher Isherwood's fine translation of the *Crest-Jewel of Discrimination:*

> There is a Self-Existent reality, which is the basis of our conscious-
> ness and ego. That Reality is the witness of the three states of our
> consciousness, and is distinct from the five bodily coverings (the
> senses). [88]

Atman is the name of this Self-Existent reality; one of its chief functions is to "witness." As with Orage's superconsciousness, the
Hindu self or *Atman* is said to be the "inner controller," the artist for
whom all phenomena make up the canvas of *maya* or illusion. In
addition to being "witness" and "controller," the *Atman* is blissful by
nature, the fountainhead of the pleasure principle. In the Hindu conception of the Self, just being conscious is a state of intrinsic value;
pure consciousness, as we learn from the third of Patanjali's *Yoga
Sutras*, isolated into its "own" form, unmixed with impressions of
the external world, is essentially blissful, intrinsically blessed. This is
a remarkable claim.

If it is true, then we don't have to *do* anything in particular to
"achieve" enlightenment; rather, it is the "karmic" chain of our do-
ings that obscures our authentic being. The Hindu formula is *satchi-
tananda:* being-consciousness-bliss. We neither have to go outside
ourselves to attain the saving state nor to acquire new knowledge.
Indeed, any particular effort we make might alientate us further from
our blissful cognitive potential.

This root bliss status of mind as such relates to the metaphor of
the mystic as witness, a metaphor we read in the light of the concept
of the OBE. Shankara and Patanjali return in various ways to the
theme of the witness, the seer, the observer, the inner spectator. The
ordinary OBE, I wish to suggest, provides a kind of spontaneous
experience of consciousness as pure witness. The more deeply rending the spontaneous cut between consciousness and its habitual
objects—as in the NDE—the more profound the potential disclosure
of the authentic properties of consciousness.

It seems there is no direct way to seize this greater reality of the Self. Letting go, renouncing, forgetting, non-doing; these are some metaphors evoking the right attitude. One knows a man who is free in this life, Shankara says, by the sign that "he has no feeling of ownership." We'll pass by the implications of this remark for economic philosophy. It would be more in line with our discussion to notice how it dovetails with parapsychological findings that "ownership resistance" is psychologically unfavorable to success in psychokinetic tasks. Not having the feeling of ownership frees consciousness to experience itself in its naturally blissful condition, according to Shankara. It also appears to be a condition for evincing the power of psychokinesis. The point is theoretically important; the consciousness that is "real being," the ground of true human felicity, is "real" subjectively. It is also real objectively, causally effective.

"Life flows by," says Shankara, but the man who is free "watches it like a disinterested spectator. He does not identify himself with the body, sense organs, etc. He has risen above the idea of duty. That is how you may know the man who is free even in this life." Nothing we can *do*, no external action, by itself can be the equivalent of the actual experience of the *Atman:* the true liberation of the spirit. The only discipline that works is being the witness, taking a stand *outside* the world. "A man who remains continually absorbed in the consciousness of Brahman is freed from the tyranny of the objective world." The whole objective world, along with the imperative for action it normally demands, is discounted, disconnected; even duty, ritual action, is spurned as ultimately valueless. We are instructed to concentrate on the One Being who is eternal bliss, to look on everything we see in the world as if it were this perfect being of bliss—an outrageous defiance of realism and common sense!

Like the surrealist, the great *Vedantin* sage is describing a technique for de-realizing the world, increasing distance, de-automatizing responses. Max Scheler, the German phenomenologist, describes this aspect of spiritual discipline as Buddha's "technique of de-actualizing the world and the self." [89] The mystic quest is thus practical, concrete metaphysics. Metaphysics here means much more than the critical examination of the most general conceptual underpinning of the world. It aims to change our experience of the world.

What surrealizes or de-realizes our ordinary sense of reality? Reducing of the idea of resistance, says Scheler. Resistance focuses on the vital impulses. "For all reality," Scheler writes, "because it is reality, and regardless of what it is, is a kind of inhibiting, constraining pressure for every living thing. Its correlate is pure anxiety, an anxiety without object. If reality means resistance, the canceling of reality can only be the kind of ascetic act by which we suspend the operation of the vital impulse in relation to which the world appears as resistance . . ." The sense of reality, the vital impulse that the Buddha called "thirst" or "craving," and the amount of resistance provide an index to the level of our anxiety. The greater the craving, resistance and sense of external reality, the greater the anxiety. For Scheler, the Buddha had a technique for overcoming suffering, a means of "canceling reality through suspension of desire," a way of making the "sensory world and the physical and mental processes disappear and fall away piece by piece, along with the sensory qualities, shapes, relations and forms of space and time." The goal state is called by Buddhists *nirvana*, blown-outness.

It is a way to induce out-of-body experience, a new kind of relation to space, as may be seen in the following Buddhist text: "Herein, a certain person, by passing completely beyond consciousness of form, by paying no attention to consciousness of manifoldness, thinks, 'Space is infinite,' and reaches up to and stays in the sphere of infinite space." This is not the whole story, but a new experience of space, a dislocation of consciousness from the body, is an important feature of Buddhist spiritual discipline. The same can be said for *Vedanta*. The *Atman*, understood as witness, radically deflects attention from the plane of life.

Conclusion
OBE Worlds: Mind as Wayward

Creating psychical distance, becoming a spectator, becoming a witness—all these metaphors for spiritual discipline speak of methods of deflecting attention from the tasks of bodily survival. In place of these tasks, we are invited to raise anchor and sail forth into Mind at Large.

Mind is on the way, it appears, refusing to be arrested, constrained, defined, predicted or annihilated. However we interpret the OB process—as a denial of death and a re-duplication of the self, as a way of sustaining the image of self and reconstituting the world during times of crisis and confusion, or as a genuine flight of the spirit into worlds beyond time and space—it attests to Mind as rebel against finitude and mortality.

The waywardness of Mind is shown in a paradox: the finest

flower of life, perhaps a factor in the origin of life, mind is nevertheless indisposed to conform to the elementary rules of the survival game. Mind, when not weighted down with the cares of matter, prefers adventure to security and loves the unknown more than it likes the familiar. Wayward mind scorns the given, the mechanical, the stereotyped. It struggles to shape novelties from chaos, to make visible the invisible. The impulse of Mind is to play with fate and chance, sometimes by seeking to master being in games of power, sometimes by seeking to purify and elevate the conditions of life itself.

The life of spirit is proof of this waywardness, the refusal of genius to submit to the rules of nature. By spirit I mean the Mind in life seeking to uncover its own secrets and unfold its own potential. Above all, the waywardness of Mind is revealed by its stubborn, many-faced revolt against death, by its unwillingness to give up the quixotic quest for the Divine Lover.

PART FOUR

ON THE THRESHOLD OF THE BEYOND

At this point, a glance backward will be helpful. We began with the idea of a modern deathcraft. Such a craft would create life-enhancing images of death. These images need to be based on positive, even if controversial, knowledge, derived, for example, from psychical research. We said that Christianity gives a key ingredient to our positive metaphysics of death: the resurrection model, which puts the accent on the transformation of earthly existence. Moreover, the need for transformation appears against the mounting nuclear crisis which, experts agree, threatens to be terminal for civilization, if not for life itself on earth.

In Part II we advanced the hypothesis of Mind at Large. The basis for this hypothesis is fourfold: first, the existence of psi; second, evidence for the survival of bodily death; third, experience of the Transcendent; fourth, the deficiencies of a mechanist theory of life. We tried to see the paranormal and transpersonal aspects of mind as part of a larger story of the evolution of life, as showing the expansion of life into ever widening circles of environment. Mind at Large, it was conjectured, expresses a tendency to create its own environment called, after Teilhard de Chardin, the Noosphere. If indeed the "goal" of life is to unfold toward a self-contained sphere of Mind at Large, then physical existence need not mark an absolute barrier to the evolution of life. The unfolding of life would not stop at the margin of physical death.

If the goal of life is continuous expansion, we can readily understand an immortality instinct in humanity; we need not be astonished at evidence for transcendent psi. The point was made that a complete *humanistic psychology should address the questions of psi potential and postmortem survival. All these, we said, are expressions of an Intelligence that pervades the evolutionary process. Survival itself may depend on a proper understanding of and cooperation with such an Intelligence.*

In Part III we looked at the out-of-body experience and tried to understand its place in a new metaphysics of death. An attempt was made to clarify and broaden the concept of the OBE, normalizing yet bringing out its spiritual implications. Mind, we said, is by nature "out of the body."

Like Alice falling down the rabbit hole into Wonderland, we may learn to sail the great ocean of spiritual being by drifting on the natural currents of the mind. Dreams, relaxation and meditation already take us "out" of the circle of routine embodied existence. Given our understanding of the OB process, we see our minds already amphibiously adrift between this world and possible next worlds. At first hesitant but with growing determination, our individual minds, unmoored from the body, launch out, here and now, to explore the mysteries of Mind at Large.

In Part IV, Chapter Seven, we turn to another source of data, which promises to further shape a new myth of the life-death connection: the near-death experience (NDE). In Chapter Eight we look at some special problems pertaining to postmortem survival; and we end in Chapter Nine with an interpretation of the near-death experience.

The NDE is the limit of the OBE continuum, the most drastic form of deflecting attention from the plane of life. In life-threatening situations, routine responses to the external world are suspended. The conscious mind abdicates, and forces of the deep unconscious are aroused. Threatened by extinction, a different system of mental functioning now comes into play. The NDE is an expression of this system.

Chapter Nine, The Archetype of Death and Enlightenment, *is where our search moves to a new level. In my view, the NDE activates a pattern of experience that fits C. G. Jung's description of archetypes of the collective unconscious. People on the verge of death often experience a typical pattern of images, effects and aftereffects. The experience is perhaps best described as a natural conversion or enlightenment process. The label I chose for this was: archetype of death and enlightenment (ADE). I attempt to show that the ADE underlies many types of transcendent human experience.*

If the ADE is a kind of holographic projection of Mind at Large, and Mind at Large has a hand in the evolution of life, then the ADE may be a prophetic projection of the next stage in the evolution of consciousness. We shall, in short, be looking at the evolutionary significance of the near-death archetype, the angel of the immortality instinct.

7

The Near-Death Experience

In the name of truth,
Are ye fantastical, or that indeed
Which outwardly ye show?

—*Macbeth*

Introduction

One day in late 1974 I was driving into Manhattan with a friend. Upon merging with traffic, we struck an embankment. The automobile careened, spun like a top across several lanes, describing a complete turn of 360 degrees. We landed unscathed on the other side of the road, escaping collision with several trucks.

During the period when the car was spinning out of control, several psychologically-odd things happened. I could see clearly the danger. It was the kind of situation impossible to imagine without flinching uncomfortably. And yet it was as if I were a spectator at an interesting show; I experienced no fear, only tranquil curiosity. Indeed, the sensation was pleasant, almost erotic. My sense of time dilated and the instant, by all odds thick with mortal consequences, swelled with a leisurely euphoria.

At the moment, we need not try to explain this episode. More important, I discovered I was somehow psychologically prepared for the emergency; a latent resource, remote from my conscious mind, was there to assist me in the midst of a life-threatening crisis. I wondered how deep and far-reaching this adaptive mechanism was and also what its ultimate significance was. I noted the discrepancy be-

137

tween my conscious image of what nearing death might feel like and
what the unconscious, spontaneous response actually was.

Later I began to study near-death phenomena. I examined old
case history collections, followed the new research and garnered reports of my own. Take, for example, the following near-death experience of a sixty-year-old Roman Catholic nun, which illustrates the
power of these experiences. It will also put us on the track of an
important theme we shall explore: the NDE as a path to universal
consciousness. The report is based on information I obtained from
three nurses from Christ Hospital in Jersey City, N. J.

Sister B. M. entered the hospital in February, 1981, complaining
of weakness and pain in her right side. She had had the pain for a
long while but had been hoping that with prayer it would end. According to the nurses' observations, the patient endured pain quietly.
Her religious medal, scapula and small white head covering were to
be on at all times; she became anxious if they were removed for any
reason.

A diagnosis of cancer was followed by surgery. The next day,
Sister B. M.'s heart rate became overly rapid and unsynchronized,
threatening her life. A "Code Blue" was called and she was resuscitated. The patient appeared to recover, spoke of her religious life, was
pleasant and cooperative except in regard to her religious articles.
She was anxious about losing them. Several days later, the patient
was sitting in bed when the nurse noticed a sudden jerking of arms
and legs, the head dropping to the right. Another "Code Blue" was
called. When the coronary care unit responded, no spontaneous res-
pirations or pulses were noted, skin color was dusky and cool to the
touch and the cardiac monitor showed a morbid arrhythmia. During
the resuscitation procedure, the nurses observed tears in Sister B.
M.'s eyes.

Again the patient recovered, but this time she described the experience she had during the resuscitation experience. First, she remembered floating out of her body toward the ceiling. "I could see my
body and everyone around me; they were upset," she said. She described how she felt herself leaving the room, surrounded by the
most complete blackness, and how she passed through a tunnel into
a dazzling bright light. There she "saw" a beautiful garden, filled
with colorful trees and flowers, and was filled with serenity and
peace. Somehow she found herself back in her body.

The Sister explained the meaning of her tears. She was trying desperately to say not to save her, that she was happy where she was and didn't wish to return to her body of pain. One of the nurses commented: "So they were tears of a different pain than we imagined."

The most interesting point in this account is that when the nurses attempted to put Sister B. M.'s medal, scapula and head covering on, she waved them away, stating they were no longer important to her, that they were only objects and that her faith was deeper now. Forty-five minutes later, the nun's eyes rolled back, her body stiffened; she went into a coma and expired three days later.

This report confirms a strong finding of ND researchers: the near-death encounter deepens the inner spiritual sense, not conventional religiosity. This is clear from the story of the Catholic nun. It is as if she caught a glimpse of the deeper spiritual reality of which her medal, scapula and habit were symbols. This does not imply rejection of the particular form of her religious faith, only perhaps that she made a deeper acquaintance with the universal foundation of all religious faiths.

A World of NDES

The near-death experience (NDE) is not the most striking anomaly bearing on death. There are two good reasons it merits special attention, however.

The first is its increased accessibility. Although psychical researchers have long been aware of reports of unusual experiences on the threshold of death, recently, medical professionals have begun to take serious interest in these phenomena. Estimates vary, but it seems that about forty percent of people who have near-death incidents also have distinctive near-death experiences. The robustness of the phenomenon was confirmed by a nationwide survey conducted by George Gallup, Jr. Based on survey extrapolations, it appears that "as many as eight million Americans, or about one-third of those who have been involved in near-death occurrences, may have felt the presence of some being or otherwise have had a positive, otherworldly experience." [90] Modern techniques of resuscitation enable greater numbers of people to return from the threshold of death. (Ironically, data are turning up, in medical settings, that challenge prevailing medical beliefs.)

Secondly, the NDE is an experience of living persons which often has profound aftereffects. In the deepest experiences of this type,

subjects are convinced of having directly seen, felt and known another world, another reality of great splendor, majesty and beauty.
The NDE, moreover, has striking similarities to a large family of deep
transformative experiences reported by all peoples throughout history. We are going to press the implications of this similarity.

Two Types of NDE

There are two types of NDE. The first consists of deathbed visions. The subject, usually ill, often bedridden, at the hour of death
suddenly has a vision. He often "sees" apparitions of deceased relatives or friends. The experience may be accompanied by an elevation
of mood. Usually, the dying person is in a state of clear, wakeful
consciousness. [10] Apparently, organic dysfunction does not correlate with these experiences. [11] The clearer, the less impaired the
consciousness, the greater the likelihood of an NDE occurring. Early
collections of deathbed visions were compiled and studied by E. Bozzano [91], J. H. Hyslop [92] and W. Barrett. [93]

The second type of NDE might arise from cardiac arrest, near-
drowning, mountain-climbing falls, suicide attempts, auto accidents
or other life-threatening incidents. Although early studies of this phenomenon exist, it was the philosopher-psychiatrist Raymond Moody
who brought the subject to public attention with his *Life After Life* in
1975. Moody formed a model of this type of near-death experience.
The common elements are ineffability, feelings of peace and quiet,
entering a dark tunnel, being out of the body, meeting with others,
having a panoramic memory of one's life, encountering a being of
light, reaching a border or limit and undergoing changes of value and
outlook. Less common but still important elements cited by Moody
are hearing transcendental music and having a "vision of knowledge."

The subsequent work of Kenneth Ring [94] supports the informal
studies of Moody. Ring describes five stages of a "prototypical" core
experience: euphoric affect, an out-of-body state, entering darkness,
seeing an unearthly world of light and entering into that world of
light. These stages seem like parts of an ordered and developing sequence; the final stages are experienced less frequently. At any one of
these stages, there might occur what Ring calls a "decisional process." The person "decides" to return to life. And this is truly a
difficult decision, since subjects often express emphatic displeasure
over being dragged back into their bodies. It is as if we are observing

a general pattern of experience unfolding itself through different people. There is never a perfect manifestation of the pattern, but different conditions allow for partial manifestations of different motifs.

In addition to the five stages and the decisional process, Ring's cases include the other features of classic near-death experiences such as meeting with others, the panoramic memory experience and so forth. On the whole, the two types of NDE, deathbed visions and close-call or resuscitation cases, are similar.

An Initial Paradox

In many resuscitation cases, the patient temporarily ceases to display vital signs. Since in such cases patients are revived, we speak of "clinical," not irreversible, death. Still, the patient, having lost all vital functioning, would, in the great majority of cases, have soon joined the ranks of the irrevocably dead, had it not been for the intervention of on-the-scene medical workers.

The fact that resuscitated patients would, without medical intervention, have died seems rather difficult to reconcile with their having any experience whatsoever. Suppose one dies in the sense that, apart from resuscitation procedures, one would not recover. Once irreversible death has begun, what biological function can we ascribe to having *any* experiences? As long as the organism is functioning, however imminent death may be, it would not be surprising if the brain continued to produce adaptive responses. For instance, Albert Heim, a geologist, described mountain-climbing falls in which accelerated mental processes were claimed; in such cases, the enhanced alertness has obvious survival value. But, from the moment the essentially irreversible process of clinical death begins, the occurrence of *any* experience seems to me paradoxical. Here, apart from resuscitation, such experiences could not be adaptive.

The Universal Pattern of NDEs

Three things about the prototypical NDE call for explanation: (a) the universal pattern they generally exhibit, a pattern that seems independent of individual variables, (b) their psi components, and (c) their profound psychospiritual aftereffects.

For the student of the natural history of the mind, the NDE appears as a distinctive finding, a coherent, spontaneous psychism. Firsthand accounts derive from all kinds of people. In case after case the same message, though coded differently, seems to emanate from a universal stratum of consciousness. What appears is a common pattern of phenomena filtered and personalized by the experiencer's cultural constructs. Osis and Haraldsson, as well as Ring, found that religious beliefs influence the interpretation, not the content of the experience. This is critical. In reading the accounts carefully, one notices that the experiencer will say he or she saw a light, and then they place an interpretation on the light: i.e., it is God, or Jesus.

Moreover, there seem to be aspects of the NDE that manifest in contexts not directly related to life-threatening situations. In short, the common pattern of near-death experience appears in a much wider variety of contexts than literal near-death. We shall look at this extended aspect of near-death imagery, affects and aftereffects shortly. The point here is that the widespread pattern under examination needs to be explained.

The Paranormal Aspects of NDEs

The paranormal side of NDEs also needs to be explained. Most of the material is anecdotal, but the cumulative effect strongly suggests the reality of the psi-dimension of NDEs. Since near-death situations generate altered states of consciousness, and altered states are psi-conducive, it is not surprising to find near-death psi-conducive.

The psi components indicate the NDEs, at least in part, express more than just wish-fulfillment or self-serving fantasy. To the extent that such experiences contain elements of genuine psi, they are oriented toward objective reality. Also, psi in general suggests the existence of an alternate, non-sensory reality, possibly related to postmortem states. This second point is of course controversial, but psi remains unexplained by physical theory and, as such, points toward the existence of an autonomous mental factor.

Psi effects related to deathbed visions. In so-called "Peak in Darien" cases, the dying person sees the apparition of a person not known to be deceased. There are a few reports of cases in which *nobody* present was aware that the person whose apparition was seen was in fact dead, thus ruling out telepathy from people at the dying person's bedside. Cases of this type are rare, but this is not surprising in view of the peculiar combination of things needed for them to occur. Most of the Peak in Darien cases come from the older literature, though Craig Lundahl [95] and Kenneth Ring [94] offer some current illustrations. The impersonal nature of dying in modern hospitals may account for the dearth of recent examples.

Psi effects related to resuscitation cases. In resuscitation cases, or other types of near-death encounter, the most commonly reported psi component comes in the form of apparently veridical out-of-body experiences. Not all OBEs, of course, contain explicit psi elements. Yet there is a common report of an OB situation in which a person near death finds himself located out of the body and later describes events.

Michael Sabom [96], a cardiologist and professor of medicine at Emory University in Georgia, recently published a book that systematically examines the OB component of near-death experiences. One hundred and sixteen persons formed the basis of this sober, medically-oriented study; ten of these encountered their crisis event under general anesthesia during surgery. Of the remaining one hundred and six cases, seventy-eight were obtained prospectively; forty-three percent of these reported a near-death experience (NDE). Sabom concludes from this that NDEs are a "common" event among those who survive near-death incidents. On the whole, Sabom's findings are consistent with those of previous researchers.

The most original contribution of Sabom's book is Chapter 7, in which the author tries to verify the OB phase of close brushes with death. Thirty-two of Sabom's patients, claiming they were out of their bodies, gave visual descriptions of cardiopulmonary resuscitation procedures performed on them during periods of apparent unconsciousness or clinical death.

To evaluate these reports, Sabom tested the idea that cardiac patients could provide pseudo-veridical accounts of CPR procedures based on "educated guesswork." He interviewed twenty-five "control" patients with medical backgrounds similar to those who had OBEs and found that twenty-three of them made at least one major error in their descriptions of the CPR procedures. In contrast to the control group, none of the out-of-body patients made any serious errors in their descriptions. Twenty-six of the thirty-two OB subjects had only general, nonverifiable details in their accounts. According to these patients, the paucity of detail was due to their being absorbed in "overall amazement at what was occurring."

Six, however, of the thirty-two, provided specific, verifiable details in the NDE reports. The procedure was to compare the patient's medical report with the account of the near-death episode. He obtained further verification, whenever possible, from relatives who witnessed the near-death event. The reader should go to the original report, but let us glance briefly here at some of the details.

(1) A security guard from Florida, for instance, was able to give the correct sequence of steps in a CPR procedure: chest thump, cardiac massage, airway insertion, medications and defibrillation. This patient rejected Sabom's use of the term "paddle" but gave an accurate description of the object itself. Sabom took this to imply that the patient was not previously acquainted with the term or the object it referred to, but that he had observed the object for the first time during his resuscitation.

(2) A sixty-year-old housewife described how an "express team" entered her room with a resuscitation cart, how her chest was thumped and an oxygen mask was placed on her face; she "observed" her carotid pulse checked, eyelids lifted to check pupillary response, arterial blood gases drawn from her hand and a nurse collecting and labeling her personal effects for a move to the intensive care unit.

(3) A forty-six-year-old laborer "observed" a nurse touching two defibrillator paddles together, a technique for lubricating the paddles and insuring good skin contact with the chest. The patient also described how everyone moved back to avoid being shocked, how his body jumped a foot high and so on.

(4) A retired Air Force pilot gave an accurate description of a fixed and moving needle on a defibrillator as it was being charged with electricity. The meter described is no longer in use but was common in 1973, at the time of the patient's cardiac arrest. During his interview, the patient used medical terms like "lidocaine pushes" and "watt-seconds," terms he had heard for the first time during his own CPR ordeal.

(5) As a last example, a sixty-year-old man, during resuscitation, was able to observe from his OB vantage point the presence of his wife and two children. The interesting fact is that his family was located some distance down the hall. According to the man's wife, whom Sabom interviewed, she and the two children came to the hospital unexpectedly and were stopped "at least ten rooms down" from where her husband was, and his face was pointed away from them at that moment. This distance factor strongly argues against the possibility that the patient, semi-conscious, glimpsed his wife and children through normal means.

Again, to remind the reader, all these detailed and rather technical observations were made by individuals who were unconscious or clinically dead. Of special interest is the discussion of hypercarbia: increased levels of carbon dioxide in the brain. Experiments with elevated levels of CO_2 are cited in which experiences closely akin to NDEs were produced: photic and OB effects, panoramic memories, ineffability, religious presences and so forth. As Sabom notes, however, we don't know if the CO_2 surplus is the cause of the near-death experience or just one of its physiological correlates. To complicate matters, in the one case where the patient's carbon dioxide and blood oxygen levels were measured at the very moment of his near-death experience, the oxygen level was *above* normal (thus ruling out hypoxia), and the carbon dioxide level was *below* normal (thus ruling out hypercarbia). In any case, hypercarbia intoxication offers a useful line of research into near-death experience, for it is a method, free of serious risk, of mimicking, fairly closely it would seem, full-blown death near-death experiences. The controlled use of hypercarbia intoxication might be usable in a modern deathcraft, perhaps in ways similar to LSD, both for expanding and mapping realms of the human unconscious.

There are also reports of OBEs in deathbed vision cases. But here the apparent separation process may be more gradual. Osis and Haraldsson write, "While still functioning normally, the patient's consciousness might be gradually disengaging itself from the ailing body." In Barrett's early study, witnesses are cited who "see" dying persons' "doubles" split off and disappear at the moment of death. This slightly premature splitting off of the psyche may explain why terminal patients often experience a sudden lessening of pain shortly before they die, although it is possible that stress-induced opiates produced by the brain are responsible.

In any case, there are gradations of depth in the NDE, as Ring's model suggests, ranging from euphoric detachment to profound absorption in transcendent worlds. Psychically, as well as physically, dying seems less an abrupt and more a gradual transition. There are clues indicating that consciousness begins to disengage itself in advance of bodily death—for instance, through dreams and mentations just prior to sudden death or the onset of fatal illness. I have records of individuals who, shortly before the onset of fatality, began to talk of deceased friends and relatives, had slips of the tongue suggesting subconscious preoccupation with them, spontaneously put their affairs in order, settled accounts, etc., as if in preparation for death.

There is an example I observed when I was visiting an elderly man, who was, in fact, not in a critical condition, after an operation. The man's wife was present; suddenly, he spoke of his mother (long dead) bringing him dinner. He meant the nurse, of course. The man died the next morning. What happened? As we know, visions of deceased relatives often presage the onset of death. In this case, it would seem as if the deceased relative "broke through" not by means of a vision but by a slip of the tongue.

Psychospiritual Aftereffects

Deep near-death experiences and deathbed visions produce profound aftereffects. Marked changes in outlook, affective states, values and life-goals are often reported. With deathbed visions, aftereffects are of short duration because the patient soon dies. Still, they are pronounced and dramatic; Osis and Haraldsson found evidence of sudden elation, inexplicable by medical factors, following deathbed visions. In the earlier case histories compiled by Barrett and Hyslop, the change in mood was often so striking that it spread to friends and families witnessing the deathbed scene.

Sabom made follow-up studies six months after the NDE and found that the changes persisted. Generally, the changes are beneficial—in some ways resembling religious conversion. Chief among the aftereffects are reduction or elimination of the fear of death and altered outlooks on the meaning of life and the nature of reality. Several interwoven points deserve special notice. NDErs experience a reduced sense of sin, a fact that disturbs some religious-minded people. The Being of Light seems disinclined toward righteous condemnation; rather, it presents itself as a Gentle Instructor. It encourages taking on the tasks of life, learning to live and work through problems; it promotes confidence that in the end, all will be well.

Some of the deeper experiencers report acquiring a sense of cosmic love. In this regard, their new value system echoes that of Plato of the *Symposium*, Dante of the *Divine Comedy* and Whitman of *Leaves of Grass*. At the same time—and perhaps to the satisfaction of the theologians of wrath—there are reports, fewer but not in insignificant numbers, of near-death meetings with demonic, hellish and decidedly unpleasant apparitions.

Psi effects are often reported as occurring during a near-death episode; they also figure in the aftereffects. In the aftereffects, however, what we notice is a shading of increased psi sensitivity into increased spiritual sensitivity. It is hard to distinguish these sharply; hence, my preference is for the term "psychospiritual." In the case of a man whose experience I recorded, the following aftereffects were noted (this person, a somewhat skeptical academic, had his NDE in 1979): being in touch with his feelings; being less egocentric, more aware of others, especially of their needs; greater psychic sensitivity (he claims to obtain impressions from touching articles belonging to people); increased perceptiveness; increased zest for life; increased energy level; and greater single-mindedness of purpose. This forms a striking array of changes.

This example is bolstered by more organized studies. For instance, Richard Kohr [97] found that near-death experiencers tend significantly to report psi and psi-related states more frequently than non-NDErs. Kohr's studies indicate a global increase of sensitivity, greater access to states of mind normally unconscious; among "psi-related" experiences are listed deeper, more subtle access to dream life, meditation and apparent memories of past lives. Mystical and more deeply meaningful experiences were also reported more frequently among NDErs. These studies were confirmed by the work of psychiatrist Bruce Greyson, who concluded: "The NDE appears to be not only psi-conducive for the duration of the experience, but psi-enhancing for the individual's subsequent life." [98] Finally, Kenneth Ring [99] has made a close study of the psychospiritual aftereffects of deep NDEs and again found a global transformation of awareness, sensitivities, values and goals.

The Interpretation of NDEs

Well, what are we to make of these strange experiences? Interpretations of NDEs may roughly be classified in two groups: reductionistic and transcendent. The former view these experiences as mainly pathological and illusory; the latter see the NDE as significant, transformative, possibly suggestive of postmortem survival. Elsewhere I have argued the case against the reductionistic interpretation [100] and so will not repeat myself here. The reader would also profit from Michael Sabom's critique of reductionistic explanations of NDEs. In Chapter Nine, I shall develop in detail my own transcendent interpretation of the near-death experience.

Let me end with the following two remarks. First, NDEs are a unique category of experiences; the core phenomenon does not correspond to anything we are familiar with such as depersonalization syndrome or drug-induced experiences. The second point is that even if they do resemble elements of some psychedelic experiences (as we shall see two chapters hence) and even if disturbances in the brain can be correlated with NDEs, it does not follow that NDEs may be reduced to illusions void of transcendent significance.

For instance, on the Bergson-James theory of the brain as a filter of consciousness, near-death, which obviously disrupts the efficiency of the brain filter, would be ideal for generating expanded states of consciousness. In other words, the fact of pathology by itself proves nothing; some theories of mind-brain might even predict that near-death would lead to expanded states of mind.

Let us admit that near-death is (shall we say "by definition") a pathological state. We cannot infer that the experiences triggered by it are themselves pathological. The best discussion of this remains William James' "Religion and Neurology," the first chapter of *The Varieties of Religious Experience*." [101] I cannot repeat the whole argument here; the reader may return to the source. Suffice it to say that James sharply distinguished the organic origin from the meaning of an experience. A long footnote argues against interpreting "religion as perverted sexuality." The fundamentalism of this school of thought is underscored, which mistakes the language of erotic metaphor for literal fact. We might just as well interpret religion as gastric malfunctioning, given the abundance of gastric metaphors in religious texts, (e.g., we "hunger and thirst" after righteousness).

"Medical materialism," James wrote in 1902, "finishes up Saint Paul by calling his vision on the road to Damascus a discharging lesion of the occipital cortex, he being an epileptic. It snuffs out Saint Teresa as a hysteric, Saint Francis of Assisi as a hereditary degenerate. George Fox's discontent with the shams of his age, and his pining for spiritual veracity, it treats as a symptom of a disordered colon."

8

The Cosmic Detective Story

*I confess that at times I have been tempted to
believe that the Creator has eternally intended this
department of nature to remain baffling, to prompt
our curiosities and hopes and suspicions all in
equal measure, so that, although ghosts . . . and
messages from spirits, are always seeming to exist
and can never be fully explained away, they also
can never be susceptible of full corroboration.*

—William James

In this chapter, we pause briefly to remark on the status of survival research as a whole. Several issues call for comment at this point in our story.

Remarks on a Peculiar Paradox

Paradoxically, the main obstacle to belief in life after death nowadays is not lack of evidence. In fact, there was never a time in history when (in relative terms) there was more organized data suggestive of postmortem survival; yet among the educated masses, the belief in survival is probably at an all-time low. Here, for example, is what Gardner Murphy concludes after years of studying survival evidence: "To me, the evidence cannot be by-passed, nor on the other hand can conviction be achieved."

In speaking of survival data, I am referring to the mediumship, apparitions and hauntings compiled and analyzed by the English and American Societies for Psychical Research. Just the material dealing with so-called "cross-correspondences," much of which remains unanalyzed and unpublished to date, comprises a small library. Nor has this material ceased to increase, as may be seen in the recent work of

Karlis Osis, Erlendur Haraldsson, Ian Stevenson, William Roll and others. It is hard to examine the best of this material without pausing and reconsidering one's preconceptions about death. Nevertheless, it is largely ignored by most present-day scholars and thinkers.

Several things at work in the background of modern life may account for this. Persons of good will and good mind are inhibited from even looking at the relevant facts, and if they do succeed in bringing themselves to look, they usually do so armed with a handful of fixed ideas designed to minimize their significance.

The Global Reign of Materialism. Perhaps one reason is a certain climate of thought: the reign of modern materialism militates against belief in survival. The official party line of the academy is that all things are at bottom material. The prevailing creed varies in expression; some of the older and cruder forms (behaviorism) are less in vogue, though identity theory, which effectively assimilates the life of mind to brain mechanisms, is the popular view among academic philosophers. The life sciences, medical and biological, remain attached to the dogmas of physicalism. So powerful is this outlook that ministers and theologians play down the supernatural side of religious experience. The idea of a mind factor enjoying autonomy and, wilder yet, surviving the death of the body, is treated as retrograde and inherently implausible, or worse, as irrelevant. Dualism, in some form essential to survival, is viewed as a dangerous heresy.

The militant secularism I speak of cuts across ideological boundaries. New age prophets of holistic paradigms no less than the common foot-soldiers of scientific materialism abstain from talk of the "beyond." Ditto for Western imports of Eastern mysticism. There is a surprising metaphysical agreement among adversaries: Soviet materialism (cynically undergirded by the pseudo-religion of Marxism) and Western capitalist materialism (undergirded by lip service to Christianity). Both superpowers run on academically supported versions of a supposed true scientific materialism. Philosophically speaking, the conflict between the superpowers is less a conflict between strangers than it is the offshoot of fratricidal impulses.

Egoism as a Way of Life. Materialism as a metaphysical doctrine implies nothing as to the way one lives. Metaphysical materialists might be unworldly in morals—devoted to lofty causes, loyal and loving to the good earth, benefactors of humanity. Conversely, professors of lofty spirituality may be, and often have been, scourges to the human race.

Still, the way people live day to day in our societies does not lend itself to belief in postmortem survival. That is, the supreme values are not only declared to be material as a matter of dry metaphysics, but they are pursued concretely in daily life. Material values are the cause of conflict, continual international politicking and military adventurism.

Practical materialism in modern cultures reduces chances for transcendent experience. In classical and archaic societies, the rite of passage offered ways to transcendence. Ego-death, incorporated into ritual, was part of the fabric of ordinary social existence. The standard rite of passage made consciousness permeable to alternate realities. Further, pre-modern attitudes toward the dead strengthened the sense of continuity with the beyond. Ancestor worship in Shintoism, for instance, or the Catholic Church's practice of saying Mass for the dead are ways of keeping alive awareness of our links with the unseen. Let us say, to simplify, that materialism as a climate of moral perception neglects the unseen pattern and stresses the visible; it supports egoism, fixation on the isolated form. Existence begins and ends at the visible boundaries of one's bodily organism; here lies the stage of the whole drama of life and death. Egoism as a way of life, a by-product of myopic materialism, inhibits alertness to the Transcendent.

Absence of a Coherent World View. This third point is interwoven with the last two. One could trace incoherence of world view to Xenophanes, who attacked the theology of Homer at the dawn of Western philosophy. Instability of world view is probably endemic to human culture since the rise of critical reason. The inability to see life as a coherent whole is especially acute today and contrasts markedly with the technical ability to manipulate the forces of material nature. Technical success has dulled the urgency for metaphysical insight.

Psi and *a fortiori* survival evidence do not fit into any comprehensive theory or world view; hence the reluctance of the scientific community to accept what appears like a mass of dubious and disconnected anomalies. Of course, the anomalies inspire *us* to question the prevailing world view. In tune with the empirical tradition, we take the realm of stubborn fact as more sacred than the realm of cherished theory.

The Parapsychological Obstacle to Belief in Survival

Having stated some general reasons for the lack of hospitality to survival evidence, we now have to look at more substantive objections. Once again we meet with a paradox: the greatest obstacle to belief in survival comes from within the field of parapsychology. Students of the best survival evidence—from the founding fathers of psychical research to C. D. Broad, E. R. Dodds, Gardner Murphy and Alan Gauld—have been driven, after eliminating everything due to fraud, poor reportage, paramnesia, cryptomnesia, etc., to choose between two options: either that some form of survival is a fact or that the appearance of survival is engineered by the extensive powers of deceptive psi from living agents. After immersing oneself in the details of the mediumship of Mrs. Piper, Mrs. Leonard and other distinguished mediums, one is driven to one or the other hypothesis; no obvious third course seems tenable.

The fact of psi permits us to believe that what looks like a message from the beyond is a piece of deception from the here and now. This option of deceptive psi from the living is said to be scientifically more respectable because it makes fewer assumptions than the survival hypothesis. After all, we know of psi among the living, the fictive powers of the unconscious, the fear of death and all the rest. We don't know about discarnate existence. Therefore, we may reject the survival hypothesis.

Obviously this approach cannot be ignored, especially when it is presented in such general terms. The problem is that there is no way the hypothesis can ever be falsified. If one is resolutely anti-survival and sufficiently imaginative, no conceivable evidence for survival need triumph in any debate. One's "reasons" will prevail over every contingency of fact.

To assume unlimited psi ability in human beings, along with the nonphysicality of psi, is already to create a hospitable climate of thought for the idea of survival. If in principle the human mind has unlimited ESP and PK (which is what super-psi implies), then the idea that our minds may survive after death seems much less far-fetched.

The claim that deceptive psi accounts for apparent survival evidence runs into another problem. There is no experimental evidence for the existence of such extensive and copious psi abilities. Anyone who knows the literature knows the piddling degree of significance shown in experimental psi situations. Yet we are asked to believe that mediums (like Mrs. Piper) or children with detailed reincarnation memories, skills and behaviors, who do poorly at ESP tests, suddenly acquire extensive, copious and complex psi abilities, exclusively in contexts suggestive of survival.

The powers of unconscious self-deception must here be assumed to be vast and relentless—an idea that might give us all pause about our favorite theories. We are all liable to be duped by that "incomprehensible enchantment" and "all powerful force" of which Pascal wrote.

"Superpsi" and Self-Deception

Rather than argue *a priori*, it is wiser to take each case as it comes and examine it for fraud, cryptomnesia, psi influence of the living, evidence for survival and so on. This is the general method of Ian Stevenson and is the basis of Alan Gauld's recent book, *Mediumship and Survival.* [102] Gauld's book is a sustained critique of the superpsi attempt to explain survival evidence. The value of this approach is to make explicit all the assumptions in specific cases where deceptive psi competes with the survival interpretation.

Take a relatively simple case, frequently cited, perhaps because it is inscribed in the legal history of North Carolina. The summary is based on the report made by W. H. Salter, who prepared the case for publication for the English Society For Psychical Research (Vol. XX-XVI, pp. 517-524), and who exchanged letters with the American lawyer engaged in the probation of the will.

In 1921 farmer James Chaffin of North Carolina died accidentally from a fall, leaving all his property to his third son, Marshall, who himself died about a year later. In June, 1925, James, the second son, began having vivid dreams or waking visions of his father at his bedside. On one occasion his father, wearing a familiar black overcoat, said, pointing to the overcoat: "You will find my will in my overcoat pocket." The coat was found in the older brother's house, and inside a sewn-up pocket was a roll of paper which read: "Read the 27th. Chapter of Genesis in my daddie's old Bible." The Bible was found in the presence of witnesses, and a new will dated January 16, 1919, was discovered, dividing the property equally among his sons. At first, Marshall's widow contested the will but backed down when she saw the documents herself. The second will, though unattested by witnesses, was admitted to probate and validated by the State. Although the Testator's action with his second will seemed odd, the lawyer assured Salter there was nothing suspect or incredible in the case.

Although it is not clear why the senior Chaffin paltered so deviously with the second will, it is easy to imagine what may have happened. Chaffin seems to have favored the third son, Marshall (shown by his first will), but was moved by duty and Bible to produce the second will. The devious, incomplete manner of disposing of the second will only reflects the farmer's lack of resolution, his wavering between duty and inclination. Writing the second will was the effect of duty, concealing it the effect of lingering inclination. Sudden accidental death prevented him from resolving his indecision. On the assumption of survival continued bickerings with conscience in the "other place" led to duty winning out.

The alternate interpretation is that young Chaffin, who stood to gain by discovering the second will, used his clairvoyance to retrieve it. (Recall that no living person knew of the existence of the secret will.) But why do all this through the halting procedure of a series of dreams or waking visions of his father? Why not a hunch or a dream or a well-timed "accident" targeted on the Bible itself? If Chaffin had been using his own clairvoyance, he would have had to have "cognized" the location of the will hidden in the Bible, because the rolled paper in the overcoat said nothing about a will. All it said was something about reading a passage in the Bible. Apart from this reading of an eleven word sentence, a feat beyond what is normally done in laboratory setting, the sentence did not even refer to the will itself. The assumption that Chaffin used his psi ability here strains credibility because it is too complicated and because it presupposes (in a man not known for any psi ability) an extraordinary and sudden capacity for psi. One opts for it only because of the presumed improbability of survival.

As the reader may have noticed, the term I have been using to name what superpsi is supposed to be doing—conjuring up apparent and sometimes quite convincing survival evidence—is "deceptive psi." In all cases of ostensible survival, the superpsi hypothesis assumes an unconscious tendency to engineer deception. Once we make this clear, we can make another assumption more explicit: where there is deception, there must be a need for deception. A clearer statement of what superpsi implies must include this qualification. Superpsi or deceptive psi in survival cases must be need-relevent. Admitting the need-relevance of supposed superpsi, we would have to restrict the range of cases to which we can apply it.

Consider the Chaffin Will Case. No one could deny the need to use psi here; young Chaffin obviously stood to gain by using his psi. But as far as we know, the need was for finding a will that favored Chaffin materially; there is no special reason to suppose there was a need to verify the persistence of his father's consciousness after death. One therefore wonders about the devious and indirect manner in which the psi worked—a series of apparitions of the father, rather than going straight to the object satisfying the need. Chaffin's need to use his psi is patent but his need for a deceptive scenario of his father's survival is not.

However, the need for deception could indeed be at work in many cases of apparent survival, as in the bulk of mediumistic cases. One usually goes to a medium expecting, hoping, needing confirmation of a loved one's survival. The mere presence of this need, of course, doesn't exclude the survival hypothesis. The point is that not all apparent survival data is even open to the superpsi hypothesis, if the need factor is absent or negligible. In the case of apparitions of the dead, we have a mixed bag and would have to take them case by case.

For instance, a teenager reported the following to me. She was about to step into the room where her father lay dead; she was distressed and disconsolate. As she approached the casket (along with her mother and brother), an apparition of her father, radiant, smiling, appeared before her. The girl's mood lifted dramatically. Clearly, need is apparent in this case.

But not all apparitions of the dead are need relevant. Consider the following (abbreviated) account of a case I investigated. A young couple moved into an apartment in Irvington, N. J., in 1979 and had been living there for six months. During that time, Grace would often wake Alan Dennis at night and say she heard the closet door opening and slamming shut. Alan usually heard nothing and, in fact, was annoyed by these intrusions on his sleep. One day, after Alan had gone to work, Claire was hanging draperies in the bedroom. Although there was no one in the house, Claire heard the living room door open and close. She poked her head outside the bedroom into the living room and saw a strange man sitting on the couch looking at her. She panicked, ran into the bedroom and grabbed the hammer; meanwhile, the closet door in the living room was heard to open and slam shut. After a while it became silent, and Claire peeked back into the living room. Nobody was there. She ran off to her mother who lived close by.

The incident caused problems between Claire and Alan, although the latter's skepticism was undermined when Claire, two weeks later, mentioned what happened to Mrs. Lewis, the woman who owned the house and lived downstairs on the ground floor. Claire was able to identify from a photograph the apparition of the man she saw sitting on her couch; he was the younger brother of Mrs. Lewis, had previously lived in Claire's and Alan's apartment and was stabbed to death in a bar in Newark nine months previously. The disturbances ceased after, and in accord with advice from a local priest, the house was sprinkled with holy water. The Bible was also opened and placed on the living room table. The couple, shaken from the experience, moved away soon after.

What are we to make of this story? After speaking with the people involved, there was little doubt in my mind of the basic accuracy of the story. Surely we cannot dispose of this by uttering the magic word, Superpsi! If superpsi is deceptive psi, where is the deception here? One could see deception at work with the teenager who saw an apparition of her father, but not with Alan and Claire. It seems absurd to say that the young couple *needed* to have this experience. It served no purpose for them at all, but was, in fact, a nuisance.

Deceptive psi seems out of court here. What then, of survival? But now comes another twist in the cosmic detective story. Perhaps, it is often said, such haunting apparitions are merely traces without consciousness, echoes of charged moments trapped in the corridors of time and space, inwardly vacant images of the living. This theory is at least as fanciful as the survival theory; it is based on no clear or plausible model I know of. If such psychic entities, ghouls lost in space, really exist, it is nothing easily digested in any case by academic materialism. But the main point is that the facts don't fit the theory; the apparition of the murdered man did not behave like a lifeless, psychic photograph; it appeared conscious and looked directly at Claire with an expression of puzzlement mingled with anger. Mrs. Lewis, the sister of the murdered man, speculated that her brother "returned" to see his newborn baby.

Moreover, why did the disturbance end after blessing the house? If this type of haunting is caused by a nonconscious eidolon stuck in the psychic ether, we wouldn't expect it to respond to intelligent discourse. If, on the other hand, we say the agency behind the phenomena was Claire's unconscious mind, then we could say that the mini-exorcism influenced the workings of her unconscious, thus bringing the manifestations to a halt. But then we run into the original problem of the motive that prompted Claire to conjure up the apparition.

This is by no means a perfect case (it would have been stronger if the apparition had been collectively seen). But it combines at least three things which, taken together, seem to me to favor the survival hypothesis. First, against "superpsi," the apparition cannot be seen as relevant to the needs of the percipient. Second, the apparition was veridical; Claire knew nothing of the former occupant of her apartment and yet was able to identify him through a photograph. Third, the apparition displayed a responsive intelligence and could not reasonably be described as appearing like a detached and mindless psychic photograph.

Reincarnation

Reincarnation is one of the oldest and most widely-held forms of belief that the human personality is not bound to the lifespan of a single body. However, it has not been since the painstaking labors of psychiatrist Ian Stevenson [103] that we have had impressive empirical evidence suggestive of actual cases of reincarnation. Based on extensive travels and on-site investigations, Stevenson has collected over a thousand cases of this type and has published detailed accounts of about fifty in a series (so far) of four books. Again, the reader will have to go to the source; we shall confine ourselves to a few remarks.

To be sure, the concept of reincarnation, as all concepts of survival, raises difficulties, two of which I will comment on here, although such difficulties shouldn't inhibit us from confronting the data. First, a logical point first made in Plato's *Phaedo:* evidence for preexistence, by itself, is not evidence for postexistence. Still, evidence for backward continuity would enhance the antecendent probability of forward continuity. The fact that something of "me" was around before my body appeared on the scene makes it easier to believe that something of "me" will be around after it is gone.

That a human mind emerges at birth along with a particular body, and yet manages to escape dissolution at the time of bodily death, seems at least curiously asymmetrical. For in that case, one has to suppose that the nonphysical basis of the person was created *ex nihilo* at the time of bodily conception, or at any rate that it acquired its potential for survivability in the course of its embodied existence. This difficulty, which might not bother Christians who believe that each soul is a special creation, is obviated by the doctrine of backward continuity or reincarnation. One might now suppose that the nonphysical basis of the person is essentially indestructible—deathless and immortal in Plato's terminology—continuous, we might say, with Mind at Large. Thus from a strictly logical point of view, reincarnation data supplement data that support forward continuity.

I mentioned a second difficulty. Suppose aspects of a personality B are continuous with a previous personality A (in the sense, say, of sharing certain memories, behaviors or skills); does it really make sense to say that *person* A has survived bodily death in the form of *person* B? Two reasons weigh against saying "yes."

(1) Being the same person presupposes some degree of continuous form. It is true that from babyhood to old age the form of a human being changes markedly, but change is gradual and relatively continuous. But the transformation from one embodied person to another (often with change of sex) is too catastrophic to justify claiming that B is the same as A. For instance, suppose my burly, gravel-voiced uncle died and reincarnated, with memories and (even say) some behaviors intact, in the form of a little girl from a nearby town. I would find it difficult, if not impossible, to think of the little girl as my uncle, no matter what memories were sharable or behaviors observable. Continuity of *personality* would therefore not entail continuity of *person;* the former may be thought of as an abstraction, but not as a substitution, for the latter.

(2) According to Stevenson, most reincarnation memories fade in early childhood. But if memory is the measure of continuity, then continuity would fail as memory failed. Survival would then be restricted to those few children who sustain short-term memories of a previous life; moreover, as the evidence indicates, it is mainly children whose previous lives were brought to a sudden and violent end that recall their past lives. This restricts the range of functional survivability to an even narrower circle.

But do non-reincarnationist views of survival handle these difficulties any better? The objection seems to be that reincarnation presupposes too sharp a break in the process of transformation to allow us to speak sensibly of survival of persons. The notion of "survival" through resurrection seems (theoretically) best to guarantee the continuity of the person; though even here, there seems to be quite a jump. If I met my uncle transformed into his pneumatic body, though more recognizable than as a reincarnated little girl, the novelty might still be quite shocking and disruptive to my sense of who I was face to face with. Indeed, according to reports in the New Testament, the resurrection appearances of Jesus were not at first recognized even by intimate disciples. Resurrection, in its own way, must count as a transformation no less formidable than reincarnation.

The same point applies to other forms of survival—for instance, survival or continuity that depends on the so-called etheric or astral body or on an even more plastic, mind-dependent dream body. However we think of survival, it implies the destruction of the familiar basis of individual bodily continuity; mind, spirit, spiritual body, whatever, no longer mediated by brain, body or the terrestrial world, must turn out to be an altogether different kind of being. There may be strands of continuity, connection, history; but, as with the fossil records of life forms, we can probably expect a "punctuated" equilibrium, sudden leaps to new forms and modes of being, if indeed the forms of conscious life do survive death. This ultimate fragility of personality may be what we are supposed to bear in mind with the Buddhistic doctrine of anatta, the doctrine that denies substance to the self or soul; or even, for that matter, with the Christian idea that our true kingdom is not of this world.

As to the second point raised about not remembering our past lives, several things may be said. Although we may not consciously remember our past lives, they may still exert a subtle influence upon us. Stevenson has suggested that phobias, philias, special talents and skills and other personality traits may be traceable to a previous life (his speculations are based on evidential case histories); these carry-overs may be quite powerful, even though we consciously forget their origins and causes. The situation is comparable to memories repressed in this life that exert powerful effects upon us. Stevenson cites examples in which memories of a previous life crop up in dreams; this raises the possibility that dreams or other altered states of consciousness do in fact put us in touch with memories of former lives, even though they may not be recognizable or verifiable as such. It is difficult to say how subtle and pervasive these nonverifiable interactions with past lives may in fact be.

Finally, we might add that among Eastern sages, it is believed that at death, or during moments of meditation, the enlightened self sees its past lives and experiences a panaroma of past incarnations just as people during near-death states experience a panorama of the events in their single lives. The wider the reach of consciousness, the more profound a spectator of all time and existence, the more one grasps the pattern of one's life and of one's lives, and ultimately, we might conjecture, of the life of the universe.

We need not take the amnesia of ordinary existence as the measure of our potential mindreach. As Plato said in the Tenth Book of the *Republic*, we have to pass through the River of Forgetfulness to enter on a new round of embodied existence. But an individual round of ordinary embodied existence may be only a small cross section of the totality of the potential experience of the self. The empirical studies of Stevenson, along with those of C. G. Jung, as we shall see later, go a way toward substantiating this metaphysical intuition, and thus of enlarging the concept of the human self.

In conclusion, many of these reincarnation cases cannot reasonably be described as need-relevant. Consider what Stevenson himself has to say about the children caught up in the reincarnation scenario:

> I wish to say that I find it puzzling that anyone should want to remember a previous life . . . Persons who remember a previous life are by no means always happier for having done so. The majority seem to me less happy than other persons until they forget their memories. As children they are often involved in painful conflicts with their parents when they remember a second set of parents, and perhaps a wife and children as well! And many of the memories recalled by subjects of these cases are of unpleasant events such as domestic quarrels, crimes, and violent death.

It makes very little sense to describe this behavior as gratifying any self-serving wishes. Like the apparition of the murdered man that caused a disruption in the lives of Alan and Claire, reincarnation memories seem more like external intrusions.

Conclusion

To review survival research as a whole is beyond the scope of a short chapter. The aim of the last two chapters has been modest: to show that we are entitled to remain open to the mystery of death. In the present chapter, the focus was on some general obstacles to accepting the results of survival evidence. Two kinds of obstacles stand out. One lies in the background of modern intellectual life: the pervasive dogma of materialism. The other comes from parapsychology itself in the form of that hydra-headed monster: superpsi.

The superpsi hypothesis is so vague as barely to qualify as a scientific hypothesis. When it is defined precisely by its deceptive and need-serving function, it seems to apply less readily to some survival evidence, such as certain apparitions and reincarnation memories. Neither does it easily apply to at least one type of mediumistic phenomenon: the so-called "drop-in" communicator. Here, a stranger to the sitter and the medium intrudes and identifies itself, sometimes providing verifiable details of its premortem existence. It is also hard to see "no-consent" cases reported in Hindu deathbed visions and "hellish" near-death experiences as the products of wish-fulfillment. These phenomena suggest external agency. One must strain to call them wish-fulfilling fabrications.

No less damaging to the notion of superpsi is the fact that there is no empirical evidence showing that living persons have unlimited psi ability. No experimental studies lead us to believe that anyone can synthesize from a diversity of sources information unknown to any living person, and reproduce attitudes, points of view, appearances of meaningful intention, and specific skills and behaviors known to belong to deceased persons. "Proof" of survival we may not have; but the mystery of death deepens, and there are good factual reasons for revising our general picture of death and the human self. There is evidence for both backward and forward continuity of the self. And psi, or if you like, superpsi, is itself the single most powerful basis for raising questions about the boundaries of the human self. Modern thought is catching up with the intuitions of the ancient Greek philosopher, Heraclitus, who said: "The limits of the soul are undiscoverable."

9
The Archetype of Death and Enlightenment

*A man should be able to say he has done his best
to form a conception of life after death, or to create
some image of it—even if he must confess his
failure. Not to have done so is a vital loss.*

—C. G. Jung

The reader will recall that we looked at the out-of-body experience from two angles: conceptual and spiritual. We found that the OB process ranges from local, "earthbound" excursions (sometimes veridical) to forms touching on spiritual life itself. Having examined the basics of the near-death experience, we now shall zero in on its meaning and spiritual content.

Beyond the abstract possibility (or even probability) of survival is the question of how the idea of survival fits into the business of living here and now. That was a point raised in the first chapter on a craft of dying; the conclusion was that a craft of dying was inseparable from one of living. So that is the question we must now ask: what is the relevance of the near-death experience to the craft of living? The NDE is perhaps compatible with survival of bodily death. But what difference does it make to the question of our existence here and now, our existence in a world stripped of inner resources and menaced by outer forces?

Let us begin by reminding ourselves that NDEs are primarily mental images experienced on the threshold of death. What kind of mental images are they? What is their function? What do they mean?

What are their aftereffects? What, if anything, do they tell us about the objective world and about our relationship to death? Are they of any special use in bringing a healing vision of death into focus? What, if any, is the evolutionary significance of this near-death imagery?

What follows is an attempt to answer these questions in the light of Carl Jung's theory of archetypes. It develops a transpersonal paradigm of NDEs which is useful for the following reasons:

(1) To begin with, NDEs are themselves evidence for the theory of archetypes, the universal patterns of imagery, affect and behavior central to Jungian theory.

(2) The theory respects the intrinsic value of the near-death experiencer, especially the sense of tremendous meangingfulness, of having encountered a supremely important *reality*. It is true that not all NDEs are tremendously meaningful; moreover, the NDE may be a complex phenomenon with multicausal origins. Nevertheless, the impact on those who have the core transcendental experience is usually quite powerful. It is to this core that the present theory addresses itself. By contrast, reductionistic theories tend to devalue and derealize the intrinsic ND experience by categorizing it as hallucinatory, illusory or epiphenomenal.

(3) The archetype theory is compatible with what psychiatrist Bruce Greyson has called a "normal neurophysiological adaptive response." For instance, evidence for temporal-limbic activity or endorphin release would be compatible with the idea that NDEs activate archetypal psychic contents. In general, the notion of archetypes, as developed by Jung, is in tune with the biological perspective; although he never fully developed his thinking here, Jung saw the archetypal layer of the human unconscious as organically adaptive.

(4) The present view complies with another point made by Greyson [104]: the need for a psychodynamic interpretation of near-death phenomena. However, there is a crucial addition: Jungian psychodynamics posits a transpersonal level of psychic reality, the level of the "collective" unconscious.

(5) The theory, unlike many psychodynamic theories, is compatible with the paranormal elements often reported in near-death research. The fifth point is linked to the fourth. The transpersonal level of psychic reality functions relatively free from the constraints of time and space, which is another way of talking about the paranormal.

(6) The archetype theory is consistent with the idea that human consciousness survives bodily death.

The theory of archetypes enables us to view NDEs as evidence for a general psychic function associated with the dying process. This function I call the archetype of death and enlightenment (ADE). It was by going beyond the NDE setting—into the realm of certain psychedelic experiences, UFO "revelations," ancient mystery rituals, dreams and so forth—that I was led to the idea of a dynamic, death-transcending psychism, latent in the collective unconscious. In coining the expression ADE, then, I am not just relabeling the NDE but naming a new theoretical construct.

The significance of such an archetype for medical science and a theory of man would be great. As Jung knew from clinical experience, "modern man"—solitary, anxious, driven, traditionless and spiritually uprooted—has lost touch with the healing symbols and energies of the deep psyche, especially the healing symbols and energies for coping with death. The NDE is a windfall clue to rediscovering the healing force within, the living answer in our own psyches to the riddle of death.

The Archetypal Nature of Near-death Experiences

The nature and origin of "archetypes" is obscure and controversial. Jung was not a philosopher, a fact he often stressed with relish, and so he was never systematic. Like Freud and Plato, his thought was always in process; there is a seminal ambiguity in his writings. Let us then just try for a good working definition of the archetype; we will illustrate its nuances by means of the NDE itself.

Archetype, primordial image, psychic dominant—Jung used these terms to refer to a dynamic and organizing psychic content, a center of psychic energy, that forms part of the ground plan of the human mind. There are similarities to the Platonic Form as well as to the Kantian categories. Jung sometimes thought of the archetype as a kind of psychic equivalent to the biological concept of instinct. The similarity lies in the a priori and nonpersonal derivation of these concepts, their regulative and ordering function on human experience. Jung repudiates the Lockean notion of the mind as a *tabula rasa*, a blank slate upon which historical or cultural contingencies can write their own arbitrary dictates. Man, in short, has an inner destiny; an autonomous principle of self-development presides over human fate. The archetypes, viewed as an organic psychic system, guide the development of the human self.

Archetypes derive from the collective unconscious. Jung distinguishes between the "archetype as such" and its particular psychic manifestation. The image that appears in the dream or myth is not therefore the archetype as such, which is never given in consciouness. Rather, archetypes are meaning-endowing psychisms; they guide, point toward the future, orient the individual in the never-ending process of self-development. Let us now look in detail at the archetypal aspects of the near-death experience.

Archetypes and Typical Situations

"There are as many archetypes as there are typical situations in life . . . [They represent] merely the possibility of a certain type of perception and action," wrote Jung. [105] Dying is one of the typical situations of life; it would therefore be surprising if there were no archetype related to dying. The archetypes express the great forms and psychic residues of the human condition, the permanent impulses, conditions and tendencies that belong to humanity at large: womanhood, childhood, heroism, wisdom, the dark side of the human soul, birth, death, rebirth and so on. We can hardly suppose a more permanent and fatal condition that imposes itself on human life than death. Now, just as even the lowest organisms are provided with mechanisms to assist in birth, growth and adaptation, so, perhaps, evolution has armed the human organism with a "mechanism" for adapting to the stage of development called death.

The archetype is a psychic dynamism that cannot be traced to the personal history of the subject. The NDE cannot be traced to the personal history of the subject either. Researchers have generally been impressed by the common patterns of the experience; typical features occur independently of personal variables such as age, sex, education, religion and culture. Apparently, when we are on the verge of death, a universal psychic pattern of images and feelings appears with a striking degree of regularity. It is hard to avoid the conclusion that the ND pattern is, so to speak, "built-in" to the deep psyche; this seems especially so when subjects are children.

Recent studies explore the near-death experiences of children. In one account, particularly intriguing from a Jungian viewpoint, a seven-year-old girl, deathly ill, heard a chorus of heavenly voices, experienced peace, went out of her body, met beings who sparkled like stars in her room, sailed through a dark tunnel at the end of which she saw a robed Christlike figure. Children, even much younger than this seven-year-old, envisioned similar archetypal near-death scenarios. It is unlikely that these images were based on personal history, on the personal unconscious or on anything learned by the subjects. They seem rather like crystallizations of the "preformed faculty" of the mind.

Fluidity and Ineffability of the Archetype

The archetypes, according to Jung, "appear under an almost infinite variety of aspects." "A kind of fluid interpretation belongs to the very nature of the archetype," he said, and further, "no archetype can be reduced to a formula . . . but they change their shape continually." This is somewhat overstated since if there were no continuity of form at all, there would be no way to pick out one archetype from another, and there would thus be no way to talk of the Shadow, the Wise Old Man, the Anima and so on. Still, there is a point in stressing that fixed labels are pale reminders of the richness of archetypal experience. The often reported ineffability of the NDE comes, therefore, as no surprise.

Archetypes mark a point of meeting between the personal and the collective experience of humankind. They are charged with a surplus of meanings and associations; they reverberate with human memories, nostalgias and aspirations. Truly to evoke these images, resonant with the passions of the human race, would take the poetic genius of a Dante or a Blake. No wonder the ordinary person returns from the NDE stammering hyperboles.

An Archetype of Transformation

Jung spoke of a category of archetype that, in addition to personified imagery (the Trickster, the Child, the Hero, etc.), consists of "typical situations, places, ways and means . . ." These he called archetypes of transformation. If the NDE is anything, it is surely an archetype of transformation; for death, symbolically and in fact, is certainly a dramatic case of transformation.

The term "archetype," be it carefully noted, does not here denote a single thing or a simple, static formula; it is a shorthand expression for a constellation of recurrent, though fluid, motifs. We find not one thing but a family of psychic processes. In the near-death experience we find personifications, guides, light-beings, deceased relatives, religious and mythical figures, voices and presences. We also observe situations, ways and places such as coming to a border, beholding heavenly (and sometimes infernal) landscapes and cities, hearing the music of the spheres, passing through tunnels, cones,

whorls, caves, soaring through darkness into the light, having prophetic visions of global catastrophe and a new age. The common
thread of the various elements of the near-death archetype is the
theme of transformation. As we shall see in our closing chapters, the
prophetic NDEs consist of powerful images of transformation on a
global scale: images of the near-death experience, the death and possible enlightenment of human consciousness at large.

How Do We Know Archetypes "Exist"?

The archetypes of the collective unconscious express themselves
through spontaneous sources: dreams, "active imagination," trance
fantasies, psychotic delusions, dreams of early childhood, etc. A
weakening of ordinary waking consciousness is a condition for their
appearance; clearly, near-death drastically weakens ordinary consciousness and so is likely to give rise to archetypal motifs. Theoretically, being near death should be optimal for activating the collective
unconscious.

The argument for archetypes has the following general form: a
subject, a child, say, or an uneducated person, has a dream. The
dream contains imagery, pictorial motifs, not traceable to the dreamer's experience but parallel to imagery and motifs found in mythology, alchemy, mystery rites of antiquity or other obscure but world-
old sources. The dream is thought, therefore, to originate from the
collective strata of the human mind.

There are other ways of explaining such cases. The most obvious
is cryptomnesia or unconscious memory. Another possibility is reincarnation memories. Ideas and images might also be picked up via
telepathy. Certainly the evidence, spontaneous and experimental, for
ESP is stronger than it is for these inherent structures of the imagination. But on the other hand, the archetypes might function in a way
that presuppose telepathy or other forms of psi. As far as I know,
little case by case analysis has been done that examines evidence of
the archetypal status of specific experiences. This lack of hard evidence accounts for the hostility in some quarters to the theory of
archetypes. In my view, however, the millions of near-death experiences, the spontaneous uniformity and universality of the imagery,
the profound similarity in the aftereffects, provide a mass of primary
evidence for the reality of this archetype of the collective unconscious.

The Autonomy of the Archetypes

Archetypes behave autonomously; they have a life of their own and "come upon us like fate." This tallies with the near-death experience in which the figures, the messengers from beyond, have a life of their own. They come like fate, apart, as the facts show, from religious beliefs and expectations; that is, the frequency of their appearances is not influenced by these variables, although, once the visions intrude, their interpretation, quite naturally, is conditioned by prior religious beliefs.

The autonomous nature of the ND archetypes is illustrated in the "no-consent" cases (otherworldly messengers who impose their wills on dying subjects) and the "hellish" visitants reported in NDEs. Osis and Haraldsson cite a case of an avowed atheist who had a deathbed vision of Christ. According to the theory of archetypes, dominants of the collective unconscious are activated to compensate for the one-sidedness of the conscious mind. According to this theory, atheism would be an extreme state of one-sidedness, a state of alienation from the powers of the unconscious. The vision of Christ might very well occur in the case of an atheist in order to compensate for a derelict psyche in the extreme.

On the other hand, most NDErs who have a vision of Christ are Christians. Yet even here, there is support for the autonomy of the near-death imagery. The literature is full of anecdotes about dying persons whose visions conflicted with their conventional expectations. For instance, they expected to see angels with wings but instead saw transfigured beings in human form. Further, we have little information about the depth of religious beliefs in NDErs. Weak, merely nominal, Christians would need to compensate for their spiritual poverty as much perhaps as atheists. In either case, atheist or faithful Christian, dying is an extreme situation, and one is liable to fall back upon the resources of the collective treasure house. Archetypes, like NDEs, are psychic reflexes. They just happen, in spite of, and even because of, the limitations of the personal ego. The archetypes of the near-death experience are harbingers of the Self that is greater than the personal ego.

According to Jung [106], [see also E. Edinger [107]], Christ is the chief symbol of the archetype of the Self in the Western world. The Self is the totality of the psyche, realized, symbolically, in the death and crucifixion of Christ. In the near-death experience of modern Westerners, there are frequent reports of visions of Christ. Often, however, what is actually "seen" is a pure light, a content without form; the Christ-form is usually projected onto this pure light.

The psychological significance of the eruption of the Self-archetype is that wholeness, symbolized by Christ, is won through "crucifixion," through death. Wholeness means welding together opposing forces, somehow taking in pain, evil, darkness and help-lessness, all that we consciously dread and wish to avoid. The epiph-any of the Christ-image in the midst of near-death is a living message from the depth of our Selves; it boldly declares that there is hope of renewed being in the menace of nonbeing. The near-death experi-ence, against the dictates of everyday reasonableness, hints of a much fuller potential for coping with death. It encourages us to trust in the power of life to transcend death.

I wish to repeat—the archetype is not reducible to the specific image and even less to the interpretation of the image. The image is more like the symbol of the archetype. The phenomenology of near-death experiences displays different symbols for the archetype of the Self. Among Christians, Christ is the chief symbol; even atheists (in a Christian culture) or persons who only experience the light without form, project the Christ image or interpretation. But in the cross-cultural studies of Osis and Haraldsson, Hindu religious figures were "seen" or projected. In Carl Becker's [108] study of NDEs and Pure Land Buddhism, cases were reported of deathbed visions of the Bud-dha. The basic function of the near-death archetype appears to be constant; the contents projected vary and depend on culture and other personal variables.

The autonomy of near-death archetypes is also evident from the following remark of Osis and Haraldsson: "It seems that apparitions show a purpose of their own, contradicting the intentions of the pa-tient." The apparitions are not projections of the personal psyche. They exhibit a purpose of their own: to "take away" the dying per-son to another world. Emotions of peace and serenity correlated sig-nificantly with these otherworldly messengers with a take-away pur-pose. Transcendental emotions, however, did not correlate with this-worldly visions or with hallucinations of the living.

This was construed by the researchers as evidence for survival. If, for the moment, we bracket this, we can at least say that the auton-omy of the near-death vision figures in the theory of archetypes.

"Otherworldly messengers" would count as "messengers" from the "other world" of the collective unconscious. Such messengers, or archetypes, proceeding from the "wholly other" regions of the collective mind, bearing their own messages with their own purposes, profoundly affect experiencers. The majesty, the fascination, the power of these emissaries from Mind at Large might indeed be so great as to rob the visionary of his or her most deeply ingrained habit: the habit, the instinct, to live. Nothing provides better testimony of the autonomy of the near-death archetypes than this.

The Numinous and the Will to Live

It often happens that, on the threshold of death, people catch glimpses of something that lures them away from life itself. Like wandering sailors who hear the song of the Sirens and drift toward disaster, those near death hear a strange melody that weakens their grip on life and makes them want to go all the way into the abyss. What could it be that reverses the instinct for self-preservation? So much anxiety is spent in the course of life struggling to fend off death, yet at the verge of death, the struggle sometimes mysteriously subsides, anxiety vanishes and life in the body becomes a reason for regret. That to which we clung so grimly all our lives, now we are all at once ready to discard.

Whatever the true explanation, we might at least be glad that nature has a few secrets up her sleeve and that she knows how to make even the dark and fearful god, Thanatos, so enchantingly irresistible. Perhaps this is done by means of endogenous opiates produced by the brain under the stress of dying. Somewhere in the secret codes of our genes there may be instructions for making dying easy, especially after the struggle for survival ceases; and if that code is part of a large ground plan which understands, as does Hindu scripture, that everything is food for everything, then there might well be provisions for making individual dying smooth and automatic at a certain point, for the benefit of the food chain as a whole. In the ecosystems of life, every death is a sacrifice for the sake of the whole; individual death is nutrition for the biosphere. Only in man is there a willful effort not to pay back dues to nature; thus are human bones and dust sealed off in urns and boxes, and nature is cheated of nutrients out on loan.

This is a possible explanation but not one that experiencers are likely to fancy. The research shows that "encounters with ostensible messengers from the other world seemed to be so gratifying that the value of this life was easily outweighed." [10] It is the messengers that cast the spell; they are bearers of meaning, seeming centers of awareness and communication. This outweighing of life's value is a prominent feature of NDEs as well as of deathbed visions. One reads and hears regularly of patients irked, angry or disappointed over being revived. Reports of these visonary wonders suggest something new. A new world is bathed in a numinous glow; its objects, beings and forms are more real, more vivid, than ordinary reality. It is not as if the dying person is merely narcotized in a dull formless contentment; it is not a blunted sense of this (painful and frightening reality) but a sharpened sense of an alternate reality.

Jung himself had a remarkable near-death experience when he had a heart attack after he broke his foot. "I felt violent resistance to my doctor because he had brought me back to life," he wrote in his autobiography. [86] Jung said it took him more than three weeks to make up his mind to live again. He regretted having to return to this "gray world with its boxes." The other world he glimpsed was fuller, not broken up into bits of time and pieces of space. "Although my belief in the world returned to me, I have never since entirely freed myself of the impression that this life is a segment of existence which is enacted in a three-dimensional boxlike universe especially set up for it." It is hard to see this shattering of one's basic sense of reality as caused by a transient dousing of the brain with endorphins. Judging from Jung's and other ND reports, the reluctance to return to life is based on the appeal of something positive in itself. The archetypes, as reservoirs of the deepest feelings of the human race, are saturated with numinous power; they fascinate and enthrall, and they might induce a sense of the unimportance of finite life, even a sense of finite life as an obstacle to infinite life. During his NDE, Jung had a vision of Zeus and Hera consummating a mystical marriage ceremony. The contemplation of such awe-inspiring images, and the cosmic feelings associated with them, might be enough to weaken the ordinary will to live.

The Feeling of Immortality

Closely related to this mitigation of the ordinary will to live is the near-death experiencer's feeling of immortality. Studies by Ring, Sabom and others cite an impressive array of positive aftereffects of

NDEs. Chief among them is a dramatic reduction of the fear of death. The fear of death would decline with feeling immortal; for Jung, this feeling is associated with the non-temporal and non-spatial collective unconscious. "The feeling of immortality," Jung wrote, "has its origin in a peculiar feeling of extension in space and time."

NDEs may induce this feeling of extension in space and time (along with the reduction of the fear of death) in at least two ways: first, by activating the archetypes. Archetypes represent points of entry into the world of the collective unconscious. Vivid archetypal experience would enhance the feeling of being extended in time and space.

Jung understood ancient deification rites as group techniques for projecting archetypal imagery: Dionysos, Persephone, Isis, etc. Using hypnotic suggestion, right-hemisphere languages, sensory overload, psychoactive drugs, trance-dancing and the like, celebrants were led into altered states, exalted visionary experiences. They experienced temporary union with the gods or archetypes, causing the extended sense of immortality.

A second way NDEs might induce feelings of being extended in space and time is by means of the out-of-body experience. We already examined in some detail the notion of the OBE. The near-death OBE covers the spectrum of OB possibilities discussed, ranging from local and veridical to those that are transcendent but unverifiable; in either case, the experience of being extended in space is dramatic and often causes feelings of immortality and diminution of death anxiety.

The aftereffects of these experiences of being extended in space are often profound and long-lasting. A twenty-eight-year-old woman who nearly died during an emergency cesarean section wrote of her experience. The result of this woman's experience was to profoundly change her sense of self-identity; she claimed to have discovered she was a spiritual being, an idea that was entirely foreign to her previously.

> I was in excruciating pain, physically exhausted, and in labor for fifteen hours. Dr. R. said, "I'm sorry, M., I'm going to have to put you to sleep." The next thing I remember was being above the room. I looked down and could see everything and everyone, including my body with Dr. R. and two nurses standing over it. I felt terrified and panic-stricken at first, but then the feeling passed. I

realized I was very big, I was taking up the whole room. I also felt very, very good. Better than I've ever felt before or since. The feeling was extreme, extreme exhilaration. I felt brilliantly, totally alive—like all my senses were tuned to maximum awareness. I was very interested in what was going on. Dr. R. yelled: "Her pressure is still dropping!" The anesthesiologist started squeezing a black rubber ball that was connected to an apparatus over my face. Dr. R. said some numbers I can't remember, and then, "OK, she's stable." His forehead had been creased above the mask and it seemed to smooth out; I could hear him letting out his breath. My husband was sitting in the corner. He looked scared and had a very sad look on his face and tears in his eyes. A nurse was wheeling in a bassinet on wheels that squeaked a little. She said to another nurse in the back: "Is everything all right?" The other nurse said, "Yup." It was like watching a movie. I started thinking the baby will be a girl, which is what I wanted.

The next thing I can remember happening was being awakened by the nurses washing me. I felt awful, shaking all over—headache, nausea. They said, "You had a girl." I asked my husband if the people said the above things and I told him what I saw. I also thought the room was very, very bright. That was the only thing he said wasn't so. It was light but not brilliantly light, as it seemed to me.

I have quoted this report in full because it illustrates both the local and veridical side of the OB spectrum as well as the nonverifiable, transcendent side. (I received a written report verifying the details of this account from her husband who was sitting in the hospital room watching his wife in labor.) There was also the expanded or ecstatic OBE, her feeling of "taking up the whole room," the extreme exhilaration, sensory enhancement and "maximum awareness." The curious, detached, esthetic attitude was also present: "It was like watching a movie." All this occurred in the presence of a brilliant light, the one thing unobserved by her husband. Although the dimension of exhilaration, expanded awareness, extendedness in space and presence to illumination were not directly verifiable, as were her recollections of things said and observed in the hospital room, they were "verifiable" in their aftereffects, in the changed sense of personal identity, the enlarged perspective of life and death.

The Bipolarity of Archetypes and NDEs

Collective psychic phenomena also involve extensions in time, which calls to mind another archetypal aspect of NDEs. The Jungian analyst Yolande Jacobi writes of the bipolarity of the archetypes: "Like a Janus head, it (the archetype) is turned both 'forwards' and 'backwards,' integrating into a meaningful whole all the possibilities of that which has been and of that which is still to come." [109] NDEs furnish plenty of evidence for this bipolarity.

First, consider the phenomenon of panoramic memory or flashback. On the threshhold of death, subjects often claim to experience their lives passing in review before them. It is as if the usual separation of time and space breaks down; past events, scattered beyond the reach of immediate consciousness, are raised from the shadows of oblivion into an enlarged present. Indeed, the notion of a present full and resonant with the presences of the past might be a useful empirical model of the idea of eternity.

Poets like Wordsworth, Pound and Eliot, and novelists like Joyce and Proust (following Bergson) made their art a rite for capturing eternity in the forms of time. The image was the vehicle for condensing the fullness and pattern of life into a concentrated presence. It is interesting to see how the medieval philosopher, Boethius, spoke of eternity in *The Consolation of Philosophy*: it is "one thing," he said, "to live an endless life . . . and another for the whole of unending life to be embraced all at once as present." The latter, Boethius asserts, is the mark of the divine mind or, we might say, of the collective mind.

This is a distinction worthy of note. The "divine" mind, the divine dimension of our own minds, does not merely survive, is not constituted by a continued succession of states; it expands its present, penetrates the depth of its own presence. This is the difference between mere survival of bodily death (which by itself gives no guarantee of quality or value) and eternity, which is the plenitude of the present, the fruit of enlightenment. "Eternity," Boethius writes, "is the whole, perfect, and simultaneous possession of endless life." Elsewhere he speaks of the divine being as "in full possession of itself, always present to itself."

These descriptions of eternity figure in Jung's concept of individuation; the individuated being is fully in possession of itself, is present to its past, the conflicts and varied energies subdued and reconciled in a higher harmony. The panoramic disclosure of the total self in the near-death experience is an empirical model of the mystical concept of eternity. Since the meaning of a given element can only be seen in relation to the total pattern, the fullness of the meaning of our lives can only be experienced in the total pattern of our experiences.

Art is one way we attempt to take hold of the total pattern; art enables us to step outside and watch ourselves (like the near-death experiencer cited above) as if life were a movie. In ordinary life, we live on the surface of time, caught in the anxiety or titillation of immediacy; but through art, mystical illumination or certain moments on the threshold of death, we experience the depth and duration of time, the presence of the present that is eternity.

Sartre, by the way, says that the meaning of a life can only be known after it is over; for as long as a person is alive, an action may be performed that could change the whole pattern of deeds that make up a life and so change its whole meaning. The near-death experience provides a glimpse of one's "eternity," the full range of the pattern, and so the drift of the meaning; but it also gives the experiencer a chance to come back and make use of the insight gleaned.

The total pattern, the bipolarity of the archetypes, not only points backward, gathering up the moments of the past into the present, but it points forward, foreshadowing things to come. And indeed, there have been reports of what Ring calls "flashforwards" in NDEs. In some cases, general future trends are forecasted; in others, there are specific elements of precognition. In the case of the woman cited above, there may have been an element of precognition. I might add here that it is a very old belief that persons on the threshold of death acquire prophetic powers. Perhaps the most interesting for our purposes are reports best described as prophetic visions of the collective fate of humankind which we will focus on later. Let us call this extension in time the horozontal axis of the archetype.

There is also a vertical, qualitative axis. Archetypes are bipolar in that they stretch backwards and forwards in time; they are bipolar in a second sense in that they have a bright and high side as well as a dark and low one. "Just as all archetypes have a positive, favorable, bright side that points upwards, so also they have one that points downwards, partly negative and unfavorable, partly chthonic . . ." [110] The bright, favorable side of the NDE is well known, but there have also been dark, chthonic encounters in the near-death state, less frequently reported. [111] Charles Garfield, for instance, found that the near-death experiences of his terminal cancer patients consisted of four types. The first was the classic experience with white light and celestial music. The second consisted of brilliant images of demonic and nightmarish entities. The third type of NDE was less brilliant but showed alternations of the blissful and the terrifying. A fourth category also involved alternations of maximal and minimal freedom in drifting through a void. The bipolarity of these experiences, their swinging on the vertical axis between freedom-brightness and constraint-darkness is evident here.

These dark, hellish visions have probably been reported less because, understandably, they were repressed. Others may have held back because their experiences did not fit into the widely publicized format. In any case, the content (devils, lakes of fire and brimstone, etc.) of these frightening visions is patently archetypal. Once we include the negative features, the NDE more clearly resembles the mythical and religious view of the afterlife. (See, for instance, Jung's [1957] psychological commentary on the *Tibetan Book of the Dead*.) The stronger this resemblance, the stronger the case for the NDE as archetypal.

Metanoia and the NDE

Reduction of the fear of death is only part of a larger pattern of transformative ND aftereffects. In cases where this larger pattern is displayed in full, the experience has all the earmarks of a kind of religious conversion. We could describe the full-fledged NDE as a natural conversion process. The convert undergoes a pervasive change of value and outlook. [112] The word for such a transformation of mind in the New Testament is *metanoia*, and it might be useful to speak of the metanoid component of the NDE. Saint Paul's experience on the road to Damascus, which had some of the classic features of the NDE, is a historically dramatic case in point.

This metanoid component of the NDE is sometimes expressed in terms of unconditional love. In the words of one experiencer: "I would describe this love I encountered in dying as 'unconditional.' It was so powerful, so complete, so forgiving, so all-knowing, so encompassing, it transcended all forms of earthly love . . ." [113] The awakening of this all-encompassing, unearthly love makes the NDE uniquely interesting from a theoretical point of view. It is a rare experience that makes for such an aftereffect. As far as the possible evolution of human consciousness, this ND-caused transpersonal love deserves our close attention.

P. Atwater describes how normal emotional relations were disturbed by her NDE. Customary attachments became an obstacle to further growth. The experience released a force that disrupted her everyday routines. A new, transpersonal dynamic of love was set in motion. *The approach of death doesn't just intensify the need to preserve the old self; it liberates forces that dissolve the boundaries of that old self.* At the gate of death, instructions for a new self are received. The restless dynamic of this new love-driven self is reminiscent of daimonic Eros and is the theme of Plato's *Phaedrus* and *Symposium.* The expansive tendency of the near-death process reflects something positive in itself, not merely the ego struggling to defend itself against extinction.

Problems result from releasing this metanoid energy and transforming love. For example, the NDEr returns from an experience she or he is linguistically unable to record, express or transmit. The framework of ordinary language totters under the stress of the Transcendent. This puts the experiencer at a disadvantage. There is not only a cultural disposition to demean reports of the Transcendent, but one also lacks the verbal appartus to make the report itself. There's a disproportion between language and experience. Now we find a similar disproportion between other social institutions and the NDE. Deep NDErs become obsessed with their experiences; it is as though a gestation has begun within them, a painful pressing outward toward new life. They complain of loneliness and find it hard to adjust to a world that falls short of the perfection glimpsed. NDErs return to ordinary life haunted by a sense of incompleteness, a nostalgia for paradise (to use a haunting phrase of Eliade).

A failure to integrate the ND revelation of unconditional love with our all-too-imperfect world may lead to psychic "inflation." The ego is "inflated" by an incommensurate psychic force. But inflation is apt to run over into deflation; obstacles to realizing the new metanoid potential send the experiencer into the valleys of depression.

Unfortunately, the liberating and the dangerous effects of the archetypes are inseparable. Given the increasing numbers of NDErs, usually in a medical setting, the problem of how to handle ND aftereffects, positive and negative, challenges the medical profession and the deep structure of the medical paradigm. In an early chapter, the metaphysical presuppositions of current thanatology were questioned. Those presuppositions dominate the day-to-day medical world, as well. Although there are signs of loosening in that deep structure, the near-death visionary has a hard time making sense of his or her experience.

Given the powerful transformative effects of NDEs and the complex and ambiguous psychodynamics, cooperation with family, clergy and medical community is needed. Failure in this will thwart the growth potential of possibly millions of near-death experiencers, now and in the future. One of the purposes of this book is to appeal to the helping community to broaden its metaphysical base of operations, to expand its paradigm of what is possible and what is effectively real in human experience. We need a helping community fully open to the helping potential already within us, a community skilled in the midwifery of souls in transformation.

The power of near-death archetypes sometimes touches those who merely allow themselves to be receptive to experiencers, according to Kenneth Ring, who has spent a great deal of time listening to NDErs. There are analogies for this sort of "direct transmission", "contact high", or *"shaktipat"* in the group dynamics of religious experience. Individuals who become living conduits to the energies of Mind at Large seem to have direct influence on others. A case of spiritual power *(dynamis)* picked up by touch is mentioned in Luke (Luke 8: 43-46):

> And a woman having an issue of blood twelve years, which had spent all her living upon physicians, neither could be healed of any, came behind him, and touched the border of his garment: and immediately her issue of blood stanched. And Jesus said, "Who touched me?" When all denied, Peter and they that were with him said, "Master, the multitude throng thee and press then, and sayest thou, who touched me?" And Jesus said, "Somebody hath touched me: for I perceive that virtue *(dynamis)* is gone out of me."

The Self and the Near-Death Archetype

On the threshold of death, the innocent ego may, for the first time, come face to face with its unknown self. This larger pattern of psychic reality submerged below the threshold of the everyday mind, but making up the fuller potential of our human identity, Jung calls the Self or Objective Psyche. This Self comes upon us as if from outside, as transcendent; Ring also thinks that the being of light, the voice, the presence experienced during near-death states, is the larger pattern of oneself. "It is not merely a projection of one's personality, however, but one's *total self*, or what in some traditions is called the *higher self*. In this view, the individual personality is but a split-off fragment of the total self with which it is reunited at the point of death." [94]

In connection with his study of alchemy, Jung remarked, ". . . the archetypes have about them a certain effulgence or quasi-consciousness. . . . and numinosity entails luminosity." So powerful are these luminous effects, symbolic and expressive of an extended consciousness, that they seem to stand outside the normal personality. Experiencers therefore believe that the "being of light" is God. "We know that an archetype can break with shattering force into individual life . . . It is therefore not surprising that it is called 'God'." The final say on this belongs to theology. The most we might say is that for the person who has this type of experience, the upper limits of the Self seem to border on the lower limits of the Divine.

In the Western tradition, to claim identity of Self (however higher) with God is blasphemous. But perhaps in light of what we are learning about the near-death experience, and what is latent in the collective human psyche, we can understand how certain individuals might be led to identify with God. Jesus was accused of blasphemy because he claimed a special intimacy with the Father. (John: 10,33) The Hindu doctrine of the oneness of *Atman* and Brahman is not shy about asserting this lofty equation. Tibetan Buddhist teachings say we must recognize that the Divine Light before which we stand in awe is a projection of the Self. The Gnostic and enthusiastic traditions of Christianity, the *Sufis* and cabalists of the Islamic and Judaic traditions, all drew their inspirations, often at great risk, from the well of this Supreme Identity.

The NDE shows that psychological experiences of such power are possible, that claims of the reality of the Divine, even of the self's identity with the Divine, were bound to occur in human history. One can also see how such archetypal experiences would, in some hardy spirits who trusted their own instincts above tradition, form the kernel of a new authority, a new interpretation of reality and a new myth of personal identity.

The encounter with the archetypes has its malevolent side, to be sure. Mix these inner urgencies with ignorance of the universals of spiritual life, spice with envy, intolerance and faction, and it is easy to see how the energies of spiritual transformation often worked their way into the ugly and tragic blunderings of history. Perhaps the study of archetypal psychodynamics could help reduce these misunderstandings and show that behind the many masks of the gods is the one eternal Self in transformation.

The Archetype of Death and Enlightenment

Let us say, then, that the NDE activates an archetype of the collective unconscious, a *constellation* of motifs that guides an enlightenment process, a passage toward greater consciousness of our Self. Let us call this constellation the archetype of death and enlightenment (ADE). The NDE is a dramatic expression of the ADE but not the only context in which it appears. Psychological, spiritual or cultural "neardeath" states may bring forth the ADE. Almost any crisis of transformation, spontaneous or artificial, individual or collective, could stir up these psychic dominants.

Near-death imagery is keyed to the process of becoming a Self. The meanings of the various images reflect the same goal or process. For example, there is the abstract image of moving from darkness to light, from unconsciousness to consciousness. Light emerging from darkness is a universal symbol. "And the light shineth in darkness; and the darkness comprehended it not." (John: 1.5) From the *Bradaranyaka Upanishad:* "From non-being lead me to being, from darkness lead me to the light, from death lead me to immortality." In the NDE, the sequence is also from darkness to light. We find the same sequence in many creation myths: in the *Rig Veda,* Hesiod's *Theogony,* the Old Testament and the Scandinavian *Eddas.* For Jews, Arabs, Germanic peoples, Celts and many others, day begins with night; darkness precedes the dawning of the light. Light is a primordial image of consciousness; it always rises from the depths of darkness.

Another common near-death image is passage through caves, canals, holes, tunnels and the like, into a clearing. This motif symbolizes birth and rebirth, passage to a new and higher plane of being. The Allegory of the Cave in Plato's *Republic* (Bk. 7) is a landmark in Western philosophy. Enlightenment is portrayed there as escape from bondage in a cave out into the light of the sun. The cave motif appears again in the Myth of the True Earth in the *Phaedo.* There is a struggle to emerge from the mist and shadow of the false earth, along with the task of learning to endure the light of the true earth. Plato's myths contained perhaps his deepest insights, the healing truths that modern philosophy has, for the most part, forgotten and which the NDE might hopefully point the way back to.

The guides NDErs meet—deceased persons, otherworldly messengers, light-beings—are personifications of the same theme: of coming to a border, of passage from dark to light, cave to clearing, bondage to release. The guides oversee the transition, the vision of wholeness and knowledge, and the return. They reveal the higher truths, encourage self-assessment, sometimes terrify into humility and prescribe the tasks of the future. The guides deepen the connection between our present and our past and future, between our own lives and those of our ancestors or offspring (as in the case of the woman cited above who foresaw the birth of her daughter). Whether the imagery is abstract (dark-light, tunnel-opening) or personal (guide, deceased relative, religious figure), the basic idea is passage from enclosure to disclosure.

The out-of-body motif expresses the same unit of meaning. Going out of the body means getting past the enclosure of embodied existence. The body itself is a cave, hole or tunnel that is escaped in the near-death experience. Dying, like being born, is a release from enclosure. One thinks of the ancient orphic formula *soma sema* (the body is a tomb); true life must then be to exit from the body. The symbolism of the NDE throws down a gauntlet before gray common sense and black scientific materialism. Dying, as it appears to the sharp but perhaps short-sighted eye of the ego, is the ultimate disaster; but before the dream-lit eye of the collective psyche, it is the gateway to self-transformation.

The enclosure-disclosure pattern has its cognitive and temporal side. The candidate for enlightenment has his past disclosed in a flashback; the future is also disclosed as symbol, probable trend or verified precognition. The enclosure-disclosure passage is also functionally equivalent to the passage from part, or ego, to whole, or Self. For instance, the ego is normally in the dark with respect to the light of the Self. Perhaps the "image" that cuts across all near-death imagery is that of Light, the symbol of consciousness. Meetings with deceased relatives, OBEs and panoramic memories are all manifestations of the "Light." They imply extensions of awareness, inroads transcending time and space.

The unifying symbol of light is not just symbolic or abstract. The light is also a literal fact, an intense, awe-inspiring *experience*. It is brilliant, dazzling, warm, peaceful, elating, vivid and sensuous. It is a pure and formless illumination and an aspect of recognizable forms: jeweled cities of light, human figures or "angels" luminously clothed, landscapes bathed in celestial radiance. The light, concrete and abstract, universal and particular, symbolizes the individuated Self, marked by a coincidence of opposites, a fusion of opposing principles and energies. Near-death experiencers are unanimous in insisting on the reality of their experience; indeed, the enhanced awareness, the fusing of opposites and fragments into a uniquely individuated self, entitles one to speak of the *superreality* of the experience. Mircea Eliade, in a study of the experience of the mysic light, wrote: "Experience of the Light signifies primarily a meeting with ultimate reality: that is why one discovers the interior Light when one becomes conscious of the Self *(Atman)* or when one penetrates into the very essence of life and the cosmic elements, or, last of all, at one's death." [54]

Archetypes are intentional, directed, dynamic. The function of the ADE is to compensate for the ego's one-sided view of death. Affectively, this means overcoming the fear of death. Existentially, it means that death promises rebirth, a change in the state of one's being. Cognitively, it signifies an expansion of consciousness. Metaphysically; reorientation toward a universal, indestructible spiritual reality. The ADE heralds a new mode of being, a new birth. In guiding the ego toward a new consciousness of Self, the ADE rescues death from the curse of meaninglessness. Here are Jung's words:

> Hence it would seem to be more in accord with the collective psyche of humanity to regard death as the fulfillment of life's meaning and as its goal in the true sense, instead of a mere meaningless cessation. Anyone who cherishes a rationalistic opinion on this score has isolated himself psychologically and stands opposed to his own basic human nature." [114]

This passage, perhaps more than any other from the writings of Jung, is the best possible commentary on the meaning of the near-death experience. But let us not fool ourselves here; the idea that death is somehow the goal of life runs totally counter to the modern outlook. It also runs totally counter to common sense. Nevertheless, this is the symbolic message that emerges from the near-death archetype, echoing the mythic claims of the collective psyche of humanity. What we call death is archetypally portrayed as the road to a greater and more fulfilling reality than what we know in life. Such a conception implies a Copernican revolution with respect to the prevailing modern view. It places the sun of the Objective Psyche at the center of spiritual reality, challenging what may be an illusion of the conscious ego: that death is a meaningless cessation.

The Near-Death Archetype in Life

Literal near-death is only one possible trigger for the ADE. Any situation threatening ego death, major life changes and transitions, might mobilize the healing powers of the ADE.

The kind of crisis and the context (near-death, dreams, mystical states, etc.) would determine which factors of the archetypal constellation came to the fore. For instance, deceased relatives are more likely to appear in a crisis of literal near-death. In nonliteral "ego-death" situations, the appearance of deceased relatives would be to no purpose. In what follows, I attempt to give some examples of the ADE in action in other than literal near-death situations: mystical phenomena, dreams, mythology, initiation and mystery rituals, psychedelic experiences and UFO "revelations." These by no means exhaust the spectrum of possible sources, but they will do for our purpose.

Mystical Phenomena. The resemblance between NDEs and mystical phenomena has been noted by researchers. Russell Noyes wrote that the mystical consciousness "seemed not so much a distinct element of the altered state under examination (that is, the NDE) but rather its more extreme progression." [115] The elements of this mystical extension cited by Noyes include transcendence of space and time, feelings of unity, loss of will, sense of truth and extreme emotion, all of which are features of archetypal experience.

NDEs and some mystical experiences are spontaneous. But some mystical experiences result from artifical practice or discipline and show a connection with near-death states. One thinks, for example, of Plato's view of philosophy as the practice of death, or of yogis who put themselves into deathlike trances. Eliade, for instance, refers to medical testimony showing that "the reduction of respiration and cardiac contraction to a degree that is usually observed only immediately before death" [40] is something yogis are able to accomplish at will. About the supernatural Christian ecstasy, one scholar wrote: ". . . the physical life approaches a deathlike state, the breathing is reduced, the heart and the pulse become slower, the vital warmth disappears, the limbs stiffen, the outer and inner senses are wholly bound. It is as if the soul, as in death, were separated from the body." [116]

These remarks show that the physiology of mystical states is similar in some ways to the physiology of near-death. But there may be no accompanying deathlike physiology; the whole process may be precipitated by purely psychical causes.

The story of the great modern Hindu mystic, Ramana Maharshi, shows the relationship between ego-death and the enlightenment experience. Ramana was in perfect health. One day he became panic-stricken that he was about to die. I quote his remarkable statement at length:

> The shock of the fear of death drove my mind inwards and I said to myself mentally, without actually framing the words: "Now death has come; what does it mean: What is it that is dying? This body dies." And I at once dramatized the occurrence of death. I lay with my limbs stretched out stiff as though rigor mortis had set in and imitated a corpse so as to give greater reality to the enquiry. I held my breath and kept my lips tightly closed so that no sound could escape, so that neither the word "I" nor any other word could be uttered. "Well then," I said to myself, "this body is dead. It will be carried stiff to the burning ground and there burnt and reduced to ashes. But with the death of this body am I dead? Is the body I? It is silent and inert but I feel the full force of my personality and even the voice of the 'I' within me, apart from it. The body dies but the Spirit that transcends it cannot be touched by death. That means I am the deathless Spirit." All this was not dull thought; it flashed through me vividly as living truth . . . [117]

In this unusual case, a psychodrama imitating death gave rise to an experience of mystical illumination. The encounter with the Self was facilitated by Ramana's not resisting the idea of his imminent death; he let go, gave up, reminiscent of some types of NDE. This act of surrender, coupled with the inhibition of normal respiration, may have triggered the experience. Voluntary or involuntary ego-surrender helps to evoke the latent powers of the Self or Total Psyche, according to Jung.

A particularly interesting recent case was brought to my attention by an experienced meditator. Mr. Norman Morris of Los Angeles, California, describes himself as professionally trained in Buddhist and Hindu yoga. Mr. Morris says that during his eleven years of intensive meditation, he had thousands of psychic experiences: trances, visions, hallucinations and so forth. On exactly one occasion, however, he had a "very, very different" experience which "was deeply moving," something unforgettable that stood out above all his usual meditation experiences. Mr. Morris explained how all efforts to reproduce his experience were in vain. Here are the details from his own written account:

> I lost awareness of my body and my surroundings. All that existed was a vast visual field which appeared dark; suddenly a whirling vortex appeared in this area. It was the deepest, darkest black I have ever seen, circular and whirling. (Mr. Morris included a drawing in his report of a black rotary pattern emanating from a center, imposed on another shade of black in the background. All in all, it makes a striking sort of black mandala.) It was "moving" at incredible speed and "I" was "moving" through it. This vortex lasted only a very brief time, and I came out the other end into a bluish turquoise landscape. I cannot adequately describe this scene; it was the most unearthly thing I had ever seen. The blues and turquoise were electric, glowing and self-luminous. I could not pick out any individual structures, though it appeared like a forested area with foliage and waterfalls made of vibrant and glowing colors. I am looking forward and down on this as if I am in the air, hovering in a helicopter. Awareness of my body, my apartment, my "self," this world had all *completely* vanished. All that existed was this heavenly sphere. The emotional component was incredible. "I no longer existed but only as an awareness. I found this heavenly sphere to be so engrossing and beautiful that I didn't want to come back. I began to feel an ending of the experience. I could not hold on to it and it ended as quickly as it had come. I found myself back in my apartment sitting in my chair.

Mr. Morris explains that he was puzzled about the black vortex and other features of the experience until he read Raymond Moody's book, *Life After Life*. But what particularly puzzled him was the fact that the experience, in so many ways like the classic NDE, occurred to him while in perfect health, during meditation, sober and awake. For my part, this experience, similar to the NDE in its basic phenomenology, implies a larger psychic mechanism that is involved in the NDE per se. Mr. Morris was nowhere near dying. The NDE seems to be only one route to the region of psychic being we are trying to map. In any case, it is hard to see the experience as the by-product of a defense mechanism of the ego.

Dreams. The dream is a crucial source of information about the ADE, since the dream is the most common inroad to the collective unconscious. In patients drawing near the end of their lives, Jung observed dreams with rebirth symbolism. The following examples are from my collection of dreams with near-death imagery. My comments are restricted to the overt near-death-related motifs. Their full, personal significance is another matter. Dreams are best understood in series, along with the personal associations of the dreamer.

Less than a year prior to his death, an elderly man dreamt he was climbing a mountain. There were three plateaus to the ascent; at each plateau he stopped—the light and surrounding landscape became brighter, more peaceful and more beautiful. At the top he experienced a wonderful happiness; some men there, who were digging in the earth, told him to go back down by following the path he took to come up. He complied, realizing he had to return something to his wife, a jacket he was holding, the first she gave him fifty years ago.

This resembles an NDE in several ways: the association of light, bliss and beauty with death (symbolized by the digging); reaching a border; and having to turn back because of a link (the jacket) with a loved one. The archetypal overtones of the tri-layered mountain is patent.

Here is another, curiously similar, example. In this case, a chronically ill woman "gave up," wanted to die and dreamt she went on a journey:

> Upon reaching a mountain I began to climb. As I climbed higher and higher, the great "cloud" that covered everything began to dissolve, and patches of sunshine began to shine through. At last I reached the top and flung myself on to the level ground, whereupon the "sun" suddenly broke out all around and permeated my entire being with healing, love, and total splendor. It was an indescribable experience of such stark truth that the memory of it seemed to have ingrained itself in my deepest being. I felt the way a person *should* feel. It was more real than anything I have ever known. [118]

The author went on to describe herself as if she were flying over meadows of colored flowers and approaching a great golden city where her departed loved ones were waiting. She then remembered leaving her cane at the top of the mountain, which reminded her of her responsibility to her (living) loves ones. With this her superreal dream ended. The author felt she had an actual encounter with God and received divine guidance, and she herself identified her experience as a "greatly expanded Jungian archetypal dream."

Morton Kelsey, an Episcopalian priest and student of Jung, wrote the book *Dreams: A Way to Listen to God*. In one story a 75-year-old Anglican priest, sick, anxious and in pain, dreamt he saw his childhood home and other highlights of his life pass in review before him. Then he saw himself sitting in his room; he looked up at the clock on the mantle, which had stopped at 11:00. The mantle changed into a doorway through which a beam of light streamed. Then the old priest rose from his chair and walked through the door into the light. After sharing the dream with his wife, his pain and anxiety vanished, and a week later he fell asleep in his chair and never woke up. The overall pattern here is similar to the archetypal NDE, and Kelsey cites the dream as an example of the numinous. The light is noteworthy, as is its aftereffect, along with the hint of foreknowledge of dying in the chair; also, the panoramic memory and out-of-body experience occur within the dream itself. Finally, it's worth noting how the tunnel-vortex motif is here transformed into a doorway.

It would be easy to multiply examples of dreams with near-death imagery, feelings and aftereffects. It seems to me that such dream and near-death experiences stem from the same matrix of consciousness and that we need one theory to account for the two sets of phenomena. This doesn't mean that NDEs are "just" dreams, mere fabrications of the personal unconscious; the suggestion is that certain dreams and NDEs derive from one collective psychic source.

Mythology. The world of myth is the world of collective dreams made public. As such, we might expect to observe in it ample traces of the ADE. One very old example will serve us here. Australian aborigine myths of the afterlife contain many motifs of modern NDEs. One tale describes the person beginning the afterdeath journey in darkness, sliding down "hollow grooves" in "a rocky, narrow gorge," entering flames (which scorched bad men), and then coming to clear spaces where the landscape is full of trees, free of undergrowth and the grass is especially green. There in the open space the spirit-traveler is said to meet dead relatives and friends. They welcome him and take him to a camp where he is dressed and painted, after which there is much shouting and play. [119]

The basic motif of enclosure-disclosure, the passage from dark to light, from part to whole (symbolized by joining and playing with the ancestors), is present in this aboriginal myth. So too is the vertical polarity of the ADE, for we are told that if the spirit-traveler has been a "greedy and quarrelsome" fellow in life, he will fail to reach the verdant camp of his ancestors. He is met by an "ugly old man," the archetype of the Shadow, and crows who pick and knock him about, leaving him scarred and disheveled. Interestingly, there are no references to anything like a pure being of light. This could mean that the idea of the individual Self had yet to emerge in the evolutionary game.

Mythology and the classics of world literature give their hints of an archetype of death and enlightenment. ADE motifs run through the deep structure of works like the *Epic of Gilgamesh*, Dante's *Divine Comedy*, Plato's *Allegory of the Cave*, the *Book of Revelation* and Tolstoy's *Death of Ivan Ilych*. Each myth or story reveals a unique perspective on the dialectic of death and enlightenment.

Tolstoy's story is worth reflecting on for a moment, for it illustrates the fierce denial of death and the inability to let go of the persona. Ivan Ilych is a judge by profession, accustomed to living by rules of rectitude and obsessed by the appearance of propriety. Pleasure, status and power are his gods; but his world begins to crumble when death steps into his life. One by one, the illusions and defenses melt away. Pain, loneliness, his selfish family break him down; his persona, his superficially personal image of reality, is broken in pieces by the onset of death. Let us follow more closely Ivan Ilych's struggle with the dragon of death that stands before the gate of enlightenment.

> For three whole days, during which time did not exist for him, he struggled in that black sack into which he was being thrust by an invisible, resistless force. He felt that his agony was due to being thrust into that black hole and still more to his not being able to get right into it. He was hindered from getting into it by his conviction that his life had been a good one. That very justification of his life held him fast and prevented his moving forward, and it caused him most torment of all.

Suddenly some force struck him in the chest and side, making it still harder to breathe, and he fell through the hole and there at the bottom was light. What had happened to him was like the sensation one sometimes experiences in a railway carriage when one thinks one is going backwards while one is really going forwards and suddenly becomes aware of the real direction.

The logic of enlightenment is strange; transformation takes place at the bottom of a black hole. It was when Ivan's schoolboy son took his hand, kissed it and began to cry that the dying judge let go and fell into the light. For an instant, the habitual impersonater became a transpersonator—with a little help from his son. He stepped out of the black hole of himself saying, "In place of death there was light. So that's what it is!" he suddenly exclaimed aloud. "What joy!"

We could say that works like this tale of Tolstoy's are "classic" because they succeed in resonating with the great healing archetypes of the collective unconscious. Of course, myths and literary works are not purely spontaneous products of the unconscious but artifacts of culture. (Even with the NDE or near-death dream, we have to distinguish between the original experience and the report of the experience.) Still, close scrutiny of these phenomena will, I believe, show the common pattern here labeled ADE. The same remarks apply to the next three examples.

Mystery and Initiation Rituals. Archaic rites of initiation are mainly ritual imitations of death and rebirth. [54] They do in a group setting what Ramana did on his own. The same can be said for the mystery rituals of Greek and Roman antiquity. There is quite a bit of material we could analyze here in light of the ADE hypothesis. We have to be selective, however, so the Eleusinian Mysteries of ancient Greece will be our example.

The riddle of those august Mysteries, which lasted well over a thousand years, comes to this: of what was the final ritual vision? What was the secret of its life-enhancing power? The effects themselves are clear from ancient testimonials. The most striking were a dramatic lessening of the fear of death, hope and belief in the reality of an afterlife, and a radiant transformation of the sense of this life.

Scholars long supposed that a special doctrine was revealed to initiates, persuading them there was a life after death. But Aristotle put this out of court when he wrote that during the rites, celebrants didn't learn anything but were "to be passive" and "to be put into a state" *(pathein kai diatethenai)*. The celebrant, in short, was put into an altered state of consciousness. The "learning" was state-specific. Again we meet with the idea that certain beliefs, not directly verifiable by the senses, are based on special experiences, anomalous states of awareness.

Three steps had to be taken in modern times to shed light on the riddle of Eleusis. The first was psychedelic research. Albert Hofmann, who discovered LSD, argued that the *kykeon*, the ritual drink used in the rites, was a potent mind-altering drug chemically similar to LSD. [120] Drinking the *kykeon* after a nine-day fast would certainly help to bring about the "state" the initiates found themselves in. The second step dealt with the archetypal content of the vision. According to Carl Kerenyi [121], the initiate experienced a beatific vision, radiant and ineffable, of the queen of the underworld: Persephone, daughter of Demeter, an archetypal expression of the vital force.

The third step was near-death research. Now we can understand the visions' aftereffects. It is no exaggeration to say that the Mysteries of Eleusis revealed the gospel, the good message of pagan antiquity, and like the Christian Gospels that lit up the overcast psyche of decadent antiquity, they endowed present existence with a new joy and pointed toward future existence with hope. Here are the words of a notable pagan initiate, Cicero: "We have been given a reason," he wrote in his treatise *On the Laws*, "not only to live in joy but to die with better hope."

In a passage from an early Greek writer, Themistios (see Kerenyi), the connection between near-death and the Mysteries was specifically cited: "The soul (at the point of death) has the same experience as those who are being initiated into great mysteries . . . At first one is struck by a marvelous light, one is received into pure regions and meadows . . . (and so forth)." For me, it is hard to avoid the conclusion that the inner world of the ancient Mysteries and that of the modern near-death experiencer derive from a common source in the collective psyche of humankind. The ancient Greeks seem, in fact, to have worked out a fairly effective method for inducing a type of functionally similar near-death experience. This, in my view, is the best hypothesis to account for the most striking effects of the rite: the reduction of the fear of death, the deepened hope and expectation of an afterlife, and the enhancement of the quality of this life.

Psychedelics. In the setting of modern psychotherapy, drugs have been used to induce initation into the mysteries of death. Ac-

cording to Stanislav Grof and Joan Halifax [123], some deep psychedelic episodes resemble the near-death experience. Given to the ter-
minally ill (or for that matter to anyone), psychoactive substances like
LSD speed up the process of ego-death. The defensive wall is shattered. ND effects turn up in drug-induced ego-death states: the life-
review, photic phenomena, meetings with supernatural beings.

A striking similarity is the effect on the subject's concept of
death. The point deserves full quotation:

> Many individuals who had the experience of death and rebirth
> sometimes accompanied by feelings of cosmic unity independently
> reported that their attitudes changed toward dying and their con-
> cepts of death underwent dramatic changes. Fear of their own phys-
> iological demise diminished, they became open to the possibility of
> consciousness existing after clinical death, and tended to view the
> process of dying as an adventure in consciousness rather than the
> ultimate biological disaster. Those of us conducting this research
> kept witnessing, to our great surprise, a process that bore a striking
> similarity to mystical initiation . . . [124]

In Charles Garfield's [124] study, people who experimented with
mind-altering drugs showed less death-anxiety than non-drug using
psychology and theology students, though they were outranked by
practiced Zen and Tibetan Buddhist meditators. Drug users, between
rational Westerners and meditating Easterners, looked on the prospect of death as a possible adventure. Indeed, drug abuse may be a
garbled search for transcendence. The problem is no doubt aggra-
vated by lack of "consensually validated" rituals of ego-death.

The modern psychedelic therapist works with individuals and,
for want of ritual (apart from the therapeutic ritual), allows the demons and angels of the unconscious to surface in a relatively haphazard way. The ancient therapist-hierophant worked under more controlled conditions: a group setting, the sanction of common
ceremonies, myths and symbols around which psychic energies ral-
lied. Participants were programmed through ritual ablutions, fasting,
psychodramas and sacrifices, ways of breaking down the ego, and
opening up to the Greater Self.

Every trick in the trade was used and it all came together in a
single package. Ancient science still hadn't "freed" itself from poetry
and religion; but, on the other hand, ancient religion had yet to split

off from "science." There are people who wish to recapture this pre-specialized wholeness. Still, it is a slow transformation; medical materialism does not favor the "holistic" methods of the ancients. Modern science has broken asunder what the archetypal vision keeps whole.

The archetypal vision holds to the unity of mind and heart, intuition and sensation, science and religion, whereas these things come apart in the dissociations of modern sensibility. Begin with the sunderment of life and death itself. The prevailing medical outlook sees death as terminal, the negation of life. The archetypal vision, like nature itself, "sees" the process of living and dying as cut from a single cloth. Living is inseparable from dying; the anabolic and the catabolic strands are intertwined in every living organism. The archetypal vision, practically speaking, invites us to explore dying as a ritual component of ongoing life instead of waiting for death to be thrust upon us from the outside at "terminal" junctions. It declares the healing venture to be part of everyday life.

UFO "Revelations." Compared with ancient and primitive societies, modern scientific culture offers few inlets to the healing powers of the collective unconscious. To be sure, these "powers" turn up spontaneously in our dreams and, as we now see, in near death. If Jung was right, we are also, in this age of science, projecting archetypes into the skies in the form of Unidentified Flying Objects (UFOs). (The possible physical realities associated with these sky phenomena are not the issue here; their psychology is our concern.)

According to Jung, UFO phenomena are signs of the end of the era. "Apparently," he wrote, "they are changes in the constellation of psychic dominants, of the archetypes, or 'gods' as they used to be called, which bring about, or accompany, long-lasting transformations of the collective psyche." [125] These sky epiphanies may, in short, be viewed as psychic by-products of the near-death experience of modern civilization.

The epilogue to Jung's book on flying saucers dealt with the case of Orfeo Angelucci, a "contactee" who had a close encounter and conversion experience. Based on Jung's account, I found almost every element in the prototypical NDE, along with the rarer phenomena such as transcendental music. Orfeo had a series of experiences in which he "saw" lights and apparitions of men and women alleged to be friends from another world. He heard voices; communications were directly mental. Orfeo felt he was about to die but also that he had transcended death. He found himself aboard a UFO that carried him away, saw a white flash of lightning, his whole life in a panorama before him, received teachings, had what Moody called a "vision of knowledge" and was carried to "heaven" where he saw wondrous landscapes and heard wondrous music. All the motifs of the NDE are present, jumbled and dressed up in space-age imagery. There were powerful metanoid affects along with plenty of ego-inflation. Again, it appears that the NDE and certain UFO experiences stem from a common source.

ADE to Evolution?

It has been noted how archetypes, being partly images of cosmic forces, analogues that link nature and psyche, may sometimes foreshadow scientific discoveries. How this works deserves study. Jung cited the idea of the archaic sun-sheel, forerunner to the invention of the wheel. He also suggested that alchemy, rich in archetypal energy, prefigured modern chemistry. Alchemy, according to Jung, also anticipated developments in modern depth psychology.

The physicist Wolfgang Pauli wrote of the influence of archetypal ideas on Kepler. Kepler's discovery of the Three Laws of planetary motion was a spinoff from search for the music of the spheres. One wonders, by the way, if this is itself traceable to real experiences of transcendental music, like those reported in NDEs; if so, it shows a curious thread running between NDEs and the rise of modern astronomy.

Pauli stresses Kepler's fascination with the archetype of the Trinity and his passion for heliocentrism, an astronomical mandala of the Self. "Because he looks at the sun and the planets with this archetypal image (the Trinity) in the background, he believes with religious fervor in the heliocentric system." [126] Guided by this image and corrected by measurement, he happens on the Laws of Motion. Discovery comes from the interplay between the archetype pressing from within and the empirical eye searching in the external world. Heliocentrism is a mandala of the Self, a picture of mind centering itself. Pursuing the mystery of the inner Self, Kepler obtained insights into external reality.

If a relationship between the transpersonal psyche and nature exists, we might wish to ask what, if anything, the archetype of death and enlightenment foreshadows. What are these extraordinary images telling us about our place in nature? Do they hint of things we have yet to discover with the tools of modern science?

The ADE strongly associates light, a symbol of consciousness, with death. The harbingers from the deep unconscious repeat in many forms the same message: death is the gateway to greater consciousness, greater being. This is encouraging for survival research. Despite the difficulties that dog the pursuit, the collective unconscious prefigures victory over prevailing doubt.

Perhaps there is a relation between religion and parapsychology analogous to the one between astrology and astronomy, or alchemy and chemistry: the former saw in a glass darkly what emerged in the light of empirical discovery. Judging by previous cases, the new discoveries will surpass our expectations. The NDE, viewed from this angle, encourages us to entertain the hypothesis, common to collective belief but ignored by modern science, that death may lead to new and possibly higher forms of consciousness.

For the Freudian school, the world of myth and archetype is largely regressive. As Freud wrote at the end of his life in the *New Introductory Lessons to Psychoanalysis*, religion is a symptom of neurotic helplessness in the presence of "reality." The Jungian outlook, which we are here attempting to develop in harmony with parapsychology, takes a progressive view of these products of mental life. A certain rationalist bias tempts one to dump the NDE into the category of *fantasy*. But from a therapeutic standpoint, such a stance already inflicts a handicap on the growth potential of the experience.

The ADE adds to our vital resources, first, through its healing function, its metanoid aftereffects. Second, the ADE, especially its near-death form, foreshadows, and effectively helps us believe in, postmortem survival. Third, the ADE is a model for the *premortem* evolution of consciousness.

We are going to return to the last point. Near-death consciousness is collective, a potential of Mind at Large. If the NDE is a projection of the Total Self, of the whole person united with the whole of higher humanity, and if the function of archetypes is to orient us toward the future, then the ADE, the millions of contemporary near-death experiences, may be guiding us toward a new type of humanity: wholer, perhaps holier and more pacific.

Consider the evolutionary significance of the near-death archetype. Humanity as a whole, it would seem from the symbolism, is going to go through a dark tunnel; at the end, it shall enter into the light of a new consciousness, a new love. All the elements in the

NDE—darkness, strange sounds, borders, landscapes, beings of light, messengers from other worlds, crises of decision, cavortings through space and time, demonic epiphanies, etc.—if the ADE prefigures rightly, must have their counterpart in the evolution of human consciousness. But if we follow this train of thought, we are led to a disquieting possibility: the counterpart of individual near-death will be *the near-death of humanity as a whole.*

PART FIVE

MESSENGERS FROM MIND AT LARGE

Our study of the NDE led to the idea of a much larger pattern of related experiences: the archetype of death and enlightenment. We now explore this death-transcending psychism in yet a wider context. We shall further probe the phenomenology of psychisms whose main function appears to be to help and encourage individuals and groups during times of crisis. Our theme is the philiac or friendly function of Mind at Large.

Chapter 10 outlines a typology of helping apparitions; Chapter 11 deals with a special example of the philiac function of Mind at Large, the "apparition" or appearance inscribed on the Holy Shroud of Turin.

After an interlude, in which we descend into the inferno of human potential to look at the prospects of global near-death, we come back to the philiac function of Mind at Large as it appears in certain recent patterns of visionary experience.

10
A Typology of Helping Apparitions

Certain facts of our mental life indicate the activity of a guiding Intelligence of benign intent; these facts, in my view, make up the empirical basis of the idea of a divine agency that loves, protects and nurtures us. The myth of such a philiac deity no doubt simplifies, and is perhaps a way of masking, the tragic complexities of life. But to play down these hints of the secret operation of a benign Intelligence might well be a serious error. We might be stifling something of our evolutionary potential.

Before we go on with our story, let us pause and reflect on the picture as it appears to be taking shape. So far the sequence is this: at the lowest rung we have isolated instances of psi and OBE; these in turn come together again as part of a more integrated, directed pattern: the NDE. However, examining the NDE we found that this was part of something larger, more inclusive, which we called the archetype of death and enlightenment.

Now we are going to mount another step and outline a general typology of *helping* apparitions. Helping apparitions, let us say, are emissaries from Mind at Large. They bring good tidings; they encourage, inspire, guide and enhance our well-being in strange and unusual ways. They are bearers of value and meaning.

General Properties of Mind at Large

Gaps in the theory of evolution inspired us to consider the hypothesis of Mind at Large. The existence of psi and the occurrence of OBEs and NDEs provided a further factual structure. The Jungian perspective which stresses certain universal, integrative mental capacities, furnished more empirical support. On the basis of these observations, we could say that Mind in general is able to transcend time and space, shows a directedness toward form and the evolution of form.

Mind at Large is *creative*. This may be inferred from its action on matter. Life itself, its new and increasingly complex forms, is a basic expression of the creative function of Mind. But the place to observe Mind in vitro, so to speak, is in Man the Microcosm. Man is the mirror of Mind at Large. To understand this, we must observe the higher mental functions of human beings. If we concentrate on the lower, the physico-chemical mechanisms of living organisms, we discover no basis for an overarching mental function. Hence, we place a stress on psi, OBES, NDEs, etc.

Creative Mind shows itself in works of the human spirit: heroic or spiritual actions, science, art, philosophy. The world of art and science, history and culture, we see as *continuous* with the evolution of the forms of life itself. The entire creative process may be viewed as undergirded by what psi scientists call *psychokinesis*. This is a fundamental datum; that is, we cannot "explain" the creative function of mind. We can describe the conditions under which it exhibits itself; but the sheer fact of creative function is a datum. We can talk in detail of the structure of the human nervous system, but sooner or later we face a gap where mind simply acts on body, where a thought, image or intention "becomes" a deed.

A word on the relation between the traditional view of Deity and the present hypothesis of Mind at Large seems necessary here. Mind at Large, clearly, is not the traditional Deity of the West. Not perfect, like the all-good, all-knowing, all-powerful God of the Jewish and Christian tradition, Mind at Large is a "god" that scientists or artists might like, an experimental divinity, like a writer or painter, accustomed to making and scratching out mistakes.

Of course, this doesn't show that the traditional view is false. Other ways of justifying it are possible. (For this the reader might turn to the works of John Hick, H. D. Lewis.) Moreover, it would make little sense to talk of *worshipping* Mind at Large. That is not the way the concept is meant to be used. Mind at Large is a conceptual grid which serves as a neutral, metaphysical prophylactic, more allowing, less constricting, less supportive of Type-A thinking.

Mind at Large is a tool for a *welcoming* metaphysics; it *offers* perhaps greater, more sublime, possibilities. In a way, the offering and welcoming metaphysics of Mind at Large resonates with the idea of God as love, eros, agape, karuna and with the idea of a friendly intelligence somehow hidden in the secret byways of a dangerous world. Those who say "God loves us" seem to sense the presence of this amicable trend in the evolution of the universe.

Mind at Large doesn't refer to any *thing*; it points only to a *process*. That is part of what is meant by saying that Mind is *creative*. God is becoming. The Kingdom of God is within us, we remember. The Kingdom is coming to be *through* us. God, being incomplete, therefore needs humanity. It is not only that God loves us, an idea that could lull us into sanctimonious smugness, but that God needs us to be *verified*.

Properties of Helping Apparitions

We base our description of Mind at Large as offering, welcoming, loving, directing, aiding, in part, on the typology of helping apparitions. "Apparition" is the best term among several possibilities in English. "Apparition," in its root sense, refers to *what appears*—a phenomenon.

What are the properties of helping apparitions? We already have some leads from NDEs, a good example of helping apparitions. Helping apparitions share characteristics of NDEs. They arise, for instance, when the rational, conscious self faces an impasse; we might say that helping apparitions tend to arise when reason can no longer come up with a rule for coping with a crisis. A willingness to admit helplessness seems to clear the way for the helping function. Helping apparitions come to the fore during times of danger, crisis and transition. It seems natural that under such circumstances our higher help would come to the rescue.

There's ambiguity, "bipolarity," in these rescue operations. For example, consider Odysseus and Circe. You may recall how Circe turned Odysseus' heedless men into swine; because the wily Odysseus could handle Circe's spell, he could enlist her as an ally in his journey to the underworld. But his ally was also potentially his worst enemy. The helping force has to be mastered. But now let's turn to examples of helping apparitions.

Myths of Helping Apparitions

Mythology is filled with supernatural entities whose purpose is to help people. Entities of the mythical imagination, however, are not easy to separate from lived experience. It seems, in fact, plausible that at least some creatures of myth ultimately derive from unusual apparitional experiences. For instance, the idea of angels may have originated from the experience of more mundane helping apparitions, mediated through dreams or ghostly phenomena.

In this section, however, we will treat helping apparitions as anonymous mythical constructs. Angels, for instance, are a good place to begin. The idea of mediating spirits between earth and heaven, richly displayed in the mosaics, frescoes and icons of Eastern and Western Christianity, may be traced back to the Old Testament and to the Babylonian myth of Marduk at war with the monsters of Tiamat; there are parallels of these intervening entities in the nikes, victories, geniuses and other tutelary agents of pagan antiquity.

Angels (the Greek word means "messenger") are named variously: in Job, servants and troops; in Daniel, visions; in Psalms, ministers and hosts; and in Revelation, spirits. The functions of angels vary. They announce coming events, as in Chapter 1 of Luke when an angel announced to Mary the conception of Jesus; they worship and attend on God, do his bidding, preside over holy places such as the Tree of Life, and protect peoples and individuals. The psychological force of the belief in supernatural agencies protecting nations may perhaps be gauged from Polish devotion to the Black Madonna. Though angels prepare, guide and protect the way of man, the idea of guardian angels looking over children is no less strong.

In the world of the Homeric epics, the gods, when they are not hindering, often help the heroes in their adventures. Concerning the heroes in the Greek epics, Bruno Snell wrote: "Any augmentation of bodily or spiritual powers is effected from without, above all by the deity." [127] According to Snell, Homer had not yet formed a fully developed concept of the personal will; hence, whenever heroic exertion occurs, it is portrayed through an image of entreating and receiving aid from a god. But another interpretation of this is possible. Homer's mythology of helping (and harming) gods may embody (metaphorically, to be sure), an understanding of a higher, transpersonal will. It seems unlikely to me that Homer didn't understand that men can exert their wills; but perhaps he knew something else that we moderns have forgotten—namely, that the Self is possessed of greater powers than the conscious ego is normally aware of.

Harbingers of Divine Intimacy

As the gods protected the heroes in the great epics, so in ancient life men sought protection under the auspices of the heroes. Nor did the hero cults become extinct with paganism. The cult of the Christian saints carried on the tradition. Consider a few examples: during crisis and distress, people pray to Saint Jude the Apostle. They invoke Saint Anthony of Padua to help find lost property. Another Saint Anthony, the desert eremite of the fourth century, gave his name to a skin inflammation, erysipelas or Saint Anthony's Fire, of which many people were said to be cured in 1089 by his intercession. Saint Christopher is the patron saint of travelers. Saint Lucy, martyred in Syracuse in the fourth century, succors diseases of the eye. Saint Joseph protects us at the hour of death. Saint Michael the archangel is an ally in the battle against temptation.

The cult of the Virgin Mary is a helping cult; the Blessed Virgin intercedes on our behalf. In the great Marian visions at Fatima and more recently at Garabandal, Mary—the medium of all graces— appears as intercessor through whom world consciousness may be transformed. Through her, one may reach the heart of the Son and the Father; she is the hidden keystone of the Holy, the Healing Trinity.

In general, the measure of sainthood is helping power; there is no place for a useless saint. The triumph of Christianity, according to historian Peter Brown in his book *Cult of the Saints*, was marked by the rise of the cult of the saint in Latin antiquity. According to Brown, the Christian cult of saints brought a new sense of personal intimacy, concrete and warmly esthetic, between people and cosmos. In the words of Theodoret, bishop of Cyrrus in the fifth century, the cult of the saints created a ring of "invisible friends" around the Mediterranean world. Remarkably, Theodoret wrote:

> The philosophers and the orators have fallen into oblivion; the masses do not even know the names of the emperors and their generals; but everyone knows the names of the martyrs, better than those of their most intimate friends.

The martyrs, who astonished the Romans with their unnatural joy in the face of death, who defied the gods of the Empire with unheard of serenity and strange new courage, were transmuted after death, at their graves and shrines, into sources of friendship, inspiration and protection. They became members of a hierarchy of invisible friends.

The cult of saints was, in a way, a fulfillment, an enrichment of the Platonic cult of Eros. Eros is the hero of Plato's *Symposium*—the supreme ally in pagan philosophy, the power that permeates living nature, a spiritual being that mediates between the human and the divine. Rooted in the body, in life itself, Eros inflames the dynamics of the spirit and impels us toward wholeness and completeness. Eros is the supreme wizard, the magus of the soul, that ferries humanity heavenward toward the holiest and brightest "apparitions" of being.

The cult of saints builds the bridge to the immortals. But now, instead of abstractly personifying the power of Eros, we have a mass movement, dating from the Resurrection, that incarnates the helping dynamic and crystallizes in the lives of remarkable men and women, heroic rebels against the "last enemy."

Psi, Archetypes, and Patron Saints

Belief in patron saints may help to liberate the psychic potential latent in us. In the first place, belief is known to be a consistent psi-enhancer. Moreover, wrong effort and ego-involvement inhibit psi. Let us suppose, to give a very simple example, that a person misplaces a valuable object. Anxious effort to find the object is apt to be self-defeating; but now suppose the person is of a religious cast of mind and relaxes, offering up a prayer to Saint Anthony; he lays the task of finding the object in the hands of an Invisible Friend who specializes in helping us find things. This might activate, indirectly through belief in the saint, a powerful psi inducer: belief. It also relieves the petitioner from being subject to undue sensations of effort and frees him from feeling personal responsibility and the fear of failure. In leaving the task up to the Saint, the petitioner, freed from the compulsion to focus on himself as the means to fulfill the task, may now attend to the goal itself and not to the means of achieving the goal.

Now according to physicist-parapsychologist, Helmut Schmidt [28], psi is a goal-oriented function. This idea is philosophically vague; operationally, however, it is clear. Consider a psychokinetic experiment with a random event generator (REG). When a subject is placed before one of these machines, all he sees is a panel of moving lights; he understands nothing of the way the machine works (i.e., the esoterica of quantum mechanics) and makes no conscious effort to influence the mechanics of the REG. Instead, his task, simple enough, is to focus on the goal or outcome—say, to make the lights move in a clockwise direction. He tries to influence the behavior of the machine simply by concentrating on the goal or end-state. He is thinking teleologically, not mechanistically. He is in the optative or wishing mood, not the indicative, subjunctive or imperative mood. In Schmidt's experiments, results were obtained at odds immensely against the chance hypothesis.

In a similar vein, the religious petitioner does not focus on *how* he might find the lost object; he just thinks of the goal of finding it and leaves it to the Saint to bother with the "how." This mindset may liberate his own clairvoyant ability to work more effectively. If he happens to be successful, faith in the power of the Saint will be reinforced.

Given this as a possible model, belief in helping powers— guardian angels, patron saints, etc.—would be self-verifying. The "truth" of certain types of religious or spiritual beliefs may therefore operate according to a special logic of self-transformation and self-verification. If this is true, the conflict between science and religion may be based on a profound misunderstanding. Much, as I will suggest in the final chapter, hinges on the distinction between conforming and transforming truths. For now, let us just note that PK in a religious setting illustrates the idea of transforming truth.

Forms of belief may change, but *some* psychic construct is essential to free subjects from the limitations of their own self-concepts. Perhaps, going beyond patron saints, the supremely self-liberating "construct" is "God." Belief in God, given the psychology of psi and the logic of self-verifying truths, is a uniquely powerful, self-sustaining and self-confirming belief. While this would only be a partial parapsychological perspective, it at least throws some light on the durability of religious belief. Religious beliefs may be durable because the more strongly they are held, the more powerfully they work; that is, the more they alter objective reality by means of latent psi.

Apparitions That Changed History

Helping apparitions have changed history. Dreams, visions and psychic appearances in general have played a complex and assorted role in the course of human affairs. To keep things simple, we will stick to a few examples dealing with the early history of Christianity. The point we shall confine ourselves to making is this: it is a fact, and one that some theories of history would perhaps be reluctant to admit, that major changes and developments in the course of human history may, at least in part, be traced back to the influence of the most impalpable, the most private and the most fleeting *inner* events.

Keeping to the birth and early development of Christianity, let us begin with the Easter Epiphany. My view is that, faith aside, we have to assume *some postmortem appearance of Jesus,* if we hope to make sense of the Christian movement getting off the ground in the first place. The disciples can only have been in despair after the Crucifixion. We know from Peter's three-time denial of Jesus something of the fear and dispiritedness of the disciples after the arrest of their Master. One has to assume some type of appearance to account for the complete reversal of attitude—the change of a small group of scattered, bewildered and defeated disciples into the impassioned core of a new religion that would help to bring down the Roman empire.

Belief in the Resurrection, the belief that death was overcome in the risen Christ, is at the heart of Christianity. Thus Paul declares: "And if Christ be not risen, then is our preaching vain, and your faith is also vain." (1 Cor.:14) The ground for this belief in the conquest of death was prepared in the ancient world by the myth of the dying and rising god.

Why did the Christian answer to the enigma of death vanquish all others, especially when Mysteries so old, august and psychically efficacious (as those of Eleusis) were available? That shrewd historian, Jacob Burckhardt, said in his study, *The Age of Constantine:*

> If we seek to realize in brief the true strength of the Christian community at the beginning of the last persecution, we shall find that it lay neither in numbers, nor in a consistent superiority in its member's morality, nor in the excellence of its internal constitution, but in the firm belief in immortality of the soul which permeated each individual Christian. We shall show presently that later paganism directed all its efforts to the same goal, but by gloomy and labyrinthine paths and without Christianity's triumphant conviction.

According to Burckhardt, Christianity won out in this competition because it "simplified" the problem. But Burckhardt doesn't explain this simplification. Perhaps the pagan initiate had to undergo a specific experience, which was costly, both financially and psychologically. In contrast, the Christian, poor or rich, simply had to *believe* the good news that Jesus was resurrected. But this brings us no closer to understanding *why*, apart from any psychologically efficacious experience, the first disciples or later Christians were *able* to believe; it doesn't explain *how* they attained the "triumphant conviction" Burckhardt alludes to. It won't do to say that Christians wanted or wished to believe, since Burckhardt's premise was that the whole of the Hellenistic world wanted to believe with equal intensity; the *need* to believe permeated the whole of the ancient world. So the question remains, why the Christian Resurrection Appearances?

That in some sense Christ appeared to his disciples after his death is taken for granted even by the most hardheaded "scientific" historians such as Charles Guignebert. Most scholars agree that Peter was the first to whom the Lord appeared. "Where?" asks Guignebert, in his study, *Jesus*. "Probably by the shore of the lake and under conditions favorable to hallucination: in the morning mist or the dazzling blaze of noonday."

But according to Scripture, the Lord appeared to *numerous* individuals: besides Peter, to James, to the Twelve, to five hundred brethren. It is also clear that these appearances occurred at different times. But this in no way daunts Guignebert, for whom all is explained by the magic word, "contagion." Thus he writes: "Contagion could only fail to be produced if all these men had completely lost their faith or if they possessed a *scientific* conviction that the appearance of a dead person was an impossibility."

I shall not criticize these remarks in detail nor the assumptions they imply, except to say that psychical research has many reports of apparitions of deceased persons that cannot easily be dismissed as mere hallucinations. A more adequate scientific study of the New Testament writings would have to take into account the findings of psychical research. A bold and informed approach to the Resurrection question, which makes use of these findings, may be found in the writings of Michael Perry. [128] Perry, for instance, puts forth (cautiously) what he calls "a telepathic theory of the resurrection appearances."

However we ultimately interpret the Resurrection story, the main point is that Christianity, apart from these first *appearances*, would never have moved beyond the defeat of the Crucifixion. The Crucifixion of Jesus was followed by a powerful appearance of *something*.

Saint Paul's Helping Apparitions

Apparitional experiences played a role in changing death and defeat into a new and vital religious movement that swept across the Graeco-Roman world. The first followers of Jesus, however, gathered in Jerusalem and viewed the teachings of the Master as chiefly for the "lost sons of Israel." It was Saint Paul who, after his conversion experience on the road to Damascus, transformed the original teachings into a universal salvation religion. The exclusively Jewish Christians of Jerusalem pretty much vanished from the scene in 70 A.D.; the survival and expansion of Christianity is traceable to Saint Paul and his conversion experience. The similarity of the latter to a near-death experience has been noted; of particular interest is that Saint Paul did not actually see an apparition of Jesus but like many modern near-death experiencers, only encountered a powerful light, audition and out-of-body experience. Here was an example of profound metanoid transformation with a major impact on history.

But the role of helping apparitions does not end here for Saint Paul. Indeed, guiding psychic manifestations oversee the development of his entire ministry. This would be in keeping with our understanding of the way helping apparitions work. Paul was not only a man in transition—he was a figure in whom was epitomized an entire age in transition. This "transitional" character of his life was both inward and outward. In 2 Corinthians, he describes his many misadventures: how he was often imprisoned, whipped many times to the verge of death, three times beaten with sticks, once stoned, three times shipwrecked and cast adrift on the open sea. A whole litany of hardships is cited: how he traveled constantly, endured thirst, near-starvation, cold and sleeplessness, and lack of clothing. He tells how he was in danger from his own people, brigands and pagans. From the sound of this, Saint Paul spent a good deal of time hovering in states near death, thus, perhaps, opening him to the power of helping apparitions.

In the same letter, we get more insight into the psychology of helping apparitions. After recounting his out-of-body experience and how he was "caught up into paradise and heard things which must not and cannot be put into human language," (2 Cor.:12), he tells how he was given "a thorn in the flesh" (it is not clear what this was) in order to prevent him from becoming proud. After pleading to be freed of this mysterious, debilitating "thorn," the Lord declared:

"My power is at its best in weakness." The power of the archetypes, of the higher directing Mind, is strongest when the ego is at low ebb and forced to renounce its claim to autonomy.

In Acts, 16, we learn that Paul was instructed by the Holy Spirit *not* to preach the word in Asia. However, one night he had a vision in Troas of a Macedonian who appealed to him thus: "'Come across to Macedonia and help us.' Once we had seen this vision we lost no time in arranging a passage to Macedonia, convinced that God had called us to bring them the Good News." Thus, as Ernst Benz remarks, it was by means of the directing agency of a dream-vision that Paul "brought Christianity to the soil of Europe."

The Case of Constantine

The conversion of Constantine in the early fourth century was crucial to the history of Christianity. The case of Constantine shows that saintliness is not a necessary condition for experiencing helping apparitions. This Roman Emperor, struggling for power with his rival, Maxentius, was opportunistic, calculating and superstitious. In his later years, his habits were effeminate; he executed his eldest son Crispus for obscure reasons and his wife, Fausta, for adultery.

In part, his "conversion" to Christianity was motivated by the wish to counter the magic of pagan spells that Maxentius was using against him. According to Lactantius, the earliest authority, Constantine was given a *caeleste signum* at the Milvian Bridge. He was warned in a dream on the night before battle to draw the monogram of Christ (the two Greek letters chi and rho) on his soldiers' shields. The battle won, the story was confirmed by Eusebius under oath. Further proof of the dream is an inscription by the Senate on the Arch of Constantine dedicated in the year 315. After this episode, Constantine was more favorably disposed to Christianity and issued edicts of toleration, which paved the way for the new sect becoming the state religion.

We see, in sum, that at major turning points in the early history of Christianity, helping apparitions played a significant role. First, there were the Resurrection apparitions, which transformed the death and defeat of the Crucifixion into the triumph of the Easter Message; then there were Paul's visions which universalized and Europeanized the Gospel; and finally, Constantine's vision played a role in converting the political power structure of the Roman Empire to the cause of the new religion.

Helping apparitions, let us recall, are related to the type of psychic presentation we have called archetypes of death and enlightenment. The property they particularly seem to exhibit is a kind of long-range directedness, obvious in the illustrations given. Helping apparitions, in this large historical context, may be seen as answers to collective crises. The cycle of pagan culture was at an end; movements, creeds and mystery religions arose in response to the NDE of ancient civilization. The Christian form of the ADE struck the deepest, most powerful chords in the collective psyche of the ancient world.

Helping Apparitions of Mystics, Saints and Shamans

The next category of helping appearances overlaps with the first; both occur in the context of explicit spiritual life. The difference is that in the present class, we stress the personal aspect of the crisis of transformation rather than the historical.

In archaic societies, the *shaman* is the go-between linking tribe with Mind at Large, the specialist in mapping and mobilizing the helping powers. Helping apparitions are common during the onset of the shaman's career, as Eliade has shown in his study of shamanism. Shamans are individuals who, for different reasons, are susceptible to the creative forces of the deep psyche. The psychopathology of shamans is widely reported; they are often sickly, morbidly sensitive, introspective, hysteroid, sometimes epileptoid and sometimes sexually deviant. At the same time, they must also be exceptionally strong, morally and intellectually, in order to succeed as shamans. Elected to the shamanic vocation by ancestry, gods or spirits, they must be strong enough to cure themselves, which is how they acquire the power to cure others.

Sickness and near-death are part of the initiation into shamanic power. According to Eliade, the traditional initiation ceremony follows the threefold scheme of suffering, death and resurrection. Siberian shamans are described as "dying" as they lie in the yurt for three days without eating or drinking. During a Siberian ceremony of dismemberment, the "candidate remains like a dead man, scarcely breathing, in a solitary place." Initiatory near-death is a factor in receiving helping power. Buryat shamans must be sick for a long time, during which time ancestor spirits assail the candidate. "During the operation the future shaman remains inanimate; his face and hands are blue, his heart scarcely beats." Eskimo shamans contemplate their own skeletons; Australian aborigines become medicine men by sleeping on graves.

We already know of the tunnel imagery in near-death experiences, so it is interesting to learn that caves are important in the initiation of North American shamans, and caves are where their helping dreams and helping spirits are encountered. It is also during these cave-descents into unconsciousness that the shaman experiences ecstatic, out-of-body states. It would seem, in fact, that shamanic initiation ceremonies act out the pattern of the near-death experience. Entering the cave of near-death puts the candidate in touch with helping powers. The bipolarity or ambiguity of helping apparitions is clear from shamanic practices. For instance (and this is typical), the animals that torture the Eskimo shaman during his visionary dismemberment later become his helping spirits.

A great deal could be said about the shamanic quest for helping spirits — about the distinction between helping spirits that manifest in animal form (similar to the European witch's "familiar") and tutelary spirits (usually the souls of dead shamans); about the use of drumming, fasting and psychoactive substances for inducing the helping visions. The main point is that shamanism represents a world-wide archaic practice of securing the aid of psychic entities whose job it is to help, heal and guide.

The pattern in the higher religions is often similar. Initiatory sickness and helping dreams occur among the masters of the Western spiritual tradition. One of the most original spiritual traditions of the West originated in the twelfth century with Saint Francis of Assisi. The story of this seraphic lover of God's creation is well known; scholars like Irwin Panofsky and Max Scheler saw in the Franciscan movement the first stirrings of the Reformation, as well as the first signs of the artistic and scientific Renaissance. So it is interesting to note that the career of Francis began with dreams and visions during sickness.

The earliest known biography of the Saint is from the pen of Thomas of Celano who wrote how Francis, "worn down by a long illness," was "enticed" by a "nocturnal vision" of glory. It seems that, at first, Francis failed to grasp the meaning of his vision, which consisted of images of military triumph and "a most beautiful bride." The bride was Lady Poverty and the warrior imagery dealt with the battle he would wage against the mundane mind.

Biographer Celano notes the change of attitude in Francis; after his mysterious warrior vision, the saint-to-be ceased to respond to natural beauty as the reputed bon vivant was wont to do. We could take this, I suppose, as a signal that he was withdrawing attention from the external world—of the process of spiritual incubation he was undergoing. We should add, however, that the esthetic quality of the Poverello's temperament was not forever lost but later reappeared in his newly individuated being. Testimony to this new form of esthetic and spiritual consciousness is the famous Canticle of Creation; here, the medieval mind begins to look on nature with a fresh sense of wonder. Like many a NDEr, the Saint withdrew in sickness from the sensory world but in the end returned to it with renewed appreciation.

It is worth noting that the great modern Franciscan, Padre Pio of Pietrelcina, seems also to have been launched, early in life, by a helping apparition which contained the image of the warrior. When the Padre was fifteen, he had a vision just before entering the Capuchin seminary in Marcone. Meditating on his vocation, suddenly he was robbed of his senses; a vision appeared to him. Writing in the third person, he writes of it in a letter to his superiors: "He saw by his side a majestic man of rare beauty shining like the sun. This man took him by the hand and he heard him say: 'Come with me because it is proper that you fight like a courageous warrior.'" The guide then led him to a spacious plain where two groups of men, good and evil, stood facing each other. A giant emerged in the foreground and young Francesco was to do battle with him. The youth held back in fear but his guide said: ". . . go forward courageously because I will stay near you. I shall help you and I won't allow him to bring you down." With this, young Francesco took courage, battled the giant and overthrew him. The guide then gave the youth a crown of rarest beauty but promptly took it back, promising he would hold one even more beautiful aside for him. The Evil One, he was told, would return "to the assault to recoup his lost honor," though help would always be forthcoming.

This was indeed a prophetic vision, for Francesco would have to endure many diabolical assaults for the rest of his life. I shall not attempt to document or try to explain these phenomena here (by, say, means of the concept of the poltergeist), but many reports exist attesting to their physical effects. Once, for instance, the young friar's fellow students heard the loud noise of bars banging in his room. In the morning, the iron bars of his window were found twisted. There are photographs as late as 1964 of the Padre bruised from these assaults; often he was unable to say Mass because of them.

The warrior "metaphor" was significant in the life of the modern

Franciscan; the helping apparitions, including the Guardian Angel, played roles in his long moral and physical struggles. Padre Pio lived in communion with the living presence of Jesus, the Blessed Virgin and his Guardian Angel—in that order. Perhaps no religious figure of recent times has done more to revive beliefs increasingly viewed, even by religious people, as superseded, demythologized. Padre Pio is an embarrassment to those who see in religion a progressive and rational manifestation of the spirit; he sends us back to the time when *myth* meant living truth.

Let us take one example, the Guardian Angel—a *mere* myth to the religious rationalist and a joke to the nonreligious. But Padre Pio took the notion of Guardian Angels quite seriously. In 1912 Padre Agostino of San Marco in Lamis, Padre Pio's confessor, performed a kind of experiment, designed to test Padre Pio's Guardian Angel. He wrote letters to Padre Pio in French and Greek (in the Greek script); Padre Pio understood neither language. According to Padre Pio, his Guardian Angel translated these letters for him and dictated letters back in French, some of which may be read in the three volumes of his collected letters. When Padre Pio received these letters, he was at Pietrelcina for medical reasons and under the care of Don Salvatore Panullo; the latter signed a deposition under oath that Padre Pio translated the Greek letters, the explanation being provided by his Guardian Angel.

Telepathy from some living source may be discounted, if Ian Stevenson and others are right; for there is no evidence of telepathic transmission of language skills. That would force us to account for the understanding of the Greek by invoking some discarnate influence, which is at least compatible with the angel theory, since angels are native discarnates by definition.

The case of Padre Pio vividly illustrates the bipolar structure of these "supernatural" psychic presentations. The more profound the struggle for spiritual mastery, the greater the exposure to unusual obstacles and opposing forces, and the deeper the mobilization of helping forces. It is known, for instance, that Padre Pio's ecstatic visions were always preceded by diabolical visions, as if the two were in some sense inseparable. The forces that would rend and destroy the integrity of the spiritual master are also linked to the release of forces that assist in his reintegration at a higher level.

We see, then, that the primitive shaman as well as the saint and mystic of the higher spiritual traditions (we have confined ourselves

to a few examples from Christianity) have recourse to the aid of helping apparitions; these individuals, like near-death experiencers, undergo a shattering of their normal ego consciousness. Assistance
from a deeper stratum of Mind is crucial to their evolution. Sometimes these guiding entities announce the onset of a special career in
spiritual service; sometimes they appear in a crisis temporarily; sometimes they become permanent collaborators or allies. In some traditions, the helping powers are deliberately courted.

This is especially true of the Native American spiritual tradition.
The first helping vision may come through sickness, as with Black Elk
when he was nine; specific procedures for renewing contact with the
guiding forces are followed. Much could be said of the American Indian vision quest, basic to Indian spiritual life. Unlike the imperial
tradition of the Roman Church, American Indian spirituality is in-
tensely individualistic.

For instance, Lame Deer, a Sioux Medicine Man, tells the story of
hanblechia, his first vision quest. A boy, he was left for four days and
nights on top of a hill, alone and without food or drink, to wait in a
pit for a vision. After some time, the boy heard voices and soared out
of his body among the stars. The voices told him he would be a
healer; he had a vision of his great-grandfather, Lame Deer, bleeding
from a shot inflicted by a white man's gun. Then he felt a power, or
essence, called *nagi* by the Sioux, a kind of inner helping double; he
felt it surge through him and fill him with joy. When he came down
from the hill after four days and nights, the boy had become a man, a
wicasa wakan, a medicine man. He took the name of his great
grandfather—the helping apparition of his great grandfather. [129]
The old American way was to rely on helping apparitions to become
fully individuated.

Helping Apparitions of Everyday Life

So far, we have noted some examples of helping apparitions in
the context of history and spiritual life. Many of these psychic presentations have profound and lasting effects on large numbers of people.
We have only scratched the surface with our remarks.

There is also evidence that extraordinary intelligences intervene
in the events of daily life. The "invisible friends" that Theodoret
spoke of back when the Roman Empire was falling apart still seem to
be in our midst.

An early student of these phenomena, the Edinburgh physician,

Samuel Hibbert, in his *Philosophy of Apparitions* (published in 1824 and reprinted by Arno Press in 1975), reserved a special chapter for "Apparitions of Good Spirits." Hibbert, an early exponent of medical materialism, was invincible in his opinion that all such apparitions are "spectral illusions . . . nothing more than recollected images of the mind." Even the eyewitness accounts of Saint Teresa's levitations are written off as due to "morbific causes." For students of the near-death experience, it is worth noting that Hibbert, writing in 1824, and reviewing treatises on "spirits" and apparitions that date back to the early 1700s, speaks of the "frequency" and "numerous communications" between dying persons and "benignant spirits." But all these are said to be the "mere phantasies of diseased imagination." Among them is the case of a Mr. John Gairdner who, in 1717, lay as if dead for two days but revived after he had been sealed in a coffin and was about to be lowered into the grave. Later that evening when the gentleman (taken for dead) revived, he "related many strange and amazing things which he had seen in the other world." I think we can guess with reasonable confidence what sorts of things Mr. Gairdner "had seen."

Gustave Flournoy's *Spiritism and Psychology*, published in 1910, also contained a special chapter devoted to "beneficient spirits." Flournoy was never quite convinced of the spiritistic hypothesis, though he took the reality of the paranormal seriously. Flournoy argues with impressive skill that what look like communications from the other side of the tomb are, in all likelihood, the "fiendish by-play of the subliminal mind." This is another way of talking about what nowadays is referred to as *superpsi*, and we have already remarked on the difficulties incurred by that view. In any case, what interests us here is the phenomenon of helping apparitions. Flournoy, apart from his views of survival, is at least struck by the power of what Myers called the "subliminal mind" and said that "things happen in the mental life *as if* we possessed in ourselves an intelligent 'incubator,' which continues to hatch out ideas and answer questions which we have confided to its care; a laboratory wisely administered, in which the ingredients placed within it are allowed to simmer and are elaborated into new products, according to our ideas and designs."

The notion of unconscious incubation is apt in some of Flournoy's examples, as, for instance, in the case of the naturalist Agassiz, who solved a problem with fossil fish by clues received in a series of three dreams. In some of his examples, however, this hypothesis ap-

pears strained: i.e., in what he calls "anti-suicidal automatisms."
Thus, he cites the instance of a man, about to jump from a window in
a fit of suicidal despondency, who was hurled back into his room by a
light that appeared between him and the window. A similar, but
more complex case, is that of Benvenuto Cellini. The great artist was
imprisoned by the Pope in the Castle of San Angelo. In a damp, dark
dungeon, his leg fractured, and overwhelmed by a sense of hopeless-
ness and degradation, Cellini contrived to kill himself by striking his
head against a piece of wood he had propped up. When all was
ready, an invisible force seized and threw him several yards away.
The next night, the apparition of a beautiful young man appeared to
him: "Let yourself be led by Him (God)," he was instructed, "and do
not cease to trust in His power." The prisoner wrote in his Bible
words renouncing his intention to commit suicide and rapidly recovered his bodily and moral strength.

More recent studies of apparitions also note the existence of a
special category of apparitions with the function of "reassuring" percipients. Thus Celia Green and Charles McCreery, British psychical
researchers, wrote: " . . . there seems to be a distinct class of experiences in which the apparition has the effect of reassuring the percipient at a time when he is undergoing some crisis or situation of
stress." [130] Several intriguing examples are given. A woman near
to giving birth was awakened during the night by the apparition of a
smiling elderly woman; the result was an unforgettable and unprecedented experience of tranquility. "The feeling I had was one I
couldn't forget as long as I lived . . ." Another person, insomniac
and under great stress, was visited by the apparition of a young
monk who said: "My child, I will give you a blessing." He laid his
hand on her head, and she fell into a sweet and childlike sleep; the
woman, not religious, "felt a different person" in the morning. Another woman (to give one more example from this collection) was
worried about her child's health; an apparition of the woman's deceased mother appeared and reassured her that there was nothing
wrong with the child. Anxiety evaporated; the doctor's diagnosis was
incorrect, and the child was indeed well. The reassuring figures are
sometimes familiar and personal, at other times strangers, bordering
on the mythical. They appear when we need them, somehow and
from "somewhere." They help.

Zoe Richmond [131] put together a collection of apparitions with
evidence of purpose. This type of apparition is theoretically important

for survival researchers, for it shows conscious agency on the part of the apparently surviving entity. In Richmond's collection, the purpose of some of the apparitions was *to help;* for example, a British General Maisey during a siege in Delhi in 1857. The General described how a voice called after him, causing him to take a sudden turn off the road; just as he left the road, the spot he was at was torn up "by a shower of grapeshot," which would have killed him. Much to the astonishment of Maisey, no one of his fellow soldiers called him. Whether we think of this as resulting from the General's own precognitive ability or the prescience of a friendly discarnate, *something* got him to move from the fatal spot.

I chose this particular case because it is similar to one from my own collection. The incident took place in 1967, in Vietnam. A young soldier was stationed in Bien Hoa; during the night, the air-raid siren rang and all personnel had to rush into an underground bunker. CG, the young man in question, did not enter the bunker but hid behind a reinforced partition outside the bunker. While crouching behind the partition, CG heard a voice: "C—come back here!" "What for?" he complained. CG didn't move but again he heard a voice call him back into the bunker. This time he got up and entered the bunker, sitting at the first support beam; once again a voice cried to him to come back. He rose and sat by the second support beam inside the bunker. "OK?" he asked. The voice ceased. In the meantime, an Air Force sergeant sat down beside the reinforced partition, at the exact spot where CG sat a few moments ago. The next moment, a rocket exploded where the sergeant was sitting, killing sixteen men, every man up to *the second support beam.* CG only suffered minor buises and later discovered no one had been calling him. The possibility that one of the dead men called him is ruled out, because none of the survivors remember anyone calling CG, although they did remember CG seeming to carry on a conversation with an invisible person.

If this warning came from CG's own precognitive ability, why all the resistance? The voice had to call him three times; after all, if CG "knew" subliminally what was coming, why play games with his own life? In any case, it certainly looks as if some rather exact information about an essentially incalculable event was involved, for the voice insisted on CG moving back to the *second* support beam, which was just beyond the rocket's fatal reach. Assuming this story is true— and having interviewed CG in depth myself, I have little reason to doubt it is true—then the "intelligence" behind the voice *knew* where the rocket would land and *precisely how far* its kill-power would reach.

I would like to end here with one more example where the apparition actually stops a person from physically moving and thereby averts a possibly fatal accident. A seventeen-year-old girl approached a red light at an intersection.

> While waiting for the light to turn green, I looked around at some children playing on the sidewalk. I glanced at the light—it had just turned green; I raised my foot from the brake, and put it on the gas pedal. The car slowly started forward. I glanced down to press the cigarette lighter. As I looked up, my mother, who had been dead since I was five, was standing in front of my car. I had only gone about five feet. I slammed on my brake. As I did, a tractor trailer ran the red light at about 40 m.p.h., and my mother was gone.

Again, was the apparition of the mother a projection from the young woman's unconscious? Or was it the saving act of a dead mother? Perhaps an altogether different way of looking at this is needed. Let us just say that these phenomena are signs of the Extended Self—the total or subliminal Self, the "higher" or "true" Self. The important thing is to remind ourselves that a Helping Potential lies hidden in the deep grain and texture of being. Perhaps we can learn to tease this Hidden Helper out of the shadows. The first step is to describe its *appearances*.

Madness and High-Minded Hallucinations

According to Wilfred van Dusen [132], the mad are privy to archetypal powers of the mind; they meet with certain good angels that Swedenborg knew in his visionary journeys. Van Dusen was a psychiatrist (for sixteen years) at the Mendocino State Hospital in California; he succeeded in getting his patients to share the intimate details of their hallucinations. He did this by treating the hallucinations as if they were real, by engaging them in dialogue. On the basis of his observations, van Dusen found (a) that there were two types of hallucination, different in function, which his psychotic patients experienced and (b) that the basic typology matched descriptions of certain spirits, said by Swedenborg to populate the planes of the afterlife.

Consistency in the types of hallucination was observed. It didn't seem to matter if the patients were schizophrenics, alchoholics, brain-damaged or senile; the basic pattern was the same. The patients generally disliked the term "hallucination" and felt they were in touch with another order of reality. According to van Dusen, all but the most advanced in madness could discriminate between their hallucinations and reality.

Patients either were assailed by lower-order voices or helped by higher-order visions. The latter were rarer and comprised only a fifth of the apparitions.

Van Dusen's description of the lower-order entities is striking. "Lower order voices are similar to drunken bums at a bar who like to tease and torment just for the fun of it. They suggest lewd acts and then scold and torment the patient for considering them. They find a weak point of conscience and work on it interminably." The lower-order hallucinations seek to destroy the patient, to wear and break him down; they do so by talking incessantly, shouting noisily and inanely, distracting their victims with fear and confusion and threatening death. They have no personal identity, though they are quick to fake one; they feed on the patient's weaknesses. They are anti-religious and try to interfere with the patients' religious practices.

In contrast, higher-order hallucinations rarely speak; they appear as light beings, communicate through symbols, are friendly, supportive and instructive. They are, according to van Dusen, "similar to Jung's archetypes, whereas the lower-order is like Freud's id." The higher-order entities even explain the function of the lower-order voices to the patients, which is to bring their weaknesses into dramatic relief. Van Dusen was convinced that the helping hallucinations "knew" more about religion and mythology than the patients, who very often were poorly educated.

For the most part, these patients fought a losing battle against the lower-order forces—which is why they were in the hospital. The duality of our inner life, the fact that each of us embodies contradictory psychic forces, is vividly displayed by this portrait of madness. Mind is at war with itself; to encroach on the mysteries of the Greater Mind is to risk war. The everyday ego with its well-adjusted persona avoids this conflict; but there is a dark side beneath our routine defenses. Even God has Satan, his adversary. Whoever enters on the journey of death and enlightenment, flirts with the powers of the spirit and needs to adopt the attitude of a warrior. The innocent or unfortunate who stray too far beyond the confines of wholesome repression are apt to be overrun by devastating forces. But even those shipwrecked by madness are assisted, if Jung and van Dusen are right. St. Francis,

Padre Pio, St. Ignatius, Crazy Horse, Buddha and Socrates, each in their own way were warriors, although the war they fought was against the demons of the Self. Unlike van Dusen's patients, however, they knew how, or were lucky enough, to use the Helping Apparitions to their advantage.

Collective Helping Apparitions

So far we've talked of helping apparitions that appear to individuals; but there is also an interesting category of these guiding forces that occur in a collective setting. If Kerenyi is right, for instance, the ancient Greeks evolved a ritual for annually evoking an apparition of Persephone, the goddess of the underworld and daughter of Demeter, during the Mysteries at Eleusis.

Our present concern, however, is with *spontaneous* collective apparitions; in modern times, the two kinds that most concern us are UFO phenomena, some of which occur in a collective setting, and the Marian apparitions, culminating in those witnessed by millions in Zeitoun, Egypt, during the late 1960s. We have already mentioned these phenomena and shall return to discuss them in conjunction with the prophetic visions of near-death experiencers in the last part of this book. Collective helping apparitions do mainly two things: they warn of coming catastrophe and they encourage people to make the basic inner changes needed to avert catastrophe. Collective helping apparitions are indications of the collective mind in transformation.

Our aim in this chapter has been to sketch a phenomenology of helping apparitions, to tell the story of our allies, the invisible friends who ring our troubled world and offer their guidance and wisdom. Mythology speaks to us of such beings: angel and jinn, fairy and familiar, gods and goddesses. The cults of the heroes and of the saints mingle truth and legend, creating healing shrines for our minds to repair to when confused, or in distress, or in need of guidance and inspiration. All these embroideries of history and imagination may be images of our own (admittedly little understood) supernormal mental powers; they may be projections that actually serve to assist in releasing these latent powers. Apparitions that spring from the hidden recesses of Mind at Large have changed history. Helping apparitions, psychically dangerous and ambiguous, are regular features in the lives of the heroes of spiritual warfare. Yet even those who do not court the higher powers often receive their help; there are helping apparitions in everyday life.

The metanoid component of Mind reaches to the peaks of spiritual aspiration and to the lowlands of human helplessness. Even in the driest gulches of human madness, a higher-order type of psychic entity may emerge and offer a helping hand. The present outline of helping apparitions extends the phenomenology of near-death apparitions. It illustrates the ADE at work, an Intelligence that appears to direct, however haphazardly, the play and upward ascent of Life.

11
The Shroud of Turin

*Whoever finds the interpretation of these words
will not taste death.*

—*The Gospel of Thomas*

A Unique Helping Apparition

For the last two thousand years, the soul of the Western world
has lived on faith in the Resurrection of Christ. Jung paid obeisance to
this psychic fact by saying that Christ embodies the archetype of the
Self for the Western world. Christ resurrected meant death transcended. It meant the Self realized, the Self gone through life's rite of
passage, but come out renewed, raised to a new wholeness. With
Burckhardt and Guignebert, we already remarked on the secret of the
historical triumph of Christianity: it was the appeal of a new vision of
death, a vision that encouraged people to do remarkable things, to
lay the foundations of a new world culture. But for that story, I refer
the reader to the books of Christopher Dawson and Arnold Toynbee.

Christianity was not alone in the competition for the mind of the
ancient world. Like our own, the age overflowed with all kinds of
cults and creeds. It seems that not creeds but actions won the day,
and the Christian martyrs' heroic handling of death converted many
Romans to the new faith. The spectacle of prisoners serenely, even
joyfully, facing death was strange and incomprehensible to pagan
Romans. One martyr inspired another; the movement seemed almost to thrive on persecution.

223

A good example is Saint Cecilia, the beautiful Roman martyr, who converted her husband to the faith on their bridal night. Both husband and wife went the way of martyred death. It certainly is odd behavior by modern standards. For many, this strange, unnatural behavior indicates a supernatural force. As for the Roman lady who died a Christian martyr, since become the patron saint of music, I would like to know what new romantic enchantment came into the world, strong enough to tame the most natural instincts: sex and the fear of death? What manner of force entered history with Christianity? What new form of energy caused a turning point in human history?

Now, any new evidence of this power must figure in revising the nihilistic myth of death. In this chapter, I examine the Shroud of Turin in light of our task of envisioning a healing metaphysics of death. In particular, I view it as a unique example—you could almost say *exemplar*—of helping apparitions and hence of the benign directedness of Mind at Large.

The Shroud of Turin is a unique helping apparition; that is, it is an "appearance" of what is alleged to be the image of Jesus on his burial cloth. Information encoded in the image, moreover, corresponds to the biblical account of the Crucifixion. It is helping, then, as a unique relic, possibly even giving an accurate yet curious type of photographic image of Jesus. Even more startling is the claim that the image on the Shroud is a type of photographic record of the instant of the Resurrection.

Historical Irony of the Shroud

One of the oddities of the Shroud phenomenon is that the paranormal elements become more apparent as scientific technology progresses. Ironically, this is happening when scientific progress seems to demand the demythologizing of Christianity. Miracles, relics—the *supernatural*—have all been pushed aside by the liberal wing of modern Christianity, in step with the dictates of secular science. Liberal Christianity, by and large, assumes that such things ought not to concern us. Thus, one minister in a liberal Christian weekly opined that current intererst in the Shroud is a sign of "infantilism."

But science and technology, when applied to the study of the Shroud, raise questions about things modernism writes off as superstitious. The Shroud, unless a lot of scientists are deluding themselves, challenges dogmas of what is possible. Consider, for instance, the following. When for the first time in 1898 Secondo Pia photographed the cloth, the camera revealed what no one could have known prior to the invention of the camera: the image of the Shroud was *reversed* in the manner of a photographic negative. This seems to suggest some photoenergetic process that would surely have been technically impossible in the days of Jesus, if indeed the strange cloth does hail from those fateful days of history. The photographic properties of the Shroud are just one puzzling aspect of a very puzzling phenomenon.

A turning point in Shroud studies came when American scientists from disciplines such as computer technology, aerodynamics, radiation physics, chemistry, optics, etc. combined forces to study the image on the cloth. In October 1978, the scientists convened in Turin for five days and nights of intensive investigation of the relic. This group is known as part of the Shroud of Turin Research Project (STURP). Many of these scientists came from such institutions as Cal Tech's Jet Propulsion Laboratory, the Air Force Weapons Laboratory, Sandia Corporation, United Technologies, Los Alamos Scientific Laboratory and the Air Force Academy. It seems ironical that these entirely *worldly* institutions, associated with inventing and developing the most diabolical machinery of destruction, should now be shedding light on the story of Jesus.

The Shroud as a Fly in Diverse Intellectual Ointments

The mystery of the Shroud is apt to irritate people of diverse intellectual persuasions. It can scarcely be welcome to most materialists. The Shroud, with its odor of Catholic sanctity, its imperial mystery, is not likely to sit well with militant secularists.

On the other hand, the Shroud might disturb many Christians. First, liberals, convinced that Christianity must be demythologized, desupernaturalized, are anxious to keep up with more respectable conceptions of truth and reality. One might wonder what the good of such a miraculous cloth could be. The social "relevance" of the Shroud may not be immediately apparent. At the other end of the spectrum are certain fundamentalists who despise the Catholic veneration of relics as a throwback to paganism.

One might guess that modern transpersonal psychologists, people busy trying to reconcile science and mysticism, would be open to the phenomenon of the Shroud. But this movement has so far kept a distance from the scientific study of the paranormal. Finally, even parapsychology has been reluctant to face the Shroud. Perhaps there is the fear of being associated with religion; parapsychology wants to achieve scientific respectability. Or perhaps there is the fear of fixing on a phenomenon too local, too eccentric for a science that nevertheless suffers from a gnawing identity crisis.

Let us lay all these scruples aside, attempt to look at the facts and follow the argument wherever it may lead.

What Is the Holy Shroud of Turin?

The Holy Shroud of Turin is a linen cloth, fourteen feet three inches long by three feet seven inches wide; imprinted on it is the image of a bearded, naked man with the wounds of a Roman crucifixion. From the way the image reveals the body, tall and well-built (familiar with manual labor) and from the way the image appears, front and back conjoined, it would appear to be a burial cloth, or *sindon*, which was wrapped around the dead body of the man. The image is extraordinary in its own right. It is the image of a dead man. Yet the face is strangely alive. It has a hieratic stillness, a sublime nobility, as we might see in a statue of an Egyptian God. It is a look of transcendent composure. The face is bruised, marked with cuts, swellings and bloodstains; yet the look is serene, the eyes closed, inwardly absorbed. The figure of death is centered. It is meditative. There is no style in the annals of art one can compare it to; an expressive soulfulness irradiates from the face. It is a remarkable image *as* an image, not inferior to Rembrandt or Leonardo. What manner of Artist gave us this icon of death and its mysteries?

The Shroud appears in history with the de Charny family at Lirey, near Troyes in France, 1353. About a hundred years later, the Duke of the House of Savoy acquired the cloth and brought it to Turin in 1578. It remains in the Cathedral of St. John the Baptist in Turin, locked away in a reliquary vault above the altar of the Royal Chapel. Sequestered in a silver casket, it is rarely displayed in public; but thanks to photography, the Image may be seen everywhere.

Assuming the Shroud to be the burial cloth of Jesus, where could such a previous relic have been for thirteen hundred years? There is little that anyone really knows about this, although Ian Wilson [133] has theorized on the Shroud's obscure past, identifying it with the Mandylion of Constantinople, renowned as being *acheiropoetos*, made by no human hand. The Mandylion was an image of Christ, copies of which resemble the image on the Shroud. However, Wilson's reconstruction is not accepted by all scholars. But this is almost secondary. Even if the Shroud's past remains obscure, its present paranormality is unambiguously before us. The Shroud's paranormality is logically independent of its history.

The Shroud as a Permanent Paranormal Object

Many problems that beset psi researchers are bypassed in the case of the Turin cloth. For instance, there can be no problem of experimenter effect, no problem with witnesses (the object is there, unequivocally, for study) and no question of it being a statistical artifact (either the image on the cloth is paranormal or it is not). The Shroud presents itself as a permanent paranormal object; the challenge to account for it is unambiguous. If there is no normal explanation of the Shroud object, then that object, transparently public, offers permanent, conclusive testimony of the paranormal.

Evidence For the Paranormality of the Shroud

There are only two *normal* ways to account for the Image of the Shroud. It is either a man-made artifact, the work of a medieval (or earlier) forger, or else it is a product of some natural process. In the latter case, the assumption would be that the piece of linen called the Turin Shroud was at least somebody's burial cloth. For instance, one of the earliest researchers, Paul Vignon [134], believed that the Image on the Shroud was a *vaporograph*, produced by ammonia and sweat mingling with oils and spices of the cloth. Apart from these two possibilities, the image would be unaccountable and, in short, paranormal.

What follows is a bare outline of the facts; a vast literature is accumulating, and there are already two scholarly journals devoted to *sindonology* (the word "sindon" in Greek means "shroud"): *Sindon*, founded in Turin in 1959, and *Shroud Spectrum International*, published quarterly in America by the Indiana Center For Shroud Studies. For an overview of the Shroud phenomenon, the reader may consult two recent books which take into account the latest scientific findings. *Verdict on the Shroud* [135], by Gary Habermas and Kenneth Stevenson, approaches the subject from a theological viewpoint and argues for the Shroud as specific evidence for the resurrection of Jesus. *Portrait of Jesus?* [136], a comprehensive study by Frank Tribbe, a lawyer-parapsychologist, presents the case for the Shroud's authenticity and paranormality in an ecumenical vein, as a challenge to all thinking people.

Historical. To begin with, there are features of the Shroud that place its origin in Palestine of the first century of the Roman Empire. The crucified man on the Shroud was pierced by nails in the wrist and not, as tradition has supposed, in the palms of the hand. Both historical research and recent experiments demonstrate this; nails in the palms of the hand would not sustain the weight of a suspended body. No medieval forger would have known this. Neither would a medieval forger have dared to portray Jesus as naked. Moreover, the body of the man in the Shroud was unwashed; the Gospels say nothing about washing the body of Jesus, and there is reason to believe that the body was indeed not washed, due to the coming of the Sabbath (Luke 23: 54-56). Also, the *Code of Jewish Law* forbade the washing of a body that had met death violently or at the hands of the state. Another point is the ponytail hairstyle common to Jewish men of first-century Palestine which is indicated by the back view on the Shroud.

Computer-enhanced analysis of the image on the Shroud shows what appear to be round objects laid on the eyes. Now it is known that placing coins on the eyes of the dead was a burial custom among first-century Jews. A specific coin fitting the computer-enhanced visual data has in fact been suggested: the lepton, issued by Pontius Pilate between 29 and 32 A. D. Another point of correspondence between the Shroud and Middle Eastern history is the three-to-one herringbone twill weave of its linen fabric. Further, in 1973, Max Frei, a Swiss criminologist and expert on pollens, examined the Shroud and found thirty-three spores indigenous to Palestine and Turkey. Gilbert Raes, of the Ghent Institute of Textile Technology in Belgium, found traces of cotton among the linen fibers of the Shroud; cotton, however, grew in the Middle East but not in Europe.

Finally, medical studies indicate that the man in the Shroud died in a short time, an idea consonant with the New Testament account of the scourgings that preceded the death of Jesus. Scourging would have weakened and so predisposed him to rapid death. A rapid death by asphixiation is indicated by evidence of forcibly contracted and enlarged respiratory muscles. These are just a few of the facts usually cited, none of which tend to support the hypothesis of a medieval fraud; on the contrary, they support the idea that the cloth comes from the Middle East at the time of Jesus.

Medical. We already mentioned that the Shroud shows a man whose *wrists* were pierced by nails, a fact about Roman crucifixion methods not privy to medieval artists, physicians or clergy, as we may infer from the way artists portrayed the crucifixion, which showed nails piercing the palms of the hands. Modern experiments show that the weight of a body cannot be sustained if impaled through palms of the hands.

The Shroud contains a good deal more medical data, none of which supports the thesis of forgery. For instance, physicians have examined bloodflows on the forehead of the man imaged on the Shroud. Rivulets of blood indicate distinctive characteristics of arterial versus venous bloodflow, the former indicated by spurts due to the heart pulsing, the latter by flows slower, thicker and coagulating more quickly. But, as Dr. Sebastian Rodante [137] notes, the difference between arterial and venous blood was discovered in 1593 by Andrea Cesalpino, again demonstrating that the Shroud contains information unknown to any possible thirteenth-century forger.

The bloodflow lines and coagulation patterns, according to Pierre Barbet [138], are in every detail natural. After death, blood separates into a watery serum and thick cellular mass; evidence for this separation is on the Shroud. The New Testament records this separation. Now the likelihood of a forger being able to reproduce with such anatomical exactitude this separation, i.e., a serum "halo effect" at the edge of blood clots and scourge marks, is small. Recent researchers confirm Barbet on the presence of clots and on the separation effect. [139, 140] Chemically and anatomically, these facts virtually rule out the possibility of applied pigment accounting for image characteristics of the blood clots. No forger would be able to reproduce imagery representing the blood clotting process.

Another inexplicable fact is that these bloodstains and blood clots appear intact on the cloth, not smeared. Removal of the cloth from the body it enwrapped would surely have smeared blood marks. Habermas and Stevenson take this as evidence for the resurrection. They reason (citing the support of California pathologist, Robert Bucklin) that the blood flowing from the wounds of the man in the Shroud would have become "loosely attached" to the linen wrapped around the body as the blood dried. "Removing the Shroud," they argue, "however carefully, would require removal of the blood clots and the disturbing of the edges of the bloodstains. Since this did not happen with the Shroud, we may assert the probability that the body left the cloth in some way other than normal unwrapping of the Shroud."

Frank Tribbe was also struck by the intactness of the bloodstains and blood clots. Thus he writes, "The permanence and sharp detail of the bloodstains logically must be attributed to the *same* paranormal, spiritual event that 'photographically' imprinted the negative body images (front and back) with such meticulous and reliable detail upon the Shroud." Of course, the absence of smudging of the bloodstains is consistent with the hypothesis that they were painted on the linen. However, none of the physical or chemical studies show the presence of paint, dye or any substance *sufficient* to account for the image on the cloth. Moreover, positive proof of blood on the Shroud has been obtained.

Physical and chemical. In the previous section, we spoke freely of "bloodstains" and "blood clots." But one of the main questions concerning the authenticity of the Shroud is whether there really is any blood on it. This is crucial for the authenticity of the Shroud.

The evidence now seems conclusive for the reality of human blood on the Shroud. P. O. Baima Bollone [141], professor of forensic medicine at the University of Turin, identified human globulins, a type of protein in blood serum, on the Shroud through the use of fluorescent antibodies. The presence of blood on the Shroud was confirmed by the American researchers, chemists J. H. Heller and A. D. Adler. [139]

Linen fibrils from the Shroud were examined by microspectrophotometry, a method used to measure and compare light radiations by wavelength. Thus, for instance, if hemoglobin (or whatever blood-related chemistry) were present in the fibrils, its characteristic frequencies would be detectable by means of spectroscopic analysis. The results of this and other tests demonstrate the presence of blood on the cloth. Heller and Adler describe twelve tests confirming the presence of whole blood on the Shroud. For example, in addition to the spectroscopic analysis just mentioned, iron was detected in blood areas by x-ray fluoresence; there were positive demonstrations of bile pigments, or protein, of albumin and so on.

These findings refute the original claims of Walter McCrone, known for his alleged demonstration that the Vinland Map of Yale

University was a forgery. McCrone thought he found substances on the Shroud that proved it was a painting. He was right in identifying the substances but wrong in his interpretation of them. For instance, the iron oxide that McCrone found is distributed all over the linen, not exclusively in the image areas, and it may be accounted for by a familiar process of retting, to which linen is usually subjected. The tiny particles of vermillion cited by McCrone are artifacts due to previous artists like Van Dyke and Reubens copying the Shroud. In any case, the particles of pigment are insufficient in quantity and inappropriately located to account for the image. Heller and Adler conclude that the image was "not produced by any pigments, stains, or dyes."

Chemically, the image is the result of dehydration and oxidation of the cellulose in the topmost fibers of the threads composing the cloth. The authors conclude that they "cannot conceive of a single simple mechanism that will also be consistent with the physical and image analysis studies." As Heller says in his recent, popular book, the Shroud remains "a mystery." [142] This, in fact, is the consensus of the forty American scientists who spent (and are still spending) thousands of man-hours on the Shroud of Turin Research Project.

Finally, let's consider some of the physical properties of the Shroud image.

Image invisible at close range. The first thing to note is simple, yet it argues against the Shroud image being a painting. The image cannot be seen at close range. It comes into focus at a distance of about four or five meters. How, then, could an artist have used brushes or other utensils physically to inscribe the marks that make the image on the linen? It is of course not *inconceivable* that this difficulty might have been overcome, but it is not easily ignored.

Photographic negativity. Quite apart from providing a convincing account of how a fourteenth-century faker could produce a perfect negative image of the man of the Shroud, there is the question of motive. Photography lay centuries in the future. What would be the point of trying to produce an image in which the shades of light and dark, rights and lefts, were systematically interchanged? What meaning could it have had for the people of those times?

Superficiality of the image. Microscopic examination of the Shroud shows that the image penetrates only the topmost fibers of the threads of the cloth. This fact must be accounted for by any theory of image formation on the Shroud. The extreme superficiality is not consistent with the idea that the image was painted on the cloth, since any paint, dye or coloring substance would penetrate, saturate and cement the fibers of the cloth. Similar difficulties face any theory that would account for the image as resulting from diffusion of gases from a dead body.

Absence of brush strokes. Once again, the microscope reveals a simple fact difficult to reconcile with the idea of the Shroud image being a painting. McCrone claims to have found evidence of paint pigments on the cloth; apart from the fact that the STURP people claim the amount and the location of the pigments fail to account for the image, the absence of brush strokes renders the idea of painting an awkward one, to say the least. For how does one apply the paint to the cloth without some tool that would register *direction* of paint flow, brushstroke or scraping? (Needless to say, the technique of spray painting was unknown to the Middle Ages.)

Thermal stability and non-water solubility. In 1532 the Shroud was exposed to a fire; water was used to douse it. The image was changed neither by the fire nor by the water; but if paints or dyes or any coloring substance made the image, some changes in it would most likely be detectable. The thermal stability and non-water solubility are therefore incompatible with the theory that the body image was formed by the application of a foreign substance like paint. Again, McCrone's claim that the Shroud is a painted forgery doesn't square with the facts.

Image independent of pressure. Theories have been advanced to account for the formation of the image that assume contact between the body and the cloth. According to this theory, chemicals that sensitized the cloth were diffused from the body, and the image appeared later. There are difficulties with this theory, in particular, the pressure independence of the image. Whatever the process of image formation, it "did not depend on pressure between the body and the cloth since . . . equal contact intensities occurred on the top and the bottom images where pressures at contact are greatly different." [135] Another point that bears thought is that thousands of linen grave cloths have come down to us from antiquity, but none of them bear anything remotely resembling the detailed photographic negative evident in the Turin cloth. Surely if this diffusion mechanism worked in the case of one dead man wrapped in a linen cloth, traces of the image-making process would be noticeable in some of the numerous grave cloths of antiquity.

Image encodes 3-dimensional information. Paul Vignon [134] was the first to notice that image intensity apparently varied inversely with the cloth-body distance. This has been confirmed by physicists, Drs. John Jackson and Eric Jumper. A microdensitometer was used to scan photographs of the image on the Shroud and this process correlated image density and cloth-body distance. The correlation was displayed as a smooth curve, demonstrating the inverse relationship originally observed by Vignon; that is, as the distance decreased, the image density increased. The next step was to convert all the points on the image to a vertical relief; this was done by means of a VP-8 Image Analyzer, which plots shades of image brightness in relation to degrees of relief. [143]

With the help of a computer, Jackson and Jumper were able to generate a three-dimensional image of the man of the Shroud. According to the physicists, the 3-D property of the Shroud image is not present in ordinary photographs; it becomes evident only when the degree of illumination from an object is a function of distance—as in a stellar photograph. According to Jackson and Jumper, this newly-discovered 3-dimensional property of the Shroud image has striking implications for the image-formation process; it rules out artistic forgery as well as models presupposing contact between body and cloth.

An Overview on the Shroud

Our first concern is with the Shroud as a helping psychic phenomenon. Even as a work of imagination, the Shroud commands our interest, as an image forged by some person, mimicking reality with such uncanny verisimilitude as to induce belief in its authenticity and play upon our hopes for redemption from death.

The physician Pierre Barbet, for instance, used the Shroud to render clear and distinct to the imagination the brutal crucifixion that the man of the Shroud suffered. The biblical narrative tells us little of the details of the personal appearance of Jesus and certainly not a great deal of the wounds, the pains and the concrete anguish of his death. If we believe the Shroud portrays Jesus, then this anguish all comes to life in the words of Barbet and other physicians who paint the picture of the crucifixion with graphic detail and color. The realistic imagery of the suffering Savior is an aid to piety; to be able to visualize this immolation is for some a spur to faith.

Such is the view of Habermas and Stevenson, who value the Shroud as a way to meditate on the death and resurrection of Christ. Now, if we are willing to entertain Jung's belief that Christ is the archetype of the Self, then by means of contemplating the Shroud image, we enter into communion with all humanity, the deep self in each of us. The medical reconstruction of this particular death and the gruesome detail of its injustice might serve as a model of all who continue to suffer unjustly. Perhaps the value of the Shroud, part of its helping function, is to bring home to consciousness the reality of the victim: the bloody host of human sacrifices lost in history.

Even more generally, the graphic measure of Christ's death becomes a measure of the horror of all human death, a pointer to our own status as subject to death. At first it is a sobering meditation. Here is no image daubed with airy pastels. It is very blunt; it shows welts, bloodstains, broken nose, the muscles frozen in the last gasp— coarse, corporeal death. Yet, at the same time, there is the mysterious face to contemplate, the eyes that seem on the verge of opening. We can meditate on the image itself, perhaps a record of a miracle, a paradigm of transformation.

Thus we have the rhetorical function of the Shroud as a helping epiphany, which is undeniable even if we assume it is a forgery. However, nothing we have said indicates fraud, especially when we look at the interplay of data: the historical, medical, chemical and physical properties of the cloth.

The helping function increases if the Shroud is thought of as authentic. If it contains a true image of the dead Christ, it would be the supreme relic of Christianity and would be an authentic aid in contemplating the death and resurrection of Christ.

The STURP scientists were unable to form a satisfactory model of how any unaided natural process could have produced the image. Vignon's vaporograph theory apparently was the easiest to dismiss; the superficiality of the image conflicts with the hypothesis of a vapor diffusion mechanism. Variants of this theory, which assume direct contact between body and cloth to account for the image, face other objections. In addition to the image's superficiality, contact theories cannot account for the 3-D property, the fact that the image is independent of pressure; moreover, no chemicals were found on the Shroud that would explain the image transfer. Contact theories fail to account adequately for the subtle shading and accurate resolution of the image. There is the added problem of explaining how the image of the hair appeared on the cloth, since we wouldn't assume that a dead man's hair would also effuse the image-producing chemicals. Finally, if we grant that the VP-8 demonstrates coins on the eyes, then there is the problem of accounting for the image *they* produced, since, once again, it makes no sense to assume that coins effused an image-producing chemical.

In ruling out a natural process to account for the Shroud image, we are left with something we can only call *paranormal*. Schwalbe and Rogers, in a paper summarizing the 1978 STURP investigation, put it like this (they don't use the word 'paranormal'): "Briefly stated, we seem to know what the image is chemically, but how it got there remains a mystery. The dilemma is not one of choosing from among a variety of likely transfer mechanisms but rather that no technologically credible process has been postulated that satisfies all the characteristics of the existing image." [143] The helping function of the Shroud image increases with its paranormality. For many, the Shroud becomes evidence for the resurrection, serving to ratify faith in the Transcendent; the faith-enhancing function of the Shroud is significant in an age dominated by faithless physicalism. The Shroud is already the cause of a growing roster of converts. For us, it is another datum in building a new metaphysics of death.

Religion and Parapsychology

Before we proceed to speculate on the origin of the Shroud Image, some remarks on the relation between religion and parapsychology are in order. These two have been flirting with each other for quite some time now; one could show that psychical research began with transcendent aspirations. Frederic Myers, for instance, one of the founding fathers, was a poet, an incurable rebel against death, a modern disciple of the religion of the ancient sage. One suspects that similar metaphysical impulses govern the quest for knowledge in the field today, although they may be concealed, even repressed. I, for one, frankly acknowledge my interest in the paranormal as a huge, sprawling mine of *counter examples* to many of the most cherished beliefs of scientific orthodoxy. I also confess an *esthetic* attraction to the surrealism of psi, useful in the *art of derealizing the idols of reality*.

Philosophy, at least as practiced traditionally, is *supposed* to question our basic assumptions about how the world works. In every age, fundamental beliefs settle into the obvious. But philosophy cultivates an attitude of distrust toward the obvious. Psi is obviously unlikely, improbable or impossible from the standpoint of orthodox science. Therefore, to practice philosophy today in good faith, to fulfill its critical function against the idols of the obvious, would seem to call for more than a sidelong glance at the paranormal. No general picture of reality would be complete without attempting to account for the anomalies of psi.

A Three-way Street

There are at least three possible relations between religion and parapsychology. In the first, religion may look to psi studies for confirmation of already existing faith. This might occur in one of several ways. It might validate the religious world view in a general way by pointing to the reality of the unseen. Or it might help to validate certain religious practices like prayer or certain beliefs associated with religion, like the belief in reincarnation. At its worst, this form of the relationship might come to religion exploiting parapsychology for its own selfish reasons.

A similar kind of relation might arise in which parapsychology looks to religion for its own purposes; psi science, if it could overcome its skittishness, might find in the jungle of religious phenomena insights into how psi works. It might get ideas for experimental hypotheses, clues to the relation between psi and personality or hints for fresh paradigms. At its worst, parapsychology could blunder into the inner sanctum of religious realities and try to digest the realm of the holy into the dry and lifeless categories of science.

The third possibility I envisage is an erotic interplay in which both disciplines mingle, each expanding its outlook and giving up some of its idiosyncratic limitations. Here is a chance for evolution, for aspects of the human spirit, long at odds with one another, coming together in a creative *coincidence of opposites.*

Theories of the Origin of the Shroud Image

Let us assume that the image on the Shroud is what it appears to be: a paranormal phenomenon, large in magnitude and in meaning. We cannot whisk this aside as a mere anomaly of statistics. Here is a psi effect bursting with meaning; it points to something beyond itself. The image on the cloth is an image of *something.* The more compelling the case for the Shroud's paranormality, the more we are driven to speculate on what this something is. So, having made a case for its paranormality, let's not repress our need to reflect on what it might mean.

Traditional. It is natural for those in the Christian faith to interpret the mystery of the Shroud as a sign confirming traditional belief. No doubt the official view is that faith cannot and must not rest on the Shroud or on any relic or supposed miracle. To do so would be to misunderstand faith, which has its own self-authenticating logic. The Shroud, at best, might be taken as a token of confirmation of faith, a gift perhaps for the needy, for those foundering on the reef of a merely nominal, reflective faith.

So one possible interpretation might be that the paranormality of the Shroud confirms the basic faith: that Jesus was the Son of God, that he died for our sins and was resurrected from the dead; in short, that everything is as tradition has basically been saying all along. On this view, the Shroud vindicates the established belief system. It is not my wish to deny this interpretation, but I can imagine that some objections could be raised against it.

In the first place, we have to distinguish between the authenticity and the paranormality of the Shroud. It may never be possible to conclude on the former—that is, that the Shroud is the burial cloth of Jesus. However much the marks on it match the unique form of death undergone by the protagonist of the Gospels, a residuum of uncertainty is likely to remain forever. Theoretically, however, science *could* reach a consensus on the paranormality of the image. By contrast, the evidence for authenticity could never be more than circumstantial. Thus, no matter how strong the case for the paranormality of the Shroud image, *whose* image it is must remain questionable.

Minimal parapsychological. Granting the paranormality of the Shroud, it seems that one is free to take an entirely low-key attitude toward the whole question. One might favor a *minimalist* parapsychological interpretation. The basic thought here would be to grant that the Turin cloth bears an image resembling the man known to history as Jesus Christ and that there is no natural accounting for this image. But one could still say that this paranormal image is *not* unique, that it is one of a class known to students of psychical research.

To begin with, Frank Tribbe devotes a chapter in his book to the *paranormal* image of "Our Lady of Guadalupe," imprinted on a cactus-fiber cloak enshrined in the Basilica of Guadalupe in Mexico City. D. Scott Rogo [15] argues in a recent book that there are many paranormal "divine images" in history, some of them quite recent. Then there is the category of "psychic photography," or "thoughto-graphy," as Jule Eisenbud [144] calls it: certain individuals seem able to project mental images directly on instant-developing film. What all this shows is that there are many types of paranormal imagery in different mediums: linen shrouds, cactus-fiber cloths, photographic film and so on.

Thus, the minimalist might agree that the Shroud is a paranormal artifact but not that it ratifies claims of Christian theology. The mini-malist would agree that the Shroud is a mystery; but so, he might say, are the "psychic photographs" of Ted Serios. The Shroud need not be seen as a sign of the supernatural; it merely takes it place among the mass of psi effects that parapsychologists accept as a chal-lenge to science.

Toward a Synthetic Outlook

I do not see how the view of a determined minimalist could be gainsaid; the situation is likened to the response to psi in general. Even admitting the probability of psi, some will *systematically play down its importance*. Others will systematically face the most radical implications. Temperament, motive, world view and other subtle variables will determine this response. And so it is with the Shroud. Psi in general—the Shroud in particular—is a litmus for revealing one's metaphysical bias.

My bias is toward novelty, synthesis, the struggle to reconcile opposites. Let me, therefore, describe a synthetic approach. First of all, it seems to me futile to invoke psi to *explain* anything. Psi is a border concept that marks the limits of current scientific understand-ing. To say that other paranormal images beside the Shroud exist tells us very little about the origin of the Shroud. All we can say is that the Shroud and other alleged paranormal images indicate the operation of a power, principle or agency unrecognized by science. The Shroud could still uniquely express that operation and be a special avenue to understanding its significance.

My thesis all along has been that psi is evidence for Transcendent Mind. This transcendent mind factor may be at work in evolution and in that phase of human evolution called history. Christianity is one current of the spiritual evolution of humanity that expresses in dra-matic, copious and powerful ways the transcendent psi factor. True, psi appears everywhere—once in a while, even in the laboratories of parapsychologists! But the most powerful showings occur in the context of intense spiritual life, as we find in the lives of great mediums, saints and yogis. In short, the psi factor *and* the spiritual factor, taken together, represent the fuller expression of Transcendent Mind.

I think we can recognize the uniqueness of the Christian vehicle of the Transcendent without accepting Christian doctrine *in toto*. Whatever we may say about other paranormal images (and the most striking, like that of the Lady of Guadalupe, seem in any case to occur in the context of Christian archetypes), the Turin image seems like a special sign of the Christian Good News.

Already we remarked on the peculiarly Christian war on the "last enemy." The Greeks, we recall, arrived at the idea of immortality. The incorporeal factor, mind or soul, was the bearer of the "real" person and survived the death of the body. The Christian moment in the dialectic of death and rebirth adds a new motif; the incorporeal or spiritual element becomes incarnate through Christ and promises to transform matter itself into a vehicle of the eternal. It is not merely that the incorporeal element *escapes* the doom of flesh but that it transforms the raw material of the "corruptible" into the "incorruptible" body.

This is a move toward wholeness, a move beyond the one-sidedness, the abstractness of the Greek ideal. We could say that Platonism is the philosophic forerunner of Mind as telepathic (independent of the body) and Christianity the forerunner of Mind as psychokinetic (transforming the body). The physical phenomena of the Christian mystics would thus constitute—as we said in Chapter 2—*signs* of transformative Mind: the stigmata, the levitations, the blood prodigies, the inedia, the incorruption, the odor of sanctity, the host of phenomena generated by saints of past and present. The image of the body of the man of the Shroud belongs to this category. Here, a dead body, not clinically dead as in our usual NDE, but "irreversibly" dead, is traced in the act of being transfigured by an unknown psychospiritual energy. Such, at any rate, is how we might choose to see the image: as part of a pattern of evidence for an archetype of death and transcendence, a messenger from Mind at Large.

The Turin Cloth and the Archetype of Death and Enlightenment

There are several ways the phenomenon of the Shroud fits with the NDE and the ADE. The Shroud configuration, as it seems *in-*

tended to be taken, is an image of victory over death. So is the ADE an image of victory over death. Christ, the archetype of the Self, is found at the center of the classic Western NDE. Christ is at the center of the Shroud; and if it was indeed a forger who fashioned that image, it was one who knew how to pluck the chords of our collective unconscious, to stir up the ancient hope in eternal life.

Whether forgery or not, the collective unconscious of the West invests the image of Christ with the aspirations of immortal selfhood, as is apparent from the archetypal NDE. Jesus is projected into the light at the moment of death; Jesus is the symbol, if Jung is right, of the process by which each person is dismembered, crucified and reborn. For Jung, becoming a Christian was an individual process. Only an individual could become a Christian; each of us has to find our own way to wholeness. No formulas will do; there are no models to imitate without heart. The path to undividedness is personal. We have to risk being abandoned, as the man of the Shroud was abandoned and as every person is in death and dying—no empty, unassimilated form, no dead weight and no dead gestures, unfelt, unlived. Jesus gave some clues and offered some help; but like the Buddha, we must be lamps unto ourselves.

Lamps—light! Here again, the ADE, the NDE, reminds us of the Shroud and of the scientific-mythical thinking slowly building up around the Shroud. How was the image formed? The theory the scientists favor is closest to their line of work: that the cellulose in the linen fibers was dehydrated by a burst of thermal radiation of extremely short duration.

One thinks of the Transfiguration, Jesus on the mountain, in which his "face did shine as the sun, and his raiment was white as the light" (Matthew, 17: 2). Elias and Moses beamed down into his presence, luminous like space gods. The Light shows itself in many places: perhaps in the *dynamis* or "power" said by Jesus in Luke's gospel to go out of his body; the light that came down in the form of tongues of flame on the Apostles; perhaps the light that people see on the threshold of death and that envelops the soul in mystical raptures. The Shroud, thus viewed as linked with this family of transforming lights, is for me a kind of space-age icon of the archetype of death and enlightenment. Meditating on it, I see the handiwork of the collective will to vanquish the last enemy: the signature of the mysterious lover we imagined waiting for us at the end of the road of life.

PART SIX

GLOBAL NEAR-DEATH?

We who are about to die demand a miracle.

—W. H. Auden

The near-death experience has been our focus for revising the picture of Mind, the thread we followed into a network of powerful inner resources. From the NDE, we spread out into a larger psychic constellation, the archetype of death and enlightenment and, further, into a typology of helping apparitions. All this, along with the data of psi, led us to hypothesize the operation of a creative Intelligence in the evolutionary process.

It is as though a Helping Intelligence would arm us with a vision of an expanded life and direct us on an upward evolutionary path. Nor can such a conception of larger purpose, of hidden pattern and secret assistance be written off as the product of vanity, for there are palpable signs, definite proddings, evidences of a transcendent causality at work around us.

In the last chapter we discussed one such sign:

241

the image on the Shroud of Turin. Some scientists believe the image on the Turin cloth to be a photograph of what could only be the most important event in history, if it really occurred—the resurrection of Jesus. In relation to the theory of evolution, such an event would express one of the most drastic leaps in organization—certainly as drastic as the leap from dead to living matter — indeed, it would be comparable to the birth of life itself. It would constitute a second birth of living matter.

One theory to account for the formation of the image on the Shroud, as we said, refers to a flash of thermal radiation; ironically, there are shadows imprinted on cement from the nuclear explosion at Hiroshima: "shrouds" of the nuclear dead. These remnants, reminders of our great destructive power, have been compared to the image imprinted on the Shroud of Turin, suggesting to some a similarity in the way the image on the Shroud and the nuclear blast shadows were made.

There is, at least in my mind, a certain psychological appeal to relating the resurrection of Jesus to the holocausts of Hiroshima and Nagasaki. If I were to formulate this vaguely felt fascination with juxtaposing the resurrection with atomic bombs and international politics, I might say something like this.

These weapons, proliferating on earth and threatening all life upon it, are powerful indeed; they can cause nameless calamities, to be sure. Still, there is a light that is higher than this life-destroying flame, a light that can restore life from death. The world may be on a collision course with catastrophe, the outcome of the hubris of scientific civilization, but the Shroud tells us there exists something strong enough to combat this evil momentum. True enough, given the realities, it will take a miracle to reverse this momentum. But the good news is that a miracle is possible. Indeed, as Auden says, *we who are about to die* demand *a miracle.*

This brings us to our last exercise with the near-death experience. We shall now consider the prospects of a global NDE. Several things make us ponder this large and gloomy theme.

The first is that the near-death process suggests a general potentiality of the human mind at large. If so, the collective basis of the near-death experience might also be the basis of enduring collective changes in human consciousness. Jung, as noted above, took the UFO experience to be a signal of the near-death experience of Western civilization, a sign that new psychic constellations were looming on the inner horizon of humankind.

But there is something else. The need to evolve has never before been so great. The evolution of human consciousness may be our only hope for survival. Technical prowess has outstripped moral sensibility. In the collective unconscious, all the demons of Christian hells and Tibetan bardos are alive and well; but they now have at their beck and call the use of Hydrogen Weapons, Lasar and Satellite Technology, the whole arsenal of modern military technology. The ancient eschatological idea of the end of the world, of a global NDE, now confronts us as a real possibility.

The lethal mixture of primitive psychism and government-backed high tech spells the need for a large-scale transformation of human consciousness. We shall stick to one model that has the merit of being grounded in empirical knowledge: the psychic changes associated with near-death.

We pursue this uneasy speculation in four steps. In the first we argue for three points, all related to the risk of nuclear catastrophe. (A) Global near-death is a technically feasible event; (B) it is morally, psychologically and politically probable; and

(C) the tendency toward nuclear war expresses the unraveling of certain premises built into the history of our technical civilization.

Second, nothing short of a global change in consciousness is likely to avert this catastrophe. No amount of clever political jockeying, no inspired diplomatic maneuvers, no unilateral gestures of good will are likely to succeed in forestalling these terrible events. Nor will the utopian dream of world government, as conceived by philosophers like Bertrand Russell, suffice to bring to a halt the unfolding logic that underlies the Armageddon syndrome. Nothing short of a new reality principle, a kind of surrealpolitik (to counter the deadly logic of Realpolitik) will be enough to do the job. Indeed, without what we can call a state-specific morality—a morality based not upon prudential calculation but upon a deeply felt sense of human, of cosmic, solidarity—without such a metanoid transformation, at least in a critical mass of humanity, the hands of the doomsday clock will sooner or later strike midnight. All this points to an evolutionary imperative.

The third step consists of examining models for the occurrence of such a massive change in human awareness. Prospects are not heartening. On the other hand, there is evidence that the collective unconscious, the intelligence that presides over the evolution of life, is unpredictable. The future contains the promise of novelty and is beyond what we can predict or imagine. Moreover, there are powerful signs of collective awakening.

Finally, there is much in our power to do: we may yet cultivate a vision of the possible, and by means of the most transparent, the most common "psychic" power—freedom—we can forge the miracle of a new earth with our own deeds. We can, at least, refuse to cooperate with our own executioners.

With a bold and hopeful vision of the beyond, we may yet discover the courage to transform the here and now. The choice is between conforming to the lethal truth of the status quo and embracing the truths of human transformation. This indeed is the final choice, collectively speaking, that we human beings are presently being forced to make.

12
Arms and the Mind

*Of these I too am now one, a fugitive from the god
and a wanderer who put my trust in raving strife.*

—Empedocles

The expectation of catastrophe is a living myth of our time.
[145] Images of the end vary; some expect the magnetic poles to shift,
earthquakes and tidal waves to sweep us under, the shores of nations
to be fractured, the boundaries of the continents transfigured. Others
envisage the death of civilization by the agency of a new ice age; or by
some mysterious epidemic or plague; or by collision with a planetary
body; or perhaps by means of an extraterrestrial invasion of malefic
entities.

Dark, frightening visions are legion. But by far, the most credible
scenario for the apocalypse is nuclear war. Indeed, the prospect of a
major nuclear war is turning into an international nightmare. Studies
show that children everywhere are literally having nightmares of nuclear catastrophe.

Technology and Eschatology

It is often said that science supercedes myth; but in military matters, it seems that science is catching up with myth. For instance, the
old mythical idea of the end of the world, thanks to science, is now
technically possible. Old archetypes take on new realities. Related

myths assume equally eerie senses of new veracity. Take the myth of
knowledge being linked with man's downfall. The story is told in
Genesis: eating of the tree of knowledge led to the expulsion from
paradise. The myth appears in Greek tragedy, with Oedipus, for instance, blinded by his passion for insight. The theme runs through
modern science fiction, Frankenstein being the paradigm of mad scientists.

As he watched the first atomic bomb explode, Robert Oppenheimer recalled words from Hindu mythology: "I am become Death,
Shatterer of Worlds." Nuclear technology makes it possible to convert the myth of the final dissolution of the world into literal reality.
Thus, in the Iranian *Zend-Avesta*, Ahura Mazda foretells the way the
earth will perish and describes the nuclear winter that today's scientists foresee: "Upon the material world the evil winters are about to
fall, that shall bring about the fierce, deadly frost," a frost so lethal
that grass will grow no more and living things die, as they retreat to
the caves and innards of the earth. The only hope for surviving this
terminal winter is to build a Vara or enclosure, a shield; for outside, it
will be a "miracle" to behold the footprint of a sheep. Iran, of course,
is a potential flash-point for atomic war, and one wonders if the ancient seers saw darkly in their prophetic glasses current trends: the
nuclear winter that would follow a nuclear war.

The creation of man is linked in Greek mythology with the battle
of the Olympians against the Titans. The genesis of the world is
drenched in imagery of mistrust and violence, of Cronos devouring
his young, of Zeus revolting against his father. In the *Theogony* (678-
721), Hesiod paints this picture of last things before the creation of
the new order of humanity:

> Then Zeus did not hold back his might any longer, but now imme-
> diately his heart was filled with strength and he showed clearly all
> his force. He came direct from heaven and Olympus hurling perpet-
> ual lightning, and the bolts with flashes and thunder flew in succes-
> sion from his stout hand with a dense whirling of holy flame. Earth,
> the giver of light, roared, everywhere aflame, and on all sides the
> vast woods crackled loudly with the fire. The whole of the land
> boiled, and as well the streams of Ocean, and the barren sea. The
> hot blast engulfed the earth-born Titans and the endless blaze
> reached the divine aether; the flashing gleam of the thunder and

lightning blinded the eyes even of the mighty. Unspeakable heat possessed Chaos.

The myth of the destruction of the world threatens to explode into reality. Does the collective unconscious have presentiments of a new humanity through global conflagration?

The Trident was a weapon of mythology—it belonged to Poseidon, the earth-shaker, nemesis of Odysseus—an instrument of godlike destructive power. It is the name now of a gigantic submarine, a monster carrying on a secret, undetectable existence in the sea, capable of destroying 160 cities in the Soviet Union. The waters of the sea, as the myths of old said, are truly the waters of death. The death-bestowing Trident prowls the oceans, deep in the great waters; but it is also in the great waters of the unconscious. It is the murderous cannibal, the incestuous beast of the id, submerged in the sea of the unconscious, submerged in ourselves.

The Technical Feasability of Global Near-Death

That the great superpowers of the world are poised to inflict mutual annihilation is a commonplace; as a cliche of consciousness, the majority accepts it with passive resignation. Everybody knows in an abstract way that each side has thousands of nuclear weapons, many of them dwarfing in destructive power the bombs used in Hiroshima and Nagasaki. Most people, however, carry on life and business as usual. It is true that there are spasmodic displays of concern, sudden flare-ups of attention and anxiety; a movie or a book captures the nation's imagination for a while, or, as in New York, June 1982, a mass demonstration against the nuclear threat stirs the feelings of the world. Still, people go back to the business of supporting the system of everyday life that, in turn, deepens the threat of global war.

It is also true that both here and abroad, there is a growing peace movement, more or less organized under the common cause of halting, freezing, reversing the arms race. It is a movement that sees the urgent necessity for action and that, by means of education, art and politics, is struggling to mount an offensive against the increasing nuclear threat. Despite this growing awareness of the crisis, despite the evidence from polls that the average person, including children, expects a nuclear war in the reasonably near future, despite the evidence from studies that this expectation is subtly changing our sense of human connectedness, our imagery of the future and of the meaning of life, despite all the conscious awareness of the "madness," the arms build-up continues. Each side continues to feel *more* threatened, *more* vulnerable, and tries to compensate by increasing the stockpiles and sophistication of weaponry. Yet every attempt to achieve security increases our insecurity; every attempt to gain advantage exposes us to some new disadvantage. The process goes on strangely out of touch with reality, even though all the moves are made in the name of "realism." It all seems to be proceeding like a dream, a lucid dream perhaps, but one from which we cannot awaken and in which our lucidity is no help in escaping the *bardo* of the collective nuclear nightmare.

The genius for devising methods of destruction is unlimited; every medium has been exploited and all the forces of nature have been put to the rack and made to serve military purposes. It ought to give pause to believers in human potential. We need to look closely at our dark side here. It's not enough to sing the praises of the Light, for the Light has an "adversary" called the Shadow. Dante's journey to paradise began in the dark wood of everyday life. Contemporary students of the "paradise" of human potential should follow Dante's lead. The visionary light that beckons us calls for admission that we are lost in the dark wood of current realities.

To begin with, let us contemplate the *totality* of our destructive potential. Based on studies made by Physicians For Social Responsibility, there is little reason to hope that we could survive nuclear war; the totality of life is threatened. The scientists who, as a body, created the Bomb, now tell us that if we use it, we shall plunge the earth into a nuclear winter. They say that an ice, colder than the ice that traps Satan in Dante's inferno, will envelop the body of the earth and that it will freeze the roots of plants and the bones of all living things.

Though all this may seem like a nightmare, we—the collective "we" of humankind—are the wide-awake creators and sustainers of this nightmare. Let us hold steadily before our minds the *voluntary* nature of the arms race. One easily forgets that the global military apparatus, engirdling the earth and threatening all life on it, is an artifact of calculating reason. Thermonuclear warheads do not materialize directly from the demons of the unconscious; they require the organized behavior of human beings. The arsenals of murder are the handiwork of careful cooperation. It is a well-paid and prestigious business linked to long-range governmental policies, supported by argument and ideology, grounded in what is taken for a coherent moral outlook. Colossal power to kill is an ordinary and integral feature of modern life, a routine necessity, like the telephone or the automobile.

The *quantity* of destructive weapons beggars imagination. This too seems to be working against us—the inability to imagine the enormity of what we are doing. The numerical data outstrip customary scales of reckoning. The danger is vaguely sensed behind clouds of abstractions; reports in mystifying jargon filter down from remote sources and secret tribunals. I get a blurry picture when I try to imagine the world-arsenal of fifty or sixty thousand nuclear weapons. You could endlessly fine-tune analysis of the chilling data, and there are experts who do this very well. Our modern day eschatologists are masters of statistics who pack their lamentations with the mathematics of megatonnage. Still, there are only vague intimations of the horror. A nuclear war might last only an hour, less time than it takes to listen to the evening news. Civilizations could convulse in the time between a few television commercials. It is a difficult trend to imagine: as the duration of war shrinks to moments, the destructive potential expands enormously.

We are lucky to have the military establishment itself to assist us in strengthening the imagination of disaster. [146] In 1964 the U.S. Army Combat Development Command commissioned a study of the comparative destructive powers of different categories of weapons, from the javelin to the hydrogen bomb. The study quantified factors related to "weapons lethality." Some of the factors studied were: (1) the effective sustained rate of fire; (2) the largest feasible number of strikes per hour and (3) the number of potential targets per strike. "A target," as Colonel T. N. Dupuy carefully defines it, "is taken to be one man." More precisely, the "target" is thus defined and quantified: "For comparability it is assumed that the men against whom the weapon is used are standing unprotected in the open in a massed formation, each man occupying four square feet of ground." Finally, (4) relative effect is a critical factor weighted into the lethality index and defined in terms of a fifty percent or more probability of the weapon killing the target-person.

The result of this ingenious analysis was the construction of a lethality index, useful for comparative historical studies. One thing is clear: in terms of accuracy, speed and reliability, the science of murder is progressing by leaps and bounds.

The javelin is at the lowest level of murderous efficiency with a lethality index of 18; or the bow and arrow rated at a paltry 20. By the late nineteenth century—well known as the century of scientific progress—the breechloading rifle attained to an index of 230. During the First World War, the field gun leaps ahead to a crisp 34,000. To make a long story short, the study awards a lethality index of 660,000,000 to a 1-megaton airburst nuclear fission bomb. The index is again wildly inflated with the 25-megaton thermonuclear "device." We have thousands of these machines of mass destruction and are making more efficient ones every day. Progress in internecine technology is truly stupendous.

The technical potential for destruction is global. It includes much more than the destruction of human beings by human beings. The human-spawned dialectic of murder threatens the life of the entire planet. Some scientists believe, for instance, that the heat from an atomic war will melt the polar ice caps, causing catastrophic floods. The planetary ecosystem is threatened by destruction of the protective ozone of the atmosphere, apart from which we are exposed to lethal radiations from the sun. In the aftermath of atomic war, bacteria, viruses and disease-bearing insects would adapt, mutate and multiply into virulent forms. At the same time, exposure to radiation will interfere with human immune mechanisms, thus making survivors susceptible to plagues and epidemics of infectious disease.

The totality of our destructive potential threatens to disrupt the genetic code of the evolutionary process. Pediatrician Helen Caldicott [147] envisages "bands of roving humanoids" that would populate the earth after radioactive assault on reproductive organs. Nor have we said anything of the nonhuman life forms, vegetation and wildlife, that would suffer from massive doses of lethal fallout, nor of the irreparable damage to the earth's waterways, soil and forests.

The war in the souls of men sucks all of nature into a general imbroglio. Scientific man has learned to make all systems of nature serve the destructive purposes of human beings. Roughly speaking, the mechanical order is the basis of conventional weaponry. Electronics is mobilized through computer technology for lethal purposes. Biological science is pressed to serve biological warfare. Chemistry does its bit for chemical warfare. The "conquest" of space falls in line on behalf of the science of murder. Laser technology is at once seized upon as a means to laser warfare. The scientific discovery of atomic power is, of course, the most dramatic example. The atomic system of nature is condemned to serve in the ranks of human military ambitions. We even hear of efforts to harness psychic power to military goals. Although this business of psychic warfare is shrouded in obscurity, misunderstanding and misinformation, the intent is clear enough. *If* the power of the psyche, through psychokinesis and telepathy, were reliably harnessable, there is little reason to doubt that attempts would be made to exploit it militarily.

All this provides a factual basis to the growing obsession with images of the apocalypse. These images are part of our collective psychic heritage. They constellate in many contexts: in dreams, scripture, mythology, literature, art and primitive ritual. The archetype of the apocalypse exhibits death and dissolution, return to primordial chaos, followed by rebirth, a fresh order of existence. The prospect of collective death and dissolution is technically feasible. Modern destructive technology thus offers to fulfill the dreams of eschatology. At least it offers to fulfill the first part about the old earth going up in smoke. This is an odd, unexpected and unwelcome coming together of science and religion.

The Lethality Index of Ordinary Reality

Nuclear war, and hence a global near-death experience, is not only technically feasible, it is politically, morally and psychologically *probable*. That is scarcely an easy thing to say; still, I think it is true. For when we look at the political, moral and psychological facts that support ordinary reality, we find little to inspire the hope that this technical potential for the final death orgy, so long and so deep in the making, will not end by actualizing itself.

Realpolitik versus Surrealpolitik

Nuclear war technology is something under control of the state, in particular under control of the "super" states or superpowers. But the morality of the state, as Machiavelli was the first to point out, is not the same as the morality of the individual. "It must be understood," he wrote, "that a prince cannot observe all those virtues for which men are reputed good, because it is often necessary to act against mercy, against faith, against humanity, against frankness, against religion in order to preserve the state." [148] Even the most benign democracies have to admit the working truth of Machiavelli's principle. The state is an entity with a life of its own, a morality of its own.

But what we observe in the world today is something more: the phenomenon of a modern superstate or superpower, an entity with abnormal, prodigious power that threatens all lesser powers, power so godlike as to make the power of the craziest Roman emperors look picayune by comparison.

In the hands of these amoral giants lies the secret of the sun, the power to scorch the earth in the name of vital interests and ideologies. All this godlike power is in the hands of small groups of men, often of low, or even perverted, moral sensibilities. This is a bizarre feature of the nuclear age: the fate of the earth lies in the hands of men who lack the godlike status to match their godlike power.

In a meditation on the "cold" war, Thomas Powers asks "What's it all about?"—the arms race, the grimacing and piling up of more and more weapons, the logomachies of the ideologues, the planning for mutual incineration. He concludes that it is about nothing or, rather, about itself; it is about power. History tells the story many times over. When one power grows, it automatically attracts adversaries, which is a natural response to cancer in the body politic. When one power grows too great, mistrust grows among the others, and the struggle is taken up to work out a balance, to contain the threat that results automatically from the excesses of power. The pattern repeats itself. Thucydides watched the game played out between Athens and Sparta; war was the outcome, the end of a cycle of civilization. Examples from history are plentiful.

The present arms race, unique in the totality of its destructive potential, is the latest, perhaps the final, turn in the spiral of massive power pitting itself against massive power; it is the game of homo conquistador, at the edge of history. So far in the spiral of history, the game of states has always been to will power; to grow when possible, to venture forth, assert prerogatives, challenge and intimidate; to arouse mistrust, bring forth insurgence and counterforce, mobilize for the climax of conflict and then triumph or suffer defeat in war. Why should it be any different in this latest episode in the great round dance of human folly?

The whole thing goes on under the name of *Realpolitik*, the curious logic of the reality of power, the logic Machiavelli spelled out lucidly and without hypocrisy. As Richard Falk [149] writes in his essay on constraining and liberating images of the world, it is a sense of "reality," a metaphysical construct that guides the goings on of power politics in the world today. But it is no longer appropriate under present nuclear circumstances.

The temptation of the state is always to seek to *increase* power; modern military and communications technology makes the idea of *unlimited* power technically feasible. The prevailing sense of realism always demands that one move to increase power, secure the superior advantage and take whatever steps are essential to protect vital interests. To think in any other way is thought to be utopian, soft, naive, possibly traitorous or downright suicidal. Given the prevailing logic of Realpolitik, the escalation of the will to power and mutual mistrust will never cease to grow. Logically, it culminates in reliance on the *balance of terror.*

Within the circle of this sense of reality, the highest appeal is to self-interest. Self-interest is supposed to be a restraining principle—a form of rationality, limited, to be sure, but useful. Self-interest may help to delay the outbreak of nuclear war, but unfortunately it cannot abolish the risk of it. The same may be said for the idea of deterrence, admittedly the most "rational" policy possible within a Machiavellian reality framework. Nevertheless, the inherent limitations, or worse, the danger of relying on *mere* self-interest, becomes starkly apparent, perhaps for the first time, in the present age of nuclear power. Indeed, over the long run, the principle of self-interest, viewed as the final word in international politics, virtually guarantees a military denouement to this long cold war drama; for the essential power struggle, and all it implies, will not have ceased—it will only have disguised and repressed itself or, at best, signed a temporary truce.

The underlying pressure to play the old games will remain the same. In this world, anyone who tries to tamper with the principle that worships power as the only realistic basis for security is seen as more dangerous than the atomic arsenals themselves. Thus in a review of Henry Kissenger's book, *For The Record*, Gaddis Smith remarks: "Love divorced from power, Mr. Kissenger is saying, may be a profound force, profoundly dangerous. Those who walk the path of love walk the path of destruction."

The threat of unlimited power automatically creates adversaries; power corrupts, and absolute power not only corrupts absolutely but creates absolute mistrust. The very idea of *any* organization possessing the absolute power over life and death that modern technology makes possible, is intolerable. It can only increase the demand for a countervailing power. This is the inevitable outcome of the standard sense of reality: extravagant power inspires extravagant mistrust.

The past forty years demonstrate the coercive logic of this reality principle in which mutual trust is inversely proportional to expanding power. Having exploded the first atomic bomb, the West automatically threatens, or is perceived as threatening, the East. In 1949 the first bomb from the Eastern power bloc exploded. The rest is history: the arms race, ever spiraling, the Cold War, cooling and heating up at turns, the stakes and risks increasing, the global massing for conflict pushing toward "hair trigger" status.

The realities of present global politics point toward a major global conflict; however that conflict commences, by conventional or by "limited" nuclear arms, the likelihood of holding back in an all-out exchange of military force, realistically speaking, is small indeed. No state that perceives itself as threatened by an adversary will hold back power it has built up and stored, sacrificed and labored to develop, prepared and planned to use for decades; it would be folly, having gone this far, not to make a last stand. It would indeed be very unrealistic to imagine any great power, in the midst of the chaos of Armadgeddon, suddenly acquiring restraint. Lord Mountbatten said in 1979: "I cannot imagine a situation in which nuclear weapons would be used as battlefield weapons without the conflagration spreading." The bottom line is that all the rational planning will be worthless. "In warfare the unexpected is the rule and no one can anticipate what an opponent's reaction will be to the unexpected." Like Zeus in the war against the Titans, there will be no holding back of strength.

My point is that the reigning Realpolitik is pushing us toward a nuclear climax; only a reversal, not of the arms race alone but of the sense of reality that dominates the thought of the world, will help here. Only a profound *inner* disarmament could impede the inertia of history.

Ironically, America, said to be the leader of the free world, is again propelling the dialectic of destruction to new and perilous heights. The twist lies in the present development of the New First Strike Triad: the Pershing II missiles in Germany, six minutes from Moscow suburbs; the Trident II, destroyer of civilizations, prowling invisibly in the seas; and the MX System, an environmental horror, a drainer of human wealth and health, launcher of sudden death across the oceans. These are weapons whose primary military function is to strike suddenly and without warning; to "decapitate" an entire nation's intelligence and control systems and so its very capacity to strike back.

How shall we expect the USSR to respond to this plan for achieving invulnerability, on the one hand, by means of the projected "Starwars" anti-ballistic system, and our capacity, on the other hand, to *decapitate* them? The very term "decapitate," with its sinister psychoanalytic suggestion of "emasculate," is bound to make the Russian generals especially uneasy. Add to this the outrageous fact that we have categorized the USSR, in a most un-Jungian and un-Christian way, as the chief, sole and central focus of evil in the world.

It scarcely bodes well for stability. On the contrary, it raises the ante in the game of nuclear "chicken" to new levels of absurdity. An adversary now has quite a bit more to worry about. The old threat of mutually-assured annihilation is being superseded by something else. In a crisis, one has to reckon on being "taken out" first; the reasoning might follow these steps. If they *can* do it, they *might* do it; ergo, they *will* do it. After all, according to what the experts calculate, these things can be done; nations can indeed be *decapitated*, reduced without warning to nuclear graveyards. Such possibilities cast uncanny shadows on the world; they pollute the psychic atmosphere.

In a grim way, something good may come of this. The First Strike Triad brings the question of trust into relief. It forces us to reflect on this mysterious phenomenon of trust, so elusive to the techniques of science and politics. Should our adversaries trust us? We have told them we cannot trust them, so why should they be so foolish as to trust us? With all this out in the open, or even implied, we have come to an impasse. Given the reduction of politics to reliance upon military technique, Realpolitik, which commands so much respect from our worldly leaders, becomes a blueprint for eventual extinction.

There is no rational content to the logic of this form of realism any more, that is, if "realistic" and "rational" are terms taken to be connected with people of flesh and blood. "Strategists cannot offer painless conflicts," Colin Gray and Keith Payne warn us in an essay titled *Victory Is Possible*; however, an *"intelligent* U.S. offensive strategy" should manage to "reduce U.S. casualties to approximately 20 million" [150] (italics added). The authors add, however, that no strategic policy that involves the risk of *more* than 100 million U.S. casualties should be acceptable. Apparently, it is deemed "intelligent" policy to plan for a "victory" in which *less* than 100 million U.S. casualties would be in the works. The use of the word "intelligent" in this context, *justifying* the possible death of tens of millions of human beings, is surely without historical precedent.

If this is the best that "realpolitik" has to offer by way of solution to the nuclear dilemma, then the reigning system of "reality" and "reason" merits careful, critical scrutiny; we shall have to demand something that goes beyond the "acceptable" sense of reality, some form of "intelligence" less cavalier about risking tens of millions of human lives for the sake of "victory." Those utopian dreams of a new spirit, a new earth, a new reality may be the last ways of escape open to us. Grim are the consequences of submitting to the prevailing sense of "intelligence" and "reality."

Let me conclude, then, that if *realpolitik*, as it has ruled the thought of men so far, is truly a blueprint for catastrophe, then something we might christen *surrealpolitik* becomes essential for survival. A politics of surreality, so called because it would appear fantastic and "unrealistic" in the eyes of the experts, would be based on three leading ideas: the transcendence of mere self-interest, unilateral affirmation of trust and a disposition to renounce power. But to what quaint spheres of human reality can we turn for models of Surrealpolitik? Surely we cannot turn to those of everyday political and economic existence.

Moral Myopia and Nuclear Mayhem

A global near-death experience is technically feasible in the sense that nuclear military technology is a real threat to life on earth. If the argument in the section above is right, there is nothing in the prevailing reality structure of international politics that would lead us to believe that the worse will not come to pass. The most that one could hope for by maintaining the balance of terror, by sustaining the threats of mutually-assured destruction, is to postpone eventual serious confrontations, one of which is likely, by all odds, to escalate to the final calamity. Unfortunately, even this deadlock in mutual terror seems to be breaking; recent developments in American policy stress concepts of limited nuclear war and more "flexible" military options, including the use of highly destabilizing defensive and "preemptive" military technologies.

If one is to look for more hopeful alternatives to change, surely the rich moral reserves of humanity offer something of promise. Granted, the "logic" of states and superstates operates, as Machiavelli said, apart from the moral demands of individual human beings. Still, it would appear that rational people, even people devoted to the pursuit of power and the cultivation of fierce self-interest, must respond to moral suasion when faced with the obvious immorality of suicidal national policies. One would of course think this was true, especially since there have been many eloquent voices of moral protest against nuclear arms since the time of their very conception; moreover, there is a plentiful supply of "insiders" from the political and military establishment, the Eisenhowers and Rickovers, whose swan songs to public life are among the most telling outcries against the threat of nuclear doom.

Yet in spite of all this, the arms race is speeding up; there is no sign of moral protest making any real difference in the actual deployment of nuclear power. The nuclear build-up remains the same, the momentum unslowed. The voice of morality, no matter how loud it cries out, is unheard by the men at the helms of power; it is powerless to divert them from their relentless onward course. The fact that the Eisenhowers and Rickovers speak up *after* they are out of office, *after* they become powerless, demonstrates the point. Indeed, it was Eisenhower who helped create the "military-industrial complex" he railed against in his farewell address to the nation; and it was Rickover who led the build-up of the nuclear navy he finally admitted was a scourge to the human race—*after* he was forcibly retired from military service.

Freud once quipped that there was nothing wrong with Christian morality except that it was practically useless. In other words, the Christian imperative to renounce power—turn the other cheek, walk the second mile — constitutes psychologically tricky terrain. It is an ideal without any libido to back it up. The same could be said about the lofty ideals, pacts and agreements of international law; as in accordance with the Geneva Convention, nuclear arms are *illegal*. The international community has already concluded that certain rules are supposed to hold in warfare; for instance, weapons or military policies that would inflict destruction indiscriminately on civilian populations are in principle forbidden by international law. Surely atomic weapons possess huge indiscriminate destructive potential, and yet they flourish like some mutant outgrowth of the human brain.

It has often been argued by such luminaries as Bertrand Russell that a world government is essential for banishing the scourge of war and the modern weapons of war. But the whole idea of nation states renouncing power and submitting themselves to a system of global intelligence strikes at the deepest fears of self-interested, power-loving and systematically mistrustful people. To what central, single body of human beings are we prepared to surrender vital portions of our autonomy? If we could manage such an act of harmonious integration on a global scale, there would be no need for a world government in the first place. The arms race, after all, is all about trying to prevent such an arrangement of a single, all-powerful, political force from taking over the world.

Now, of course, the proponents of world government would claim that the central intelligence agency they have in mind would be composed of disinterested men and women, devotees of universal reason, with the well-being of every human soul at heart. Even if we were to suppose that such an elite bureaucracy were in secret training in the academies of ShangriLa, there would still be the problem of concretely securing power and using it to persuade or coerce the rest of unenlightened humanity.

In short, we come back to that old dilemma of Plato, who long ago warned that the human race would never cease coming to grief until wisdom and power become intimately allied. Plato, when he finally got around to trying out some of his ideas with Dionysius, the tyrant of Syracuse, barely escaped with his life. In any case, the whole idea of putting stock in a world government may be misguided; and if one is a reader of Dostoevski's Legend of the Grand Inquisitor, it may even smack of something more sinister than the arms race. Perhaps it would be more to the point to stress Max Scheler's [89] idea that the higher the spiritual value, the less power it has to coerce the world; the "power" of higher ideals depends on the generosity, the receptivity and the courage of individuals to make them come to life. It is we who have to endow the great ideals with life and libido, for they have none of their own; they are only projects, so to speak, of a higher world, of the next stage of our psychosocial evolution.

The idea of deterrence is flawed; it can only inflame the lower forces that drive us. It cannot be relied upon to activate the ideals. The ideals — ones that are essential for survival in our "reality"-infested world—do not compel or coerce; they draw us on and out of ourselves, in the manner of Goethe's Eternal Feminine.

The trouble with everyday morality is its myopia. It's alright as far as it can see, but it barely sees a few inches beyond its nose. I remember Frank Terpil's mother being interviewed on television. Frank Terpil made a handsome living selling arms (in a distinctly treasonous setting) to the likes of Idi Amin. Yet Frank's mom could only see what a nice boy her son was, how enterprising he was in grade school when he sold his first machine gun to make some pocket money. No doubt there was merit in Frank; but the overall demerit seems to have escaped the motherly perception. The tiny spot in the foreground, warmed by instinct and feeling, glows brightly; but the large, no less real, background is a huge blind spot. There is a sense in which it is hard to charge moral blame here, for one can respond morally, as sensorially, only to what one can see. The general idea that *other* sentient beings have nice qualities, and even have certain *rights*, may sit as a vague concept somewhere in us; but it may not impress itself too vividly on the whole person.

This makes me wonder if the medieval philosophers were onto something when they spoke of intuition or intellect *seeing* universals with a degree of concreteness that we deny to our nominalist abstractions. When Jacob Boehme first heard the word *Idea*, he had a vision of a beautiful garden. Perhaps Plato had something like this in mind when he spoke in mystical hyperboles of seeing the Idea of the Good, which, he said, was above existence itself. In other words, the ideals our politicians and preachers invoke as supreme may rise, at best, to the level of abstract counters; they rarely attain to an esthetically-felt sharpness. Perhaps we let the bombs multiply because we cannot imagine a world without them; that is, we cannot *see* the Idea of a better world with the details, the smell, the color, and the hum of a real garden with real dew on real flowers.

Morality is powerless when divorced from esthetics; esthetics is hollow without the directing eye of spirit. The morality of everyday life is an abstraction from God, love and beauty. Frederich Schiller, German romantic poet and friend of Kant, made this point in the *Esthetic Education of Man*. [80] The education of political man must be an education of the whole person.

The morality mouthed by those at the head of the nuclear power establishment is not the morality likely to stop the march toward nuclear disaster. For it is that uninspired, abstract and counterfeit morality that the bastions of established power continually exploit to maintain the dead hand of the status quo. A different kind of "morality" is needed, something that might not even look like morality, for it would surely have to be something that ran against conventional morality, even against conventional legality.

For instance, when Daniel Berrigan commits an act of civil disobedience and splatters blood on the nose cone of a nuclear weapon, he is breaking the law and is obviously out of tune with the morality of the workers in the General Electric plant. He is out of tune with the law-abiding citizens who are making the bombs. He is also disposed to renounce power, for to commit civil disobedience is to risk bodily incarceration. This kind of civil disobedience might count as a type of Surrealpolitik. Daniel Berrigan, and others like him, are among the rare practitioners of this art form.

To be disposed to renounce power is also a sign of an attitude toward death; since death is the ultimate power over us, every gesture of self-surrender is a gesture of freedom from bondage to the fear of death. To preserve life, we may have to come to grips with the ultimate fear of death. Needless to say, I am not alluding to such mottos of monumental idiocy as "Better dead than Red" (nor to the opposite, "Better Red than dead"). What I am saying has to do with the greatest problem raised by the arms race: the problem of inner disarmament. After all, the arms race is supposed to be about security from death. Do we not prepare for hideous death and destruction because we wish to avoid hideous death and destruction? A runaway fear of death spurs the arms race; it is an absolute need to be secure from the fear of death. Perhaps only a morality that was wed to a consciousness free of the morbid fear of death and, as a consequence, free of the morbid need for security, would be strong enough to renounce the weapons, to take the right steps and mobilize the right forces needed to begin the inner and outer disarmament of the world.

But again we come back to the theme of surrealpolitik, the idea that a new attitude toward power is needed, a different governing sense of what is real, ultimate and important. Nicolas Berdyaev, a Russian philosopher who lived through the Russian Revolution, understood the impotence of ordinary morality, of the rhetoric of high-sounding morality, for coping with the Communist will to power. Berdyaev [151] maintained that the liberal philosophy of the West is spiritually and morally unable to halt the spread of Communism, which the Russian thinker saw as a godless messianic movement, a religion capable of inspiring self-sacrifice without love, a kind of millenial dream of perfection and justice that tramples on the inwardness of individual persons.

The Communist plague—and hence the nuclear rent in the world—"is a reminder and denouncement of an unfulfilled duty, of the fact that the Christian ideal has not been achieved." Communism draws its strength from the failure of the official Christian morality of the West to respond to the demands of social justice. If Berdyaev is right, the whole rationale of the arms race is based on a vicious circle; and the point is not to fight Communism but to cease betraying our own ideals. The customary way of fighting Communism seems "calculated rather to strengthen than to weaken it. It gives new arguments to its defenders." The way to combat this *spiritual* plague is with authentic, "integral Christianity: not rhetorical, tattered, decadent Christianity, but renascent Christianity, working out its eternal truth towards consistent life, consistent culture, consistent social justice." What this means in practice is "to leave off supporting capitalism and social injustice" rather than add to the injustice that increases the appeal of Communism. Berdyaev's remarks of 1931 speak to people of today who believe, for instance, that by supporting repressive regimes to further our "vital" interests, we only stoke the fires of Communist insurgents and increase international tension.

But Berdyaev, in asking the Christian liberal power bloc of the West to forsake capitalist morality and impartially pursue social justice is asking for a miracle, a spiritual revolution. To undermine the appeal of Communism and thus to create a deep global disposition toward detente, we shall have to return to (or evolve toward) an "integral" spirituality, a surreal attitude toward power. Short of this, the ugly abortions of the spirit, the forces that thrive on decay, will flourish. Berdyaev chalked the future up to the mystery of man's freedom but saw no reason to exult in optimism.

Rumors of a Death-Instinct

The fragility of the moral imperative needs no heavy underscoring; the chasm between our moral potential and the immorality of the world is obvious. The truth is that we cannot separate morality from psychology.

The state, Plato said, is the psyche writ large. Whatever we do, say and think is in some final way mediated by the psyche; our arms are extensions of our minds, and the bombs and missiles do ultimately materialize from our minds. A discussion of doomsday and evolution, therefore, leads back to the central theme: Mind. Is there any good news from the psyche about prospects of escaping nuclear near-death?

Unfortunately, if we look at what students of human behavior have to say—including ethologists and biologists—we are faced with a disconcerting array of observations and theories. With such gloomy notions as the death-instinct, neurological paranoia, dislocated aggression, psychic numbing, archetypes on the rampage, etc., it is hard to envisage progress toward peace.

Psychoanalytic theory, to begin with, suggests that we are bent on destroying ourselves, that this sickness of the human self is tied to the process of becoming "civilized," an unavoidable offshoot of the evolution of culture. The suicidal neurosis of mankind would seem to be a toxic side-effect of living a "normal," "adjusted" life.

We owe to psychoanalysis the insight that we are not masters in our own house; indeed, our worse *enemy* is in our own house. There are forces within us that are opposed to life. Freud, like Jung, went back to mythology, to the earliest thinkers, borrowing from Empedocles the idea of two cosmic forces, Friendship and Strife (*Philia* and *Neikos*). Eros and Thanatos were the names Freud gave to the warring psychic forces: the life-instinct and the death-instinct.

We needn't examine the theory of the death-instinct here. The evidence for it, for example, in Freud's *Beyond the Pleasure-Principle,* is weak. Nevertheless, it is a useful way of referring to a mass of empirical data, suggesting a common nexus of causes that runs deep in the human condition. As a myth, the death-instinct is a counterpart to the Devil; the Devil, like the death-instinct, is the Spirit that continually negates. Both constructs point to something devoted to spoiling the quality of life. The curious thing is the way it disguises itself and mingles with high ideals.

"The philosophical act par excellence is suicide," wrote the romantic poet, Novalis, a thesis acted out by Stoics like Seneca and Marcus Aurelius. Denial of the life-instincts mixes with philosophy and religion, with high spiritual ambitions. The spirit that continually negates, the self-destructive force within, is subtle and many-faced. The theme of philosophy and suicide reminds us of Albert Camus who brashly said that self-slaughter was *the* philosophical problem. Kirilov, the quintessential hero of Dostoevskian extremes, killed himself to prove he was free. Suicide was his way of marking off a *new stage of evolution.* Kirilov reminds me of the Skoptski sect, Russians who took scripture literally and mutilated themselves, trying to force their way into the Kingdom of God. Self-destructive tendencies mingle with aspirations of transcendence. This is perhaps true of asceticism, a refined form of self-conscious suicide.

Self-destructive behavior may be allied to deep (and twisted) longings for another world, another reality. The mass suicide in Jonestown, Guyana, shows how easily people can be seduced by the rhetoric of transcendence. Rough counterparts to the Guyana self-massacre exist in the annals of history. Causes, great and small, regularly attract victims of self-immolation. Lofty ideals lure men to their destruction. Many a Nazi youth went down to dusty death spellbound by Wotan's magic sounding through Hitler's lips. The Japanese *kamakazi* pilots of the Second World War trace their life-negating heroics back to the venerable Samurai tradition of *bushido.* Buddhist monks in Vietnam made themselves holocausts, protests against American military intervention.

It is surprising how cheaply people hold their own lives, especially if one takes into account the kind of thing Karl Menninger, in *Man Against Himself,* calls "chronic suicide": the chronic invalids, the alchoholic addicts, the sociopaths, the professional complainers, malingerers, martyrs — people who slowly kill themselves by poisoning their bodies or the quality of their lives. Other writers like Theodor Reik [152] implicate masochism in the war people wage against themselves; pain becomes compulsively wed to pleasure and, by degrees, dislocates itself from pleasure entirely. The need to torture oneself ends by serving occult needs, thus allowing people to play into the hands of the dark forces.

Parapsychology adds a dimension to the talk of masochism, chronic suicide and death-instinct with *psi-missing,* the notion that we use our psi abilities to injure and thwart ourselves, should that be our dominant need. The eternal losers would not then be victims of fate but engineers of their own ruin, with a little help from unconscious psi. Once we see that psi can work on behalf of our self-destructive instincts, we can agree with Jule Eisenbud [153] that we resist psi in fear of our own possible power as death-and-ill wishers. Indeed, psi power and the death-wish make an insidious couple; even more unsettling is the thought of the death-wish conjoined to atomic power.

Plain outright suicide is on the rise, as the facts and figures show; teenagers in America seem particularly prone to performing the supreme philosophical act. Concerning the lure of thanatos, the near-death experience we have dwelt on throughout these pages may be important.

I would call attention to the possibility that suicides, outright or chronic, might have some unconscious presentiment of the intoxication of the near-death rite of passage; a vague, free-floating intuition of euphoric OBEs might, under special circumstances, ease the way to death-baiting behavior. Stories of romantic death pacts in which love, ecstasy and death dangerously cohabit could play off such unconscious allurements. So might the compulsive risk-takers, those who wax heady by playing at the edge. One gets more than a whiff of this in the life of Ernest Hemingway, whose close brush with death left him with fond memories and led him, if John Updike [154] is right, to bizarre exploits of violence and even murder. There is, in fact, evidence that some suicides do anticipate a transcendent experience; D. Rosen's [155] study of survivors who jumped off the Golden Gate Bridge and lived to tell the tale confirms this. In one case, the Bridge (itself an archetype of transition) was perceived as the way to a golden world of transcendence; and indeed, the failed suicide describes with the usual glowing superlatives his inner state while falling to probable death.

What interests us here is how all this translates into the doomsday question. The myth of an evil principle, a dark destructive force with eschatological potential, is entrenched in the collective psyche. But the mixture of destructive psychic tendencies and great technological power makes our current situation historically unique. In a brilliant book on this subject, *Life Against Death* by N. O. Brown, the author puts it like this:

> Freud was right: our real desires are unconscious. It also becomes apparent that mankind, unconscious of its real desires and therefore unable to obtain satisfaction, is hostile to life and ready to destroy itself. Freud was right in positing a death instinct, and the development of weapons of destruction makes our dilemma plain: we either come to terms with our unconscious instincts and drives—with life and death—or else we surely die. [156]

Back in 1950 (Brown's book appeared nine years later) the Dutch psychiatrist, Joost Meerlo, also wrote of the dangers of the Bomb and the suicidal tendencies of the human race. "Even with such immense technical power in his hands, man feels incapable of coping with his fate. He does not know how to deal with the danger of the Bomb mainly because, unconsciously, this danger attracts and fascinates him. So strong is the suicidal tendency in us that we can easily turn our technological tools and toys against ourselves." [157] Meerloo's point is that guilt and helplessness are apt to create suicidal panic; his book, which is on panic, gives many shocking examples in war and life of people driven to jump like zombies into the abyss. The specter of the Bomb itself inspires feelings of helplessness and threatens to hypnotize us into suicidal submissiveness.

Different writers stress different aspects of the potential for global suicide. Meerloo picked out guilt and helplessness; more recently, Robert Jay Lifton has focused on psychic numbing before the threat of nuclear death. Lifton has also connected the Bomb with the problem of transcendence and finds a danger in the image of transcendence linking with the bomb itself. He suggests something quite startling: that in the absence of adequate imagery of transcendence, the bomb itself might become the image of transcendence.

> We have descriptions of the sense of awe and transcendent power and even beauty experienced by witnesses of bomb tests and by both perpetrators and victims of the two atomic bombings of cities. These provide glimmerings of—for some, enticements toward—experiencing the inexperiencable. In psychological terms that could mean overcoming one's imagery of extinction and radical future-lessness by means of what may be perceived as the only form of transcendence worthy of the age, that provided by the weapon itself. [149]

If Lifton is right, the danger of the Bomb is increased by the prevailing dogma of annihilation, the lack of a viable image of transcending death. The pathology of the prevailing death imagery may increase vulnerability to the destructive forces within. It becomes harder to resist the pull of the imagery of extinction. If this is so, it underlines the need to dig deeper into ourselves, deeper than the darkest depths of the Freudian unconscious, if we wish to rediscover a healing imagery of death. In the absence of that higher imagery, imagery strong enough to overcome the despair of "radical future-lessness," there is the danger that our vulnerability to the bizarre enchantment of transcendence by nuclear death deepens.

There is a danger of millenial psychosis. Lifton deals with the problem in a chapter on nuclear fundamentalism. Oddly enough, it surfaced in 1982 with Admiral Rickover expressing his belief that nuclear war was inevitable, and his musing that a "better species" might come after us. Rickover uttered an extreme proposition of surreal politics when he said that getting rid of the Defense Department was the best thing we could do to increase our security. But to speak of a *better species* that would hopefully spring from the ashes of atomic holocaust shows a leaning toward millenial fantasy.

Certain collectively ingrained beliefs influence our behavior by playing on age-old hopes and dreams. One of those dreams is that at the end of a thousand-year cycle, the world is supposed to change radically or come to an end. But the expectation of the end is also the hope for a new beginning. One wonders if the many people, often children and youth who polls say expect nuclear war in the near future, are not responding to such ideas percolating in the collective psyche. Suppose that the collective psyche is primed periodically to experience large-scale breakdowns and renewals. In traditional cultures, such a need might be satisfied through various rites of passage. The danger arises that in our de-ritualized and de-sacralized culture, such needs might unconsciously seek profane and more disastrously literal outlets.

Given that the quality of global life is indeed becoming impoverished, along with the assumption that a collective psychism is priming us with images and expectations of the end, we have further reason for concern about the present conflict between the superpowers. The millenial dream is a major expression of the archetype of death and enlightenment, raised to cosmic proportions. The danger of this archetype of death and rebirth is that, with the help of Western technology, it has the power to historically actualize itself. The archetype in question is very old. We find it in the ancient epic of Gilgamesh, the hero who crossed the "waters of death" in hopes of capturing the secret of immortality. It is possible that collective presentiments of such a journey across the "waters of death" are presently constellating in our historical, profane and increasingly unstable consciousness.

We need to consider the possibility of such a deadly interplay between our inner and outer life. All the ingredients of a lethal mix are present: instability of external circumstances, powerful but unchanneled internal needs and a technology able to translate spiritual chaos into material catastrophe.

Paranoia Against Metanoia

Throughout this book, we have used the term *metanoia*, borrowed from the New Testament and referring to the deep and pervasive change of outlook that often follows the experience of ego-death. By changing a prefix, we come to another word suggesting an opposing mental syndrome, one that figures in our discussion of the push toward global near-death: *para*noia. The Soviets are often said to be "paranoid," though I do not think that they have exclusive rights to the term. As far as our discussion of the increasing probability of nuclear war and hence almost certain global near-death, the question of paranoia merits a brief excursus.

Militarism would never flourish were it not justified by fear and suspicion of those who are—or only seem to be—our adversaries. The distinction has a way of getting blurred in day to day practice. In an atmosphere of prolonged fear and hostility, the distinction between a "real" and a "perceived" threat is sometimes hard to maintain. As William H. Kincade admitted with surprising candor:

> Such is the nature of strategic planning and the state of mutual fear, however, that whatever scenario can be conceived as a possibility, even a remote one, is usually perceived as a threat. *When 'threat' is used here, therefore, it connotes the perception of a threat.* (Italics added.)

Thus, in the military world of strategic planning, the distinction between possible and real, imagined and occurrent, threat evaporates in the sultry atmosphere of mutual fear. A nuclear war might erupt on the basis of what, in effect, was the hallucination of danger. The inability to distinguish between real and imagined threats is one mark of the "paranoid" personality. When, moreover, mutual fear is enhanced by mutual aggression, the resemblance to paranoia becomes more striking.

The term "paranoia" and its variants, "paranoid" and "paranoiac," have entered the general vocabulary. "Paranoid" is used to refer to a state of extreme, unreasonable suspiciousness, though when international tensions increase, it is often difficult to draw the line between reasonable and unreasonable. Would it be unreasonable, for instance, for the men in the Kremlin to be "paranoid" knowing that, according to the U.S., they are the chief focus of evil in the world, or knowing that we refuse to renounce the first strike option; are at present developing a New First Strike Triad; and are planning to develop a "Starwar" anti-ballistic invulnerability?

In such an atmosphere, suspiciousness will predominate, and it is impossible to predict what action or remark is liable to be *perceived* as threatening. It is this ambiguity, this hair trigger, flash-point mentality that is perhaps the greatest present danger. A politics of the surreal would have to search the origins of this mentality and try to discover ways of disarming it.

If we go back to Book Nine of Plato's *Republic*, we find a portrait of the tyrant, and though the word "paranoid" is not specifically used, the resemblance to modern descriptions is noteworthy. To begin with, the tyrant perverts the erotic. He is a man driven to act out his dreams, derelict of restraining reason, unable to discriminate between reality and fantasy. For him, too, the distinction between perceived and actual threat has dissolved. Inwardly divided, at odds with the world, the tyrant is a faithless and friendless being. He is preoccupied with carefully marking out and showing favor with his friends while always sharply fixating upon and berating those who are not; but this is only a symptom of his deep proneness toward infidelity, his inability to be friends with himself, which Plato said in the *Republic* was the essence of injustice.

The tyrannic soul, slave of unfulfilled desires, lives in constant fear of those whom he oppresses, "full of terrors and alarms." The unhappiest of beings, governed by unnamed forces within, he feels compelled to dominate all forces without. For Plato, the tyrant's insatiable quest for power is a way to make up for a deformed erotic capacity. The tyrant, at bottom, is the great unsatisfied lover. Much of this, by the way, resembles Wilhelm Reich's portrait of the fascist mind, also a product of deformed eroticism. The general theme went to the heart of Herbert Marcuse's critique of the "tyrannical" dimension of modern capitalist society. Marcuse and Reich, like Plato, understood that psychological categories were also political categories (Plato's state as soul writ large) and that if we want to change the repressive power structure of the world, we have to change the psyche of humankind. The disposition to renounce power, the shift toward a more trusting and less violent and exploitative lifestyle, here depends on a revolution in basic human relations.

It was Freud who gave the classic psychoanalytic interpretation of paranoia. Based largely on the celebrated case of Schreber, Freud understood paranoia as an unconscious defense against repressed homosexual wishes. The mechanism of paranoia, as Freud describes it, is quite interesting, especially if we disentangle it from its exclusively homosexual focus.

A homosexual wish, "I love him" undergoes a series of denials, repressions and transformations. First, "I love him" becomes "I do not love him—I *hate* him." But an internal feeling is disposed to become an external perception. It is thus further transformed, by the mechanism of projection, to "He hates me, is persecuting me." In the world of psychoanalysis, the law of contradiction is overturned, and affirmation becomes negation. Love is mangled into hate. The subversion of logic and concealment of truth happens via projection, which is a way of getting rid of an intolerable, inner contradiction. "In delusions of persecution the distortion consists in a transformation of affect: what should have been felt internally as love is perceived externally as hate."

It may be worth noting here that war and warlike activities (which include a fair share of paranoia) are mainly pursued by the masculine half of the human race. If Freud is right about paranoia, then part of the psychic roots of war may lie in the defensive attitude of men who cannot cope with their unconscious need to love other men. In our age of nuclear warfare, an involuntary phallic symbolism of missile weaponry offers some food for thought.

To entertain this hypothesis, however, we need not confine ourselves to a homo*sexual* conception of love. We might, in a broader vein, say that the paranoia that nourishes masculine warlike tendencies is the result of denying homo*eroticism*. Homoeroticism, let's say, means strong emotional bonding between members of the same sex. Platonic, sapphic and whitmanesque models come to mind, along with the agapaic and chivalrous love that nurtured the Christian tradition. Since such emotional bonds are always liable to produce regressive homosexual associations, they are naturally exposed to the risk of repression. This *generally contracted capacity for love* would make a fertile matrix for paranoid thinking.

The Freudian account of paranoia brings something else out. In paranoia, libido withdraws from the external world. "I do not love you," becomes "I do not love anybody, anything." But the libido must go somewhere, so it fixates on the ego. Thence arises the megalomania of the paranoiac. Delusions of grandeur are the obverse of delusions of persecution. One way to sustain delusions of grandeur is to acquire power, a way of ratifying the infinite love of the ego and mollifying the infinite fear of the other.

There would then seem to be a strong link between the need for power and deficiencies in the erotic sense of reality; the greater my ability to love, to open myself out in trust before the world, the less need have I for power, the symbol of the potency of my ego. All this contrasts sharply with metanoia, in which the ineffable overflows the boundaries of the ego, and the importance of symbolic power is diminished. Metanoia is the psychic antipodes of paranoia.

Psychoanalysis has stressed the *systematic* character of paranoid delusions and their protective function. Once the libido or life-force is withdrawn from the world and focused with mad intensity on the ego, the outside world is seen as more threatening. The paranoid mode is ruled by a self-contradictory logic: attraction is perceived as repulsion—love, as we remarked earlier in connection with Kissinger, becomes a dangerous path to destruction. The paranoid world view, if we may so speak of it, demands the exclusion of the irrational—of the erotic. They threaten to break through the wall of repression. Paranoia is totalitarian; it wants to keep everything under the surveillance of its sharply focused light and does not feel comfortable in the presence of shadows and ambiguities.

Sandor Ferenzci, a radically-minded Freudian, made an interesting comparison: "Philosophical systems that seek to explain rationally the whole order of the world, leaving no room for irrationality (i.e., for what is not yet explicable) have been, as is well known, compared with the paranoiac delusional systems." The paranoid mentality thus locks itself into the straight-jacket of the system.

This contractedness tallies with descriptions of totalitarian oppression. Here, for instance, is what Jacobo Timerman has to say about his Argentine oppressors: "The chief obsession of the totalitarian mind lies in its need for the world to be clearcut and orderly. Any subtlety, contradiction, or complexity upsets and confuses this notion and becomes intolerable. Whereupon an attempt is made to overcome the intolerable by way of the only method at hand—violence." [158] Or, take another example, an eyewitness account of life in the German concentration camps. Eugen Kogan writes of the men who volunteered for Hitler's Elite Guard: "Their minds were enclosed by a hard shell consisting of a few fixed, dogmatic, effortless, simplified concepts underneath which lurked a flood of inchoate emotionalism." [159]

The paranoid cognitive style is brilliantly narrow and forcefully exclusive, as David Shapiro shows in his book, *Neurotic Styles*. [160] The contraction in capacity for love leads as well to a contraction of intellect and world view. Paranoid suspiciousness betrays a fear of contact with the newness and strangeness of things; intelligence turns into an instrument of *defense* rather than of discovery. One thinks at once of the "defense system," so increasingly central to the "security" of the modern state. The danger we have to consider in the light of these reflections is that scientific intelligence, which is the crowning achievement of the modern world, in serving the aims of the military, is becoming an instrument of the paranoid cognitive style.

To counter this dangerous tendency, science, I believe, needs to return to its roots in Greek philosophy, which, as the etymology of the word shows, was guided by the love of wisdom. In a word, the challenge is to *eroticize science* before science falls completely under the dominion of the paranoid will to power.

But before we push all this too far from ourselves, consider this. If we are to take Sartre's analysis of human relations seriously, the potential for paranoia is rooted in the nature of ordinary consciousness itself. Let us use as our text some words from a chapter of *Being and Nothingness* [161] entitled "The Look." Sartre writes: "Thus being-seen constitutes me as a defenseless being for a freedom [that is, for Sartre, another conscious being] which is not my freedom." When the Other *looks* at me, I become an object for that Other. *How* I am objectified and *that* I am objectified escapes, in principle, my power to control. I am defenseless against the freedom of the Other. The Other may think of me as he will, secretly despise me, inwardly hold me in contempt. Indeed, even insofar as he admires and places a positive evaluation on me, he does so in such a way that I remain an object for him. I remain defenseless—even against his *good* will.

It is easy to see how I might assume a paranoid stance toward the Other, for I can *never* be sure of what the Other is thinking of me. In the absence of that certainty, I am free to project the worst possibilities. In principle, I can never verify what the Other is thinking of me, how he is transforming me into an object. The thought that I am inescapably *exposed* to his look—to his secret judgment—is by itself enough to intensify my mistrust of him. Normal relations thus contain the seeds of paranoia, for all normal relations presuppose an essential defenselessness. All human relations, no matter what the overt structure, involve a basic vulnerability. The freedom of other human beings is always liable to be seen as a threat, an invisible danger, as something that might negate, objectify and possibly over-whelm me. Ordinary consciousness is therefore latently paranoid.

The paranoid potential is latent in ordinary consciousness; it is at work in the way civilization takes its routine toll on us through the perversion of the erotic; through a truncated version of the ego and what is thought to be its vital interests; and through a narrowing of the intelligence for defensive and aggressive purposes. Paranoia, in this sense, is shown by Freud to be the unavoidable fruit of life in higher civilized society. The gloomy prognosis in *Civilization and Its Discontents* is that repression of the life force leads to aggression and guilt. Wars will only increase with the advance of civilization, which demands continual sacrifice of the life-instincts to the demands of the prevailing reality-principle. So, while civilization lays the psychic groundwork for war, it also promotes the technical means to give full vent to the hostilities it creates. If Freud is right, civilization, as it is evolving, based on repression and high technology, is its own worse enemy. Meerloo's and Brown's belief in a collective suicidal tendency is confirmed.

Others, like Konrad Lorenz, have traced the increase of human violence to the frustration of aggressive behaviors which, at least at one time in the history of our animal evolution, served an adaptive purpose. Once again, the culprit is man-made civilization, which ag-gravates biological aggression, though it fails to provide adaptive out-lets for it. And once again, the technical side of civilization magnifies the danger of forces within us.

Man must therefore evolve into a new kind of animal with a new kind of civilization; for in its present condition, driven by surplus aggression and armed with a murderous technology, it is slated for extinction.

Arthur Koestler [45] and Paul McLean [162] have theorized on what they call the "paranoid streak" in man deriving from certain flukish developments in the human nervous system. The main idea is that the human animal suffers from a dissociation of the cognitive and feeling centers of the brain; hence, there is the tendency to feel pervasive and objectless fear and suspicion for no good objective rea-son. Victims of this schizophrenia of heart and mind become prone to hunt for scapegoats, "causes" and other convenient abstractions onto which to project their free-floating terrors and hostilities. Whatever the explanation—twisted libido or cognitively dislocated fear and aggression—the possibility of a "paranoid streak" in humankind is something we cannot afford to ignore. It ranks very high among the stumbling blocks to our psychic evolution. The real conflict, then, that threatens the world today is not between East and West, Communism and Capitalism; it is the conflict between the paranoid and the metanoid potentials of the human animal at the crossroads of evolution.

13

The Thanatos Conspiracy

*I do not know what horrors may be in store for us,
but no one can doubt that, unless something very
radical is done, scientific man is a doomed species.
In the world in which we are living, there is an
active and dominant will towards death which has,
so far, at every crisis, got the better of sanity.*

Bertrand Russell

For forty years the great powers have been preparing for war.
Never before in history has such destructive power been readied for
use. It is agreed that its full use will certainly cause irreparable harm
to life on earth. The mythology of the end is on the threshold of
exploding into stark reality. We have been musing on the odds
against all this happening, looking at the question from different angles and wondering what resources offer hope. The result so far has
been discouraging.

Of course, there are things in the works: peace and human potential movements; changes in the official stances of religious communities, in the medical, legal and teaching professions; coalitions of
women, preachers, ecologists, radicals, liberals, conservatives, dissi-
dent communists and new-age capitalists. But none of this has
slowed the momentum of the arms race one iota; mammoth outlays
for the new weapon systems are on tap, the routine rhetoric and
doublespeak goes on as usual. There may be lulls in the rhetoric of
belligerence, but they do not reflect a real trend toward peace.

Reflecting on the large patterns, one is obliged to agree with Russell that in a crisis we usually let the will to death dominate the will to

277

sanity. As Mazzini said, history is no party to our cause. The lesson of history is that when nations prepare for war, they make war. Of course, world leaders agree: atomic war is not acceptable as a way of resolving political disputes. The planet-destroying arsenals are justified by their deterrent uses. Yet there seems little in current morals and politics to inspire confidence in these demurrings. Political "morality" is admittedly no respecter of persons; personal morality, however lofty notionally, lacks libidinal foundations. Indeed, normal psychology only increases our misgivings—the human soul is divided against itself, as much, perhaps, in love with death as with life. Against all claims of reason, self-interest and morality stands the insidious lure of the death-instinct. Above and beyond politics and ideology, steeped in the hidden byways of our civilized way of life, is something else with which we have to reckon: the thanatos conspiracy.

What I mean by the *thanatos conspiracy* is an extension of what Edward Thompson [163] describes in an essay, "Notes on Exterminism, the Last Stage of Civilization," and of what Robert J. Lifton and Richard Falk mean by "nuclearism." [149] These authors see in the nuclear peril an addiction to a *syndrome* of moral, political and economic attitudes and practices. The nuclear peril is the logical conclusion of a way of life, the self-destruct denoument of a civilization.

Thompson writes that the Bomb creates a "field-of-force which engenders armies, diplomacies and ideologies, which imposes client relationships on lesser powers and exports arms and militarisms to the periphery." The Bomb draws everything into its orbit and casts a spell on the whole world; a component of a weapons *system* manned and bolstered by a social *system*, it organizes a vast work force, research and academic centers, special skills and intricate security systems. This industry of death acquires its own self-justifying dynamic and generates the need for its constant self-advance. The profit motive and bureaucratic inertia contribute to the exterminist momentum, quite apart from the ideologies of the "central human fracture." Nuclearism, while widening the world split, ironically becomes a kind of religion we rely on for "security." The Bomb becomes the idol to which we sacrifice the wealth of nations.

The Bomb, as Thompson says, symbol and active force, is driving us to the final stage of civilization, the conclusion of a long-evolving network of premises; it is a symptom, the most fatal, of a deeper disease. We had our hint already from Empedocles and Freud: the Bomb is the symptom of the cancer of the death-instinct. It has already begun to "explode"; it has been sending its fallout on the winds of the earth for a long time. Lifton puts us on the trail of the diagnosis when he says, "The sustained destruction of nature by our poisonous industrial substances takes place before our eyes as a kind of prefiguring of a final, natural Armageddon." There is an underlying connection between the assault on the environment and the deployment of nuclear weapons. It is part of the same pattern, the same logic of exterminism; it is part of a conspiracy of the death-instinct, the genius of thanatos, deep-rooted in evolving man, the eternal adversary against life, and known under many guises of the mythical imagination.

Nihilism, as Nietzsche said, the uncanniest of guests, is standing at the door. He brings dark tidings and casts a shadow on familiar places, chilling the air with fearful presentiments. In what follows, I describe some notes from the nihilist-exterminist motif; the important thing is that each note is linked together and that *together*, they make the songs of the Sirens of Thanatos.

Materialism as Nihilism

There is a link between the way scientific philosophy evolved in Western civilization and the growing risk of nuclear war. Modern science—since Galileo's new physics—thinks little of ends, purposes and values. It aspires to ideals of pure objectivity, quantifiable truth and high predictability. The human perspective—the internal world of "secondary" qualities—is pushed aside, irrelevant to truth. About the metaphysical implications of the Galilean revolution in physics, Edwin Burtt wrote, "Man begins to appear for the first time in the history of thought as an irrelevant spectator and insignificant effect of the great mathematical system which is the substance of reality." [164] Now it is open to us to demonstrate our "relevance" in the scheme of things by learning to act upon the forces of the "great mathematical system" of nature. Performance is the measure of scientific truth, the measure of our metaphysical status in the world. Science, a method of intervention in nature, becomes a means for reasserting our identity in the presence of cosmic indifference.

Edward Teller, developer of the hydrogen bomb and believer in its uses, once said that "we would be unfaithful to the tradition of

Western civilization if we shied away from what man can accomplish." [165] Teller associates making the hydrogen bomb with fulfilling the duty of Western civilization.

The H-bomb simulates the solar creation of energy. Western science has captured the secret of the sun. We could almost feel we recovered our ancient link with the gods. We know how powerful we are by the measure of our capacity to threaten all life on earth. We are becoming the gods of death, destroyers of worlds, as Oppenheimer said when the first nuclear bomb exploded.

Seen in this way, the Bomb marks the closing of an evolutionary cycle. Western civilization, a product of planetary life, can trace its birth back to the sun. Yet from the sun, it has captured the power to destroy itself, to cancel the labors of billions of years of cosmic evolution. Thus the Fall as defined biblically is complete: Adam has eaten of the tree of knowledge, known the power to inflict good and evil, and is thus like god. The Bomb brings us to a watershed in evolution. According to orthodox biology, life began by chance; ironically, it may end by plan.

Of course, it makes no sense to blame "science" solely for the current impasse. Still, we may ask—is there anything in the scientific enterprise, as it developed in the Western world, that paved the way for this complicity with terminal nuclearism? Is there something in the Western way of doing science that lends itself to degrading, threatening life on earth?

There is a trend in science—not to be identified with science as a whole—a kind of totalitarian will to explain, reduce and control all things by means of physical concepts. This trend, since the Renaissance, has been successful in stamping its image on every aspect of life. Modern science evolved in such a way that it came to hold as suspect the reality of subjectivity, feeling, inwardness and privacy—consciousness itself. This, I believe, is the cornerstone of a general pattern of destructive invalidation. Reality materialized does contract our sympathies and deadens us to the diversity of being.

Behaviorism—still an imperious voice in psychology—sounded the death knell of consciousness, pronounced it a useless vestige of superstition and banished it from scientific discourse. If consciousness is reduced to an epiphenomenon, a shadow being, it is not likely to fare well after life. Materialism decrees personal extinction in the Beyond. Science provides the machinery hastening extinction here and now. Nihilistic science is totalitarian.

The negation of the living earth by nuclear weapons is prefigured in the negation of consciousness by materialist metaphysics. Animism, the philosophy of primitives, respects the rivers, forests, mountains and oceans—because they are *alive*. By contrast with primitives, Nature is a dead affair to modern science. For us it is easy to strip-mine Mother Earth. Animism, respecting the globe as a living entity, is the opposite of modern materialism, which reduces life to mechanism, banishing consciousness itself.

The germ of tyranny already lay in the thought of Democritus. Nothing exists, he said, but atoms and the void. This is a bold leap of intuition that simplifies the wild profusion of the world's phenomena. It is at once the glory and the malady of the human intellect—the will to proclaim that nothing exists *but* one particular kind of thing. The dream of modern science is to catch the butterfly of the universe in the fist of a single theory. I choose, for the moment, to highlight the sinister side of this venture.

Consider the following interrelated phases of the quantitative way of organizing reality, a way that ends by invalidating color, queer irregularities, unrepeatables and anomalies. We need to look at the total pattern. The roots of the machinery of mutual annihilation are habits of thought, deeply ingrained in the abstractions and categories we use to shape our vision of the world:

(1) Begin with the secularizing of existence. The credentials of the sacred derive from certain special revelations of consciousness. To deny the reality of consciousness is to deny those special revelations and, hence, to desacralize the world.

(2) Next, the world of native lifestyles, customs, beliefs and myths suffers from the same contempt. The culture of the computer, fast food, the automobile, etc. forms the template for a world culture; the ways and means of native traditions are dismissed.

(3) Third, if there is contempt for cultural pluralism, there is a more terrible contempt for the plurality of life forms. The opulent variety of nonhuman life forms suffers dearly at the hands of clever *homo technicus*. Since the creatures of air, sea and land are just complex machines—soulless and unconscious—shouldn't they be properly *utilized* to satisfy our needs, real or imaginary? Why demur to incorporate animal *material* into our factories, our industries, our systems of profiteering? The nonhuman, of course, are defenseless against our guns and exploding harpoons.

(4) Fourth—and needless to say—the inanimate, the "environ-

ment," is there, at hand, "raw material" to be exploited. An aboriginal, an animist—one who imputes consciousness to stones and rivers—might scruple over exploiting nature; but a materialist true to his philosophy never would. Materialism is the great leveler, the philosophy of a dead universe.

Indeed, if everything is *matter*, then everything is *material*—material *for* someone, accent on the dative case. The invalidation of consciousness justifies melting down the plurality, the diversity of being into raw material for human consumption. A homogenized universe is the final product, a universe in which a kind of legalism of the abstract intellect dominates diversity and individuality.

The dialectic of destruction is a distortion, a tragedy of cosmic dimensions. Its aggressions and agonies penetrate beyond the human sphere, and are a scourge to the whole planet. Human destructive potential is no petty, local affair. The whole of creation groans from this sickness, this infection of being from the virus of exterminating reason. Nihilism, the power of negation, proliferates like nuclear weapons, the activity of soulless brains in concert.

Consider this piece of ugly irony. Materialist science threatens the material basis of life. The material quality of life is eroding as a result of the arms race; vast labor, wealth and resources, diverted from human needs, are shunted into the gorge of the nuclear Leviathan. The culture of the Bomb, the dangerous apex of scientific materialism, is an enemy to material life. The cruel diversion of resources from the needs of material life foreshadows the total devastation of life, the culmination of nuclear nihilism. This perversion of priorities, this real and present wasting of life's precious resources, is a prominent part of the thanatos conspiracy.

The Triumph of the Secular

Materialism leads to a secularized world. There is little breathing space for the age-old dimension of experiencing the sacred. The sacred dimension calls us beyond ordinary life. It sets up boundaries; stop here, it proclaims—you may go no further. For instance, the ethics of Kant, based on the sacred kingdom of ends, on the sharp distinction between ends and means, does not allow one to think, as our military planners do, of sacrificing one hundred million persons or intrinsic ends to ideological victory.

The person of presecular societies lived the basic categories of life—space, time, nature, work, sexuality—in a distinctive way. All objects and events are possible openings into another world: the house in which you live, work, marriage and dying. Human life, from the sacred perspective, is a rite of many passages, a ritual of many deaths and rebirths. The sacred mode of being overflows with chances for inner growth. Every juncture of existence, the minor by-ways and the major gaps and impasses, offers openings to a life-enhancing source. The most negative of events, illness, chaos and death, allow, in a sacred world, for renewal, reintegration on a higher plane.

The sacred universe lives by the law of compensation: if you fast from the senses, you may obtain the gifts of the spirit; if you embrace suffering aright, you court supernatural joy; if you know how to let go, surrender the obvious advantage, learn perhaps the craft of dying, an alternate resource becomes available, the promise of a new kind of power, an abundance of new life. The world, according to the sacred view, is a complex symbol, a living conduit to a greater, un-seen well of being.

Modern secular man has little taste for this. No longer a mystery to contemplate, an invitation to love, a path to a wondrous journey, the universe becomes an endless puzzle to solve; for technology, it becomes a stupendous factory to exploit.

The triumph of the secular condemns the average person to a world of diminished meanings. Sex becomes gratification, play a tranquilizer, work the getting of wages. It now becomes possible to think of our appearance on earth as essentially devoid of meaning, the upshot of millenia of random atomic mutations, the aimless play of chance. The materialist conception of death as annihilation mirrors the conception of life as void of meaning. Nullity seeps into our im-ages of life and death. The idea of nuclear holocaust is the logical endpoint of a dead universe without meaning; it looms before us as a kind of vengeance against ages of vain human aspirations; and it mocks the impotence and hollowness of ideals of progress and per-fectability.

Knowledge of the world is incomparably richer from the discov-eries of natural science; but the world of possible experience, in may ways, has pitifully shrunken. The road of transcendence, the high-way to the world's sacred realities, is blocked; science has erected a sign on it that reads in large letters: DEAD END. So, in a sense, the

Bomb has already dropped; we live in a spiritual wasteland contaminated by the fallout of unmeaning, polluted from the stench of dead gods and rotting ideals.

The Erosion of Indigenous Lifestyles

In a conflict between two cultures, the one armed with superior technology usually prevails. The culture of the Native American fell before the European musket. The countries with the biggest guns write the history books, define peoples as "civilized" or "savage," draw the maps that peg parts of the world as "third" or "developing."

Ours is the century of the refugee. There are millions of dislocated people in transit from their native lands and homes—people living in camps, on boats unable to disembark, on borders between hostile countries, in reservations, gulags and concentration camps. In the great cities of America, lost amid lush forests of high-risers, there is a growing nation of the homeless. Being physically uprooted from one's native land is only an extension of being spiritually uprooted from one's native tradition. Exiles in inner space end as exiles in physical space.

The world is crowded with exiles, refugees of technocracy: Native Americans, Tibetans, Eskimos, Vietnamese, Cambodians, Australian Aborigines, Africans. The list could be extended indefinitely—human beings whose traditional way of life, material and spiritual, has been uprooted by "progressive" ideologies backed by invincible technology.

Native beliefs and customs embody philosophical statements, general forms of life. They represent centuries of cultural evolution, patterns of adjustment to varied environments. Yet the march of our nuclear civilization is sweeping the forms of native life into oblivion. But these forms of life, victims of technocratic nihilism, may have things to teach us.

Consider, for instance, the Papago Indians of the American Southwest whose song magic controls their use of power. The warriors of this gentle tribe, who adapted themselves to their desert world, used song magic to gain and master power. "He must train himself for its use and through all his life go in fear that his dreadful weapon may turn against him," wrote Ruth Underhill [166], who lived with the Papago in the 1930s. One would like to see a comparable wisdom among our own military and political big chiefs, a little more in the way of "savage" scruples about the dangers of power.

The uprooters are themselves uprooted; we live as refugees from our own traditions. We are refugees in our own land because the culture of the Bomb has displaced the culture of our ancestors; we worship the idol of the Bomb, trust in its power as the basis of our security. The culture of nihilism has put up a barrier between ourselves and the helping powers of our native traditions. Extinction of species of spiritual life also foreshadows nuclear extinction. The homogenization of world culture is a deadly side of the thanatos conspiracy.

The Assault on Nonhuman Life Forms

Technocratic man, the greatest hazard to wildlife, has diminished what is by destroying many species of life by hunting, by industrialization, by intensive agriculture or by the elimination of the natural habitat of animals. Countless species of life have been extinguished or are threatened with extinction. This is yet another foreshadowing of the final nuclear extinction.

Zoologists say that the appearance of man coincides with the disappearance of many animal species of the Pleistocene era: giant birds such as the teraton of North America, the flightless superswan of Europe, the elephant bird of Madagascar, the dodo of the Islands of Mauritius and the twelve-foot-tall moas of New Zealand. Man is the being that makes other beings *disappear*: this destroying magical feat occurs inwardly in the mind, in acts of conceptual annihilation, and outwardly on the plane of life, in acts of material annihilation.

For example, primitive tribesmen, employing newly discovered flint weaponry, descended from Siberia through Alaska and the Americas and devastated, within a thousand years, a fantastic variety of wildlife that once flourished here. The asphalt tar pits of La Brea in Los Angeles, California, preserve traces of many of these prehistoric creatures: huge short-faced bears and coyotes, giant long-necked camels or llama, saber-toothed cats and giant lions, enormous bison and sloth, mastadons and shaggy, red-haired mammoths, four-hundred pound beavers and other giant herbivores. It was a primal foretaste of the carnage to come.

Hunting, and the development of hunting skills, played a significant role in the evolution of man. But certain forms of hunting for sport, especially as we observe in the modern world, point to problems in the pathology of human destructiveness. Consider, for instance, the sport of hunting as practiced by certain oil-rich shieks of the Middle East. The hunters and their guests normally set out in the hot gravel country in air-conditioned Cadillacs. A fleet of jeeps follows, while planes reconnoiter ahead to spot game. The total hunting envoy of jeeps, Cadillacs and planes is in radio communication. Once game is located, the jeeps herd the animals together until they are within range of the hunters, who rake them down with World War II air-cooled .50 caliber machine guns. Thus, plutocratic hedonism adds to the momentum toward extinction.

Not all the violence committed against wildlife can be ascribed to the pure fun of hunting. A good deal of the killing can be laid up to mundane commercial need. The plight of the whale, the largest creature ever to inhabit the earth, is a case in point. The slaughter of whales has increased in recent years. With the help of huge fleets equipped with sonar, helicopters and explosive harpoons, the Japanese and the Russians have reduced the eight species of these mysterious creatures to near oblivion. The Atlantic grey whale is now extinct. The blue whale, an animal remarkably similar to man in body temperature, circulatory system and brain and eye structure, is also nearly extinct. Americans are among the largest importers of whale products; the Leviathan of biblican repute ends up in our paint cans, transmission fluids and cosmetics.

The assault on nonhuman life forms shows the totalitarian drift of man-centered technology. The human population is swelling to unmanageable proportions at the cost of other life forms. Unsacred scientism has not only depopulated the universe of the supernatural, but it is relentlessly diminishing the inhabitants of the natural world. The beings above and those below us in the hierarchy of nature are equally victimized. The conspiracy is consistent.

The Subjugation of Nature:
Protagoras versus Standing Bear

The technocratic credo is perhaps best summed up in the words of the ancient Greek Sophist, Protagoras: "Man is the measure of all things." The idea may be flattering to us, but it has been a curse to the rest of the natural world. If the lakes, rivers, air, hills, valleys and trees that girdle the globe, all the nonhuman inhabitants of earth, could speak with their own voice, they might say: "No, dear philosopher, the whole earth, the living system of the world, is the measure of all things."

The devastation of the planet's physical body, like the erosion of "archaic" and traditional cultures and the decimation of wildlife, is linked to the undermining of sacred realities. People of traditional societies experience the sacred in the natural environment, which shapes their behavior toward it.

The Native American way of life, before the arrival of European settlers, was holistic in outlook. Chief Luther Standing Bear [167], once an interpreter in Buffalo Bill's Wild West Show, spoke eloquently of the sacred kinship of being, a kinship unknown to modern rationalism. According to Standing Bear, the old people of the Lakota, a western tribe of the Sioux, literally loved the earth and reclined on the soil "with a feeling of being close to a mothering power."

For us, the idea of "mother earth" is little more than a quaint metaphor. The Indian experienced the soil as a "mothering power," a source of nourishment. A sense of personal kinship defined and imposed limits on his relationship to the earth. Standing Bear continues: "It was good for the skin to touch the earth and the old people liked to remove their moccasins and walk with bare feet on the sacred earth. Their tipis were built upon the earth and their altars were made of earth."

Home was a way of connecting with the earth; religion celebrated the sacred power of the earth. The old Indian, Standing Bear says, healed himself with the life-giving forces of the earth; when he sat upon the ground, he could "think more deeply and feel more keenly" as well as "see more clearly into the mysteries of life and come closer in kinship to other lives around him." By living in reverent communion with the earth, the Lakota enhanced psychic powers, sensitivity to the natural kinship of living forms. A listening attitude toward nature increased general perceptiveness.

But with us it is different. Warm kinship with earth is bad business. In line with the credo of Protagoras, man is the measure of value on earth. Man is the engineer who, in Bacon's prophetic words, puts nature to the rack. Our common mode of speech with nature is in the imperative mood; our usual manner is to command and appropriate, rarely to listen. But isolation from the healing, sensitizing earth aggravates hostility and paranoia; witness city dwellers who exist screened from nature in boxes made of steel and concrete.

Living in harmony with nature encourages trust between humans and other living creatures. Says Standing Bear:

Kinship with all creatures of the earth, sky and water, was a real active principle. For the animal and bird world there existed a brotherly feeling that kept the Lakota safe among them, and so close did some of the Lakota come to their feathered and furred friends that in true brotherhood they spoke a common language.

The Native American's kinship with the earth enabled him to feel safe in his environment. The feelings are quite different in our denatured societies: fear, distrust, cruelty toward wildlife and deafness to the language of living things.

The most serious consequence of losing touch with the earth is explained by Standing Bear: "The Lakota was wise. He knew that man's heart away from nature became hard: he knew that lack of respect for growing, living things soon led to lack of respect for humans too." Man, torn from the mothering power of earth, becomes hard, insensitive. We see this growing hardness in our lack of respect toward the flora and fauna of nature: the whale, the baby seal, the gorilla; forest, mountain, sea; the humans. It is all of a piece. Hardness, psychic denseness, cold pragmatism; these are no respecters of persons, animals, minerals or vegetables.

The degradation of traditional lifestyles and mythologies, and the exploitation of natural resources, are cut from the same logical cloth of unsacred scientism. The exploitation of natural resources and of humans stems from the same root: the hardened heart of which Standing Bear spoke, the computational mind cut off from nature's life-giving, mothering power. By reducing nature merely to extended matter, depriving it of personality, of any status as an end or "thou," modern materialism creates a psychic paradigm for aggressive objectivity toward things in general. It undermines the imaginative kinship with nature, reducing it to neuter objects, using it as material to satisfy human needs. The Native American does not, as Protagoras and Bacon, absolutize the human perspective.

The Suicide of the Spirit

The aim here is not to detail the erosion of the sacred or the assault on the ecosphere. Rather, we had raised the question of a widespread, long-evolving pattern of destructiveness, the climax being the mounting menace of nuclear catastrophe. Science itself, as developed and used in the Western world, figures in this conspiracy. The nuclear threat to life itself became possible with the help of science.

Science has been used to coarsen our inner environment and to abuse the outer environment. Again, recall the most prominent, and perhaps the strangest, symptom of this conspiracy against life: science's view of consciousness itself. Consider, for example, a statement from a distinguished biologist:

> Let us try to describe ourselves exactly to each other. We shall find that we can do better then by trying to speak of ourselves as inhabited by a number of pseudo things such as consciousness, mind, experience and the rest of them.

Or this from a philosopher:

> Contemporary science, in short, does not seem to require the notion of 'experience,' and is getting to the brink of rejecting it, in effect, as 'unreal' or 'non-existent.'

As far as losses linked to unsacred scientism, this is the last word: loss, invalidation of experience, consciousness itself; the evacuation of inner reality; reduction of the human to the mechanical.

The Homogenized Universe

The reduction of man to a machine completes the building of the nihilist monolith. The work of homogenizing the universe, in principle, is hereby accomplished.

The great spiritual traditions, by contrast, see the universe as multi-leveled, man an inhabitant of many mansions of being, a sojourner between sense-worlds and the (normally) invisible realms of spirit. In the eyes of tradition, a human being is not just a physical object trapped in time and space but a road to other dimensions of being. Human being is portrayed as dual—mind and matter—or as tripartite—mind, matter and spirit.

The words of the Renaissance thinker, Pico della Mirandola, express the idea of our existence as a meeting place of many realities. It is a classic statement on human freedom from the *Oration on the Dignity of Man*.

> Taking man, therefore, this creature of indeterminate image, He (God the Creator) set him in the middle of the world and thus spoke to him:

'We have given you, O Adam, no visage proper to yourself, nor any endowment properly your own . . . We have made you a creature neither of heaven nor of earth, neither mortal nor immortal, in order that you may, as the free and proud shaper of your own being, fashion yourself in the form you prefer. It will be in your power to descend to the lower, brutish forms of life; you will be able, through your own decision, to rise again to the superior orders whose life is divine.'

We who are in the midst of great transformations in earth history might remember Pico's words. It offers a vision of ourselves existing at the crossroads of different dimensions of being. Harmonious with the modern conception of evolution, of life as an open-ended process, it invites us to steer the course of our own evolution. Pico's words help formulate the final choice facing us at this turning point in the survival game. We are beings of indeterminate form, unformed formers, imageless imagers of future selves. We may descend to brutish nuclear barbarism or rise to a life in tune with our divine potential.

14
World With a Flower in Its Mouth

The unleashed power of the atom has changed
everything except our ways of thinking. Thus we
are drifting toward a catastrophe beyond
comparison. We shall require a substantially new
manner of thinking, if mankind is to survive.

—*Albert Einstein*

Nothing less than a world-wide spiritual revulsion
against the Satanic Kingdom would give us any
chance of bringing the military riders down.

—*Edward Thompson*
LETTER TO AMERICA

The last two chapters dealt with the probabilities of nuclear disaster; this one deals with models of spiritual revolution. The probabilities of the former are high; hence there is a need to focus on the "substantially new way of thinking" Einstein wrote of and, more recently, on Thompson's "world-wide spiritual revulsion."

In a play by Luigi Pirandello, *The Man With A Flower In His Mouth,* a man emerges from a doctor's office with a fatal diagnosis. Possessed by this knowledge of impending death, the world lights up for him, the smallest things swell with significance; the doomed man's awareness changes radically, a conversion of consciousness takes place. The physicians of culture have diagnosed our world, our civilization, and found it suffering from the fatal disease of nuclear nihilism. Ours is a *world*, a civilization, with a flower in its mouth.

291

Groundwork for the Miraculous

The nuclear debate is the crucial debate of the 1980s. Either we resolve it or we ourselves will be dissolved in the final conflagration. I believe, however, that we need a holistic perspective on the nuclear peril; no piecemeal analysis of symptoms will do. We have to get to the cause of the disease.

Therefore, instead of making recommendations for dealing with specific symptoms, I sketch a theoretical framework for learning to do what must be done—*whatever* that may be. The general potentiality for a new kind of action is at issue here; it is a kind of groundwork for the miraculous.

It may be that escape from our dilemma, however self-caused, is no longer in our power, that help must come from outside the system. As in the NDE, at the moment one acknowledges helplessness, the higher resource, operating outside the ordinary mind, comes to aid.

We have been talking about certain resources of creative energy, new affective potentials and immensely-broadened intellectual sympathies. Access to a larger reality is a real possibility; unfortunately, there exist no easy formulas for mobilizing our transcendent allies.

Nevertheless, I am convinced that without somehow tapping into these deeper springs of our being, no path that we choose will lead us out of the dark wood. Apart from increased attunement to our inner resources, *any* course of action we take is likely to fail to really advance us toward peace.

Practical people are always telling us *what* to do; they often neglect to say *how*. Human beings have an invisible, inner side—a holistic politics would underline this fact. Native American culture understood that a good warrior must also be a good medicine man. Time at the computers in the Pentagon is not enough; there must be periodic retreats to the kiva and the sweat-lodge. Another way of saying this is that politics—our programs for bettering the world—must become "state-specific." They must flow from particular inner dispositions, qualities of mind and sensibility.

The problem is not being *disposed* toward disarmament; everybody says they want peace, but what is really in our hearts? That is another question. The truth is that we cannot disarm under conditions of mutual mistrust and hostility. Hence the present search for models of inner transformation that would dispose us toward genuine peace.

The form of this book is itself a gesture toward transformation. The way the thought and imagery is woven together is an exercise in holistic thinking. Our dialogue must be large, democratic. Books of healing intent should mirror in form the goals they espouse. In thought we unite first. And so in these pages, we listen to many voices from many camps of thought, from many times and stages of history; we try to make of this listening a meeting of minds, hearts and spirits—East and West, science and religion, humanist and transcendentalist, ancient and modern—shorings up from the past, visions of the future.

Models of Transformation

Since the threat of global near-death is the product of a "systemic" pattern, only a systemic revision will help us cope with the threat. A tremendous force is driving us to a precipice; only a tremendous force can stop us from hurtling over the edge. A transformation. A revolution. An evolution. A new consciousness. A new reality. Miraculous metanoia. Slogans, visions and paradigms multiply, showing vital signs of the immortality instinct, rumblings in the collective unconscious.

No wonder there is a growing literature of modern, scientific prophetism. Tone and style may differ, but the prophetic strain is unmistakable. The common theme is clear: we are in the midst of a crisis of unprecedented proportions, but a new consciousness is emerging, or must emerge, if we are to see it through to the light at the end of the tunnel.

Models for transformation range from political revolution to psychospiritual evolution. Our assumption is that political change, apart from inner change, will in the long run not help. A new attitude, a new consciousness, a new rhythm of being is called for.

The attraction of the archetypes in our futurist thinkers has assumed the form of a fascination with the concept of the paradigm: the living integrative myth that guides the life of whole communities. Writers like Marilyn Ferguson [168] and Ken Wilbur [169], each drawing on different traditions, struggle to integrate massive quanta of data into new patterns, images and paradigms, new circuits of numinous energy for pulling us upward from the Eden of our Lorenzian beginnings to full-blown Godhood. We are creating paradigms of our own future evolution, setting up lodestones to magnetize our higher spiritual energies.

The collective will to live, the collective intelligence and imagination, is working hard these days to conjure up healing visions. It is a global book of the dead to which we are trying to give shape, a manual for the bardo of nuclear death and transfiguration. Models of transformation are prescriptive, composed in the optative mood. Like the magic songs of the Papago Indians, they describe desired events. They are resonators of the collective unconscious, agitators of goal-directed processes, sparkers of hopeful mutations.

As we shall argue in the final chapter, in one sense they are neither true nor false, for their function is not to describe, or correspond to, existing states of affairs. Their real function is to evoke states of affairs; they are expressive, not impressive, truths. Indeed, in the bardo of life and death, in the open, fluid, dissipating field of the evolutionary process, truth is not fact, done, but forging, fabricating. Truth here at the edge of history is not a matter of computational intelligence; truth engages the whole person. Truth is troth, betrothal to the unborn, the unknown god.

Psi, Archetypes, Near-death: The Stuff of Psychic Evolution

We need to be exact about what sort of psychosocial evolution is needed:

1) Above all, a *new* type of radicalism, one that attains to global dimensions—a *spiritual* radicalism—is required.

2) By global dimensions, I mean that this spiritual radicalism must somehow attain to a critical mass, one that forms a new power bloc and helps to constitute a *disposed system* toward peace.

3) This must express itself in a new understanding of reality—a new metaphysics. Just as the revolutions of the nineteenth and early twentieth century were preceded by the thought of Locke, Rousseau and Marx, and just as, to take a crucial historical example, the rise of the new Christian civilization was preceded by the teachings of the New Testament and the early Church fathers, so a post-nuclear civilization must be preceded by a *new global metaphysics of life and death*.

Let us consider some types of "mechanism" for such psychosocial evolution. It would take a separate book to describe and critically analyze possible models. We therefore focus attention on models concerned with the data used in this book: psi, archetypes and near-death experiences. This is an approach with one advantage: it is empirically based.

The notion of critical mass is central; doubtless, there are people of good will, even enlightened people, but somehow they fall below the mark necessary to ignite a general shift of consciousness. They remain a minority. Yet qualitative shifts might suddenly take place; neurologist Ragnar Granit [170] relates the rise of consciousness to a numerical critical mass of neurons. A certain degree of material complexity has to be reached before consciousness may emerge. This critical complexity factor allows us to predict the emergence of a global brain, a unified earth consciousness; the critical number is ten billion—atoms to form a cell, cells to form a self-conscious brain and humans on earth to form a new consciousness. The process on earth is being speeded up by the rapid spread of an electronic network linking billions of individual brains, slowly giving birth to the global brain. The technical foundations for *sharing* a new consciousness do, in fact, seem available. Instantaneous global intimacies are technically feasible and, in fact, are daily fare in the media. Again, though, there is the question of who is dictating what the global brain thinks: Corporate America, the Soviet Bureaucracy or what? Clearly, an open future is here.

If there is an artist-god looking to reshape and advance the cause of life, the targets it can act upon most effectively are systems excited by internal fluctuations. PK, for instance, is more likely to act on dice tumbling in indeterminate motion than dice sitting stably. Thus the dissipation of societal norms, a part of increasing nuclear instability, may be a factor in the formation of a new adaptive consciousness. The hold of the old, nonadaptive forms of consciousness has to be shattered. The problem is whether in shattering the old forms, life on earth will also be shattered beyond recovery.

The shattering of the old forms of consciousness might come about through global near-death. Global near-death might, in a fearsome way, turn out to be a good thing. This, of course, is not what we had hoped for; we were looking for models of radical spiritual consciousness that would *prevent* global near-death.

Global Near-death and the New Consciousness

Let us for a moment look at some possible relations between global near-death and the emergence of a new consciousness. The first difficulty lies in forming a proper analogy between individual and global near-death. We know that in the former, striking changes of consciousness often occur. We also know that these changes are not peculiar to individuals but express latent collective potential. How, then, might we imagine our collective potential awakening? Well, in some sense it must relate to collective near-death. The near-death experience, as we've seen, is a model for a natural conversion process. The metanoid potential of the deep near-death experience could, under conceivable circumstances, be awakened *en masse*.

A collective change of consciousness might arise from a collective NDE. This might occur in one of two possible ways. In the first, the changes would come *after* global cataclysm. In the second, *before*.

Consider the first, and hardly enticing, possibility. If we are looking for a model in which people are suddenly transformed, become deeply disposed toward peace, we find it, ironically, among the *hibakusha* of Hiroshima and Nagasaki: the first victims and survivors of atomic attack. The modern city of Hiroshima has, in fact, become a symbol of the quest for peace. Scattered everywhere are monuments and bronze tables that read: *This is our city. This is our prayer. Building peace in this world, or O God of evil, Do not come this way again. This place is reserved for those who pray for peace. And on the Peace Park memorial where the names of the A-Bomb dead are inscribed: Let all souls here rest in peace, for we shall not repeat the evil.*

But are the *hibakusha* a possible model for the collective transformation in question? There are difficulties in using Hiroshima and Nagasaki as models for what might happen in a *global* war. In the aftermath of the 1945 atomic blasts, there remained an outside world. The bombings were essentially local affairs. In a global nuclear exchange, there would be no outside world; the whole planet would be imbroiled. Destruction would dwarf that of 1945, encompass the whole of Northern Hemisphere civilization, possibly the whole biosphere.

Oddly, the totality of destruction could be taken as boding well for prospects of collective transformation. For after Hiroshima and Nagasaki, Western civilization remained intact. Indeed, for some, the use of the bomb seemed proof of the greatness of the Western Way, proof of a new power for winning just wars. Enthusiasts imagined that the bomb might become an instrument for enforcing stable international relations. The 1945 atomic attacks demonstrated the special potency of Western civilization.

But the next nuclear war would be a different affair. A *global* nuclear battle would, by contrast, leave Western civilization in ruins. It would be impossible to construe such a disaster as victory in any human sense. The failure of Western civilization would be visible for all survivors to contemplate.

A nuclear denoument of Western civilization is a poor model for the road to global expansion of consciousness. More reasonably, one may expect a vast contraction of consciousness; consider the two likely types of nuclear war survivor.

First are the Japanese *hibakusha*: survivors near enough blast-point to sustain injury, immediate or long term. The chief response of the Japanese, according to Robert Jay Lifton [171] who made a close study of Hiroshima survivors, was psychic numbing. "I would suggest now," Lifton writes, "that psychic numbing comes to characterize the entire life-style of the survivor." Reports on the psychological response to other types of collective catastrophe, like plague and the modern concentration camp, agree with this description: the victim is zombified, anaesthetized.

Collective catastrophe produced marked changes in the reality-sense of survivors. "With such events, so radical is the overturning of the sense of what is 'real'—of what must be psychologically absorbed—that the survivor's mental economy undergoes a permanent alteration, a psychic mutation." For the most part, however, the mutations Lifton described are toward decreased awareness; victims become depersonalized, shut off perception of what is happening to them and act as if they are detached, unfeeling observers. The psychic mutation described by Lifton is not the kind that stirs our hope for the future of humanity.

In classic paradigms of psychic transformation, self-numbing can be seen as a halfway stage; it corresponds, by way of grotesque caricature, to the phase of withdrawal from the world. With *hibakusha*, however, introversion was forced, a consequence of shock. In strategies of self-transformation, however, introversion is deliberate.

The Japanese victims were psychically mutilated, although some *hibakusha* emerged heroic, transformed beings. In one case, a woman apparently acquired healing power. She described the encounter with the bomb as "the greatest event in my life"; it drove her toward the mystical recesses of her being. Her comments say something about the psychology of conversion: "I thought I had come to the extreme point—the very end—and there was absolutely nothing to depend on but religion."

Others emerged from the bomb encounter with a sense of mission. "This sense of a special 'mission' made possible by a 'miracle' was widespread among *hibakusha*," Lifton writes of someone he interviewed. "Regarding himself as one 'obliged to serve . . . in a higher cause,' he described feeling 'a new source of light, which allowed me to recover myself and surge back . . . a call to keep on living.'"

Reports of this type of missionary response suggest that some *hibakusha* reached levels of consciousness similar to the classic NDE. Perhaps if numbing to outside reality is carried far enough, one might retreat to archetypal levels of consciousness and draw the powers of transformation. But this was not typical among atomic bomb survivors.

There are, moreover, marked differences between the A-bomb survivor and the classic near-death survivor. In near-death, vital signs temporarily disappear, but the patient revives. The longer the "clinical" death, the deeper and more powerful the experience. The near-death experiencer is often restored to well-being. This contrasts sharply with A-bomb survivors. The atom blasts and the damage inflicted did not result in massive numbers of clinical death and resuscitation. But clinical death—the temporary absence of vital signs—is, by and large, the condition of the change of consciousness under consideration.

Two other things argue against atomic megadeath being a likely avenue to collective psychic transformation. First, there is a heavy burden of guilt suffered by *hibakusha*—guilt because they survived and others didn't. Survival was itself a source of psychological problems. Nothing like this happens in a typical near-death case. Secondly, *hibakusha* could never be sure about their survival. Many died slow, lingering deaths. All suffered anxiety from subtle and latent effects of exposure to radiation. This, again, is unlike cases of clinical resuscitation. In sum, *hibakusha* are a poor model for the evolution of human consciousness. It is also the least appealing, for obvious reasons.

But not all survivors of a nuclear holocaust would be *hibakusha*. There is a second type. Sticking to the American scene, we can imagine patches in the hills of West Virginia or Oregon, untouched by direct blast effects or radioactive fallout. We can imagine survivors far enough removed from centers of widespread destruction, who would attempt to build a new life.

They offer little hope as founders of a new type of humanity. Not having been directly touched by catastrophe, the main concern will most likely be personal survival. But basic services of civilized life will have broken down. Food and water will be scarce, contaminated, and communication and transportation systems disrupted. Under such circumstances, it is hard to imagine that law and order will prevail, far less the refined amenities of social life. This class of survivors is likely to descend to what Hobbes called the *state of nature:* a condition of war of all on all.

Of course, the psychic world we are trying to envisage is historically unprecedented. Perhaps we could compare it after the fall of the Roman Empire. But the suddenness, the totality of a global nuclear war hardly favors the comparison.

A clue to the mental world of survivors may lie in new publications dealing with so-called "survivalist" tactics. "Survivalists" are people who expect the imminent collapse of civilization. They believe, often with religious ardor, in a coming catastrophe: massive economic breakdown, natural or man-made war-begotten cataclysm. They are building their hideaways in the remoter woodlands of the South and of the Far West, in the hills and deserts of the Southwest. Many are urban dwellers anxiously studying techniques for survival in the wilderness. For these far-seeing people, reliance on firearms is the key to preparations for doomsday.

A glance at a recent issue of *Shooter's Survival Guide,* a publication meant as a guide for doomsday, is telling. The cover features a photograph of a well-dressed, middle-aged business executive—with a machine-gun strapped on his back! The caption reads: "White Collar Survival Tactics." The array of "survival" information is considerable: articles, ads, editorials, letters on high-powered survival guns, survival knives, methods of making your own survival bullets, setting man-traps, using tear-gas, "paralyzers" and so forth. I quote from a spunky article entitled "The Hardcore Survivalists." "The real survivalist," we are told, "has no more trust in police than he does with the rat packs he believes will be coming after his supply of food, water, ammunition and firearms . . . There will be no law other than the law of the jungle. It's a case of 'me and them.' "

This view of the future brings us back to the theme of realism. Survivalists are nothing if not "realistic." Grammar is on the wane, the tone shriller, but they express the unvarnished psychic reality of people who think of their fellow humans in distress as "rat packs."

Here is the paranoid distrust, the reduction of the world to "us" and "them," the contempt for the rule of law and confidence in firearms. If survivalist fantasies reflect the probable psychic reality of the post-Armageddon populace, again there is little to strengthen our hope in the advent of a higher consciousness. On the contrary, it is this very "rat pack" mentality which is driving us to the brink of disaster. The bardo of the paranoid survivalist is full of wrathful deities in ambush. Those whom we see as rat packs, and treat as rat packs, are likely to become rat packs.

Here is how Vico [172], in *The New Science*, describes the last stages of a culture ridden by civil disorder:

> For such people, like so many beasts, have fallen into the custom of each man thinking only of his own private interests . . . Thus no matter how great the throng and press of their bodies, they live like wild beasts in a deep solitude of spirit and will, scarcely any two being able to agree since each follows his own pleasure and caprice. By reason of all this, providence decrees that, through obstinate factions and desperate civil wars, they shall turn their cities into forests and forests into dens and lairs of men. In this way, through long centuries of barbarism, rust will consume the misbegotten subtleties of malicious wits that have turned them into beasts made more inhuman by the barbarism of reflection than the first men had been made by the barbarism of sense.

In Vico's scheme, there are two kinds of barbarism: one based on sense, the style of primal humanity; the other upon the refinements of intellect, the style of advanced civilization. The old way was frank and open, seen in the savage outbursts of enraged Achilles, grieving the death of his friend, Patroklos. The new way is sly, covert, but "more inhuman." It conceals itself under "soft words and embraces;" one thinks of "survivalists" who invoke their civil rights to justify owning Magnum 44's. The arms race, itself, is the ultimate example of the barbarism of reflection. For here we witness an unprecedented build-up of a science of murder, calmly, deliberately, under the cloak of soft-spokenness and reasonableness. It is a system, a vast network, of subtle and "malicious wits."

Neither *hibakusha*, nor so-called survivalists, are promising candidates for our new metanoid world, at least not in the short run. It is conceivable that after a nuclear holocaust, scattered nuclei of transformed beings, barbarians of sense, inspired by the helping powers of Mind at Large, might seed a new consciousness, one that will blossom centuries hence. One recalls the monastic orders, centers of learning and meditation, that grew among the ruins of the Roman Empire. The new consciousness may thus arise gradually, haphazardly, a far-off spring after a long nuclear winter. Centuries may pass, but the Terror would trace its effects in the minds of future generations. Nuclear cataclysm would be the most dramatic and the most drastic stimulus to hasten the next step in the evolution of human consciousness. The sheer immensity of the disaster would reverberate in the collective psyche of humankind. Evidence that the old consciousness—that is, the prevailing consciousness of today—*was radically corrupt* would be apparent to all. The lesson will be written in letters brilliant enough for the blind to see: *the colossal burn-out of Western civilization.*

Conclusion

Only a radical spirituality, a new metaphysics strong enough to command a new kind of courage and solidarity, will overturn the system of the nuclear warriors. The NDE, a clue to an unknown system of inner resources, and touching on the deep structure of the human mind, led us to this curious meditation on the Bomb itself as a possible trigger of transcendence.

Now a second model for nuclear enlightenment depends on the mind alterations taking place *before* catastrophe. It sometimes happens that people have transformative near-death imagery before or without actual bodily harm. Awareness of impending loss of autonomy, an attitude of surrender, may set into motion the first flickers of these images. By analogy, the vivid premonition of catastrophe might activate the reordering mechanisms of the deep psyche; we might then escape our bad fate and buy a lesson in enlightenment cheaply.

It is then possible that the collective human psyche is in transformation even now, as we inch toward global disaster. We may be sensing a probable future subliminally and are already in process of evolution. Latent energies, oriented toward survival, are perhaps at this very moment awakening in us.

In the next chapter, we examine some signs of these mass stirrings of the collective unconscious—signs that the obscure forces of the archetype of death and enlightenment may be awakening on a collective scale—a premonitory response to a probable collective future.

15
A Morphology of the Apocalypse

Today, the goddess is no longer worshipped. Her
shrines are lost in the dust of ages while her
statues line the walls of museums. But the law or
power of which she was but the personification is
unabated in its strength and life-giving potency.

—Mary Harding
Woman's Mysteries

Prophetic NDES, UFO Revelations, Marian Visions

The collective unconscious of humankind is in a state of unrest. The Bomb is causing Mind at Large to reverberate with monitions of disaster and visions of a new earth.

Let us then examine three types of prophetic visionary experience: near-death visions—especially the "prophetic" subset; UFO "contactee" cults; and visions of the Blessed Virgin Mary. All follow a common pattern and stem, I conjecture, from the same adaptive mechanism of the collective unconscious: they are part of the configuration called the archetype of death and enlightenment. What might all this mean for the evolution of human consciousness? Are there indeed evolutionary stirrings in the collective psyche at the present time? Comparing these visionary experiences, perhaps the reader will be persuaded that there are.

A point before proceeding—we focus on the deep levels of these experiences; few NDErs have the apocalyptic imagery discussed here. Likewise with UFO and, to an extent, Marian visions. However, at their deepest, the experiences converge in collective content and proclaim the same planetary message. Here we find evidence of

303

a single intelligence at work, a single set of messages from Mind at Large.

To begin with, the phenomena have lately intensified; in different ways, each is a reaction to the growth of science. The most recent, the NDE—already entrenched in the popular mind—is due to progress in resuscitation technology. UFO contactee cults took quantum leaps into the public eye in 1947, at the dawn of the nuclear age. The UFO mythology is a mythology of science, gussied up in ideas of extraterrestrial civilizations, future worlds and higher technologies. Our last example, the visions of the Virgin Mary, increased during the nineteenth century—a century of science, skepticism, progress, technology and revolution.

UFO mythology, let me add, is allied to science fiction; "little green men" are entities of fiction *and* of UFO experience. We meet them in fairy and occult lore, as Jacques Vallee showed in *Passport to Magonia*. [173] *Close Encounters of a Third Kind*, *E.T.*, *Star Wars*, *Superman*—such movie mythologies have beaten all box office records because they hit nerves of the collective mind. In each of them, as Robert Short shows in *The Gospel From Outer Space* [174], the scientific imagination becomes a screen for projecting the archetype of the savior god. The gods project themselves into the most unlikely places; they have begun to invade the Hollywood dream machine.

What follows extends the typology of helping visions sketched in Part Five. Prophetic NDEs, UFO contactee cults and Marian visions: let's look at them in light of (1) the *content* of the vision, (2) the *context* in which it arises, (3) its main *function* and (4) its *aftereffects*. We are going to find some interesting parallels.

One last point—we already noted the moral ambivalence of archetypal experiences and should not be surprised to find sinister overtones in these trends. This is probably most apparent in some UFO cults, especially if we are to believe Jacques Vallee. We needn't look at these patterns as rigidly deterministic, however. They are forms of possible psychospiritual evolution, not blueprints of the inevitable.

The Content of the Visions

There are many points where the three types of vision overlap in content. We confine ourselves to three. In each we find reports of meetings with powerful, transformative light beings; second, there are prophecies of global cataclysm; third, the visions point beyond the darker prospects to a New Age of the Spirit.

Light Beings

Light, more than anything in these experiences, is the focus of personal transformation; as we saw in the chapter on the ADE, "enlightenment" is not just symbolic but visceral, "energetic." It does "work."

In the spiritual near-death visions, light beings are often met. Indeed, Moody's "being of light" has become a key trope in the new mythology of death. (The Coptic Christians who witnessed the Lady in Zeitoun (1968-71) refer to her as the "Mother of Light.") Sometimes this being of light is invested with name and form, but often not. Rather, a quality in the light marks the illumination experience: it is loving, all-embracing, all-forgiving. Experiencers say that this light, however dazzling, doesn't hurt the eye.

Anyone acquainted with near-death stories will note the likeness to the Marian experience. Writes John Delaney [175] in *A Woman Clothed With The Sun*, "Without exception, Our Lady's appearances are accompanied by brilliant light—light of an unearthly intensity but which despite its brilliance did not hurt the eyes of those experiencing the vision." Conchita, in her Garabandal diary, described her visions of a mysterious Lady of Light at age thirteen: "Suddenly, there appeared to me a very beautiful figure that shone brilliantly but did not hurt my eyes at all." [176] Similar accounts of the light are plentiful in NDEs.

As in the near-death experience, the identity of the light being is often unclear. The apparitions begin as clouds or balls of light and then assume a form. At first, the light being was said by the Garabandal children to be Saint Michael. Later, the figure of Mary crystallized. Lucia, one of the child visionaries of Fatima, describes in her *Memoirs* the Lady as "all of light, more brilliant than the sun dispensing light, clearer and more intense than a crystal cup full of crystalline water penetrated by the rays of the most glaring sun." Yet at first, the Lady announced herself simply as "from Heaven."

In the UFO visions, light beings also appear, in the guise of space brothers and ultradimensional emissaries. They, too, are luminous beings. One gets the impression that this light, apart from what it does or how it feels to the visionary, is at least a symbol of consciousness. In any case, unusual photic effects are often reported in the UFO experience; for instance, one group believes it communicates with the Higher Beings telepathically on a "tensor beam," a kind of mind-light beam with odd spatial properties.

The connection between UFOs and (in particular) the Fatima phenomena has already been noted by UFOlogist and astrophysicist, Jacques Vallee. In *The Invisible College*, Vallee explores the links between Marian and UFO visions.

Vallee, like Jung, stressed the psychic side of the UFO phenomenon, playing down the idea of UFOs as machines from outer space. This, I should say, is also our assumption. The theological side of Marian visions, as well as the possible "extraterrestrial" factor in UFO visions, is a matter on which we suspend judgement. It is the phenomenology, the psychological significance of these events that concern us, especially their status as archetypes that stir the dynamics of the collective unconscious.

To illustrate the UFO-likeness of events at Fatima: one witness, Maria Carreira, said, during a 1923 inquiry, that she heard "the same buzz when they talked and the same mounting of a rocket at the end." Then there are the odd luminous effects. To begin with, the Lady's apparition was preceded by a light being who announced himself as an "Angel of Peace"—a beautiful, illuminated figure of a youth. The appearance was accompanied by flashes of light and thunder-like sounds.

In April, 1915, Lucia, Jacinta and Francisco were playing at the entrance to a cave when they heard the rumble of a powerful wind—the latter is, as Vallee notes, "a constant in UFO behavior." I would add that rumblings and buzzings are also a feature of NDEs. The light appears, the sounds are heard, at the foot of a cave. Caves and grottoes often are settings for Marian visions. Again, cave and tunnel imagery are common in near-death encounters.

Lucy, eight years old, was the first link in the chain of Fatima events, since it was she who, while saying the rosary, first envisioned the cloud of light from which the Angel of Peace emerged. The rosary, a powerful mantra evoking the Blessed Virgin, would help to induce an altered state of consciousness; it is an established fact of parapsychology that altered states favor the occurrence of psi events. All these are ideal conditions for the emergence of archetypes; recall Jung's point that children, or anyone in an altered state (dreams be-

ing the best example), are most likely to meet with archetypal entities.

Vallee links the UFO to the Marian vision; both seem also linked
to the near-death experience. In the chapter on The Shroud, we described effects of supernormal light; again with the Fatima phenomenon, we find photons on the rampage, a trick of some divine pin-
wheel meant to stretch the rational mind to breaking point. Consider
this, for example.

On the last day in the Fatima cycle of apparitions, October 13,
1917, extraordinary light phenomena were witnessed not only by the
three child visionaries but by an estimated 70,000 witnesses, some of
them miles from the Cova da Iria. Many of the witnesses were hostile
and skeptical. It had been raining heavily and everybody was
soaked—photographs exist of the amazed crowd holding umbrellas
in their hands. Shortly after midday, before this vast and mixed multitude, thick gray clouds suddenly parted and rolled away like the
curtains of a stage. The sun emerged in a clear blue sky, glowing like
a silver disk, unnaturally muted in its brilliance. For a moment, the
multitude was enchanted by this oddity in the heavens.

Then the apparent disk began to rotate rapidly—three times, it
was said—and blood-red streamers flew from the rim, sending waves
of warmth and colorful lights shimmering on the countryside. Suddenly the disk plunged erratically downward; many fell to their
knees in terror, believing it was the end of the world. The disk, however, stopped short and rose back into the sky in the same irregular
way. When it was all over, many "minds were blown" and many
strange healings were said to have taken place. The sun was back to
normal, but the whole countryside, and everybody present, was suddenly dry. As for the movements of the disk, based on eyewitness
accounts, it looked like the zigzag "falling leaf" motion of UFOs.
Hence the legend of the sun "dancing" at Fatima.

Thus we have *two* kinds of light experience, the private and the
public. This mysterious light that comes to raise our consciousness
likes to straddle the normal categories of inner and outer, subjective
and objective. Perhaps it means to challenge our dualistic paradigm
of self, our insular ideas of I and the other, of inner me and outer
world. In the presence of this higher light, the routine boundaries of
reality seem to fade away.

In 1971, Brad Steiger published a book, *The Aquarian Revelations*

[177], which, like the work of Jacques Vallee, documents UFO mediums, individuals who claim to be channeling prophetic information from various Space Intelligences. The likeness to ND and Marian prophecies is again striking. Light is a central symbol of the UFO Aquarian Revelations. One group called the Light Affiliates centers on a Space Intelligence called Ox-Ho. The archetypal Light permeates Ox-Ho's teachings. We hear of a *solar* government that we must rally around and of a *light* shield that we can learn to use to protect ourselves in the coming spiritual wars.

Here is a sample of Ox-Ho's Aquarian Revelations, in which the theme is Radiance and Love. The message is virtually identical with that of current near-death visionaries and could easily have come from any one of them:

> Radiance is the giving forth of the Light which expresses Love. Radiance is the beam that shines forth from one who is loved, or who gives love, and is a way of demonstrating in material form the very expression of love itself . . . in light is love, in love is peace, in peace is brotherhood, in brotherhood is eternal love which shines forth for the radiation of the entire Universe.

And so it goes, anonymous and universal, sounding the ancient themes and clothing them in bland metaphors of space science.

Here, before the ND visionaries, were widely scattered groups who, sensing the threat to life on earth, were using the symbols and imagery of deep near-death experiencers. This, as I said in the Chapter on the ADE, shows that the NDE is part of a larger experiential pattern, unknown to orthodox life science but possibly significant for survival. If we are to understand the meaning of UFO, ND and Marian visions, we need to focus on this total underlying pattern.

Ox-Ho, curiously, refers to the Fatima prophecies. It is generally known that the Catholic Church has not revealed part of the Fatima prophecies, supposed to have been made public in 1960. Why the secrecy? Could the prophecy be embarrassing to the Church? According to the Ox-Ho revelations, "The entity who appeared at Fatima foretold the coming downfall of all religions which were not true to their beliefs. The message was intended to inform the people of the coming changes in the organized churches so that they might become spiritually aware and know that the transition was needed and was not the wrath of God." In 1961-1965, the Garabandal prophecies said that priests and cardinals were heading for perdition and, more specifically, that there would be only two more popes after the present one, thereby making Pope John Paul II the last. And after that, what? The end of the world? A woman Pope? Radical reorganization of the Church?

Like UFO epiphanies, Marian visions seem, to use Jung's phrase, to signal "the end of an era." The year 1960 indeed marked a period on the threshold of tremendous change in the church—e.g., Vatican II, along with many defections or challenges to church authority. The secret Fatima prophecy may have been feared as encouraging even more radical change. The Ox-Ho "revelation" about Fatima recalls Berdyaev who made a similar point over fifty years ago: that Communism would be the scourge of a *false* Christianity. The downfall of Western institutions would result from a failure to evolve creatively, a failure to understand and live by their own truths and ideals.

Global Catastrophe

All three types of vision project what the facts of military technology portend: global catastrophe. The near-death visionaries, like the UFO seers, foresee an earth convulsing with poleshifts, earthquakes and tidal waves; they see a world tottering on the edge of economic collapse or nuclear war. In these prophecies, catastrophe itself is holistic. That is, outer disaster is pictured as caused by inner chaos, geology as somehow subject to the moral forces of humanity. It is the wrong inner "vibrations" that are causing the earth to tremble.

These images of apocalypse also picture postmortem calamity. For instance, the Fatima children had a vision of hell, of "lost souls . . . tumbling about constantly in the flames and screaming with terror." This corresponds to the hellish visions reported, infrequently to be sure, in NDEs.

Images of apocalypse are general and specific. Sometimes where specific, later events suggest genuine precognition. Elements of precognition are best illustrated in Marian prophecies. In 1830, Catherine Laboure was told by Our Lady that "Monseigneur the Archbishop" of Paris would come to grief as part of the growing political upheaval. Archbishop Darboy was in fact murdered in 1870. So did Archbishop de Quelen twice have to flee for his life during the revolution which erupted shortly after this 1830 vision. Further, Archbishop Affre was shot to death on the barricades in 1848. This particular preview seems to have had multiple confirmations.

At Fatima, several events suggest precognition. The children foretold a "miracle" that would occur on October 17, 1917, at noon; this was confirmed by spectacular displays that occurred that day. The Lady told them that Francisco and Jacinta would die very young; that another war (the First World War was not yet over) "would begin in the reign of Pius XI"; that it would be heralded by an "unknown light" in the night sky; that the Church would be persecuted; that Russia would spread a godless ideology, fomenting wars and religious persecution; that several nations would be *annihilated*. All these but the last seem to have come true. For example, the prophetic sign of impending war: on the night of January 25, 1938, the sky in Europe and part of North America lit up with a brilliant display of the northern lights. As for the one yet unfulfilled prophecy of nations being annihilated, it would have made little sense to speak of whole nations being annihilated in 1917. Unfortunately, in the light of nuclear weaponry, it is not at all difficult to imagine the annihilation of entire nations today.

A New Age

But, as we might predict from the ADE, there must be light at the end of the dark tunnel. These visions, however bleak in outlook, give us the signal to go forward, to trust in life. Whatever monsters lie in ambush on the road ahead of us, the last signal is a green light. Like the apparition that faced Saint Paul on the coasts of Europe, the message is: cross over! The near-death prophetic visions tell of the advent of an age of peace, love and brotherhood. The same theme runs through the UFO contactee literature: a New Age, an Aquarian Age lies at the end of the road of our current woes. Both near-death and UFO visionaries speak of a coming "Golden Age." Marian visions, too, see a new age of peace—beyond the smoke and rubble.

A contactee cult called the Solar Light Center published in its Summer-Fall 1969 *Starcraft* journal a list of its leading principles. These include belief in a "Cosmic Christ"; "belief in the expression of universal love, compassion and understanding as the true basis for world peace"; "belief that a spiritual Light is being sent to uplift Earth and raise the frequency level of all cells, all atoms, in preparation for the coming change" and so forth. People of the Solar Light Center believe that a special "Light energy" is being received that will result in a "transition to a higher frequency" of "vibrations" and thus a new Golden Age. This is remarkably similar to Kenneth Ring's work on near-deathers who engage in similar talk of "vibrations" and "frequencies" and an evolutionary "Kundalini energy." Sensations of burning are said to follow both prophetic NDEs and UFO contactee visions; and so are there odd physiological effects in the Marian encounters. Apparently, the Light that burns supernatural images in souls, in burial cloths and tilmas, leaves its trace in living bodies too.

Steiger sums up the teachings of the Space Brothers (translate "Beings of Light" for NDErs): "Man stands now in the transitional period before the dawn of a New Age. With peace, love, understanding and brotherhood on man's part, he will see a great new era begin to dawn." As far as the hopeful side of the apocalyptic morpheme, the Marian visions are slightly less sanguine, more realistic, in a way, and more specifically ideological. Whereas ND and UFO visionaries see the troubles of the world in a general "denseness" of "psychic frequencies," the Marian apocalypse, though equally general in its appeal to our higher human potentials, refers more specifically to the need for a "conversion of Russia," thought to be a unique locus of ideological depravity.

Marian Visions and Feminism

The content of Marian visions raises a special question. Marian visions, of which over two hundred were claimed between 1928 and 1971 are, I believe, an aspect of a general awakening of certain dormant, often repressed, energies of the human psyche. I am referring to the energies, the qualities, the sensibility, associated with the multiplex archetype of the feminine.

Broadly, that is, psychologically understood, the Marian experience resuscitates the earth goddesses of antiquity; the Marian age reconnects modern spiritual sensibilities with the age of Eleusis—the ancient mysteries, a world in which the divine was experienced in relation to certain collective feminine realities. Under the emperor Valentinian, official Christianity, rooted in Judaic male chauvinism, wiped out the cult of the godesses in the fifth century. Entrance to the feminine psyche was apparently blocked. By contrast, the old Greek religion always stayed open to this vital aspect of the total self.

The Kore, maiden daughter of Demeter, like Mary, was also a virgin. Ravished by the God of Death, the Mysteries re-enact her recovery and celebrate the return of spring. They relive the resurrection of the Feminine Psyche and strive to raise from wintry death apparitions of new life. Our near-death experiencers also tell of strange springs of bliss, mysterious flowerings of body and soul. The social visionary Marcuse struggled to shape-shift a new reality principle symbolized by Orpheus, a being of the feminine psyche and the god whose music can make the lion lie down with the lamb. Great poets know the power of this flute call of the soul, the power of the Eternal Feminine, guide of Dante and Goethe. We hear it again, the return of the repressed, in the voices of modern Marian visionaries.

In our search for models of collective transformation, we've hit on something important: woman power, woman consciousness. Anchored to politics, to the massing of new blocs, forces and counterforces, this powerful but arrested dimension of the total human Self is crucial for spiritual radicalism. Perhaps the right deployment of the Feminine Counterforce offers a way beyond the old dichotomies of "right" and "left"—a move toward the politics of a healing Center.

What is the general, universal significance in the call to Marian devotion? For one thing, it means responding to "the angel of peace," cultivating the life-nurturing love of the mother. The esoteric meaning of the Marian visions, I suggest, lies in a general awakening of the archetype of the feminine, a force that, in addition to what it means for women, also touches on the potential of the complete man: the total human Self.

This is not the place to review the phenomenon of modern feminism. I will, however, hazard this remark: the process of empowering the feminine archetype, if carried out authentically, would exert a powerful influence on planetary life. The experiment, as far as I can see, has already begun. New evolutionary possibilities are emerging, energies long held in bondage by rigid ideas of sexual specialization, by patriarchial repression, and are slowly being released on a worldwide scale. The psychology of the feminine archetype, a rich field by contrast with the simple social stereotypes, offers important clues to understanding and furthering the evolution of human consciousness.

Two things, at least, should be said. First, as Marina Warner notes in her study of the myth and cult of the Virgin, *Alone of All Her Sex*, the adulation of disembodied purity degrades women by not respecting their natural sexuality and humanness. The danger, as always with archetypes, is to blanket individuals with abstractions; an obvious example is that old favorite, the madonna/whore projection. On the other hand, only a fundamentalist interpretation of "virgin" would force us into such a clumsy position. In "esoteric" psychology, virginity means androgeny: a quality of wholeness, freedom. It is not something you lose but something you gain, something that enlarges your personal identity.

The second point is that the total feminine archetype is complex: nurturing, life-affirming, peace-loving, yes, but also cunning, dangerous, seductive, daring, artistic, sensual, earthy, etc. Says Karen Rosenberg, "Just when we were beginning to get a sense of the cultural and psychological variety of women's experience, we are told to stop and contemplate the female as harmonious whole." [178] It won't do here to project grandiose savior ideals, which could become a way of destroying the experience of women as persons. In any case, the nurturing, life-enhancing energies of the feminine archetype are in all persons, women and men.

The feminine motif in the ADE helps us see an underlying connection between the mystery cults of antiquity, the Marian visions of modern times and the growing women's movement. Viewed as ultimately stemming from a single consciousness, they suggest a new psychospiritual power emerging on the global scene. The menace to the biosphere, much the brain child of patriarchal modes of consciousness, is arousing the feminine side of the human psyche. We are, I believe, witnessing a spontaneous self-healing of the collective mind, an attempt to redress a dangerous imbalance, a groping to awaken the divine *Shakti*: the feminine force Tantric yoga says sleeps like a coiled serpent at the base of the spine.

One last point—earlier, we discussed materialism in its nihilistic guise. But there is another type of nurturing, sacred materialism—the *mater*ialism of mother earth, of the old Greek and Native American traditions. Etymology is our clue for recovering a lost unity—*mater*, the Latin root linking matter and mother. The Marian visions, thus interpreted in an authentically catholic sense, herald a life-supporting materialism of the New Age.

Function of the Visions:
A Network of Magi

What is the main function of these extraordinary experiences? The answer is clear. In all, it is to warn and to transform. Apocalyptic visions deal in futures. Eschatology is probablilistic, catastrophe is conditional. The ultimate message: it's up to us; a bright and multicolored flag, against a dark horizon, waves us on to action.

Images of ruin rise up from the misty deeps of the world soul; the rough beast slouches toward Bethlehem to be born. In an age foreshadowing nuclear winter, we are all summoned to be magi, to form a network of magi, to hazard the desert and follow where strange stars lead. These lights that flash from the heaven of Mind at Large inspire us to say farewell to the old, the life-denying self. They give us glimpses of where we could go and charge us with the energy to go there. The function of the visions is pretty much the same: to grant courage to change in heart and soul, to sacrifice the gift of ourselves to the infant god of our own higher future. They help us to make the final choice, to take the leap beyond death to new life.

Context

Life and the Forms of Life in Extremis

In the last heartbeat before eternity, the soul sends up its messages of guidance and consolation. The universal adaptive mechanism of the ADE is awakened in life-threatening situations. This is clear in near-death visions. In very deep near-death visions, the adaptive information goes beyond the personal; it addresses the transpersonal and takes the form of a general apocalypse. UFO revelations entered a new phase in 1947 in the wake of the first atomic bombings, events bound to cause a stir in the collective consciousness. UFO revelations, in my view, are part of a response to the increasing risk of nuclear war. They register perturbations in the collective psyche.

UFO and near-death visionaries are clear on this: their visions are given to assist humanity at large in the transition to new forms of life. The earth itself is in transformation; we need to learn to adapt to a new earth because the old earth is passing away. Churned out by the collective unconscious, the vision is a map of global near-death and inner transformation. It is also a response to a life-threatening situation. The species, not just the individual, is on the threshold of near-death. Indeed, all species of life are threatened; hence, catastrophe is pictured in geologic imagery. Person and planet are at risk; this type of prophetic imagery is "designed," it would appear, to provide a perspective with survival value.

But in addition to person and planet, there are forms of culture and spirit; these too are "near-death." The thanatos conspiracy, the leveler and homogenizer of the human spirit, saps the roots of vital forms of life. Thus, not only were Native Americans placed on "reservations" by the white conquistadors, but their forms of spiritual life, rooted in reverence for the land, were also destroyed. Yet as the culture died, it created movements, prophetic visions and new art forms. For example, the Ghost Dance of the plains Indians was inspired by Wovoka, himself a near-death visionary. Similar patterns occur in other messianic religions of the oppressed.

Marian visions are a response to a life-threatening situation; the life of a people's spirit is at stake, however. A collective form of spiritual life may be "near death." Take for example the hailstones of Remiremont in 1907, said to be imprinted with an image of the Virgin (see Rogo, 1982, pp. 141-158) or the recent Marian sightings in Medjugorje, Yugoslavia. Here, as in most Marian settings, are circumstances of political upheaval, repression, persecution, spiritual deadness or indifference. The community is attacked from without or crumbling from within; but death of the spirit is in the air. The visionaries rally to the cause. There is conflict. It is war, the fundamental war of the spirit. The visionaries are persecuted (officials threatened to boil the Fatima children in oil!); but they hold out and, in the end, are vindicated, get their message across, often with the aid of psi wonders. The group is renewed, reordered, revitalized; the group consciousness is resuscitated.

Evolution is punctuated by sudden appearances of novel and unforseeable forms of life; we should expect the same with the psychospiritual evolution of humankind. We cannot predict what new life-saving, life-enhancing forms of spiritual life will emerge to help us to adapt to a weapon-infested environment. So much we can say with confidence. The three patterns we are looking at now offer clues for imagining forms of consciousness with this kind of adaptive value, forms based on the internalizing of *detente*.

Mind at Large as Democrat

If the collective mind is working through this morpheme of the apocalypse, we might expect wide receptivity to the message. And indeed, UFO sightings, like NDEs, are a global phenomenon. They occur to all kinds of people. UFO contactees come from all walks of life, all ages, all countries—likewise with near-death experiencers. Mind at Large is democratic, respects neither rank, nor privilege, nor status, nor wealth, nor power. Our mysterious angel of death and transformation is liable to pay anyone a visit. Marian visions also have a global reach—France, Italy, Portugal, Spain, Lebanon, Egypt, Yugoslavia, etc.—and though they seem confined to Catholic populations, there are growing exceptions, as in Beirut at the Sirian Church of Saint Paul and, most notably, in the spectacular sightings of Zeitoun which were photographed and witnessed by multitudes.

Zeitoun is a small town outside Cairo, a place where legend says the Holy family stopped while in flight from Herod. One evening in 1968, apparitions of the Marian Goddess were seen by two Moslem mechanics. The usual pattern, in which children and Catholics are the visionaries, was broken. It was the most remarkable display of Marian apparitions in modern times. Millions of all religious persuasions observed the strange luminous apparitions of Mary, Joseph, Christ Child, dovelike and other aerial pheonomena. The sightings were of unusual duration, sometimes lasting up to six hours. The period in which these frequent and prolonged sightings took place stretched from 1968 to 1971. They were attended by well-documented healings.

The democratization of the Marian archetype was the culmination of a progression. Notice the sequence of Virgin appearances.

Some Marian Visions Since the Nineteenth Century

Time	Place	Number of Percipients
1830	Paris	One young woman.
1846	Salette	Two children.
1858	Lourdes	One young woman.
1871	Pontmain	Two boys first, then a group of children.
1879	Knock	Fourteen people, mixed population.
1888	Castelpetroso	Two women, then five hundred witnesses.

Time	Place	Number of Percipients
1917	Fatima	Three children, the Virgin; up to 70,000 witnesses to other light phenomena.
1961-65	Garabandal	Three children, prophecy of events to be witnessed by whole earth.
1968-71	Zeitoun	Hundreds of thousands of witnesses, all ages and faiths.

This chart only touches on some of the most well-known cases, but I think it will do to show a definite trend. The number and range of percipients is clearly increasing, as is the duration of the experience. At Fatima, appearances were spaced on a monthly basis for six months, longer and more regular appearances than anything in the nineeenth century. In Garabandal and Zeitoun, during the second half of the twentieth century, the duration of the experiences increased significantly again: first, overall, apparitions in a given location recur over a period of years, and, in the spectacular case of Zeitoun, they last individually for hours.

The nineteenth century marked a period of increase of Marian visions, mainly in France, a traditional stronghold of devotion to the Lady, and where the war between modernism and traditionalism exploded in the French Revolution. Visions of the Holy Virgin again multiply in the early twentieth century and then again in the second half of the twentieth century. If Marian visions are *part of a collective psychospiritual process,* and if life forms continue to be increasingly threatened as we near the end of the twentieth century, then it is reasonable to predict that even more spectacular aerial apparitions will occur in the future.

Indeed, since the threat to life is global, we might predict a global apparition, *a global experience of the transforming light.* Notice that the prophecies of Garabandal speak of just such a thing.

(For the record, the Bishop of Santander and the Holy See concluded that nothing supernatural occurred in Garabandal, which, however, hasn't weakened interest in the cult.) According to predictions, something will appear simultaneously to all inhabitants of the earth. Details are obscure; it is, however, supposed to take place in three stages: a warning, a miracle, a chastisement. The effect will be tremendous; some will experience profound terror, even death. Its function, in plain words, will be to change our minds, to "convert" us.

The global scope of the prophecies may be seen from Conchita's own words. The "miracle" is going to take place *para convertir al mondo entero*—"to convert the whole world." There is also a warning that will precede the miracle. "The warning is a thing that comes directly from God and will be visible throughout the entire world, in whatever place anyone might be." It will be "like a revelation of our sins and will be seen equally by believers and nonbelievers and people of any religion." It will be "like a purification," "a sort of catastrophe," and "we shall see the consequences of the sins we have committed." The warning will be something "supernatural and will not be explained by science." The miracle will leave a trace, a "sign that will remain forever at the pines . . . that we will be able to photograph, televise and see, but not touch. It will be evident that this is not a thing of this world but from God." The sign will be comparable to "rays of light" but will not be a natural light phenomenon.

Now if none of these bring about a change of heart in humankind, there is yet a *chastisement* to come. In June of 1962, Conchita and the other two child visionaries were observed "shrieking in terror," waving their hands, as if to ward off the sight of something horrible. One of them cried out: "Oh! May little children die rather than experience this!" [176] It is not hard to suppose that this Garabandal nightmare vision was like the nightmares children are nowadays having of nuclear war. Children might well be unwittingly sensitive to global trends.

It is as though the Helping Intelligence is getting more desperate and feels driven to intervene on our behalf. Perhaps these prophecies are voicing, in their own spiritual dialect, a message for the whole human race. Clearly, the same message is coming from other sources. The different forms begin to merge into one form and seem to be struggling to break out of the molds of ancient sect and ideology. Hence the archetypes of Christianity are erupting into Moselm cultural space (as in Zeitoun and Beirut) and, into the Communist world (as in Yugoslavia), stopping, paralyzing the mind (as happened to Bernadette Soubirous and some UFO contactees), reviving ancient beliefs, funneling transforming energies into the world.

Nor need we underestimate the power of this collective spiritual energy. When we consider the prodigies of Fatima—the ability to reduce a crowd of 70,000 to abject terror, to create the illusion of the sun plunging to the earth, to part the clouds, to dry up the rain, to fan the earth with sudden heat and to turn a Portugese countryside into a

colorful electric circus—the Garabandal prophecy of a global apparitional experience seems less fantastic. Something quite powerful appeared in Fatima to overwhelm the minds of the most hardened and
hostile skeptics. Or when we consider the sheer massive publicity of
supernormal power that displayed itself in Zeitoun, again the Garabandal prophecy seems less fantastic.

Reflect for a moment on the utility, given the growing nuclear
crisis, of such a global illumination: instant panoramic memory, a
quick fix on the collective "consequences of our sin"—a vision perhaps of the horrors of nuclear war. It is not hard to imagine some
Helping Intelligence, some agency of Mind at Large, preparing to
engineer such a show for the human audience.

Aftereffects

But we have yet to remark on the aftereffects of these experiences, a subject we can deal with only in brief. Again, similar patterns
exhibit themselves. The experiences change people's sense of value,
truth and reality. The following statement about UFO contactees
could be made about NDE and Marian cases: "Families and friends of
the contactee report that he is literally a different and changed person
after his alleged experience. Higher intelligence and perception are
often mentioned, as well as a seeming increase in ESP or psychic
abilities." [177] NDE, UFO and Marian seers all show sharp changes
in spiritual values; they see a new world of love, brotherhood and
peace coming. They show, as Steiger says, a new trust in a "higher
intelligence"—what we might call Mind at Large—the "mind" of life
anxious about the survival, the ongoing evolution of life on earth.

Aftereffects include an increase in psi ability; if this is true, we
may take it as evidence for this "higher" intelligence at work. On
general grounds, psi probably works best when it works transcen-
dently, that is, toward the benefit of the race as a whole. There are
indications, for instance, that talented psychics like Edgar Cayce were
unable to use their gifts directly for themselves and, in general, that
ego-bound activities are self-defeating in psi-land. Healers, saints and
yogis, as instruments of the universal enlightenment process, do, as
a matter of fact, seem to show the most powerful psi abilities.

In any case, researchers [99], [98], [97], offer evidence that near-
death experiencers are more disposed to have, or at least to notice,
psi or out-of-body experiences, or to be more sensitive to the spiritual
world that seems naturally linked with them. There are different

ways of accounting for these correlations. One possibility is that the near-death encounter, especially when it is very deep, puts the subject in touch with the collective, evolving tendencies of the race. In other words, psi may work best when it is serving the interests of evolution, pointing to the higher adaptive potential of human beings.

Among the aftereffects of great Marian visions is the building of shrines, churches and cathedrals. Shrines, such as Lourdes, sometimes become the center of unusual and even paranormal healings. Lourdes, for instance, has its own medical staff that decides, according to the rather strict standards of Lambertini, on the status of claimed miracles. Some of these, as with Pierre de Rudder's materialized legbone, are in a category of their own and quite defy normal accounting. [15] More recently, in the late '60s, are many reports, some well-documented medically, of miraculous healings in Zeitoun. Congenital blindness and advanced cancers are said to have been healed during collective visions of the Mother of Light. [179]

All this seems in harmony with what we said in Chapter III: that psi is part of a transcendent system of functioning and that, probably, the lower the level of psychosocial evolution, the greater the likelihood of safety "restrictions" on psi output. Whereas, the higher the spiritual evolution, the greater the tendency for psi to manifest. Moreover, if psi is linked to evolution, as some biological thinkers believe, psi may manifest more readily during periods of evolutionary crisis. The function of the psi—healings in Zeitoun, for instance—is not just to aid suffering individuals; it is also to strengthen the conscience, the consciousness of the race. The Coptic Christians, at the time of the apparitions, were, as a minority, religiously and hence politically threatened by Moslem and Communist forces; the visions of the Mother of Light helped them, as a people, to deal with their oppression.

Unusual psi powers may become increasingly available as *global*, not merely *cultural*, near-death approaches and thus as the evolutionary imperative becomes more stringent. However, psi, as our code word for certain radical extensions of the human personality, promises no secret substitute for military or technical power. It offers something quite different. Call it the sanction for a new way of being in the world, a basis for a different kind of sensibility, a living consciousness expanded to embrace the oneness of all life forms. This would be the most important potential suggested from the study of NDEs, the key to a new collective mode of being.

Missionaries and Transforming Forces

Psi, as with Padre Pio and Sai Baba, is a tool for transition, for building the Noosphere. An extended social sensibility is common to the three types of experience. Our visionaries change their own lives; they also feel a sense of mission toward others. In one case of a powerful NDE reported by Kenneth Ring, the "Light" told a woman, in these "exact words":

> With the gift you have now received, go forth and tell the masses of people that life after death exists; that you shall all experience my PROFOUND LOVE! Love is the key to the universe; you must all learn to live in peace and harmony with one another on earth while you have the chance. This will be a very difficult task for you, my child, a huge undertaking, but you shall do it. You are loved. [99]

Who or what is this Light? One might invest it with any identity or just think of it as the voice of humanity. But *if* the Light assumed the identity of the Virgin Mary, the message would pass as Marian. The address, "my child"; the Christian idea that *we are loved*; and that spreading the message of this love will be "very difficult", "a huge undertaking," is unmistakably Marian. The Marian visionaries, at Fatima and Garabandal, for instance, were forewarned of difficult times; but they too were encouraged to trust. "In the end, my Immaculate Heart will triumph," the Lady of Light declared to the children of Fatima in 1917.

Christ, in his cosmic aspect, appears often in the UFO revelations. And where there is Christ, you will find his apostles. Again, from Steiger's study of the Aquarian Revelations: "The flying saucer missionaries are quite unconcerned about their personal welfare and are barely heedful of the needs of their families." The idea of mission is a feature of prophetic-apocalyptic traditions; if we are observing, as I believe we are, the effects of a long-range Higher Intelligence operation—initiated by the collective mind in response to probable eco-catastrophe—then the missionary component makes sense and won't slacken as we approach end-time.

The missionary goal of transformation requires energy. The archetypes of transformation release psychic energy. Ring calls it kundalini and observed specific symptoms of this force, like sensations of heat, in some of his subjects. UFO contactees often complain of odd sensations, heat being commonly mentioned. The idea of a vital force, of a cosmic *elan* in Bergson's terms, is old and widespread. One could list the names, ki, mana, odic force, animal magnetism, orgone energy, etc. Parapsychology gives us psychokinesis. In the Christian tradition, it is called the Holy Spirit; and Charismatic Christianity is awakening to this force en masse today.

Indeed, it seems right to look at this awakening of Charismatic Christianity as part of the same current of Marian consciousness. We observe some radical thrusts of the Healing Spirit—in the form of the theology of liberation, the civil disobedience movement and the Catholic Bishop's Letter, which reverses an antiquated position on war, challenges authorities who worship the idol of the Bomb and links up with progressive thinking the world over.

A mission to change the global mind needs organization, a mass core of enlisted warriors of the spirit and, perhaps, a new technology. The NDErs are the newest group of our visionaries; already they are beginning to network under the aegis of IANDS, The International Association for Near-Death Studies, whose headquarters is located in Storrs, Connecticut.

As for UFOs, Vallee suggests there is an occult organization, which includes masters of espionage and psychic technologies, manipulating the mind of mankind. He is unclear about the source of this occult intelligence operation and is open to the possibility that it is quite mundane. Vallee feels we need to make sense of the apparent *control system* revealed in UFO phenomena. An intelligence does seem to be systematically trying to mold us anew, perhaps to assist in our much-needed evolution. But Vallee senses something malevolent here and cites sinister links with Right Wing enclaves, and other intrigues. Like a good science fiction writer, Vallee plays up the mystery and suspense; but there is no evidence for such a secret organization.

Still, the basic insight remains: the UFO phenomenon *does* look like a control system; it is, however, more easily explained by the machinations of Mind at Large. We already have evidence suggesting the reality of archetypes and psi. The similar pattern of UFO and Marian visions with prophetic and profound NDEs argues for a psychic origin of these experiences. The pattern reveals the activity of collective intention, an intelligence with creative power and, contrary to Vallee, benevolent but not all-powerful. (A malevolent side *is* always possible, however.)

As for the Marian visionaries—they are part of the oldest "occult" organization in the Western world: the Catholic Church. This, too, had its sinister side, its inquisitions and auto-da-fes. But a powerful creative energy lies in that ancient psychospiritual network, and we observe it at work today in many forms and places.

The numbers factor is worth noting. A 1982 Gallup Poll showed that about seven or eight million Americans have had NDEs, which translates, globally, into even greater numbers. Another 1973 Gallup Poll on UFOs is interesting. Fifteen million Americans claim to have seen a UFO. The percentage believing them real has risen from 46 per cent in 1966 to 54 per cent in 1973 to 57 per cent in 1978. We have already called attention to the growing spiral of Marian phenomena, spreading in extent, duration and access to public perception. According to a Blue Army publication, the Fatima-based organization claims twenty-two million adherents, all committed to the belief that the way to right the world is through psychospiritual power, namely, prayer. All this, taken collectively, implies a growth of an unusual degree of *belief* potential in large masses of humanity. Goatishly inclined rationalists like Vallee see in this a menace to human dignity, as if it implies automatic slavish submission to the dark forces.

A parapsychologist would be interested in the creative potential of mass belief. It is known that belief and expectation are psi-creating; on a mass scale, we do not know what psychokinetic forces could be released—enough perhaps to conjure a global near-death experience! Admittedly, this is a radical speculation; but somehow this enlarged belief potential may help to create a New Age consciousness, a deeply understood, deeply felt anti-nuclear way of life. The high belief index itself is nothing to fear; *what* people believe needs to be worried about.

Suppose there is a growing corps of *warriors of the rainbow,* to use a Native American phrase. What sort of technology is available to combat the world managers of the death-instinct? Given that the new missionaries of Mind at Large are gaining access to transforming forces, what of the job of speeding up our collective transformation? Obviously, we need a "technology" that gets to the minds and hearts of the "enemy" within. Vallee refers to an occult "psychotronic" technology—methods, developed by the Czech researcher, Robert Pavlita, for utilizing "bioenergy." The Marian tradition, too, has its spiritual "technologies": the scapular, the miraculous medal, the rosary. All these depend on the intercession of the Virgin, the "mediatrix of all graces." Many extraordinary claims exist, uninvestigated by science, about these psychospiritual technologies.

There are two other points on spiritual technology. First, secrecy:

The Marian visionaries keep us in a state of suspense, expectation and ambiguity. Certain prophecies are not made public. Near-death visionaries are vague and say they forget the details of their visions of knowledge. Their "forgetting" is akin to the "secrets" of the Marians—a way of creating suspense, intensifying expectation and keeping the future indeterminate.

Another method of creating psychic tension is to manipulate sex energies. We already noted the "kundalini" effects of NDErs. One order of UFO contactees, the Order of Melchidezak, which traces itself back to the high priests of the Old Testament, abstains from sexual emissions to obtain spiritual-revolutionary power: in a word, tantric or platonic sex yoga. The cult of the Virgin may be seen as a type of Tantric yoga. Rightly used, this energy needn't be a candidate for neurotic repression. It *could* be used to expand the erotic sense of reality. Moreover, this form of Marian Tantrism—many of the Catholic saints were masters of it—is probably linked with psi abilities.

In Catherine Laboure's vision of 1830, the Blessed Lady was seen standing on a globe over a green, gold-spotted snake. Whoever masters the sexual impulse—the snake under the Lady's foot—will also use the world as a footstool: an Icon of Catholic Tantrism. The esoteric sense of "virgin" is here indicated; the Lady and the Snake are one. The Snake is mastered, male energy fused with female. Or, conversely, in devotion to the Marian Icon, the female energy is discovered in the wholeness of the male Self. The cult of Mary, esoterically taken, is a quest for sexual wholeness. It is an old quest. In the Gnostic Gospel according to Thomas, it is said that we "enter the Kingdom" when we "make the two one, the inner as the outer, the above as the below, and the male and the female into a single one." It would be a powerful ally against divisive forces, to discover the "virgin" within, the true virility, the healing energies of the whole Self.

Eastern *Tantric* yogas, as well as the Church's teachings on sex, go back to the oldest shamanic traditions; they are based on fusing intelligence with our vital instincts. To bring down the empire of thanatos will not be easy; among many possibilities is new thinking about sex, the tremendous force of the life-instinct. Eros, root of spiritual transformation, is precious stuff in the experiement of life. We hardly understand its evolutionary potential. If the death-instinct is gaining ground, we might turn to traditional sex yogas. We might learn to mobilize new energies for spiritual warfare.

Metaphors of Mind at Large

Let us then meditate on the mediatrix, the mothering power of our collective mind. We need to build a poetics of science—shape hieroglyphs of the soul to stir, gather and direct the energies of creative evolution. The treasure is hidden within the cave; but certain guardians block the entrance. We lack the passwords to help our passages.

These visionary phenomena are like passwords—like metaphors of Mind at Large. *Metaphor* comes from a verb meaning to "carry across." Let us tie ourselves to these rafts of Mind at Large and use them to ferry across the ocean between the old and the new age.

To beat the conspiracy of the death-instinct, we need a discourse on miraculous method. Not Descartes but Rimbaud. The New Age must begin in fantasy, for the old age is dying of reality.

16

Truth in Transformation

One thought fills immensity.

—Blake

Verum et factum convertuntur.

—Vico

Who knows whether the faithfulness of individuals here below to their own over-beliefs may not actually help God in turn to be more effectively faithful to his own tasks.

—William James

Many futures are latent in the womb of time. We have traced the shadows of a dark future and, in the last chapter, a brighter form of things to come. A higher consciousness is within us. It may appear in the experiences of mystic and poet, ascetic and shaman; in vision quests and ancient mysteries; in the dreams, psychedelic and near-death encounters of ordinary people; in sky epiphanies at the crossroads of history. The symbols, landmarks and signs are all about us. We need to decipher the meanings, glimpse the pointers through mists of current sensibilities.

In the last chapter we marshalled evidence for these phenomena in the guise of NDE, UFO and Marian visions. The common theme was collective death and rebirth. The study of this morpheme of collective transformation adds a dimension to the nuclear debate. It suggests that a major collective change in human consciousness is an empirical possibility. Apart from such a change, chances of reversing the arms race are probably quite small. A new inner empowerment is essential before we can learn not to rely on military power for security.

Hence, we pursue this difficult probe into the collective psyche for signs of hope. The NDE was our inlet into a larger sea of psychospiritual potential and offered a credible model for collective spiritual transformation.

As the probability of nuclear holocaust increases, upheavals in human consciousness are also likely to increase. Nowadays, predictions and prophecies of the future are epidemic. Some emanate from fancy think tanks; others appear under the rubric of futures science. Much is based on biblical prophecy and stirs up millenial fantasies. Prophecy is itself often a catalyst in unstable social processes. For instance, growing numbers of evangelical Christians see events in the Middle East, along with the prospect of nuclear war, as part of God's plan for Judgment Day. Such views may lead to opposing peacemaking efforts. Prophecy, in this sense, can be dangerously self-verifying. We need to understand this category of self-verifying truths. In this sense, "poetry" is part of the process of psychosocial evolution. We need then to focus on the poetics of evolution.

The Poetics of Evolution

"Winning" at this point of the survival game calls for a poetics of evolution. The metaphysics of Mind at Large is "poetic." It affirms the possibility of our psychospiritual evolution. Let us then place the notion of evolutionary poetics in the context of choices facing us today.

In this book, we have attempted to form an alternate picture of the phenomenon of death, based on psi and death-related phenomena. We constructed a model of psychosocial transformation, a kind of evolutionary scenario, and pitted it against the scenario of probable nuclear catastrophe. The evolutionary scenario grew from the attempt to understand the psychic resources for dealing with death. The model of collective transformation was based on observations of individual transformations.

Holy war-mongers aside, people want to avoid nuclear disaster; but people are constrained in their thinking about what is possible. Chained to constricted world views, we submit to the lethal status quo. Faced with a "higher" vision of reality, we respond with passive skepticism: "How could such things really be true?"

As I acquainted myself with the facts of the military build-up and began to see a kind of conspiracy of the death-instinct, I sometimes felt despair. Somewhere along the line, I decided despair was a temptation I had to resist, knowing that we are all up against a simple choice: either to respond to the call of life or succumb to the lure of death. There was "evidence" to justify both views: nuclear fatalism and high optimism for the future.

Finding myself under the spell of a defeatist idea of truth, I had to build, at least in a makeshift way for myself, a new raft of truth to sail the sea of existence. Philosophers, prophets and scientists have grappled with the idea of truth for ages; but the quest for a saving truth becomes crucial under the shadow of the doomsday clock. We need to drop a lot of useless baggage and get to the healing heart of truth.

Consider an outline of two general outlooks—one that expresses that of the established power structures; the other, more sympathetic to the active minorities who believe in alternate worlds. The terms are my own; others may use their own lingo. The "poetics" are the same, however.

OLD METAPHYSICS OF THE BOMB	NEW AGE METAPHYSICS OF DEATH AND ENLIGHTENMENT
Realism and realpolitik.	Surrealpolitik.
Paranoia.	Metanoia.
Security through clinging to ideology.	Security through trust in universal higher consciousness.
The best weaponry is material, based on manipulation through force and terror; appeal to lowest psychic forces.	The best weaponry is spiritual, based on rational diplomacy and understanding of basic human needs; appeal to highest psychospiritual forces.
Mind is epiphenomenon of individual brain.	Brain is epiphenomenon of Mind at Large.
Life after death a wish-fulfilling illusion.	Life after death a probability.
Human nature essentially fixed in its limitations.	Human nature in process, unlimited in its evolutionary potential.

We could extend the list. The point is that items on each side of the page form a pattern, an outlook. For instance, a strict materialist is not likely to put much stock in a higher consciousness for security; for him, security is apt to lie in weaponry, in manipulation of the "lower" mind. Is there a clear sense in which we can say that one outlook is "true"? We could argue for or against any item on our lists; surely, we are free to play down one kind of evidence or play up another. But we cannot, on the whole, say that one outlook is "true" and another "false." Outlooks may rest on particular propositions, atoms of unambiguous truth and falsehood; but the outlook as a whole—the metaphysics or paradigm—runs on different logical rules. Outlooks are communal activities in which things are *made* true. Hence the epigraph for this chapter from Vico: what is true and what is made are convertible.

Conforming and Transforming Truths

Certain fundamentalist habits of thought are a stumbling block to exploiting our inner potentials. A rigid sense of truth gets in the way. But if we hope to adapt to the dangerous world we have created, we are going to have to change our raw perceptions of truth and reality. One way is to distinguish between conforming and transforming truths.

Some Philosophic Notes

A struggle has been under way between two camps of truth seekers, two concepts of truth: one conforming, the other transforming. Hegel's distinction between *Vernuft* and *Verstehen* shows this nicely. There is, according to Hegel, a conflict between Reason *(Vernuft)*, creatively responsive to the living flow of history, and Understanding *(Verstehen)*, the fixed categories, the frozen conceptions of reality that express partial insights of the past. To the extent that Spirit or *Geist* is evolving toward the future, it opposes our partial perceptions of reality. Reason is an instrument of transforming truth; understanding merely conforms to what is.

An early sign of war in the history of truth was Vico's critique of Descartes. Descartes saddled us with the computational model of conforming truth: whatever could not be filtered through the grids of linear logic, he degraded in truth status. The insights of a cross section of human experience became absolute truth to which all thought was condemned to conform. In *On the Study Methods of Our Time,* written in 1709, Vico [180] denied that the Cartesian method was an adequate model for all science and concepts of truth. Vico struggled to revalidate, resacralize history, art and religion. But, according to Vico, you had to explore the "modifications" of your own mind to rediscover the truth values of "barbaric" psychic realities.

If we wish to *verify* the new metaphysics, the "reality" of the new collective psychospiritual force field, we must explore the modifications of our own minds. We must become authentic individuals to "verify" the prophetic truths of Mind at Large. If we hope to give new blood to new ideals we must be ready to enter into honest dialogue with our own deep fears and longings. The elusive goal of peace cannot be secured without first exploring the labyrinth of our own selves. The source of peace lies hidden in the tangled underbrush of our unexplored selves.

For Vico, as for Hegel, the founding, the evolution of civilization, springs from a creative form of truth: a poetic metaphysics. New societies are founded by the archaic imagination, by poets whose intellects have not been "rusted" by soul-deadening reflection. To be sure, the Cartesian conception of truth was transforming and became the basis for founding a new technical civilzation. But the total poetic truth of humanity was deconstructed, invalidated. Vico's attack on Descartes was an attack on the *inhumanity* of conforming truths.

One could rewrite the history of philosophy from the viewpoint of conforming versus transforming truths. The distinction has been drawn before; nuclear nihilism forces us to face it anew. Nietzsche knew the vital function of fiction. Dionysos embodied his archetype of poetic transformation, not Apollo whom he identified with a Socratic perversion of instinct, a destruction of imagination. The only truths are truths that enhance life; the wisdom of "lies" is above the knowledge of conforming truths.

The struggle on behalf of life-enhancing truth was waged by William James, student of the nuances of truth and of the nuances of consciousness. In particular, he was intrigued by the notion of self-verifying truth, where holding a belief is itself a condition for confirming the truth of a belief. The example he gives might be of interest to a surreal politician.

Trust, he says, is self-verifying. Imagine the following. There is a holdup in a train. How is it possible that one man, even armed, could keep a trainload of people in abeyance? The armed man assumes no one person trusts his fellow passengers to risk intervention. If all

trusted each other to make a first move, what bandit would dare to
face being overwhelmed by the mass in concert? The power of arms
rests on certain patterns of collective belief. Shatter that belief and
you shatter the power of arms.

For Cantwell Smith, the central focus of religious truth is the individual person; religions as creeds, as true or false, are destined for
extinction. The New Age, beyond creeds and ideologies, will root
itself in a common source of piety and good will, a personal relationship with the Transcendent. According to Smith, it is

> dangerous and impious to suppose that Christianity is true, as an
> abstract system, something 'out there' impersonally subsisting,
> with which we can take some comfort in being linked—its effortless
> truth justifying us, and giving us status. Christianity, I would sug-
> gest, is not true absolutely, impersonally, statically; rather it can *be-
> come* true, if and as you or I appropriate it to ourselves and interior-
> ize it, insofar as we live it out from day to day. It becomes true as we
> take it off the shelf and personalize it, in dynamic actual existence.
> [181]

What Smith says of Christianity as an abstraction is also true of
the New Holistic Paradigm, true of a New Age Metaphysics of Death
or of any ideal or paradigm we choose to entertain. The idea of transforming truth helps us look at old problems in new ways. For instance, instead of parapsychologists and anti-parapsychologists being obssessed with the quality and degree of evidence for particular
claims, we may stress the transforming truth potential of psi data—
learn to *act* on the basis of a theoretically enhanced belief in our creative potential, both individual and collective. Transforming truth
roots itself in the creative power of spirit.

It is an old dictum of spiritual philosophy, a common New Age
belief, that thought, desire, creates reality. Psi science, testimony of
the saints, observations from daily life, all these attest to this power of
belief. Beliefs are transforming truths. What, then, are the beliefs we
cherish most, the hopes, the visions we are transforming into reality?
If it is true that the collective mind is unconsciously creating the
present, as well as foreshadowing the future, and if it is true that each
of our individual minds counts in the final drift of Mind at Large,
then each of us, individually and personally, has a hand in shaping
the future of life on earth. Our thoughts are subtly changing into
things; our thinking is a "thinging."

In the current planetary perspective, transforming truth is all. We have glimpsed a better world. The question is: how to "make it come true?"

Hidden and Unhidden Choices

Choice permeates the fabric of our mental life. We begin by choosing what we use in our construction of reality. We focus on particular sets of data and push others into the background—the orthodoxies of science, the revelations of mystical life, the doctrines of theology, the insights of philosophers or psychologists, the data and theories of parapsychology. Or we shape a new pattern from different sets of data. Outlooks are shaped by this initial choice.

We favor one hypothesis or another. For one person the evidence for a haunting may be dropped as coincidence, overheated imagination; for another, it's suggestive, worthy of further consideration. This follows from the first choice. If you ignore psi data or UFO data or "miracle" data, then individual cases of these types won't carry much weight. From the first, often unconscious, choices springs a powerful dynamic.

There are criteria and methods to guide our choices. But we fall back upon choice again; for it's an open question—*what* criteria and *what* methods we choose in our search for, our construction of, reality. The whole enterprise of knowledge is riddled with hidden choices, impelled by secret fears, desires and ambitions. The quest for truth is never impartial; even God selfishly wants us to conform to his truth.

Transformatives

A trend in Western thought rebels against conformist epistemologies: theories of knowledge, dating from Aristotle, define truth as a relation of conformity of subject to object, statement to state of affairs. According to the conformist conception of truth, a statement is true because it conforms to a given state of affairs.

Another species of truth is based not on conformity but on "transformity." Now the state of affairs conforms to the statement. The "statement," or belief in the statement, transforms the reality. Illustration: "God is love." Clearly, this is not a statement to which any obvious state of affairs corresponds. Call it a "transformative" whose truth value lies in the way it helps us to act upon indeterminate states of affairs. Seen strictly in the light of conforming truth, we dismiss "God is love" as meaningless. Yet those who believe it is true might be disposed to act in conformance with *it*; they might even change the world so that it increasingly made sense to say that God *is* love. If we act as if we believe that God is love, the world will perhaps begin to look *as if it is true* that God is love.

Survival and Transforming Truth

Transformatives are handy in the survival game. Place the concept of truth itself in the context of evolutionary theory, of healing the nuclear cancer of our civilization

Truths, myths of self-transformation, are verified by living them; if they are not lived, they are not true, and we are not true to them. If we save the myth, the myth will save us.

The truth of saving myth is a creative act; it differs from the truth of statements that merely assert matters of fact. If it is true that the sky is blue, it is because the sky is indeed blue; one reports on a state of affairs. Here truth mirrors the reality of the world. But other beliefs are becoming true; such budding beliefs are sometimes self-verifying. For example, if I incessantly mistrust you, treat you as untrustworthy, I increase the likelihood of you behaving in bad faith. Conversely, acts of trust increase the likelihood of calling forth trustworthiness. Live the myth of trust, and truth will forge, not merely mirror, reality.

The choice is between the conforming truths of the arms race — "realism", "rationalism", "deterrence", "the lessons of history", etc.—and the transforming truths of the metanoid mind, the creative energies of life, a New Age and so on.

I choose to believe that life is negentropic, erotic, and that the "force" of life itself will inform my transforming truths. We have to get past the roadblocks of conforming truth. We are tied to the corpse of conforming truth, immobilized by the hypnotic drumbeat of the thanatos conspiracy. If we give ourselves to the aims of a larger, richer life, the truths we embrace will awaken the energies of transformation.

Psi and Transformatives

The idea of transforming truth gains an ally from parapsychology. Indeed, I am tempted to say that parapsychology is mainly the study of transforming truths. Thus, believers in psi have more psi experiences and hence confirm their belief in the reality of psi; nonbelievers ("goats") score below chance. This so-called "sheep-goat" effect, though marginal, predicts the occurrence of psi. [182] It applies to the average person who has no special spiritual or psychic gifts. It applies more dramatically to the inspired who truly believe it possible to move mountains: the great saints, yogis and adepts who make "miraculous" psi.

Cases of apparent precognition may be types of *self-fulfilling prophecy*. In parapsychology, a sharp distinction between precognition and psychokinesis cannot easily be drawn; it always seems possible that when we have foreshadowed or foreseen the future, we have in fact had a hand in causing it to come about. Our forewarning dreams and apparitions may as much show what is already stirring to life within ourselves as they show the future.

Here the blurring between precognition and psychokinesis is *apropos*. Marian, UFO and NDE prophetic visions of catastrophe and rebirth are best seen as expressing trends toward probable states of being, images, perhaps, for mobilizing adaptive behaviors. It is better to reject their fatalism and take them as spurs to rousing human potentials.

An important experiment in group psychokinesis, reported in Owen and Sparrow's *Conjuring Up Philip* [183], touches on the question of transforming truth. The purpose of the experiment, conducted by a group from the Toronto Society of Psychical Research, was to conjure a ghostly apparition through a special group psychological technique.

They made up a story about a mythical personage called Philip. For one year, they meditated on "Philip," struggled to make their fantasy tangible. At first they sat and meditated calmly on their mythic Philip, rehearsing his tale of love betrayed, revenge and untimely death—the stuff of many a haunting. Results at first were poor. But the time spent was not altogether wasted; a strong sense of solidarity developed among the researchers.

After studying the work of Kenneth Batcheldor and Colin Brookes-Smith, English scientists who worked in the psychology of PK production, the group changed their tactic; gathered in a circle, as in a Victorian seance, joking and singing, they dropped all self-conscious striving. Meanwhile, still focused on the goal, they merged freely, in a skillfully-induced mood of self-surrender, with Philip's myth.

The new tactic worked, and "Philip" was duly conjured. He did not quite make it as an apparition but succeeded in making his presence known *physically* by sounds of no recognizable frequencies, and by levitating various physical objects. The results were noted repeatedly by competent observers and were recorded on tape and video.

The implications of this experiment are tremendous. It adds a new dimension to the idea of transforming or self-verifying truth. Perhaps in this experiment we gain a hint as to how the Divine, the Transcendent, discloses itself to us. It *needs* us. The collective we, believing, create the miracle, the various epiphanies and auditions of Mind at Large. Substitute "God" for "Philip," religious believers for the Toronto group and we have a new basis for understanding and exploring the world of "religious" realities, a world of transforming truths.

The Toronto experiment demonstrates the power of transforming truth, the power of the group mind directly to alter physical reality. "Philip" offers a clue for understanding the collective apparitions of Mary, discussed in the last chapter. We are, more than we might think, the subtle artificers of the world we inhabit. What "fiction," what "Philip," what god or goddess, shall we choose to *verify*—to make true? That is the final choice.

The Inner Arms Race

My aim here has not been to review the politics, economics or history of the arms race; nor to outline specific ways of bringing it to a halt; but to study the impact of the increasing probability of nuclear war on our collective psyche; and to show that it is stirring up powerful forces within us. These forces are real and can change our lives.

In this chapter, we sketched a theory of truth, a poetics of conscious evolution. The old truths have sustained the old death-oriented civilization. We need a new truth, a new model of truth, for a new civilzation. The healing truths of the future cannot be conforming truths; they cannot be based on what has failed. They must be truths with the power to transform us; they must be lodestars of our higher potentials.

Is a real New Age dawning? A sign would be the arms race stopped, reversed, the energies of death transmuted into the energies of life. When that happens, we'll know a New Age has begun.

But the arms race reveals a history, a way of life. It is the sinister flower of high technical civilization—a symptom of cultural schizophrenia, of intellect dissociated from heart and soul, of the ego and its abstractions on the rampage. To stop and reverse it, we'll have to go beyond politics, economics and ideology; the arms race speaks to our need for a new way of life on earth, for a transformation in the spirit.

In response to all this, there are perhaps three schools of thought. First are those who believe we must begin by working on our selves to discover the source of peace within; in this search for inner peace, we are told, we begin to work on our private acre of immediate reality, patiently spreading from neighbor to world at large.

Second are the peace activists. All kinds of peace groups are springing up on a world-wide scale. It is said that in the Bay Area of California alone, there are over five hundred groups of peace activists. A strong awakening of Christian conscience may be seen the world over, a pro-life stance revealed in coherent revulsion against the anti-life of our medical, economic, social and military practices. The human potential movement is addressing itself to the job of peace—there are peace workshops, peace meditations; talk of creating a new peace paradigm, recognition that peace must be waged on many fronts: ecological, economic and philosophical.

There are grass-roots movements like the nuclear freeze. Scores of cities and counties in the United States have declared themselves nuclear-free zones by ordinance, town meeting or referendum. People are calling for disinvestment of city funds in the stock of nuclear weapons manufacturers. The range of peace-oriented actions is wide and various: door to door canvassing, writing letters to government officials, nonviolent civil disobedience, war-tax resistance and so forth. Whether you attach a bumper sticker to your car or camp with the women at Greenham Common against the cruise missiles, options for action are available.

One has only to distinguish the inner and outer models to see that a third, which embodies both, is best. For it's plain that inner transformation without action will never set the banners of the New Age flying. Nor will our activists succeed in bringing peace into the world if they are not at peace with themselves.

Each of us has a role to play in the great survival game. If we become numb and passive in the face of the challenge, we unwittingly join in the conspiracy of death. The good news is that a real psychospiritual force, is awakening in the world today—an expression of Mind at Large, the guiding intelligence of Life itself. It draws its strength in part from individual minds, from what each of us does and thinks.

Whatever path you choose, whether from the inside out or from the outside in, the goal is the same: to realize that in the final matters of life and death we are animated by a single light. The one Light is not just a metaphor but a loving power, a living energy.

The threat of thermonuclear war is a spur to human evolution. Nothing is certain about the future, and conditions are ripe for the unexpected. It would be odd this late in the game not to feel malaise; but there are grounds for hope too. If we cast a cold eye on all high dreams and utopian visions, we only abort the birth of the possible. But if we choose to believe in the vision of a new age, we may thereby hasten its coming. Faith in the future stems from the past; evolution teaches that anything can happen. Out of chaos, miracles are sometimes born. Who can guess what new form of life, what angel of transformation, awaits us in days to come?

CODA

There is a place beyond the flatlands of the human soul—a place of many names. Poets evoke it in images and rhymes; musicians trace echoes of its uncanny chords. Dreamers catch glimmers of its otherworldly light. Philosophers search for it on frail ships of reason. Mystics claim to be regular sojourners to this far country of the mind. The heroes of myth and the heroes of history are haunted by longings to conquer this final citadel. The catechisms preach to us of it. Shamans and monks, children in their magic games, devise ways of teasing out its mysteries, tasting its sacred powers. Those who skirt at the edge of the world in mishaps of near-death come back stammering tales of its ineffable charm.

And now at this dangerous hour of history, the shamans of science have begun the search. They search beyond the end of the known world, the place beyond Ocean, the Waters of Death.

From many sources we catch notes of one melody. From all times and cultures, a Certain Same Message is being tapped out from the timeless depths. Strange hints and beckonings, a manuscript in a bottle tossed up from unknown seas, pregnant hieroglyphs scratched on ancient stones: all are a festival for archeologists and astronomers of the Mind.

339

And yet, some say this place is in our very midst, that we only need to change our ways of seeing, if we wish to contemplate the fabulous beauty. Yet despite this nearness and presence, it remains far away and we feel its absence. For however close it lies to our breast, we hesitate before an enchanted boundary. For at the gate of the great treasure stand guardians whose glance can paralyze mighty warriors.

Now though this place is far away in its nearness and terrible in its beauty, and though the road there is crooked, near mapless and strewn with pitfalls, the journey is always undertaken.

And travelers tell tales.

Always we hear of light, surpassing the sun in splendor but gentle as love itself. The one radiance radiates into many forms, many landscapes of the soul. We behold it in strange disguises: now smiling as Jesus or Aphrodite, now awe-inspiring as Persephone or Yama. The one great light wears the clothing of culture and is suited to the affections of the beholder. The primal blaze breaks into images of jeweled cities, emerald lakes and trees, sapphire skies.

In the gardens of Mind at Large, all fruit and flowers fall freely from the Tree of Life—no wily serpent, no trumpet blasts of indignation, and no voices of angry thunder. From this light, some say ethereal strains of music pour. Here at the end of the dark tunnel, each intimate moment is restored: our lost sisters and brothers, our fathers and mothers, each friend and lover who touched us once, revive in this world of light. There, the travelers say, time blends into space and all space is present to the heart's eye. There the first dawns mingle with nights of the future. The old grow young and the end is the beginning.

There we are re-minded and re-collected and enjoy the vision we tried to get by means of patient study. We find in that place everything we misplaced, toys of childhood and deeds of old age, memories we lost and hopes to which we dared not cling to. Justice reigns in this place of gathered time, where all things are said to walk in friendship. And in this place—this secret kingdom—all tears will be wiped away, all fear struck from the heart, and death will be no more.

Such are the tales told by travelers.

REFERENCES

1. Sorokin, P. *The Crisis of Our Age.* New York: Dutton, 1941.

2. Wolman, B. B. *Handbook of Parapsychology.* New York: Van Nostrand, 1977.

3. Krippner, S., ed. *Advances in Parapsychological Research.* Vols. 1-3. New York: Plenum, 1977.

4. Wheatley, J. M. O. and H. L. Edge. *Philosophical Dimensions of Parapsychology.* Springfield, Ill.: Charles Thomas, 1976.

5. Braude, S. E. *ESP and Psychokinesis: A Philosophical Examination.* Philadelphia: Temple University Press, 1979.

6. Plato. Hamilton, Edith and Huntington Cairns, eds. *Collected Dialogues.* New York: Random House, 1966.

7. Taylor, J. *The Rule and Exercises of Holy Dying.* New York: Arno Press, 1977.

8. Beaty, N. L. *The Craft of Dying: A Study in the Literary Tradition of the Ars Moriendi in England.* New Haven and London: Yale University Press, 1970.

9. Evans-Wentz, W. Y. *The Tibetan Book of the Dead.* New York: Oxford University Press, 1960.

10. Osis, K. and E. Haraldsson. *At The Hour of Death.* New York: Avon Books, 1977.

11. Greyson, B. Organic brain dysfunction and near-death experiences. Presented at the American Psychiatric Association 135th Annual Meeting, Toronto, 1982.

12. Brown, N. O. *Love's Body.* New York: Vintage Books, 1966.

13. Cruz, J. C. *The Incorruptibles.* Rockford, Ill.: Tan Books, 1977.

14. Thurston, H. *The Physical Phenomena of Mysticism.* London: Burns Oates, 1952.

15. Rogo, D. S. *Miracles.* New York: Dial Press, 1982.

16. Lowith, K. *Meaning in History.* Chicago: University of Chicago Press, 1958.

17. Cohn, N. *The Pursuit of the Millennium.* New York: Oxford University Press, 1981.

18. Marcuse, H. *Eros and Civilization.* Boston: Beacon Press, 1966.

19. Feuerbach, L. *Thoughts on Death and Immortality.* Berkeley: University of California Press, 1980.

20. Jung, C. G. *Psychological commentary.* In Evans-Wentz, op. cit.

21. Wolff, R. P. *In Defense of Anarchism.* New York: Harper & Row, 1970.

22. Kübler-Ross, E. *Death: The Final Stage of Growth.* Englewood Cliffs, N. J.: Prentice-Hall, 1975.

23. Becker, E. *The Denial of Death.* New York: The Free Press, 1973.

24. Myers, F. W. H. *Human Personality and its Survival of Bodily Death.* London and New York: Longmans, Green, 1903. (2 Vols.)

25. Rhine, J. B. *Extrasensory Perception.* Boston: Bruce Humphries, 1934.

26. Beloff, J. *The Existence of Mind.* New York: Citadel Press, 1962.

27. Palmer, J. Parapsychology as a probabilistic science. In Roll, W. *Research in Parapsychology: 1979.* Metuchen, N. J.: Scarecrow Press, 1980.

28. Schmidt, H. Psychokinesis. In Mitchell, E. D. and J. White. *Psychic Exploration: A Challenge For Science.* New York: Putnam's, 1974.

29. Murphy, G. *Three Papers on the Survival Problem.* New York: American Society for Psychical Research, 1945.

30. Beloff, J. *New Directions in Parapsychology.* Metuchen: Scarecrow, 1975.

31. Benz, E. *Evolution and Christian Hope.* New York: Doubleday, 1966.

32. Randall, J. *Parapsychology and the Nature of Life.* New York: Harper & Row, 1975.

33. Taylor, G. R. *The Great Evolution Mystery.* New York: Harper & Row, 1983.

34. Thorpe. W. H. *Science, Man and Morals.* London: Methuen, 1965.

35. de Chardin, T. *The Phenomenon of Man.* New York: Harper Torchbooks, 1965.

36. Schrodinger, E. *What is Life?* Cambridge: University Press, 1969.

37. Hitching, F. *The Neck of the Giraffe.* New York: Mentor, 1982.

38. Gould, S. and N. Eldredge. Punctuated equilibria: the tempo and mode of evolution reconsidered. *Paleobiology* 3 (1977).

39. Smith, J. M. *Evolution Now.* San Francisco: Freeman, 1982.

40. Eliade, M. *Yoga: Immortality and Freedom.* New York: Bollingen, 1958.

41. von Bertalanffy, L. *Problems of Life.* New York: Harper Torchbooks, 1960.

42. da Ripabottoni, A. *Padre Pio da Pietrelcina.* Foggia: Centro Culturale Francescano Convento, 1974.

43. Bergson, H. *Creative Evolution.* New York: Random House, 1944.

44. Hardy, A. *The Living Stream.* New York: Harper & Row, 1965.

45. Koestler, A. and J. R. Smythies. *Beyond Reductionism.* Boston: Beacon Press, 1969.

46. Sheldrake, R. *A New Science of Life.* Los Angeles: Tarcher, 1981.

47. Morris, R. L. Biology and Psychical Research. In Schmeidler, G. R. *Parapsychology: Its Relation to Physics, Biology, Psychology, and Psychiatry.* Metuchen, N.J.: Scarecrow Press, 1976.

48. Morris, R. L. Tacit communication and experimental theology. In Morris, J. D. and others. *Research in Parapsychology: 1974.* Metuchen, N. J.: Scarecrow Press, 1975.

49. Bergson, H. *Matter and Memory.* London: George Allen & Unwin, 1962.

50. Sidgwick, H. and Committee. Report on the census of hallucinations. *Proceedings of the Society for Psychical Research* (1894).

51. Stevenson, I. *Twenty Cases Suggestive of Reincarnation.* Charlottesville: University Press of Virginia, 1974.

52. Bozzano, E. *Dei Fenomeni di Telecinesia in Rapporto con Eventi di Morte.* Verona: Casa Editrice Europa, 1948.

53. Caycedo, A. *India of Yogis.* Delhi: National Publishing House, 1966.

54. Eliade, M. *The Two and the One.* New York: Harper Torchbooks, 1965.

55. Rao, R. Theories of Psi. In *Advances in Parapsychological Research 2, op. cit.*

56. Honorton, C. Psi and internal attention states. In Wolman, *op. cit.*

57. Braud, W. G. Psi conducive conditions: explorations and interpretations. In *Psi and States of Awareness.* New York: Parapsychology Foundation, 1977.

58. Tart, C. *States of Consciousness.* New York: Dutton, 1975.

59. Stanford, R. Conceptual frameworks of contemporary psi research. In Wolman, *op. cit.*

60. Palmer, J. Extrasensory perception: research findings. In Krippner, S., ed. *Advances in Parapsychological Research 2.* New York: Plenum, 1978.

61. Unamuno, M. *Tragic Sense of Life.* New York: Dover, 1954.

62. Rank, O. *The Double.* New York: Meridian, 1979.

63. Harrington, A. *The Immortalist.* Millbrae, Cal.: Celestial Arts, 1977.

64. Hafen, B. Q. and K. Frandsen. *Faces of Death.* Englewood, Colorado: Morton Publishing Company, 1983.

65. Goodman, L. *Death and the Creative Life.* New York: Springer, 1981.

66. Hick, J. *Death and Eternal Life.* New York: Harper & Row, 1976.

67. Arendt, H. *Between Past and Future*. New York: Viking Press, 1961.
68. Sheils, D. A cross-cultural study of beliefs in out-of-body experiences. *Journal of the Society for Psychical Research* 49 (1978).
69. Mead, G. R. S. *The Doctrine of the Subtle Body in Western Tradition*. Wheaton, Ill.: Quest, 1967.
70. Osis, K. and D. McCormick. Kinetic effects at the ostensible location of an out-of-body projection during perceptual testing. *Journal of the American Society for Psychical Research* 74 (1980).
71. Irwin, H. Out of the body down under. *Journal of the Society for Psychical Research* 50, 785 (1980).
72. Blackmore, S. *Beyond the Body*. New York: Granada, 1983.
73. Ullman, M. and S. Krippner. (with Vaughan, A.) *Dream Telepathy*. New York: Macmillan, 1973.
74. Morris, R. L. The use of detectors for out-of-body experiences. In *Research in Parapsychology 1973*. Metuchen, N.J.: Scarecrow, 1974.
75. Brookes-Smith, C. Recent research in psychokinesis. In Pearce-Higgins, J. D. and G. S. Whitby. *Life, Death & Psychical Research*. London: Rider, 1973.
76. Barber, T. X. and S. C. Wilson. The fantasy prone personality. In Sheikh, A., ed. *Imagery: Current Theory, Research, and Application*. New York: John Wiley, 1982.
77. Bullough, E. Psychical distance. *British Journal of Psychology*. Vol. 5 (1915).
78. Kant, I. *Critique of Judgment*. New York: Hafner, 1961.
79. Price, H. H. Some philosophical questions about telepathy and clairvoyance. In *Philosophical Dimensions of Parapsychology, op. cit.*
80. Schiller, F. *On The Aesthetic Education of Man*. New York: Ungar, 1965.
81. Marcuse, H. Art as a form of reality. In *On the Future of Art*. New York: Viking Press, 1971.
82. Chipp, H. B., ed. *Theories of Modern Art*. Berkeley: University of California Press, 1969.
83. Rhode, I. *Psyche*. (2 vols.) New York: Harper Torchbooks, 1966.
84. Husserl. E. *Ideas*. New York: Collier, 1962.
85. Streng, F. J. *Emptiness: A Study in Religious Meaning*. New York: Abingdon Press, 1967.
86. Jung, C. G. *Memories, Dreams, Reflections*. New York: Random House, 1961.
87. Orage, A. R. *Consciousness*. New York: Samuel Weiser, 1978.
88. Prabhavananda and Isherwood, C. *Shankara's Crest-Jewel of Discrimination*. New York: Mentor, 1970.
89. Scheler, M. *Man's Place in Nature*. Boston: Beacon Press, 1961.
90. Gallup, G. Jr. *Adventures in Immortality*. New York: McGraw Hill, 1982.
91. Bozzano, E. Apparitions of deceased persons at deathbeds. *The Annals of Psychical Research* (1906).

92. Hyslop, J. H. *Psychical Research and the Resurrection.* Boston: Small, Maynard, 1908.

93. Barrett, W. F. *Deathbed Visions.* London: Methuen, 1926.

94. Ring, K. *Life at Death.* New York: Coward, McCann & Geoghegan, 1980.

95. Lundahl, C. *A Collection of Near-Death Research Readings.* Chicago: Nelson-Hall, 1982.

96. Sabom, J. *Recollections of Death.* New York: Harper & Row, 1982.

97. Kohr, R. Near-death experience and its relationship to psi and various altered states. *Theta* 10 (1982).

98. Greyson, B. Increase in psychic and psi-related phenomena following near-death experiences. *Theta* (1983).

99. Ring, K. *Heading Toward Omega.* New York: William Morrow, 1984.

100. Grosso, M. Toward an explanation of near-death phenomena. In Lundahl, C., *op. cit.*

101. James, W. *The Varieties of Religious Experience.* New York: Longmans, Green, 1913.

102. Gauld, A. *Mediumship and Survival.* London: Heinemann, 1982.

103. Stevenson, I. *Twenty Cases Suggestive of Reincarnation.* Charlottesville: University Press of Virginia, 1974.

104. Greyson, B. The psychodynamics of near-death experiences. In Greyson, B. and C. P. Flynn. *The Near-Death Experience.* Springfield, Ill.: Charles Thomas, 1984.

105. Jung, C. G. *The Archetypes of the Collective Unconscious.* Princeton, N. J.: Princeton University Press, 1971.

106. Jung, C. G. *Aion.* Princeton, N. J.: Princeton University Press, 1959.

107. Edinger, E. *Ego and Archetype.* Baltimore: Penguin Books, 1974.

108. Becker, C. The centrality of near-death experiences in Chinese Pure Land Buddhism. *Anabiosis* 1 (1981).

109. Jacobi, Y. *Complex, Archetype, Symbol in the Psychology of C. G. Jung.* Princeton, N. J.: Princeton University Press, 1974.

110. Jung, C. G. Psychological commentary. In Evans-Wentz, *op. cit.*

111. Rawlings, M. *Beyond Death's Door.* New York: Thomas Nelson, 1978.

112. Flynn, C. Meanings and implications of NDRr transformations. *Anabiosis* 2 (1983).

113. Atwater, P. M. H. Coming Back. *Vital Signs* 1, 4 (1981).

114. Jung, C. G. *Structure and Dynamics of the Psyche.* Princeton, N. J.: Princeton University Press, 1978.

115. Noyes, R. *Dying and mystical consciousness.* Journal of Thanatology 1 (1971).

116. Arbman, E. *Ecstasy or Religious Trance,* Vol. 2. Stockholm: Scandinavian University Books, 1968.

117. Osborn, A. *Ramana Maharishi and the Path of Self-Knowledge.* New York: Weiser, 1973.

345

118. Skaar, M. My personal encounters with death. *Vital Signs* 2, 1 (1982).

119. Robinson, R. *Aboriginal Myths and Legends.* New York: Hamlyn Publishing Group, 1969.

120. Wasson, R. G., A. Hofmann and C. A. P. Ruck. *The Road to Eleusis.* New York: Harcourt Brace Jovanovich, 1978.

121. Kerenyi, C. *Eleusis: Archetypal Image of Mother and Daughter.* New York: Pantheon Books, 1967.

122. Turyn, A., ed. *Pindari Carmina cum Fragmentis.* Cambridge, Mass.: Harvard University Press, 1952.

123. Groff, S. and J. Halifax. *The Human Encounter With Death.* New York: Dutton, 1977.

124. Garfield, C. Consciousness alteration and fear of death. *J. Transpersonal Psychology* 7 (1975).

125. Jung, C. G. *Civilization in Transition.* Princeton, N. J.: Princeton University Press, 1964.

126. Pauli, W. The influence of archetypal ideas on the scientific theories of Kepler. In C. G. Jung and W. Pauli. *The Interpretation of Nature and the Psyche.* London: Routledge and Kegan Paul, 1955.

127. Snell, B. *The Discovery of the Mind.* New York: Harper Torchbooks, 1960.

128. Perry, M. *The Resurrection of Man.* London: Mowbrays, 1975.

129. Lame Deer and R. Erdoes. *Lame Deer Seeker of Visions.* New York: Simon and Schuster, 1972.

130. Green, C. and C. McCreery. *Apparitions.* New York: St. Martin's Press, 1975.

131. Richmond, Z. *Evidence of Purpose.* London: G. Bell, 1938.

132. van Dusen, W. *The Presence of Other Worlds.* New York: Harper & Row, 1974.

133. Wilson, I. *The Shroud of Turin.* New York: Image Books, 1979.

134. Vignon, P. *The Shroud of Christ.* Westminster, 1902.

135. Stevenson, K. E. and G. R. Habermas. *Verdict on the Shroud.* Ann Arbor: Servant Books, 1981.

136. Tribbe, F. C. *Portrait of Jesus?* New York: Stein and Day, 1983.

137. Rodante, S. *Shroud Spectrum International.* Issue No. 1, 1982.

138. Barbet, P. *A Doctor at Calvary.* New York: Image Books, 1963.

139. Heller, J. H. and A. D. Adler. A chemical investigation of the Shroud of Turin. *Canadian Society of Forensic Science* Vol. 14, No. 3 (1981).

140. Miller, V. D. and S. F. Pellicori. Ultraviolet fluourescence photograph of the Shroud of Turin. *Journal of Biological Photograph* 49/3 (July, 1981).

141. Bollone, P. B. *Sindon* 30. Turin: December, 1981.

142. Heller, J. H. *Report on the Shroud of Turin.* Boston: Houghton Mifflin, 1983.

143. Schwalbe, L. A. and R. N. Rogers. Physics and chemistry of the Shroud of Turin. *Analytica Chimica Acta* 135 (1982).

144. Eisenbud, J. *The World of Ted Serios*. New York: Pocket Books, 1968.

145. White, J. *Poleshift*. New York: Doubleday, 1980.

146. DuPuy, T. N. Quantification of factors related to weapon lethality. In *Historical Trends Related to Weapon Lethality*. U. S. Army Combat Developments Command, October, 1964.

147. Caldicott, H. *Nuclear Madness*. Brookline, Mass.: Autumn Press, 1979.

148. Machiavelli, N. *The Prince and Selected Discourses*. New York: Bantam, 1966.

149. Lifton, R. J. and R. Falk. *Indefensible Weapons*. New York: Basic Books, 1982.

150. Gray, C. and K. Payne. Victory is possible. *Foreign Policy* 39 (1980).

151. Berdyaev, N. *The Russian Revolution*. Ann Arbor: University of Michigan Press, 1971.

152. Reik, T. *Masochism in Modern Man*. New York: Farrar, Straus, 1941.

153. Eisenbud, J. *Paranormal Foreknowledge*. New York: Human Sciences Press, 1982.

154. Updike, J. *Hugging the Shore*. New York: Alfred A. Knopf, 1983.

155. Rosen, D. Suicide survivors: a follow-up study of persons who survived jumping from the Golden Gate and San Francisco-Oakland Bay Bridges. *Western Journal of Medicine* 122 (1975).

156. Brown, N. O. *Life Against Death*. New York: Vintage Books, 1959.

157. Meerloo, J. *Patterns of Panic*. New York: International Universities Press, 1950.

158. Timerman, J. *Prisoner Without a Name, Cell Without a Number*. New York: Alfred A. Knopf, 1981.

159. Kogan, E. *The Theory and Practice of Hell*. New York: Berkley Books, 1980.

160. Shapiro, David. *Neurotic Styles*. New York: Basic Books, 1965.

161. Sartre, J. P. *Being and Nothingness*. New York: Washington Square Press, 1966.

162. Maclean, P. D. *The Paranoid Streak in Man*. In Koestler, A., *op. cit.*

163. Thompson, E. P. Notes on exterminism, the last stage of civilization. *New Left Review* 121 (1980).

164. Burtt, E. A. *The Metaphysical Foundations of Modern Science*. New York: Doubleday, 1954.

165. Lifton, R. J. and E. Olsen. *Living and Dying*. New York: Bantam, 1975.

166. Underhill, R. M. *Singing For Power*. New York: Ballantine, 1968.

167. McLuhan, T. C. *Touch the Earth*. New York: Random House, 1941.

168. Ferguson, M. *The Aquarian Conspiracy*. Los Angeles: Tarcher, 1980.

169. Wilbur, K. *Up From Eden*. Boulder: Shambhala, 1983.

170. Granit, R. Reflections on the evolution of the mind. In Elvee, R. *Mind in Nature*. San Francisco: Harper & Row, 1982.

171. Lifton, R. J. *Death in Life: Survivors of Hiroshima*. New York: Random House, 1967.

347

172. Vico, G. *The New Science*. (Trans. Bergin, T. G. and Fisch, M. H.) New York: Doubleday, 1961.

173. Vallee, J. *Passport to Magonia*. Chicago: Henry Regnery, 1969.

174. Short, R. *The Gospel From Outer Space*. San Francisco: Harper & Row, 1983.

175. Delaney, J. J., ed. *A Woman Clothed With Sun*. New York: Image Books, 1961.

176. Pelletier, J. A. *Our Lady Comes to Garabandal*. Worcester, Mass.: Assumption Publication, 1971.

177. Steiger, B. *The Aquarian Revelations*. New York: Dell, 1971.

178. Rosenberg, K. Peacemakers and soldier girls. *The Nation* (April 14, 1984).

179. Tadros, M. B. *Forty Miracles of the Lady Virgin*. Cairo: Coptic Orthodox Church, 1976.

180. Vico, G. *On the Study Methods of our Time*. New York: Bobbs-Merrill, 1965.

181. Smith, W. C. *The Meaning and End of Religion*. New York: Harper & Row, 1978.

182. Schmeidler, G. R. and R. A. McDonnell. *ESP and Personality Patterns*. Westport, Conn.: Greenwood Press, 1973.

183. Owen, I. M. and M. Sparrow. *Conjuring Up Philip*. New York: Pocket Books, 1977.